T0391025

Environmental Economics Research and China's Green Development Strategy

Series on Chinese Economics Research[*]

(ISSN: 2251-1644)

Series Editors: Yang Mu *(South China University of Technology, China)*
Fan Gang *(Peking University, China)*

Published:

Vol. 19: *Environmental Economics Research and China's Green Development Strategy*
by Zhang Youguo
translated by Xu Hao, Xie Linlin

Vol. 18: *The Transformation of China's Economic Development: Perspectives of Sino–US Economists*
by Yang Wandong, Zhang Jianjun, Huang Shudong and Zhu Andong

Vol. 17: *Income Distribution and China's Economic "New Normal"*
by Wan Haiyuan and Li Shi

Vol. 16: *Research on Efficiency and Fairness of Resources Allocation by China's Governmental Administration*
by Sheng Hong and Qian Pu

Vol. 15: *Industrial Overcapacity and Duplicate Construction in China: Reasons and Solutions*
by Li Ping, Jiang Feitao and Cao Jianhai

Vol. 14: *Reforging the Central Bank: The Top-Level Design of the Chinese Financial System in the New Normal*
by Deng Haiqing and Chen Xi

Vol. 13: *Social Integration of Rural-Urban Migrants in China: Current Status, Determinants and Consequences*
by Yue Zhongshan, Li Shuzhuo and Marcus W Feldman

Vol. 12: *Game: The Segmentation, Implementation and Protection of Land Rights in China*
by Zhang Shuguang

*For the complete list of volumes in this series, please visit
www.worldscientific.com/series/scer

Series on Chinese Economics Research – Vol. 19

Environmental Economics Research and China's Green Development Strategy

Youguo ZHANG

Chinese Academy of Social Sciences, China

中国社会科学出版社
CHINA SOCIAL SCIENCES PRESS

World Scientific

Published by

World Scientific Publishing Co. Pte. Ltd.

5 Toh Tuck Link, Singapore 596224

USA office: 27 Warren Street, Suite 401-402, Hackensack, NJ 07601

UK office: 57 Shelton Street, Covent Garden, London WC2H 9HE

Library of Congress Cataloging-in-Publication Data
Names: Zhang, Youguo (Economist), author.
Title: Environmental economics research and China's green development strategy /
    Youguo Zhang (Chinese Academy of Social Sciences, China).
Description: New Jersey : World Scientific, [2019] | Series: Series on
    Chinese economics research ; vol. 19 | Includes bibliographical references.
Identifiers: LCCN 2019012716 | ISBN 9789811202902
Subjects: LCSH: Economic development--Environmental aspects--China. |
    Environmental policy--China. | Environmental economics--China.
Classification: LCC HC430.E5 Z435238 2019 | DDC 333.70951--dc23
LC record available at https://lccn.loc.gov/2019012716

British Library Cataloguing-in-Publication Data
A catalogue record for this book is available from the British Library.

This book is published with the financial support of the project of China Classics International
(经典中国国际出版工程)

《环境经济学研究新进展: 中国绿色发展战略与政策研究》
Originally published in Chinese by China Social Sciences Press
Copyright © China Social Sciences Press, 2016
Translated by: Xie Linlin, Xu Hao

For any available supplementary material, please visit
https://www.worldscientific.com/worldscibooks/10.1142/11347#t=suppl

Desk Editor: Tan Boon Hui

Typeset by Stallion Press
Email: enquiries@stallionpress.com

Preface

Ecological progress has become an indispensable aspect of the Chinese-style socialist construction, and the only way leading to it, apparently, must be one of green development which incorporates both economic and ecological benefits. This book, as a part of the research results of the innovative project, "A Research on Green Development Strategy and Policy", sponsored by the Chinese Academy of Social Sciences, and as one of the achievements of the key disciplinary fields (technical economics) of the Academy, conducts an in-depth research with a combination of qualitative and quantitative methods on crucial issues concerning the strategy, route, and policy of China's low-carbon development. The book contains four parts in addition to the introduction.

Part I, consisting of three chapters, deals with green development strategy. Chapter 1 discusses the necessity and rationale for China to treat climate change as one of the concerns of its state strategy; Chapter 2 deals with the problems of uncertainties, technology, and path lock-in that must be addressed in the strategy of energy development; and Chapter 3 reports a dialectic analysis of the appropriateness and inadequacy of China's energy-conserving target.

Part II, comprising Chapter 4–7, discusses the path of green development. Chapter 4 analyses the ways to decrease per capita carbon emissions for China from two perspectives, i.e., economic development and technological progress. Chapter 5, using the United States as a case study, investigates the influence of agricultural productive models on environment. Chapter 6 explores the development route for low-carbon trade on the basis of quantitative analysis of the amount of embodied carbon in China's trade. Chapter 7 calculates the visual water consumption in China's foreign trade and analyzes a development model for water-saving trade.

Part III, which includes Chapters 8–10, takes on several fundamental issues in policymaking for green development. Chapter 8 discusses the methods for environmental evaluation, one crucial issue in policymaking for green development. Chapter 9 focuses on the introduction of environmental factor into efficiency (productivity) evaluation and proposes an operable evaluation method. Chapter 10 analyzes the calculating methods and principles for greenhouse gas emissions.

Part IV reviews and evaluates the policies for green development and comprises Chapters 11–14. Chapter 11 makes a systematic review and provides an outlook of China's environmental policies. Chapter 12 investigates the influence of water fee adjustment on industrial water-use efficiency. Chapter 13 evaluates the general and structural effects of carbon emission intensity constraints. Chapter 14 evaluates the potential influence of different taxing standards for carbon tariffs on China's economy and carbon emissions.

The authors responsible for each chapter are as follows: Youguo Zhang for Introduction; Yisheng Zheng, Youguo Zhang, Yuhong Li and Xiao Zhang for Chapter 1; Yisheng Zheng for Chapter 2; Yuxin Zheng for Chapter 3; Youguo Zhang for Chapter 4; Yuhong Li for Chapter 5; Youguo Zhang for Chapter 6; Xiao Zhang for Chapter 7; Xiao Zhang for Chapter 8; Yuhong Li for Chapter 9; Yuhong Li and Yisheng Zheng for Chapter 10; Youguo Zhang for Chapter 11; Jing Li and Xiaocan Ma for Chapter 12; Youguo Zhang and Yuxin Zheng for Chapter 13; Youguo Zhang, Shilin Zheng, Li'an Zhou and Guang Shi for Chapter 14.

Contents

Introduction: Coordinating Ecological and Economic Construction With Green Development

*Institute of Quantitative & Technical Economics,
Chinese Academy of Social Sciences*

In the Report of the 18th National Congress of the Communist Party of China (CPC), ecological progress, together with economic, political, cultural, and social progress, has become one of the five aspects in the overall plan of socialist construction with Chinese characteristics. Promoting ecological progress aims at building a beautiful country, achieving lasting and sustainable development of the Chinese nation. It is a long-term task of vital importance to people's well-being and China's future.

1. Promoting Ecological Progress Is in Line With the Marxist View of Ecological Environment

The relations between man and nature are governed by the law of unity of opposites, and promoting ecological progress is in line with the Marxist view of ecological environment.

First, human beings are a part of nature and cannot survive without nature. This is not hard to understand: for the sustenance of human life and metabolism, we incessantly depend on nature for air and food. Marx, in the *Economic and Philosophic Manuscripts of 1844*, points out that "nature, insofar as it is not itself a part of human body, is the inorganic body of human being. Man lives on nature. That is to say, nature is his body, with which he must remain in continuous intercourse if he is not to die. That man's physical and spiritual life is linked to nature means simply that nature is linked to itself, for man is a part of nature." Moreover, according to Darwin's theory of evolution, the process which produces the human race is the evolutionary process of apes in nature. Thus, Engels, in *Anti-Duhring*, states that, "Man himself is a product of nature, which has developed in and along with its environment."

Second, nature provides an important source for human wealth. It was commonplace in ancient times when the productive forces of human beings were still underdeveloped that they lived entirely at the mercy of nature: when Mother Nature turned out to be favorable for crops, they lived prosperously otherwise they suffered from famine. The accumulation of human wealth then largely depended on natural conditions. In a capitalist society, human productive forces have seen unprecedented development. As Marx and Engels said in the *Communist Manifesto*, "The bourgeoisie, during its rule of scarce 100 years, has created more massive and more colossal productive forces than have all preceding generations together." Yet even in this case, human wealth could not be produced without nature. Marx points out in *Critique of the Gotha Program*, "Labor is not the source of all wealth. Nature is just as much the source of use values (and it is surely of such that material wealth consists!) as labor, which itself is only the manifestation of a force of nature, human labor power." Furthermore, in the *Economic and Philosophic Manuscripts of 1844*, Marx says, "The worker can create nothing without nature, without the sensuous external world. It is the material on which his labor is manifested, in which it is active, from which and by means of which it produces."

Finally, man plays a dynamic role in their relationship with nature. Man may actively put nature at his service, while nature retains a massive reactive power against him. Engels points out in *Dialectics of Nature*, "The animal merely uses its environment, and brings about changes in it simply by its presence; man by his changes makes it serve his ends, masters it." As mankind entered into the epoch of capitalism, the great development of productive forces changed, to a large degree, the relation between man and nature with man's ability to change and master nature enhanced. For instance, man now may establish water conservatory facilities to deal with flood and drought, to divert water from a long distance, and to produce a large amount of hydropower. However, "let us not flatter ourselves overmuch on account of our human victories over nature. For each such victory nature takes its revenge on us", stresses Engels in *Dialectics of Nature*. With the significant development of productive forces, man has become more confident and more active, in the face of nature, while simultaneously, his activities lead to more destruction of nature. Depletion of resources caused by human activities and disasters brought about by environmental pollution are now posing a serious threat to human survival and development, for which human beings may pay the price of comfort, health, reproduction, and even life. For instance, the top 8 public environmental hazards of the 20th century caused by environmental deterioration now have become an ingrained part of the painful memories of mankind.

In short, man cannot live without nature even for a moment, and thus must adopt a dialectical materialistic attitude toward nature, trying to grasp the laws of nature and base his activities on them. Engels has warned mankind in *Dialectics of Nature* that "at every step we are reminded that we by no means rule over nature like a conqueror over a foreign people, like someone standing outside nature — but that we, with flesh, blood and brain, belong to nature, and exist in its midst, and that all our mastery of it consists in the fact that we have the advantage over all other creatures of being able to learn its laws and apply them correctly." At present, human productive forces have achieved development that is unparalleled in history. If protection of ecological environment is not taken very seriously and activities are not carried out according to natural laws, man tends to easily conduct his activities in an unsustainable way, causing severe damage to the ecological environment. On the other hand, the continuous deterioration of ecological environment harms human survival by leading to various disasters, which may result in the extinction of human species. Man destroying natural environment is actually destroying his own "inorganic body". The call for promoting ecological progress demands human activities to be conducted in line with natural laws, which reflects the Marxist view of ecological environment. It also meets the demands of the times, and is inherent in the realization of the well-rounded development of a person.

2. CPC Has a Tradition of Appreciating Ecological Progress

The CPC has a tradition of appreciating ecological progress. On October 11, 1955, Comrade Mao Zedong, when talking about comprehensive planning and leadership enhancement for agricultural cooperation in a summary speech delivered at the Sixth Plenary Session of the 7th Central Committee of the CPC, pointed out, "Economic planning of countryside includes by-work, handicraft, diversified operation, comprehensive operation, short-distance wasteland clearing and immigration, supplying and marketing cooperation, credit cooperation, banks, technology promotion stations, and so on. Besides, there should be greening of barren hills and villages. I think that barren hills of the north in particular need greening, and can be greened. Comrades from the north, do you have the courage to do it? Many lands of the south also need greening. It would be a nice thing to see greening in various places of both south and north within several years. It is a beneficial issue to agriculture, industry and all sides." In August, 1958 Mao Zedong said at a large meeting of the Political Bureau of the Central Committee that "we need to green all the rivers and mountains of our motherland, to make it something like a garden; it should look beautiful everywhere, natural looks should be changed", "villages and cities should be greened and afforested, look like gardens; there will be Summer Palaces and Zhongshan Parks everywhere."

An inscription by Deng Xiaoping for the People's Liberation Army (PLA) Summary and Commendation Conference for Tree-Planting and Afforestation in November 1982 read, "Plant trees and advance afforestation, green motherland, and benefit future generations". He formally commented on a report by the Ministry of Forestry on the national voluntary tree-planting movement on December 26, 1982, saying that "the work should be continued for 20 years, with each year showing an improvement on the previous, each producing more solid work than the previous. To guarantee time-efficiency, a practical and feasible system of examination, commendation and punishment shall be established." In September 1995, Jiang Zemin pointed out in the article "Correctly handle some significant relations in socialist modernization" that in the drive for modernization, sustainable development should be treated as a major strategy with population control, resource conservation, and environmental protection as top priorities; population growth should match developing social productive forces; and economic construction should be coordinated with resource environment, resulting in a beneficial cycle. In 2000, Jiang Zemin emphasized in the article "Pushing forward the socialist cause with Chinese characteristics in the new century" that great importance should be attached to ecological progress and environmental protection so that, with long-term efforts, the hills of China will be forever green and the rivers of China will forever flow, and the resources of China can be put to sustainable use.

The report of the 16th Party Congress clearly stated that as human society entered the 21st century, we started a new phase of development for building a well-off society in an all-round manner and speed up socialist modernization. In line with the new situation of building a well-off society in an all-round manner, the Third Plenary Session of 16th Central Committee of the CPC proposed that reform of the economic system should be deepened with "putting people first, establishing a comprehensive, coordinated and sustainable view of development", i.e., the Scientific Outlook on Development, as a guiding idea and principle. Sustainable development is inherent in and required by the Scientific Outlook on Development, which aims at facilitating the harmonious relationship between man and nature; realizing the coordination between economic development and population, and resource and environment; sticking to the development path of civilization of progressive production, wealthy life, and clean ecology; and ensuring generation-by-generation sustainable development.

The report of the 17th Party Congress proposed that the development pattern will be significantly transformed; we will quadruple the per capita GDP of the year 2000 by 2020 through optimizing the economic structure and improving economic returns while reducing consumption of resources and protecting the environment; promote a conservation culture by basically forming an energy- and resource-efficient and environment-friendly structure of industries and pattern of growth and model of consumption; we will have a large-scale circular economy and considerably increase the proportion of renewable energy sources in total energy consumption; the discharge of major pollutants will be brought under effective control and the ecological and environmental quality will improve notably.

The report of the 18th Party Congress further proposed that promoting ecological progress is a long-term task of vital importance to people's well-being and China's future; faced with increasing resource constraints, severe environmental pollution, and a deteriorating ecosystem, we must raise our ecological awareness of the need to respect, accommodate to, and protect nature; we must give high priority to making ecological progress and incorporate it into all aspects and the entire process of advancing economic, political, cultural, and social progress; and we must work hard to build a beautiful country and achieve lasting and sustainable development of the Chinese nation.

3. Green Development Contributes to a Coordinated Development of Ecology and Economy

3.1. *Economic development of China increasingly restricted by the resource environment*

It seems a recent development of these past few decades that depletion of resources and environmental deterioration has become of general concern to mankind. However, from the perspective of history, the two issues never stop threatening human survival and development. For example, in ancient times, the demise of the once prosperous Maya civilization and the ancient city of Loulan in China was linked to environmental deterioration. More recently, the top 8 public environmental hazards caused by environmental deterioration have now become an ingrained part of the painful memories of mankind. Lately, the issue of global climate change has given rise to endless debates from all walks of life. Up till now, it can be said that depletion of resources and environmental deterioration are not temporary and local issues any more, but a major security problem on a global scale-concerning human survival and development.

China, the largest developing country in the world, is now on the road to the great renewal of the Chinese nation and peaceful development. The unexpected global issues of resource and environment security, however, make it a complicated and difficult matter. Globally, a major cause of the increasing restriction of resource environment confronting the economic development of China is that developed countries have consumed a huge amount of resources that the earth provided during their industrialization and urbanization period, and at the same time, transferred a large number of pollution-intensive industries to developing countries, who thus have only very limited capacity to utilize the resource environment for their modernization. If the route of industrialization and urbanization pursued by most developing countries is the same as that of developed countries, the remaining resources may not be able to sustain us for long. Even developed countries despite in their industrialized and urbanized status, have felt a scarcity of resources. A well-known case in point was the 1973 oil crisis, which led to skyrocketing of oil price. After that, gone were the days of cheap oil prices, which was followed by a sharp decline of the growth rate of global economy.

The eye-catching economic boom of China started with the Reform and Opening Up in 1978, when the global scarcity of resources had already made an impact. Speaking of China, it takes up only a relatively small percentage of the ore reserve of the world, despite its complete use of ore varieties and in total quantity. In terms of ore resources per capita, China is not ore-rich, but poor in reserves, proving a limited guarantee for social and economic development. Now, over 30 years since the Reform and Opening up, the economic scale of China and the whole world has expanded fundamentally. Rapid growth on the basis of such an expanded scale of economy will undoubtedly put more strain on resource supply. The issue of China's resource security has thus become ever more severe. In the meantime, environment security has made itself felt in all aspects of development. Over the past 30 years since the Reform and Opening Up, "the environmental issues that showed up in different stages in the over-100-year industrialization of developed countries concentrated in China with the characteristics of being structural, complex and concentrated."

3.2. *Unsustainable extensive economic development*

Since the Reform and Opening Up, China with its large population base has achieved, all through to the present day, a rapid growth in economy and fast advancement in industrialization and urbanization. At the beginning of the Reform and Opening Up, China was obliged to exact more than normal use from natural resources so as to obtain the capital necessary for development, because of its small amount of primary capital and very limited foreign investment. It seems somewhat necessary that the economic model then would be extensive, and inevitable in that the rapid economic development thus brought about would make the base of China's natural resources ever more fragile and cause serious damage to the environment. While the over-consumption of resources by developed countries and their transference of polluting industries overseas constitute the important external factors giving rise to the issue of resource and environment security of China, extensive economic development serves as the internal factor.

On the one hand, extensive economic development accelerates the consumption of China's resources. Faced with a lack of funds, local governments, for the sake of economic development, often control and bring down the prices of immovable or hardly movable resources such as ores, water, and land, making these a big attraction for liquidity factors especially capital, necessary for economic growth. In the meantime, China has the need to advance urbanization, and infrastructure investment will also increase correspondingly, which can only be accomplished by increased resource supply. For this purpose, in an underdeveloped economy, governments often have to adopt policies bringing down the price of resources to achieve rapid urbanization and to improve the people's livelihood. But to achieve this measure, the huge public infrastructure investment would have become an incubus for government. All these factors combined account for the relatively low price of resources in China. Thus, it is hard for some resource-exporting areas to benefit from their resources and to change the unitary economic structure of resource exploitation. Furthermore, over-exploiting has turned from bad to worse, and some areas have run out of resources ahead of time.

On the other hand, extensive development causes severe environmental pollution. More often than not, industries which are resources-intensive are also pollution-intensive. With less developed environmental techniques, the environment of China is increasingly polluted. Commensurating with its economic growth. In spite of having comparatively fully formed policies for environmental protection, the deteriorating tendency of China's environment is difficult to turn around, as the deep cause lies in extensive economic development. The thirst for GDP growth makes many local governments reduce or cancel their "restraint mechanism" on potential investors. With GDP growth as a requisite task, protection of the resource environment is overlooked and relevant environmental standards and regulations are loosened, carelessly enforced, and sometimes even revoked. For their part, departments in charge of environmental protection, with an unclear status especially in local governments, are handicapped by the current system in exercising their power and function. Many environmental bodies in local governments suffer from problems of being understaffed, a lack of funds, and outdated equipment. It is difficult for them to carry out effective supervision and management, facing an already large and increasing number of objects to be supervised and managed. Many companies thus ignore environmental laws and regulations.

3.3. Green development is a must

What is worrying is that China still holds on to extensive economic development with investment of capital and materials as a focus. Recently, the economic growth of China has started to depend less on resource environment, but generally speaking, such dependence is crucial notwithstanding the change. Within a foreseeable period of time, China, for rapid and further development of economy, will consume more resources of various kinds and emit more pollutants. With an ever enlarging economic scale, China is facing more resource constraints, running the risk of unsustainable resource environment. It is thus imperative for China to solve the problems of resource and environment security, which is an inherent demand in and a requisite for building a well-off society in an all-round manner.

Despite the fact that the influence of resource environment on economic and social development has long been well recognized, major theories of the West for economic development are yet to fully appreciate the importance of the resource environment. Before the scarcity of the resource environment was felt, they held that resource environment had a limitless capacity of supply, and hence no special attention was needed thereto. When the scarcity became evident, as represented by oil crises, they turned to the idea that man-made capital together with the technological progress would substitute for natural resources and environment, with a full appreciation of the scarcity of the resource environment still wanting. There is no denying that these ideas may be justified for developed countries. Yet for developing countries, whose number and population account for the bulk of the world, the increasing scarcity of the resource environment cannot sustain their development if they seek to rank among developed countries by sticking to the old way of modernization of industrialized countries.

This is a noteworthy issue, especially for a big developing country like China. On the one hand, scarcity of various resources and events of severe environmental pollution frequently occurred, showing that if China continues on the path of present extensive economic development, the available resources may run out and environment capacity may collapse under this huge burden before China accumulates enough man-made capital to supersede the resources and environment capacity necessary for economic growth. On the other hand, if China, a developing country with the largest population in the world, can effectively solve the problems of resource and environment security, it is tantamount to guaranteeing resource supply and living environment for one-fifth of the world's population.

Green development serves as a way to realize coordinated development of ecology and economy. The essence of green development is to integrate ecological progress into economic development, making it one of the inherent demands and constraints of economic development, thus facilitating the change of the growth model, making it more in line with natural laws and realizing coordinated and unified development of both ecology and economy.

First, the Marxist view of ecological environment calls for respect for nature, conforming to nature, and protecting nature. It does not ask human beings to be inactive, or to live entirely at the mercy of nature, but to actively put nature at their service by transforming nature according to natural laws. China is currently at the primary stage of socialism with the principal problem of the society still being how the ever-growing material and cultural needs of the people can be satisfied with outdated social production methods. The report of the 18th Party Congress thus still stresses that taking economic development as the central task is vital to national renewal, and development still holds the key to addressing all the problems we have in China. For economic development, it is necessary to combine human labor and nature, to dominate nature and develop productive forces, to create material wealth, and finally to achieve prosperity for all people. These are demanded by Chinese-style socialism, and by the current task of building of a moderately prosperous society in all respects.

Second, ecological progress needs economic development as a necessary material basis. For example, ecological progress demands implementation of the strategy of a development priority zone, which can only be done and facilitated on the basis of large-scale infrastructure investment and transfer payment. As another example, protection of ecosystem and environment, which is essential for ecological progress, may involve major projects of ecological restoration such as comprehensive treatment of desertification, stony desertification, and water and soil erosion; water conservancy construction for enhancing the capability to prevent floods, combat drought, and drain waterlogged lands; and building of disaster prevention and reduction systems to heighten the ability to defend against meteorological, and geological disasters and even earthquakes. Such projects call for stepping up efforts to protect the ecosystem and environment, and also need large-scale investments in terms of personnel, materials, and funds. Without material wealth generated by economic development, these measures for ecological and environmental protection would have been impossible.

In brief, ecological progress by way of green development, which aims at solving the problems of resource and environment security, not only provides a basic safeguard for the scientific development of China and building a moderately prosperous society in all respects but also serves as a highly instructive model for developing countries, and thus makes a great contribution to the sustainable development of humanity. The call for ecological progress and green development thus highlights a major strategy of China in addressing the severe problems of the resource and environment situation currently, and in building a moderately prosperous society in all respects.

4. China's Green Development Is Confronted With Challenges

It is obvious that China is obliged to choose green development, which decouples economic growth and resource and environment overconsumption. In order to ensure the building of a moderately prosperous society, the pursuit of green development, however, should not harm the stable and rapid economic growth, should continue to ensure the employment and income growth of the people, and should be in line with the basic conditions of China such as maintaining its economic power, technological level, and regional productive structure. China faces many difficulties in its path to achieving these goals. These are summed up in the following.

4.1. *Weak resident consumption, rigid demand of investment, and poor basis for demand optimization*

The transition from relying mainly on investment and export to relying on a well-coordinated combination of consumption, investment, and export, as proposed in the report of the 17th Party Congress, is not only conducive to optimizing final demand pattern, strengthening the basis for economic growth, and fending off economic risk but also to facilitating the disconnection between economic growth and the resource environment. However, one cannot be optimistic about the current situation of the demand pattern. On the one hand, a long-term mechanism of expanding resident consumption has not yet been established. In the first place, the economic growth of China was largely dependent on investment for many years. For the accumulation of capital, the price of other economic factors including workers' salary has been distorted to a certain degree. This leads to a slow increase of resident income, especially the income of residents in rural areas, constituting a major constraint for consumption expansion. Second, for want of a well-established system of social security and public service, increasing preventive savings for the purposes of later life, health care, housing, unemployment and education for the children dampens the expansion of resident consumption. On the other hand, there is still rigid demand for investment in China. Even though China has made great improvements in infrastructure in recent years, it is unable to meet the demands economic and social development. Large-scale construction and investment are still needed. For some areas in Central and Western China in particular, inconvenience in transport proves to be a "bottleneck" for economic and social development. In the meantime, the level of modernization still has large room for improvement, which correspondingly demands large-scale urban construction and investment. Besides transportation and urban construction, a huge amount of investment is called for in infrastructure projects such as irrigation and water conservancy, environmental protection (sewage water treatment network and pollution monitoring system, for instance), and city renovation. In addition, large-scale investment is needed in the installation, promotion, and updating of machines and equipment so as to enhance technological progress, and especially to raise the level of resource conservation and environmental protection. Due to these rigid demands for investment, capital formation will continue to account for a major percentage of the final demand of China.

4.2. *Inability of service industry to substitute for secondary industry in the short term*

The economic growth of China crucially depends on the secondary industry, with its percentage in GDP far exceeding the world average and the averages of various other countries (as classified in terms of income), while the percentage contribution of tertiary industries is well below the world average. The transition from secondary industry, serving as the major driving force, to the primary, secondary, and tertiary industries jointly driving economic growth, as proposed in the report of the 17th Party Congress, will clearly contribute to the disconnection between economic growth and resource consumption and environmental pollution. To realize the said transition, however, two challenges must be met. The first is that China, in the current stage of rapid industrialization and urbanization, has a great need for secondary industry. As mentioned earlier, China has a demand for infrastructure and updated machinery and equipment, which necessitates both investment and the products provided by secondary industry. The second challenge is that internal and external forces for promoting tertiary industry are not strong enough. The major propelling power for the tertiary industry is resident consumption, which as indicated above, expands slowly and weakly. It is thus hard for resident consumption to boost the tertiary industry in a limited and short period of time. Also, international demand may not serve as a power to propel the tertiary industry in a limited and short period of time as China's international competitiveness in tertiary industry is weak. Thus, there is still a long way to go for the tertiary industry to substitute for the secondary industry in its role in economic development, including boosting economic growth and promoting employment. This is more clearly seen in Central and Western China. Despite the wish to change their development model and efforts to seek and try different ways to optimize the industry structure, many areas in Central and Western China find it difficult to come up with an industry which can be a substitute for the secondary industry. It is even harder for these areas to transform the model of economic development.

4.3. *Underdeveloped technology of resource utilization and environmental protection, and a lack of policies in relevant fields*

In light of the heavy dependence on investment of basic productive factors such as resource, investment, and labor for economic development, the 17th Party Congress treats "the transition from relying heavily on increased consumption of material resources to relying mainly on advances in science and technology, improvement in the quality of the workforce and innovation in management" as one of the three transitions in the transformation of the model of economic development. The technology of resource exploitation and utilization, however, is still underdeveloped, which constitutes one of the major difficulties for China to disconnect economic growth with resource and environment. For instance, in terms of energy utilization, there is a severe lack of advanced technologies, and a plethora of backward technologies, whereby the energy efficiency of China lags behind the world top level by 10%, while the energy consumption per unit of high energy-consumption product is 40% above the world's top level. Moreover, some current policies pertaining to the resource and environment are not favorable to the improvement of relevant technologies. First, the pricing mechanism is not well-established for the enhancement of reasonable utilization of resource and environment. The prices of some resource products fail to reflect the scarcity of the resources and the supply and demand relation in market. For some other resource products, costs for their development at the initial stage, pollution treatment, and exit when the resources are depleted are not fully represented in the prices. External costs for enterprises to develop and utilize resources have not been internalized. Second, there is a lack of policies for providing incentives to technologies of high resource- and environment-efficiency. It is not entirely due to a lack of technologies that low energy efficiency and serious pollution are evident in China. It is also because fiscal and revenue policies and other market mechanisms are not fully established so as to encourage research and development, production, and use of energy-conserving and environment-friendly goods, and to repress the production of high energy consumption and high emission goods. This exerts an unfavorable impact on research and development and promotion of energy-conserving and environment-friendly technologies, devices, and products. A good deal of clean and efficient energy technology has not been widely put into use.

5. Overall Plan for Promoting Green Development

China is persistently committed to ecological progress, which is in line with the Marxist view of ecology. The 18th Party Congress attaches even more importance to ecological progress, which, as a major strategic plan to deal with the current severe ecological condition, meets the demands of the social and economic development of China. For ecological progress, the transformation, utilization, and protection of the ecological environment should be conducted according to natural laws so as to provide more favorable conditions for the survival and development of the people, that is, ecological development and economic construction should be organically combined. The 18th Party Congress further proposes that ecological progress should be incorporated into "all aspects and the whole process of advancing economic, political, cultural, and social progress". It not only shows that ecological progress has become an indispensable part of building socialism with Chinese characteristics, but also points out a direction for ecological progress. "Striving for green, circular and low-carbon development", as stressed by the 18th Party Congress, can be seen as specific implementations of the strategy of ecological civilization. With a view to solving the challenges confronting China's green development, we propose the following lines of thought in line with the specific demands as proposed by the 18th Party Congress concerning economic development and ecological progress:

5.1. *Actively promoting the green transition of production models*

First, we should advocate and encourage circular economy and actively establish regional circular economy systems, especially ones internal to the secondary industry, so that the green transition of the secondary industry can be driven forward.

Second, we should vigorously promote production- and livelihood-oriented modern service in order to meet social demands, and effectively facilitate the integration between manufacture industry and service industry so as to meet the needs of the people for structurally upgraded consumption and to promote the harmonious development of the society.

Finally, we should actively cultivate and develop strategic emerging industries and optimize and upgrade the industry structure. Some regions in Central and Western China, in particular, should take their own regional features into account and develop relevant strategic emerging industries so that their industry structure can be fine-tuned, economic competitiveness be enhanced, the gap between these regions and Eastern regions be narrowed, and local security problems of resources and environment be tackled.

5.2. *Optimizing requirement models and initiating the transition of economic development models at the source*

First, we should further the reform of the income and distribution system, endeavor to increase the income of residents, especially those in rural areas, establish and perfect the system of public service and social security with a purpose to enhance resident consumption power and livelihood, and actively cultivate a green consumption model.

Second, we should strengthen planning and management in investment and attach great importance to livelihood projects so as to ensure the effectiveness of investment in infrastructure and reduce to a minimum the negative impact of infrastructure construction on resources and environment.

Finally, we should heighten the level of opening up. On the one hand, we should encourage the export of high-tech, high value-added, and high-end service products, and limit that of resource- and pollution-intensive products, with a view to optimizing the structure of export products, endeavoring to turn exportation into an important driving force in the development of emerging and service industries and in the economic transformation, and a favorable factor in dealing with the security problems of resources and environment. On the other hand, against the background of resources and environment scarcity, we should have a more thorough and complete plan for strategy implementation, a deeper understanding of the times, and actively obtain necessary resources in the international market.

5.3. *Establishing and perfecting policies, institutions, and mechanisms favorable to green development*

First, we should step up our efforts to establish a state system of innovation and support green development with innovative technologies. As a matter of fact, innovation is indispensable, not only to circular economy but also to modern services and strategic emerging industries. Quickening our steps to establish a state system of innovation and to support green development with innovative technologies can serve as a fundamental path and a long-term strategy to deal with security problems of resources and environment.

Second, we should establish and perfect a price-forming mechanism favorable to resource conservation and environmental protection. Prices that fully recognize the scarcity of resources and external costs can substantially turn the current trend of resource and environment abuse. It has also been pointed out in the Report of the 18th Party Congress that we should deepen the reform of prices, taxes and fees for resource products, and establish a system for paying for resource consumption and compensating for ecological damage, a system that responds to market supply and demand and resource scarcity, recognizes ecological values and requires compensation in the interest of later generations, and that we should carry out trials for trading energy savings, carbon emission rights, pollution discharge rights, and water rights.

Finally, we should establish, perfect, and resolutely enforce laws and regulations concerning resources and environment, build an administrative system that contributes to the protection of resources and environment, and actively involve the public in the process and give full play to their initiative.

Part I

Reflections on
Green Development Strategy

This part reflects on the green development strategy of China and includes Chapters 1–3.

The first chapter discusses the necessity and the rationale for China to treat climate change as one of the concerns of its state strategy. The necessity lies in the fact that China needs to take climate change as an opportunity to focus on and actively participate in the possible worldwide revolution of energy technology. Also, the transformation of the current economic development model can start by making this a focus. For this, China should, first, express to the international community its notions and methods as regards climate change; second, make efforts to turn to a self-controlled and sustainable development model; and third, treat the problem of climate change as a point of departure to reach a consensus among all sectors of the society on long-term development strategy.

Chapter 2 deals with the problems of uncertainties, technology, and path lock-in, which must be addressed in the strategy of energy development. Uncertainties mainly stem from the potential choices of technological innovation plans. Different plans may lead to major differences in the future. China must actively consider the problem and explore an endurable and sustainable development path and model, rather than blindly follow the beaten track of industrialized countries. In the field of energy conservation, China should endeavor to break such barriers to innovations of energy technology as "technology lock-in by market", "rent-seeking" activities, and "nonfeasance", promote rational consumption models, and at the same time respect the law governing industry structure upgrading and should not blindly pursue "structural energy-conserving", in order for energy-conserving policies to be coordinated with economic development, ability building, and environmental protection of China.

Chapter 3 deals with a dialectic analysis of the appropriateness and inadequacy of China's energy-conserving target. It suffers from an obvious theoretical deficiency, and a defect in practice — to take energy consumption intensity as an indicator of appraisal for the energy efficiency of different areas and departments. A "brake-slamming" practice that aims at lowering energy consumption intensity by a large margin in a short period of time will be harmful to its long-term reduction, and to the long-term development of China. The appraisal and management of energy efficiency for different areas must be conducted on a material-based energy consumption indicator at the level of products and industries, rather than on the currently used area-based energy consumption intensity. In order to actually relieve the pressure of resources and environment, China should extend its measures of energy conservation and emission reduction from the field of production to that of consumption.

Chapter 1

The Long-term Strategy of China to Deal With Climate Change[1]

Yisheng Zheng, Youguo Zhang, Yuhong Li and Xiao Zhang

Institute of Quantitative & Technical Economics,
Chinese Academy of Social Sciences

Recently, China has been presented as "the biggest trouble-maker"[2] by Western media in terms of climate change, and also as "the most important partner"[3] in the state strategies of Western countries. This is because

---

[1] A brief version of the present chapter has been published in *China Economic Times*, January 6, 2000.

[2] The fact that China's energy consumption and CO_2 emissions have increased rapidly, that China becomes the world's largest emitter, and that its emissions per capita exceed world average turn the country into a target of propaganda and criticism of Western media. Given the historical responsibility of developed countries, the international community has already reached the consensus on the principle of "common but differentiated responsibilities", which also provides hope and serves as a basis for the world to solve the problem of climate change. Some Western countries, however, do not actually want to honor their promise to help developing countries in terms of technology and capital (which constitutes the premise for the latter to carry out their responsibilities), not to mention the combination between slowing down climate change and truly changing their production mode, lifestyle, culture, and current unjust international relations. They thus place too much emphasis on problems at the phenomenal level and even blame others, especially China, the rapidly rising country, in the name of morality for climate problems. Global cooperation to deal with climate change faces the danger of a major failure. There were signs even before the Copenhagen Conference that some Western countries were not only expecting the failure of the Copenhagen talks, but also preset China as the scapegoat.

[3] In the international talks for climate change, the US government is pushing China to the front in a different way: it is trying to pull China into its own circle — "cooperation between the world's two largest emitters" — so as to bypass the European Union and

the growth rate of CO_2 emissions in China has repeatedly exceeded the expectations of international energy agencies, which thus already lands China as the world's biggest emission country; also, international capital can hardly ignore the huge market capacity of the country. Meanwhile, China, as a developing country, is also one of the major powers to protest against and to call for a change of the unfair practice of developed countries in matters of climate.[4]

China is now in the process of industrializing, but does not enjoy the resource and environment conditions of developed countries when they started to rise. China is under intense international pressure for its greenhouse gas emission reduction, with its goals of modernization not yet realized. This is undoubtedly an unparalleled challenge. The challenge is two-fold: to achieve the goal of development, and to achieve it under the situation where resources and environments pose serious concerns, a situation quite different from that enjoyed by Western developed countries.

We then have to not only protect our rights to development, but also cherish these rights. To protect the rights is to assert equal rights to development in the international community, and to cherish them is concerned with the basic strategy of China, that is, regardless of the uncertainties in international cooperation on climate change, China will not limit the problem to energy strategy, but combine measures to deal with climate change with the transformation to a self-controlled and sustainable development model.

---

influence the international agenda in this "joint" way. In this way, the US may, on the one hand, display their efforts to the domestic and international audience in influencing China's emission reduction, and, on the other hand, seek special cooperation with China, the largest market for new energy technologies.

[4] Although some Western countries have assumed leading roles, their efforts are limited in that they are determined to avoid changes of the *status quo*, mechanism, and system of the distribution and use of resources of the world. Some even explicitly express their determination not to change their way of life (e.g., the US). Unlike developing countries, as regards many issues related to "mitigating climate change", developed countries could but would not do it. They would not give up the practice of changing measures of "saving the planet" to a game of interest. It is a truly worrying fact that climate change is less a natural disaster than an artificial calamity.

1. The Relation Between Climate Change and the Economic Development of China

First, developed countries may capitalize on climate change and innovation of energy technology to restrict the development of China, and thus widen the gap of economic development between them and emerging economies. The lock-in of the development model with that of developed countries as the only choice constitutes a major barrier to the technological innovation of China. In the recent decade, in contrast with the bumpy process of greenhouse gas emission reduction, developed countries stage an arms race in the research and development of energy technology. Regardless of the discussions concerning the causes and consequences of climate change, a substantial revolution in energy technology may as well break out.

For instance, with the prospect of oil depletion, international oil companies are stepping up their transformation to energy companies of a comprehensive nature, actively promoting renewable resources, developing new energy technologies, and participating in emission reduction of greenhouse gas. Some European countries have already achieved many new technological results.

In the United States, a new pattern, which was passively formed in the financial crisis, but quite in line with the international attitudes toward climate change, and with a view to economic growth in the era of new energy and to safeguarding the dominating position of the country, is taking shape. Once "a lack of room for low-carbon energy or carbon emission" emerges, the US government may probably draw on its special political influence, financial position, and advantages of new energy technology to form a new international hegemony and international trade mechanism with long-term profits for the country.[5] In the new situation where the problem of climate change makes its impact, some countries

---

[5] During the Bush administration before the new energy policy in the United States, the government-supported research and development of new energy resources had a huge investment. However, the traditional fossil energy giants, which have long been considered conservative, have actually carried out and completed the transformation from thinking to technology and planning. Obama's new energy policy only ignited these potentials in a orderly way, cleared up further institutional barriers for it on the basis of a competitive

may lag behind, and even be reduced to a position of being exploited and controlled. Those countries that have too little space for their own choice and too little free means in international cooperation, especially those that swing from one side to another in their own development strategies, are most likely to miss their development opportunities and lose their original advantages or development momentum in this resource "reshuffling".[6]

In contrast, China's technological progress and industrial upgrading have not broken through some barriers of the lock-in of development mode, for example, the problems of economic relations between the central and local governments as intensively reflected in the fiscal and taxation system, the restrictive effect of the excessively export-oriented economic structure on the upgrading of economic structure and enhancement of innovation capability, and so on. The reason why China, while proposing ecological civilization, is increasingly involved in the Western-style development path of high energy consumption and high material consumption is that it has actually not overcome these barriers, and even strengthened them intentionally or unintentionally. This has greatly weakened the independent abilities of innovation and coordination of China, and these abilities are the only strengths that we can forever rely on in dealing with the certain and uncertain challenges of the future.

Second, in fact, even if there is no climate change problem and no pressure for China to commit to emission reduction, the present development model of China is still difficult to sustain. Climate change is not the only environmental problem confronting China. Many environmental problems have not received the same international attention as climate change, but are essentially related to the survival of over one billion people in our country.

Take water pollution as an example. In recent years, drinking water sources in China have been troubled by the problem of water pollution, which is getting worse. Pollution incidents frequently break out, and drinking water safety for residents is severely jeopardized. According to

---

market, and continuously coordinated interest relations. These are all prerequisites for the technological revolution.

[6] "Whoever cannot master energy cannot master his own future." (Barack Obama). That is, whoever loses his autonomy over energy cannot control his own future.

the "Monthly report on water quality of centralized drinking water sources in 113 key cities of environmental protection" issued in June 2006 by Central Environmental Monitoring Station, China, water quality in 16 cities is not up to standard, accounting for 14% of the key cities; 74 drinking water sources do not meet the standards, accounting for 20.1% of the drinking water sources in the key cities; 527 million tons of water do not meet the standards, accounting for 32.3% of the total water withdrawal in the key cities. According to the study of our research group, with the increase of urbanization rate, the domestic water demand of urban residents in China will be at least 2–3 times that of the current level in 2030. With the current scale and speed of water pollution, it will be very difficult to ensure the safety of drinking water in China for a long period of time in the future.

The overall deterioration of the environment will intensify social conflicts, and the shortage of energy and resources will put sustained economic development under an unprecedented and severe test. Will China's future be like the US, Germany, or Japan of today? In 2005, energy consumption per capita for China was 1.5 tons of standard coal. If it reaches 9.8 tons of standard coal, which is the current level in the US, China will consume 13 billion tons of standard coal, which is equivalent to the energy consumption of the whole world in 2005 and 57 times the scale of China's new energy (hydropower, nuclear power, and wind power) in 2008. If it reaches the current level of Japan or Germany, China will still need to consume more than 6 billion tons of standard coal. Future China thus cannot be a country like the US or any other developed country, but must explore new development concepts and strategies based on its specific conditions.

Third, the "surgical CO_2 emission reduction scenario" under the traditional development model may produce even worse results. In China, some regard the issue of climate change as pure "foreign interference". They believe that as long as China is not bound up too soon by the international commitments to emission reduction, the country can continue with the present development momentum and achieve the goal of modernization. Once the inflection point of the Kuznets curve is reached, all problems can be solved. There is also an opposing view: China need not worry about being committed to emission reduction too early, because it may force the country to directly adopt latest technology, give full play to the low-cost advantage of backwardness, and realize emission reduction by strides.

Our research shows that the above two views each have their own theoretical rationale and supporting forces, but both fail to fully recognize the particularity of the development path of China. The two conflicting views may in reality collide and mix into a "two-skin" situation: on the one hand, the present model of economic growth is continued; on the other hand, foreign energy technologies and equipment are widely adopted. This local-surgery-like low-carbon scenario is likely to be counterproductive, rendering China excessively dependent on and restricted by foreign technology and making it tend to ignore social balance and environmental problems other than greenhouse gases in the process of highlighting "low carbon".

In short, an important issue facing China's climate policy is not about whether China will save energy and reduce emissions in the future, but about whether it will "improve the environment under a new development model" or "save energy and reduce emissions under the current development model". The former means that no matter how uncertain climate change is, China can develop autonomously, harmoniously, and sustainably. This is a longer-term choice with less chance of regrets. With the latter, it is difficult for China's development to get out of the passive situation in some cases.

Those who do not consider the future are not wise enough to consider the moment. In order to truly change the mode of development, China cannot blindly imitate and follow the footsteps of developed countries to deal with its unique difficulties as a developing country. China cannot solve problems by having a mindset of creating problems. While learning from the experience of developed countries, China should also treat it as a long-term development strategy to seek an opportunity to break away from the lock-in of the traditional development path. This is the dual wisdom China should consider in dealing with climate change. This does not mean refusal of industrialization and material input, but encouragement of a creative spirit by which to initiate innovation with Chinese characteristics, and also having a realistic attitude by which to distinguish advantages and disadvantages. Otherwise, it is very difficult for China to get out of the trap of extensive growth, to gain freedom of development in a future world full of uncertainties, and even more difficult to make its due contribution to mankind as a rising power of ecological civilization.

2. Long-Term Strategies to Deal With Climate Change

2.1. *China should present its ideas and methods in dealing with climate change to the international community, and make its own historical contributions in terms of thoughts*

First of all, to enable the Chinese people, who make up 20% of the world's population, to lead a well-off life is the ultimate goal of the development of China. The emergence of a "two-type (that is, resource-conserving and environment-friendly)" harmonious society is in itself the greatest contribution to the sustainable development of the world.

Second, China should firmly join the Third-World countries and those who care about the fate of the world in resisting and criticizing the selfish and unjust behaviors of some developed countries on the issue of climate change and promoting the formation of a more equitable international order. The US, which accounts for 5% of the world's population, is now consuming 22% of the world's energy, and its behavior in international affairs, especially climate change, are disappointing. Historical experience shows that, without profound worldwide justice in the use of resources and freedom of development, it is impossible to change the long-term trend of "partial improvement and overall deterioration" of the world's environment, to create a generally clean world and to reach a peaceful, stable, and sustainably solution to the problem of global climate change. If those countries that have long occupied and squandered resources disproportionate to their population continue to ignore this problem, they may further lose their moral status. China should continue to strengthen international cooperation and endeavor to promote beneficial interaction on issues of justice and environmental issues.

Finally, we should advocate and realize sustainable consumption and production modes, and firmly oppose luxury consumption. First, energy consumption will probably increase in the future, because there are still quite a few people in China who live at a lower standard of living, and thus we need to reserve room for more carbon emission for such people. Second, active measures should be taken to restrict those who luxuriously consume energy, including the new luxury groups of China. Third, China should provide a rational guide to consumerism and set up the worldwide banner of opposing the imitation of the American way of life and advocating for sustainable consumption.

2.2. *China should work hard to turn to an autonomous and sustainable development model with active adjustment and preparation during the transitional period*

At the Copenhagen Summit, China showed to the world its determination to reduce greenhouse gas emissions. China's coal-based energy supply structure and its national conditions at the stage of industrialization, however, determine that considerable efforts must be made to achieve emission reduction targets. The next decade can be viewed as a transitional period for China to deal with higher emission reduction targets. The country should hurry up to carry out policy adjustments and system construction in various related fields to strengthen the ability of the whole society to adapt to risks. We should not single-mindedly seek the polish of indicators, and in the course, miss the opportunity of innovation and transformation. During the course of development, the country has various choices, ranging from equipment renewal, technology type, urban and rural development planning to life style and system arrangement. We should take care to avoid ignoring and giving up these choices in pursuit of short-term interests. It is otherwise inevitable that China will be locked in the existing international system of division of labor. We should cherish the rights to development, create conditions for the transformation to an independent low-carbon development, avoid falling into the above-mentioned "passive" reduction after 2020, and lay a foundation for China to turn to an independent and sustainable development path. A few forward-looking adjustments are detailed in the following:

(1) In structural adjustment, the degree of export-oriented economy of China should be adjusted to a more reasonable level. At present, China excessively relies on exports and foreign capital to promote economic

growth and employment. For a big power, it is fairly passive, and this is undesirable in the long run. China should carry out the transformation to "meeting domestic demand" slowly and unswervingly, and make it more in line with overall sustainable development, rather than meet the short-term interests of special departments and interest groups. It requires adjusting and straightening out a series of domestic relations, including industry structure, fiscal and taxation policies import and export policies, and supporting financial reforms.

(2) Improve the pattern of technological progress. After more than 30 years of economic development, China should be able to achieve self-reliance in major technologies. For this purpose, we attach importance to international technology transfer on the one hand, and on the other hand, we should build and develop our own innovation capability. In terms of technology selection, we should not only develop and master "high, fine, and sharp" technologies in key fields or industries, but also select some environmentally friendly technologies that attract the labor force and enhance employment in the field of general consumer goods production. Taking the basic conditions of China into consideration, the goal of technological progress cannot be too simple. Large-, medium-, and small-sized enterprises should be mobilized to work with a joint effort to form a diversified, multi-leveled and multi-formed pattern of technological progress. Measures should be taken to prevent three kinds of unfavorable situations: first, the "foreign seeking" line of thought that favors foreign investment is not conducive to healthy competition and the growth of domestic enterprises. Second is the "one leg" development pattern in technology that seeks size and scale. A rough practice of focusing on the "big" and ignoring the "small" needs to be prevented. Third is the preference for top-down, single-handed, and centralized decision-making, which restricts local technological innovation, curbs technological diversity, and leads to loss of traditional wisdom.

(3) Establish economic, cultural, and social mechanisms that lead to sustainable consumption patterns. Sustainable consumption refers to "providing services and related products to meet the basic needs of mankind, improving the quality of life while minimizing the use of natural resources and toxic materials and minimizing the waste and

pollutants generated during the life cycle of services or products, thus not endangering the needs of future generations" (United Nations Environment Program). The consumption pattern of China should be suitable for its national conditions of lack of resources and large population, and still more in line with the fact that a large number of Chinese people live below average standard. Energy conservation and emission reduction in China should go one step further to guide consumption, and this includes imposing high luxury tax on high energy consumption, such as large housing and large displacement vehicles; laying out strict requirements of low energy consumption for urban planning, encouraging for example public transportation; and so on. Chinese people should carry forward the traditional virtues of thrift, and the country should strengthen the construction of socialist culture and morality, and advocate that those who get rich first live a rich but not extravagant life, and lead others to become rich together instead of, in terms of values and lifestyles, closely following the Western way of consumerism and luxury consumption.

The above three adjustments are important and difficult, which will impact the habitual mentality, interfere with the vested interests of some groups, and even increase the current difficulties and pressures. It is by no means a job for a few experts and administrative departments. The historical mission of promoting the formation of a new development model is a national event involving more than one generation. The active participation of the whole society and an open and transparent decision-making process will have an inestimable impact on improving decision-making, heightening the level of innovation, and promoting the concept of sustainable development of all citizens.

3. Climate Change as a Point of Departure to Reach a Consensus by All Sectors of the Society on Long-Term Development Strategy

The Copenhagen Conference is over. The following facts have been made clear.

First, in the face of possible disasters caused by climate change, human society has made a lot of effort, but so far it has not been able to think as a community of interests. We should continue our efforts to promote global cooperation.

Second, it is not that the energy resources of the earth are not sufficient to maintain human existence, but that they cannot maintain the way of life human beings are pursuing today. Compared with developing countries, developed countries have almost all the advantages. However, their worries about "free rides" of developing countries in climate cooperation exceed their fears about common disasters of mankind. Their desire for interests exceeds their determination to take responsibility, and they do not want to put "common but differentiated responsibilities" into actions of emission reduction, which falls well within their capability. They could but would not do it.

Third, environmental effects caused by the rapid expansion of China's economy have become a global topic. The energy consumption per capita for China is only 15% that of the US. Some Western media, however, have exerted enormous international pressure on China regardless of the fact that China is a developing country. These media obviously do not lack analytical skills, but lack the courage to be fair. While exaggerating and criticizing the total environmental impact of China, they also admire and want to make use of China's huge open market. This double attitude toward China shows that Western countries are really concerned only with their own interests, ignoring the happiness of the Chinese people. The pressures created by such selfishness, arrogance, and prejudice will only strengthen the determination of China to pursue an independent road to sustainable development.

The Copenhagen Summit has attracted the unprecedented attention of the Chinese people. It makes us strongly feel that there is an inextricable link between China and the world. Facing complex external challenges, only vision and self-improvement can enable the Chinese people to realize their long-cherished wish to live a happy and dignified life and to make a unique historical contribution to the coexistence and common prosperity of the whole world.

Chapter 2

Uncertainties, Lock-In, and "Energy-Conservation First" Strategy: A Discussion on Methodology

Yisheng Zheng

Institute of Quantitative & Technical Economics,
Chinese Academy of Social Sciences

1. Coping With the Turning Point: A Reconsideration of "Energy-Conservation First"

1.1. *Uncertainties*

In China, few people openly deny the necessity of "energy-conservation first". In a seemingly uncontroversial atmosphere, "energy-conservation first", however, may easily turn into an empty notion of "political correctness". As a result, one might not be that confident when it comes to actual actions. As to what extent it is necessary to conserve energy, there are certain consensuses, but more are yet to be established. Some established consensuses are as follows: (1) It is generally believed that in China, as there is increasing pressure about the world environment (especially the climate problem), there is also an increasing pressure of domestic environment and energy resources. The central government has already made emission reduction and energy conservation (instead of GDP) as hard restrictive indicators during the 11th Five-Year Plan period. (2) The energy potential of China does not seem able to relieve the pressure on energy supply. The consensus, however, has weaknesses: There is a wide gap between local governments and the central government (many local governments do not feel the macro-pressure). More importantly, we have not paid enough attention to how to understand the impact of these pressures, and especially how to deal with future uncertainties.

Human beings have never before realized that they live in a world full of uncertainties (in the human world, uncertainty has never been as prominent as it is now). Take energy as an example. (1) Even if a common agreement tends to be reached about the authenticity and scientificity of global warming and its influence on human life, there are still many uncertainties as to how different countries should adapt to the new situation and share responsibilities thereof. (2) We have many substitute choices of energy resources for fossil fuels, and some of them may well be the eve of a major new energy technology revolution. This includes: a) new energy, such as that from nuclear fusion and combustible ice; b) low-carbon energy technologies, such as carbon recovery and storage, and nuclear energy; c) development of renewable energy. But no one is clear about the time of commercial breakthrough (when will these technologies be commercialized)? (3) Even with fossil fuels, despite the remarks about the depletion of oil, once there is the possibility of cheaper access to energy from outside, or price fluctuations, it will inevitably induce the parties concerned to take chances. Some think to themselves: What is the meaning of striving to conserve these fuels? Shall we stick to our plan and continue to conserve energy, or flow with the trend and adjust at any time? Undoubtedly, it requires wisdom to make decisions under uncertain conditions and a clear line of thought to grasp the long-term interests in a changing situation. It is very difficult for a big country to always have its decision-making at optimal. What is more realistic is the common understanding of major principles in a more general sense. In terms of energy strategy, two questions concern us the most: (1) What is the greatest risk to China? (2) What is the most valuable strategic opportunity for China?

1.2. *What is the worst case scenario that we should endeavor to prevent?*

The pressures on the environment (including the international pressure of climate change) and resources (such as energy security) may bring some hard constraints for us. These hard constraints on the total amount of energy will be a precondition for energy conservation. However, against the background of uncertainty, it is hard for us to confidently determine the necessary or suitable amount of energy to be saved, even though such an estimation is of great significance. What is more certain is that both the reduction of fossil fuel supply and the advent of international environmental pressure will have a great impact on the economy and the existing energy-based system of China. The impact will come to China sooner or later. It can be said that the question is not whether you want to build an energy-conserving society, but whether you move toward it actively or passively. The question is not whether you need to transform your energy system, but whether you transform it smoothly or with chaos? The adaptation to a new energy system will start sooner or later. The most important question is probably whether China's response strategy is timely and far-sighted. Will historical opportunities be lost? Is the adaptation costly? Starting from this point, we have conceived four scenarios: scenario A is the consequence of a lack of adaptability when the world does not have cheap traditional energy. This scenario is BAU — a situation of general technological progress that does not give priority to energy conservation. Scenario A1 concerns the shutdown of a large number of enterprises under the new price system and the inevitable "planned distribution of energy". This will lead to self-importance because of possession of energy; cause separation of powers; deepen social conflicts; result in economic collapse; and may even lead to division. Scenario A2 is about immediately obtaining new and easily accessible cheap energy, and no crisis follows. Scenario B is about an immediate slowdown of the economy, which leads to reform of the production and consumption structure according to a reasonable energy consumption target, or enforcing total quantity control with the goal of entering into a low-energy-consuming society sooner. Scenario C starts with tapping the real potential, focuses on the cultivation of comprehensive capabilities, gradually expands and strengthens the energy system that adapts to the new price system, makes the transition as smooth as possible, and turns to an energy-conserving society.

The logic of this chapter is: With an energy-conserving society as the inevitable result, the difference is whether the transition is active or passive. When it comes to passive emergency "energy conservation", there is not much left for us to discuss. What we need is precisely a strategy of "early preparation and smooth transition" in order to reduce the risk of national development and avoid the worst-case scenario A1. We yearn for scenario C and need C as a development model. As for the big transition that is likely to come, it concerns the rise and fall of a country on whether it is prepared or not. Therefore, the key task is whether we can adjust the energy-economic system in time, and the real question is whether we have the ability to undertake such an adjustment and whether we can continuously expand it.

1.3. *What are the strategic opportunities most important to us?*

As most of our problems or dilemmas can be attributed to "underdevelopment", most of our opportunities also stem from it. More and more people find it self-deceiving to handle the deterioration of environment and resources (energy) under the original development model. Since the conditions of population, environment, and resources are inherently harsh for China and the country lost its historical opportunity to consume the world's non-renewable energy and environmental space at a low cost or with no scruples, which was the situation in countries that developed early, China cannot and should not develop along the old path of industrialization. As long as we can get rid of the pseudo-historical view that one can only develop by following the steps of forerunners, as long as we can receive the applause for our rapid development with a clear mind, and as long as we can get over the temptation of lifestyle of industrialized countries, especially the US, it is not difficult to realize a simple truth: a large portion of our hope for survival and development comes from the reality of our underdevelopment. This is, we still have quite a lot of choices for technical routes and equipment. We have not yet adopted an Americanized consumption pattern. We have not completed the urbanization process. The history of evolution is full of path dependence, but there are also forks in the road, and some new choices (perhaps not active) do not belong to or favor pioneering countries but rather belong to or favor late-comers.

From a historical perspective, this may be a real opportunity for "new industrialization". Speaking of "comparative advantage", this may be said to be our biggest, long-term, and real "comparative advantage", not "cheap labor" and not "low environmental standards". We can turn to a new, clean low-carbon energy system at a lower cost than Western countries. We can adapt to a new era with less historical burden. We may be the earliest and largest market of some new energy form, at least in some respects. However, the period of historical opportunity is limited. It is a major bifurcation point in the evolution of history. Opportunities are valuable, and once lost they will not come back again. Therefore, the most significant goal of China's energy strategy should be "timely transformation of energy system".

2. Can We Overcome the Forces that Hinder Our Transformation? — A Reconsideration of the Challenges Confronting "Energy-Conservation First"

After confirming that "energy-conserving first" is secondary to the goal of "timely transformation of the energy system", the question now becomes how to make it feasible. Briefly, from the production side, there are three ways to save energy: saving energy by economic structure, improving technical efficiency, and directly reducing production consumption. From the consumer side, there are also three ways: improving energy efficiency of consumption, changing lifestyle, and directly reducing the demand for consumption. China has been carrying out energy conservation and related policies (including changing the mode of economic growth) for decades. The design of the new policies should not leave the experience aside, that is, it must carefully examine what problems have been encountered and what problems are being encountered in the practice of policies in the above-mentioned energy-conserving ways. For the sake of simplicity, three ways should be discussed here: first, technological upgrading and consumption rate increase; second, changing of the way of consumption (life); and third, structural energy conservation. From the perspective of capability of energy system transformation, we focus on the following questions: What hinders us from turning into an energy-conserving society? Where do all kinds of "inertia" come from?

2.1. *What hinders the renewal of technologies?*

The energy-conserving policy of China can be said to be dominated by technological upgrading. For this purpose, the relevant departments in China have made efforts over the years in terms of price, management, and other incentive policies, which lead to a clear improvement of energy and technological efficiency. However, the long-standing problem of "lack of motivation" has not been solved. The author believes that this is due to three problems.

2.1.1. *Technology lock-in of the market is the root cause*

Many bottom-up models are based on the choice of "regretless technology" (i.e., technically and economically feasible) and cost totaling. Their macroeconomic conclusions, however, often prove impractical and over-optimistic, though some empirical studies show that there are indeed many companies enjoying a "win–win" situation of environment (or energy conservation) and economic benefits. Why is this? We can generally blame the poor policy environment, and attribute it to the fact that some social costs have not been included. But from a systematic point of view, we should pay special attention to the problem of "technology lock-in". "Technology lock-in" refers to the refusal of enterprises or industries to replace or improve existing technologies — they lack motivation, preferring to use existing technologies, even though energy-conserving technologies prove more beneficial at current market prices. That is to say, they are no longer able to survive without the existing technical systems, which makes the whole technical system extremely inert. What causes the lock-in is the interconnection and mutual need of various links in the technology system, as well as the interaction and mutual assistance between technology and related institutions. A complex system between technology and institutions has been formed. No link in the system is an independent unit, and all of them co-exist and co-evolve within the process by interdependence and mutual reinforcement. Once locked, that is, once the complex system of technology and institutions is formed, it cannot be easily replaced and give way to new substitute technology, although the latter is often superior to existing technology. Some Western scholars have clearly attributed the slow diffusion of clean energy technologies to "carbon lock-in" — the industrialized countries have fallen deep into the existing techno-economic system of petroleum energy (for example, large electric power system and small car transportation system), in which all links are locked, from production to life, from companies to government institutions.

Obviously, China also suffers from market and technology lock-in which is even more serious and more complicated. Some enterprises or sectors of China, when updating technologies and equipment, blindly pursue short-term benefits and do not pay enough attention to their energy efficiency, connectivity with the new generation of technologies, learnability, and compatibility. As a result, a large number of equipment and technologies have been imported and reimported. They are generally more advanced than those of China, but soon will become outdated in exporting countries. Once such production capacity is introduced, it will be in service for decades, and a huge system will be formed consisting of the supply of raw materials and a series of supporting projects. If what is introduced is high-energy-consuming technologies and is difficult to connect with the future technology system, it may constitute a technology lock-in that is unfavorable to future development, repelling new technology, even if it has better environmental economic benefits (under the new price structure). The challenge for our enterprises is to overcome their short-sightedness and reject some well-renowned "advanced but declining technologies" (especially those from multinational corporations with strong economic and political influence). Such technologies may lock us in. What is to be guarded against is less the selfish strategy of multinational corporations than the possibility that domestic interest groups pursue their own interests at the cost of the whole nation.

Market and technology lock-in not only narrows the "space of regretless choice" at a micro-level, but also serves as an important factor affecting macroeconomic strategy, for undoubtedly energy prices are low from the perspective of energy conservation. But why does such a situation subsist for a long time? From a macroeconomic perspective, economic growth (in terms of GDP), especially the growth of some export products and "high value-added industries" such as automobiles, is to a certain extent supported by resources such as low-cost energy. It can thus be said that they have always been protected by policies, which in turn interact with the low price of fuels in consumer goods so as to form the reality of low tolerance. With the exception of energy conservation and environmental protection departments, the dominating sectors of society do not care about the social costs (such as environment and destruction of resources due to low recovery rates) incurred by excessive energy consumption. The low market price, which ignores social costs, does not reflect the value or scarcity of such resources as energy. It only reflects the current dominant position of capital in various factors of production, especially the prominent position of some energy consuming industries. Lying behind the GDP growth, which is pushed by the seemingly "natural" market forces, are some industries implicitly subsidized by huge social costs. At present, China is not resolute in adjusting and raising energy prices (including taxes), precisely because the driving force is not enough to change the industrial development pattern supported by low prices for many years (and the worldwide interest pattern based on such prices). This is the root cause that hinders us from getting rid of the "pattern locked by the current market price system". This kind of problem is more associated with the "problem of market failure".

2.1.2. *The game of "direct rent-seeking" is not over yet*

With a lack of protection of natural resources — either due to a lack of clear definition of rights (property rights, use rights, income rights, etc.) or of realization capability, or due to a lack of effective supervision — preemption of public resources has become a strategic choice that is far more preferable than enhancing efficiency. That is, if some investments and developments utilize resources by possessing free public or unknown resources, then the more resources are utilized, the more public resources will be occupied (see the authors' article "Joint production model"). Thus, a game pattern is formed: whoever occupies and uses more resources is the winner of the competition, that is to say, "wasters benefit". This is manifested in the knowingly repeated low-level production and construction in the crude exploitation of energy and mineral resources. This kind of behavior produces a kind of "super market demand" for resources, that is, the excess demand for resources promoted by the system. There are other related economic phenomena: in state-paid projects, the demand is greatly exaggerated (e.g. the demand for water resources in water diversion projects and the scale of pollution control projects); the competition between local governments for GDP growth leads to economic policies that put too much emphasis on investment and exports (instead of using consumption to guide economy). This is more gross waste than the above-mentioned market failure. However, GDP achievement, government behavior that is oriented toward self-interest, and its "rent-seeking" behavior are precisely the forces that hinder us from getting out of this situation. All these problems are related to the fact that the government has not actually turned to public management and public finance, related to the condition of a semi-market economy. We may thus call these "pre-market problems".

2.1.3. *The factors restricting our energy-conserving technology renewal are related to unbalanced development*

The dual economic and social conditions have formed two industrial sectors in China: one is the more advanced industrial sector located mainly in major cities, namely, the first industrial sector; the other is the "inferior and small industrial sector" located mainly in rural areas, namely, the second industrial sector. The second sector is backward in technology and economy but performs certain social functions. Over the years, equipment in the first industrial sector have been continuously upsized and their efficiency increased. However, to a certain extent, the progress has been discounted in the overall effect due to the gradual transfer of backward equipment to the second industrial sector.

Instead of arguing about "at which point of development we are now standing" in terms of the Kuznets curve, it is better to find out our real problems and practical starting points — is there not a shortage of examples where things could have been done but never have been?

2.2. **What are the obstacles to controlling consumer demand?**

The most powerful consumer groups in China are blindly and comprehensively imitating the lifestyle of developed countries. Many people admit in the abstract that the latter's way of life should not be the direction of

China's development, but still move toward it recklessly. Lifestyle is the final determinant of the composition of economic demand and supply system. Once formed, it is difficult to pull back due to path dependence. We should not be led into this road by the dream of a Western lifestyle. This is another bifurcation to be guarded against, which we are about to enter into and be locked in. The problem, however, would be better broken down into several parts than treated as a whole. The first situation is irrational waste. We have the potential to overcome waste. In the first place, the government is perniciously used to ostentation and extravagance. There is a lack of effective supervision over the public use of public resources, and then there is also the social mentality of vying for and flaunting in terms of consumption. The second situation is the dominant influence of consumerism, especially the continuous and almost endless guidance, education, and stimulation of the consumption patterns of developed countries to the new middle-income groups (not to mention the high-income stratum) in China. The third situation is that the consumption level of over one billion people in China does not need to be suppressed, but needs to be developed, including the impact of urbanization on the lower strata and farmers. Special attention should be paid to the fact that China's resident consumption should not be compressed in principle, but due to the large increase, special measures should be taken to prevent low-level duplication.

It is easy to overcome irrational waste, but it is difficult to overcome consumerism, which is the biggest challenge we face. What we want to challenge and get out of is the centuries-old concept of market consumption. In an era when human beings are trying to measure and reduce their "ecological footprints", we cannot accept the old concept that consumption is an "individual right", which is not subject to discussion and change, just as enterprises cannot be left without any social responsibility. One of the specific challenges at present is that even if China can successfully realize the new macroeconomic orientation of relying on consumption to drive the economy, there is still a huge gap or conflict with our concept of saving. The shift from investment-driven growth and export-driven growth to "consumption-driven growth" is undoubtedly a major progress.

This can be confirmed by the success of the "National Income Doubling Plan" which began in the late 1950s. This, however, poses a new challenge to the energy-conserving policy. The upcoming change will definitely make energy conservation a more important and urgent issue. It requires encouraging new lifestyles in a timely manner and formulating policies of guiding consumption as soon as possible so as not to get into the mire of consumerism. This is a critical historical moment.

Energy conservation always starts with less controversial points (e.g., "win–win" and "no regrets"), and becomes more difficult when there is no other way out. Generally speaking, exploring new resources (especially accessible public resources) has the topmost priority, and this is followed in order by improving energy efficiency and consumption pattern transformation, and reducing the amount of living activities is probably a helpless choice. For those countries which have sufficient funds, strong capability of technological innovation, and powerful consumer rights, efforts will be made in preemption, exploring new resources and improving technological efficiency. The latter two ways, that is, consumption pattern transformation and reducing the amount of living activities, will be of less focus. Although there is reasonable room for energy consumption to rise in China, the country would have to face up to the choice of consumption guidance and control. This is the fate that weak countries have to endure.

What can we do to bring the people back who are being indulged in consumerism? Strictly speaking, consumerism is not simple a "waste", but a pattern of life–production lock-in. According to consumerists and their behaviors, energy conservation looks like energy reduction. Only irrational waste is what is commonly called "waste".

2.3. *"Structural energy conservation" should not be mixed with other energy-conserving policies*

The so-called "structural energy conservation" is an ambiguous term. Some people regard it as the result of artificial adjustment of economic structure, which is sometimes understood as adjusting the investment–consumption structure; sometimes as adjusting the structure of primary, secondary, and tertiary industries; and sometimes as adjusting industrial structure (especially the policy to suppress high energy-consuming industries). Others also view it as a reduction in energy consumption derived from natural changes in economic structure caused by economic growth. The understanding of structural energy conservation concerns changes in the industry structure as brought about completely by plans and arrangements or purely by spontaneous economic development.

The share of structural energy conservation can hardly be ignored. Regardless of whether structural energy conservation comes from government plans or market forces, estimations of both predictive and regressive economic models show that its influence is considerable. For example, the World Bank believes that changes in economic structure took up 70% of the force to slow down environmental pollution in the 1980s in China. The Development Center of the State Council also holds that 70% of the force to slow down the increase in energy intensity (in the same period) should be attributed to changes in economic structure.

Yet structural energy conservation is difficult to observe. This is because first, people have different understandings of its exact meaning, and thus it is difficult to clearly attribute energy conversation to a given factor. The difference between different speculations is mainly due to different assumptions.

Moreover, structural energy conservation as a policy is extremely difficult to control. Can the economic structure of a big country (e.g., investment–consumption structure, primary, secondary, and tertiary industry structure) be adjusted arbitrarily? It is only possible to say that when a policy has worked, it must be in line with the tendency of the times in a relatively long-term structural evolution process. The main forces to form and change a structure come from the more basic level of economy: system, endowment of natural resources and population, international environment, and development level. Economic strategies (such as policies to adjust industrial structure, especially policies to suppress high energy-consuming industries) are also largely built upon them.

We cannot attribute the economic structure of a big country to a single factor, and we cannot ignore the fact that change in economic structure comes from an organic process of interaction and combination of these factors. What the input–output table reflects is only one aspect or angle of the economic building that is susceptible to quantitative descriptions, and such descriptions are often static. It reveals the connection between economic sectors, but it cannot simulate the process of structural adjustment and also fails to tell us the cost of the changes and their feasibility. Some experiences of China show that the correlation between structural energy conservation and structural policies is much weaker than expected. For example, repeatedly suppressing high energy-consuming and high environment-polluting industries (such as shutting down "inferior and small" enterprises) over a long period of time has not achieved satisfactory results. The existence of "rebound" shows that there is still an economic need for them: banning them here and now will result in them springing up elsewhere, in another way. If such limited and intensified structural adjustment does not lead to desirable results, the result of a deeper structural adjustment is even less optimistic.

Taking the unexpected results into consideration, we should admit that economic structure is not something that can be fully controlled by policies. The decrease (or increase) in energy consumption intensity caused by the process or fluctuation of economic development should not be treated as an indicator for achievements (or failures) of politics. In short, energy-conserving policy should influence structural change as far as possible, but it should not be denied that it is not sufficient to bring about structural changes, let alone control them. Certainly, we do not mean that we cannot resist or do anything about the economic structure as reflected by the world division of labor other than adapt to it. What we mean is that we should not mix structural energy conservation with other energy-conserving policies.

3. Firm Policies With Uncertainties: A New Viewpoint of Energy Conservation

As explained before, energy conservation is aimed at promoting a timely transformation of the energy system, and the biggest challenge to it is whether the influence of technology, consumption and path dependence (lock-in) in economic structure can be overcome. We also explicate that the difficulty in formulating a firm energy-conserving policy lies first in the various uncertainties and, second, in the decentralized nature of energy-conserving work. The new idea of energy conservation should be targeted at these problems. In short, the new strategy can be called the "strategy of getting out of lock-in under uncertainties", because some lock-in states can be alleviated and avoided. The strategy will be focused on the following points.

3.1. *Chinese energy-conserving policy should concentrate on capability development*

On the one hand, politics and economy change very fast. Experience has shown that our forecast of economy and energy consumption over the past 30 years is quite inaccurate. Considering the changes in the world's economy and environment and their integration into one body and mutual influence, and technological development and the difficulty of predicting major technological breakthroughs, human beings have increasingly made decisions on the condition of uncertainties. On the other hand, for a big country, a major policy like "energy-conserving first" needs to be stable and firm. It can be neither too rigid nor too soft. Then how to do it? What makes this problem even more complicated is the fact that important measures are always lagging behind in effect, and immediate measures always fail to produce sustainable effects. The fact is well known, but many policymakers and researchers suffer from being uneasy and too eager for immediate effects and quick profits.

The most long-term value is capability. We shall have consequential results for sure, such as the amount of fossil energy saved and the quantity of pollution reduced. We may, however, always be in a passive situation if all efforts are made to meet standards (whether they are set by ourselves or international agreements) without considering their subsequent and overall impacts. Of course, we have firmly replaced backward projects by technological upgrading, and results have been achieved, but this is not enough. The capability that we are talking about does not simply refer to strengthening current competitiveness (such as cost-effectiveness level), but includes the compatibility to expand the existing production and consumption modes and make them susceptible to continual improvement in the future. Special emphasis is placed here on the capability to understand the period of opportunity and adjust the pattern of one's own interests. China is the largest market for new (or low-carbon) energy systems in an international competition when the world has begun to adapt to the "post-petroleum energy era". It is in itself a huge strategic resource for China.

Everyone wants to seize this great historical opportunity as early as possible, because it is beneficial to seize it, but harmful if let go. And it is we who should cherish it the most. Like other natural resources, it is a resource for progress to a capable host; to an incompetent host, it is a resource for others, nothing to himself, and sometimes even a curse.

3.2. *"Conservation" should become the common will of the whole country and the whole society*

Although "energy-conserving first" is in fact demanded by the times, which requires opportunist-like flexibility, it is also a firm pursuit of an ideal goal to establish an energy-conserving society that can develop sustainably in the future. Before setting up goals, such as total energy conservation (including pollution emissions), energy consumption of GDP, and technical unit consumption, and in what scope and in what ways to achieve these goals, the concept of energy conservation should be established in the first place. The country needs to adopt a historical view and stand fast so as not to be influenced by short-term economic growth. With the pursuit of GDP as a principle, energy-conserving strategy based on transformation can provide no way out. Since energy conservation involves problems of a different nature (e.g., pre-market problems, market problems, and post-market problems), it requires various methods (ranging from economic system reform and cultivation of technological innovation environment to promotion of social concept transformation) and different social forces. Energy conservation can only be achieved by the concerted efforts of the whole society. If it only stays at the stage of establishing policies by the central government and implementing these policies by local governments, no profound network of social movement can be formed. Without such a network, continuous process of system reform, technological innovation, and concept transformation will not only find it difficult to succeed but may also run the risk of being terminated halfway. Obviously, all links in the process require national will and consensus. The most important manifestation of the national-social will is that it has the power and the ability to overcome the strong resistance that hinders the country from getting out of or not slipping into the situation of production and consumption lock-in, and especially has the way to adjust the established pattern of interests. It should also be manifested in the promotion of an overall and continuous adjustment of the financial system, tax policy, financial system, local development strategy, and foreign economic policy, until the root cause has been dealt with, and the elements of the system that encourage waste are completely eliminated. Energy conservation under the current development mode is extremely limited, but this is only the beginning. As long as we start to dispense with the overdependence on the original energy systems which inefficiently utilize a large amount of fossil fuels, greater potential can be tapped.

3.3. *Energy conservation requires a systematic view*

First, the energy-conserving policy should be further coordinated with environmental policies. Energy conservation is important, but it should not become a closed system of policies, pursuing an absolutely independent goal. It must coordinate with those policies that have complementary relation with it, including clean (e.g., low-carbon) energy policies, environmental policies, and policies to save water and mineral resources. In developed countries, the relationship between energy policy and environmental policy is getting closer and closer. In a certain sense, there is a trend of environmental dominance. Considering the national conditions of China, it is not necessary for China to do so for the time being. However, the new energy-conserving policies should strengthen the connection, communication, and coordination with environmental policies, as they will otherwise restrict each other, leading to a waste of social and administrative resources.

In some developed countries, energy conservation and environmental policies are closely connected, and such a connection is even dominated by environmental requirements to a certain extent. This is because the environment directly affects the quality of life, international relations, and international agreements. Many environmental standards naturally become hard indicators, that is, they become ends — they are ends rather than means. For China, there will also be rigid requirements from the international environment in the future (it will not be an energy efficiency requirement, but may be an environmental requirement, such as total amount of emissions or total amount of energy consumption close to it).

Second, the energy-conserving policy should conform to the principle of general equilibrium. The principle of policy balance refers to the principle of focusing on general effects and being responsible for the ultimate and overall goals. For example, the trend toward duality of technological progress should be considered in the overall energy-conserving assessment. The influence of backward technologies that are not easy to monitor and have been transferred out of large cities and large-sized enterprises, and the social costs of shutting down these "inferior and small" enterprises, should also be taken into consideration in the overall policy. Do not repeat the old stories to the effect that "cities are promising and villages are deteriorating". We should establish the principle of general equilibrium in policy design to replace the principle that blindly encourages "localization (local or sectoral maximization)", and we should establish the concept of "opportunity cost" to replace the "all-or-nothing principle" in project evaluation.

Third, the energy-conserving policy should protect diversification, which is a principle of the "anti-lock-in strategy". Innovation is the soul of building a conserving society and the only way to deal with the major uncertainties and get out of some situations of being locked-in. Therefore, protecting diversity should become an important objective of policy so as to protect the creative spirit and expand the development space of new equipment and new modes. We must change the mentality of blindly seeking big size, protect local and decentralized technologies and designs, and suppress the force of monopoly, which is often source of lock-in.

Fourth, the removal of various barriers to energy conservation should be treated as one of the most important tasks of the government. Policies and standards should be not made out of consideration of easy administration and operation of a given department, but in favor of energy-conserving and innovative enterprises, helping them remove various obstacles. We take "technology lock-in" as the main focus of our policy. The reasons for this are as follows: (1) The problem it aims at is harmful and long-standing, and in particular need of resolution. The focus is not technological updating, but to find out obstacles. (2) Reality — our concern is not to increase investment in general, nor to single-mindedly advocate unrealistic technologies, but about the "feasible range" where efforts may lead to success. (3) The principle is to strive to achieve the highest point in the feasible range — to choose the most promising technology in this range. (4) It is likely to get out of the difficulty in the debate on the stage of development and seek a breakthrough point in the dilemma — neither falling into the old road of realism nor hanging in the pursuit of a new road of development with no idea of where to start. Theoretically speaking, this is a "real move" to clear the confusion caused by the "stage theory of development". We are trying to show that it is better to start from this problem than be engaged in empty talks about transforming the mode of growth.

4. Some Suggestions

First, energy conservation requires macro-policy adjustments. For example, in principle, policies should not protect low energy-efficiency industries, should not subsidize GDP growth in any way, and should encourage higher energy tax. China should step up its efforts to restrict the production of and shut down high energy-consumption enterprises. This is, of course, a trade-off, and there will be a cost. In the short term, the cost may overshadow the output. It cannot be completely avoided, either from the macro or from the micro point of view. In this sense, energy consumption per unit of GDP should not be treated as a major hard indicator, for it is self-contradictory in that on the one hand it encourages energy conservation and on the other hand it encourages an increase in GDP. The indicator proves a negative direction for places and industries that have the conditions to reduce energy intensity by increasing GDP. It is not conducive to controlling total energy consumption and environmental quality deterioration that is positively related to it.

Second, new reforms should be carried out in technical evaluation. In the first place, third-party assessment should be insisted upon without giving up "insider assessment". Second, new principles and standards should be established, taking uncertainties and technology lock-in into consideration.

It is foolish and unrealistic to attempt to accurately distinguish the origin and makeup of energy-conserving effects (whether it is the impact of macroeconomic changes, or general equipment updates, or changes of the original inefficient technical route), but it is absolutely necessary to pay attention to them and treat them differently. It is in itself a matter that may be energy-consuming and fruitless. It requires an in-depth study on how to do it. For example, how to guide enterprises to prefer advanced energy-efficient technologies to applicable technologies? How to change the regretless range of choices for enterprises? At least, those "advanced large companies" (some of them are multinational) do not deserve our best comments, if they delay the choice of better technologies with the excuse of good energy consumption indicators. Of course, it is difficult to evaluate the cost of technology adoption. Only with the idea of respecting but not worshipping can success possibly be achieved. An energy-conserving policy with capability as its focus represents a new generation of policies. Is it not understandable that it should be difficult?

Third, an authoritative agency should be established for communication between departments, such as a committee for the communication of economic–energy–environment departments.

Fourth, a system of broad social involvement should be instituted.

Chapter 3

Reducing Blindness in Energy Conservation and Emission Reduction: Some Reflections on the Indicators of Energy Consumption Intensity[1]

Yuxin Zheng

Institute of Quantitative & Technical Economics,
Chinese Academy of Social Sciences

China is now in the industrialization stage of rapid economic growth. Against the background of global warming and with the huge pressure of resources and environment, China has stepped up its regulation of energy conservation and emission reduction in recent years. After the 11th Five-Year Plan, a sharp drop in energy consumption intensity continues to be treated as a binding indicator in the 12th Five-Year Plan. Among the major countries in the world, China's attitude toward energy conservation and emission reduction is active. However, we should also be soberly aware that although China has made great efforts in energy conservation and emission reduction and has made remarkable achievements, there are still many areas both in understanding and in practice worth thinking about and improving. Facing these problems squarely and deepening the understanding of the targets and their regularity of energy conservation and emission reduction will be beneficial to the healthy development of

---

[1] The simplified version of this chapter was published in the 9th issue of *Study and Practice* in 2011 and was reproduced in full text in *Xinhua Digest*.

energy conservation and emission reduction in China and to the realization of the sustainable development strategy.

1. Energy Consumption Intensity, as an Efficiency Indicator, is Deficient

China takes energy intensity (energy consumption per unit of GDP) as an indicator of energy conservation. Obviously, energy consumption intensity is used here as an indicator of energy efficiency. The basic way to conserve energy and reduce emission is to improve energy efficiency. Apparently, it is logical that people want to achieve GDP growth with less energy consumption. Moreover, energy consumption intensity does reflect to a certain extent the macro-efficiency of an economy's energy consumption and is widely used at home and abroad. Yet an in-depth examination reveals that energy consumption intensity as a measure of energy efficiency has obvious defects. It cannot effectively reflect the level of energy conservation of the whole society. It is thus an obviously flawed practice to simply use it as an indicator for energy conservation, and to treat its decrease as rate of energy conservation.

1.1. *Energy consumption intensity is not a suitable indicator for energy conservation*

Energy consumption intensity reflects only the dependence of economic activities on current energy consumption and is not suitable for use as an indicator in energy conservation evaluation. Taking a look at the definition expression of energy consumption intensity, it is easy to see this point. The definition expression of energy consumption intensity is the ratio of current energy consumption to current GDP. Obviously, there is no consistency between input and output in this indicator, for current energy consumption does not represent all energy input, and current GDP does not equal the entire output of current energy consumption. Thus, energy consumption intensity cannot fully reflect the efficiency of energy consumption. To be precise, the intensity of energy consumption reflects only the degree of dependence of economic activities on current energy consumption.

The main reason why energy consumption intensity is often used as an efficiency indicator is that people often neglect the fact that the output flow of economic activities lags behind its input flow, and current input and current output do not exactly correspond. We'd like to call attention to the following two basic facts.

1.1.1. *Current energy consumption is not only the source of current GDP but also the source of future GDP*

Current energy consumption will not only contribute to current GDP, but also to future GDP. Thus, current GDP reflects only a part of the contribution of current energy consumption, and the contribution of current energy consumption to future GDP is not included.

For example, the energy consumed by infrastructure construction and other investments in fixed asset contributes not only to current GDP, but also to future GDP through condensation in fixed assets for a long time to come. Ignoring the contribution of current energy consumption to future GDP is a sign of lacking understanding of the time lag in output.

Obviously, energy efficiency as reflected by the ratio of current energy consumption to current GDP is not adequate. The fact that energy consumption intensity cannot reflect the contribution of current energy consumption to future GDP will lead to an overestimation of current energy consumption per unit of GDP. Generally speaking, the actual energy consumption per unit of GDP will be highly overestimated for economic activities that have long-term benefits, and for developing economies which are mainly driven by energy-intensive investment activities.

High investment rate is a stage feature for China, a country currently at the stage of primitive accumulation, which is an energy-intensive process.[2] High energy intensity is thus quite normal. At present, the main problem of China's economic development is not the high investment rate but the low efficiency of investment. Due to poor management, there are serious problems of unreasonable investment structure (excessive in some

---

[2] In China, it is generally believed that economic growth as driven by investment accounts for its low quality and unsustainability. It follows as a result of lacking understanding of the laws of economic growth at the current stage of development.

cases and insufficient in others), frequent mistakes in decision-making, low quality of projects, and poor economic benefits. For example, the level of urban planning in China is relatively low, and urban construction pursues ostentatious effects, concentrates on superficial aspects, and tends to lean to large-scale demolitions and reconstructions. In the meantime, water conservancy facilities and public facilities in cities, such as environmental protection facilities, public transportation, and underground engineering, are obviously lagging behind. A large number of buildings feature low-quality, poor energy conservation and have a short service life.[3] China eliminates its production capacity too rapidly. Seemingly, GDP grows very quickly, but the wealth accumulated is quite limited. There is no doubt that changing the situation constitutes an important aspect of improving energy efficiency and reducing waste.[4]

One of the prerequisites for changing this situation is to adopt a long-term view. The benefits of current investment and current energy consumption should be examined in a longer period of time. The limitation of energy consumption intensity as an indicator wrongly directs too much attention to short-term benefits, neglecting the long-term benefits of energy consumption. In fact, in China, a country at the stage of primitive accumulation, only a small portion of current energy consumption serves the current period — most of it contributes to long-term future development. At present, China adopts a hard hand in regulation, demanding a significant reduction in current energy consumption intensity, which is likely to neglect the long-term effect and effectiveness of investment. The practice actually encourages short-term behaviors, providing opportunities for lowering construction standards (such as energy-conserving standards and environmental protection standards) and jerry-building. It is not helpful in solving the problem of low investment efficiency and unreasonable structure, and is even likely to aggravate the situation. The current energy consumption intensity may be temporarily lowered, but in the long

---

[3] The average life span of buildings in China is 25–30 years, while in developed countries the average life span of buildings is longer, 132 years in the Great Britain, 85 years in France, and 80 years in the US. See http://news.sina.com.cn/c/2010-04-05/231820011742. shtml.

[4] It will also prove significant in reducing the financial risks of China.

run, and in general, more energy will be consumed. Future generations will thus be forced to bear more costs, including those of energy consumption. In fact, just taking a look at the fact that the drainage system of London built more than 150 years ago still functions well while most cities in China are often paralyzed by heavy rain, we will have a clear understanding of the situation.

1.1.2. *Current GDP involves not only the contribution of current energy consumption but also that of previous energy consumption*

As current GDP cannot reflect the total output of current energy consumption, current energy consumption cannot reflect the total energy consumption of current GDP either. In fact, current GDP depends not only on current energy consumption, but also on previous energy consumption. Previous energy consumption contributes to current GDP through condensation in infrastructure and other fixed assets. Therefore, the energy actually invested in current production includes both current energy consumption and the accumulated energy consumption condensed in fixed assets. Certainly, the ways in which the two (current energy consumption and cumulative energy consumption) contribute to production process are different. It is a complicated issue to calculate the service flow of energy input corresponding to current GDP, which we will not discuss here.

One of the fundamental differences between developing countries and developed countries is that developing countries are small in capital stock, while developed countries are large in capital stock. It can be taken to mean that compared with developing countries, GDP of developed countries enjoys greater contribution from energy and other resource consumption condensed in capital stock. Moreover, energy consumption is not only condensed in the huge capital stock possessed by developed countries, but in fact in all developments of modern civilization, including scientific and technological advantages, high educational level, good environment, and so on. The current low energy consumption intensity in developed countries is based on a large amount of energy consumption in history. Therefore, if energy consumption intensity, which ignores past energy consumption and reflects only current energy consumption, is taken as an indicator to examine energy efficiency of current GDP, it will definitely lead to an overestimation of energy efficiency in developed countries and an underestimation of energy efficiency in developing countries. Obviously, energy consumption intensity cannot correctly reflect the differences in energy efficiency between countries at different stages of development.

In China, the comparison between China and developed countries in terms of energy consumption intensity[5] provides the basis for the judgment that China is enjoying low energy efficiency and excessively consuming energy, which leads to an overestimation of its potential of energy conservation. This judgment is one-sided and blind in some spots.

1.2. *Regional comparison of energy consumption intensity is unreasonable*

Energy consumption intensity of different regions and different economies lacks comparability, and a simple comparison is unreasonable. If we examine from a spatial dimension the input–output relationship as defined by energy consumption intensity in different regions, it is easy to find that energy consumption intensity cannot correctly reflect the relationship between energy consumption and output of these regions. In fact, energy consumption in a given region provides the source of GDP not only for that region, but also for other regions. Energy consumption intensity of a certain region cannot display its contribution of energy consumption to the GDP of other regions, nor can it display the contribution of energy consumption of other regions to the GDP of this region. Therefore, simply taking such an indicator to assess the energy efficiency of a region and the level of energy consumption in different regions is one-sided and unreasonable. There is no doubt that using the indicator for the purpose of regulation does not help the rational allocation of resources throughout the country. In fact, the complexity of economic activities makes it impossible for us to accurately determine the reasonable value of energy intensity in various regions. There is a great blindness in such a regulation.

---

[5]The energy consumption intensity of China in 2006 was 4.3 times that of the US and 9 times that of Japan, according to data from the Internation Energy Agency.

There is a huge gap in energy consumption intensity between different regions in China, but it does not mean that the same gap holds in energy efficiency between different regions. The difference in energy consumption intensity between regions is related to the difference in development level and technology, but it is mainly determined by different industry structures. The industry structure of a region is a result of resource allocation across the country, with some focusing on heavy industries, some on light, and some on energy-intensive ones. It is also closely related to the location and natural resources of the region and the national layout of industries. It is thus not appropriate to simply compare energy consumption intensity of different regions.

In an era of economic globalization, known as the "world factory", China sells a large number of products abroad and also imports a lot. China is generally at the end of the global chain of industries. High energy consumption and low value-added products take up a major part of the exports of China, while in the imports low energy consumption and high value-added products are in the majority. Energy consumption condensed in exports is far greater than that condensed in imports, with a considerable portion of China's energy consumption being finally consumed by overseas consumers. The rapid development of China's foreign trade has the effect of widening the gap in energy consumption intensity between China and developed countries. This pattern of international division of labor and the resulting gap in energy consumption intensity are to a considerable extent related to prices of production factors, investment environment, comparative advantages, and the efforts of multinational corporations to optimize the allocation of resources in the world. One cannot draw a simple conclusion to the effect that China enjoys low energy efficiency.

In order to eliminate the non-comparable elements between countries, purchasing power parity (PPP) is often a method used to adjust GDP when making international comparisons. Since PPP is significant to tradable products and appears arbitrary to other products, it can be used for reference only. When PPP is used to calculate energy consumption intensity, we can see that the gap between countries will be greatly narrowed. As can be seen in Table 3.1, according to the conventional GDP calculation, the energy consumption intensity in the US is 0.21 and that in China is

Table 3.1 Major energy indicators in China, Japan, and the United States (2006)

	China	US	Japan
Primary energy supply per capita (toe/capita)	1.43	7.43	4.13
Primary energy supply per unit GDP (toe/thousand US$ in 2000 price)	0.90	0.21	0.10
Unit GDP (PPP) primary energy supply (toe/thousand US$ PPP in 2000 price)	0.22	0.21	0.15

Note: PPP refers to purchasing power parity; "toe" represents a ton of standard oil equivalent.

Source: IEA website, http://www.iea.org/stats/index.asp.

0.90. With the PPP method, the intensity in the US is still 0.21 and that in China is 0.22 after conversion based on the US. It can be seen that there is little difference between the two countries. The rationality of using the result to illustrate the gap between China and the United States in energy efficiency is still dubious. This further shows the defect incomparability of value-based energy consumption intensity as an indicator for energy efficiency and energy conservation.

1.3. *Reasonable methods for assessing energy efficiency and energy conservation*

The assessment of energy efficiency and energy conservation should be carried out at product level and industry level by using physical-quantity-based energy consumption indicators. As analyzed above, energy consumption intensity reflects only the degree of dependence of economic activities on current energy consumption, and cannot fully reflect the efficiency of energy consumption. In the meantime, there is a lack of comparability between different regions and different sectors. In short, energy consumption intensity is a suitable indicator to assess energy conservation across regions and sectors.

Strictly speaking, when used as a measure of energy efficiency, energy consumption intensity is only significant among homogeneous or replaceable products. Heterogeneous products of different performances and properties usually have different energy consumption intensity. The difference is largely caused by physical characteristics or technical properties of different products, which are not subject to change. If these different and irreplaceable products are all essential, then we can hardly say that producing products of low energy consumption intensity is more energy efficient than producing those of high energy consumption intensity. It is obviously against economic laws to indiscriminatingly assess different products by energy consumption intensity, to harshly reduce energy consumption of high-intensity products, and to blindly suppress the production of high energy-consuming products regardless of market demand.

In fact, the complicated input–output relationship across regions and sectors makes it difficult to accurately determine relatively reasonable values of energy consumption intensity for specific regions or sectors. It is, therefore, difficult to decompose energy consumption intensity according to different regions and sectors. The reasonable method to assess energy efficiency and manage energy consumption is to apply physical-quantity-based energy consumption indicators at the product level and the industry level. This thus requires a series of well-established industry standards, energy consumption standards for products, and a solid basis for energy accounting. We should vigorously promote an energy auditing system, step up the formulation and improvement of national standards for energy-consuming equipment, and improve enterprise energy-conserving measurement, accounting, and statistical systems. For such purposes, it is necessary to adopt scientific, standardized, and refined management, as without this effective and reasonable results would hardly be achieved in energy conservation and emission reduction only by simply relying on energy consumption intensity and its level-by-level decomposition.

2. It is Inadvisable to Excessively Pursue a Sharp Drop in Energy Consumption Intensity Within a Short Period of Time

Although energy consumption intensity has obvious defects as an indicator for energy efficiency, it is still significant as an indicator for the proper regulation of total energy consumption. When it is used as an indicator of total energy consumption and for trend management within a specific range, it should be noted that the change of energy consumption intensity has its own principles. It is not always "the lower the better". It is inadvisable to excessively pursue a sharp drop in energy consumption intensity in the short term.

2.1. *No certainty exists for energy consumption intensity to sharply drop within a short period of time*

Historical data show that in the process of industrialization, the long-term change of energy consumption intensity for most countries has undergone an inverted U-shaped curve, first rising and then falling with the economic development, while that for a small number of countries has taken the shape of an inverted W, i.e., there are two or more peaks (e.g., South Korea).

It is easy to understand that most developed countries have undergone an inverted U-shaped energy consumption intensity curve. Industrialization is a process of capital primitive accumulation and urbanization. At the initial stage, energy consumption will grow faster than economy due to large-scale infrastructure construction and corresponding development of high energy-consuming industries, which leads to an increase in energy consumption intensity. With the development of industrialization, the accumulation of capital, and the improvement of infrastructure, high energy-consuming industries will start to take up a smaller proportion in the national economy at a certain stage, while the proportion of high-tech and service industries will gradually increase. In the meantime, along with technological progress and the improvement of energy efficiency, the growth of energy demand will naturally slow down and become slower than economic growth, resulting in a decrease of energy consumption intensity.

When an even higher level of economy is achieved, the proportion of the processing industry will further decrease, the degree of informationization will become higher and higher, and the energy consumption intensity will become further lower. Here, an advanced structure of industries will largely account for the rapid and sharp decrease in energy consumption intensity, and such a structure follows as a result of economic development, the improvement of the people's income level, and the concomitant changes in demand structure (the increase in the proportion of high-value-added products). A significant increase in the people's income level is actually the power source for structural transformation.

It is worth noting that the inverted U-shaped change from monotonic rise to monotonic fall in energy consumption intensity for most developed countries is the long-term trend, but no similar pattern is found in the short term. Data show that energy consumption intensity of various countries increase or decrease with frequent fluctuations. Its short-term trend is "fuzzy" and uncertain. That is to say, there is generally no strict monotonic increase or decrease within a year or an even shorter period of time. Even in the middle and later stages of industrialization when energy consumption intensity goes along an obvious downward trend, uncertainties of economic activities still frequently bring about fluctuations or temporary increases, which is, in general, quite a normal phenomenon.

For example, on the whole, since the late 1970s, the energy consumption intensity of China is in a period of great decrease. It, however, sharply rebounded in the years 2001–2005. During this period, the Western Development Strategy of China was comprehensively implemented, housing reform gave rise to great development of real estate industry, urbanization accelerated, China acceded to the World Trade Organization (WTO), initiating a surge in foreign trade, and the rapid increase in the scale of infrastructure construction promoted the development of heavy chemical industry. Taking these facts into consideration, we cannot simply say that it is abnormal that the energy consumption intensity increased in the period instead of continuing to fall along the downward trend.

It is not difficult to understand that the energy consumption intensity of an economy is not determined by exogenous factors, but by the stage of development and current conditions of operation. Its trend is subject to the needs of economic growth and objective economic laws. Total energy consumption control for the purposes of overcoming market failures and realizing energy conservation and emission reduction cannot be done in violation of economic laws. Specifically, it seems inappropriate to set a macro-goal of energy consumption to be achieved in a short period of time without leaving any room and to require economic activities to strictly comply with it. During the period of the 11th Five-Year Plan, in order to achieve the planned goal of energy conservation, some places even went to the extreme of limiting electricity supply to the detriment of normal production and life. From a macro point of view, we should try our best to avoid setting short-term binding energy-conserving targets, and take short-term fluctuations into full consideration when setting long-term targets of energy conservation and emission reduction.

During the period of the 11th Five-Year Plan, the task of reducing energy consumption intensity was basically completed. If the period of the 12th Five-Year Plan sees intensity energy consumption continue to decrease dramatically, China will experience a major monotonic drop for ten consecutive years. We cannot say that it is not possible. But we have to be prepared for possible fluctuations. Various factors show that during the period of the 12th Five-Year Plan, there are many uncertainties in energy consumption intensity. If possible fluctuations are to be ironed out, stricter administrative measures have to be taken and higher prices need to be paid. This needs to be carefully weighed and judged.

2.2. *Excessive pursuit of a sharp drop in energy consumption intensity within a short period of time will do harm to the long-term development of China*

China, a country at the stage of primitive accumulation of capital, is fundamentally different from developed countries in terms of capital stock per capita. The capital stock per capita of China is only one-tenth of that of the US. And the situation varies greatly between regions and between urban and rural areas in China. There is still a long way to go for China to complete primitive accumulation. Large-scale investment is necessary, and fixed asset investment, especially infrastructure construction, is generally energy intensive.

In fact, only a small part of the energy consumed in the process of primitive accumulation is enjoyed by the current generation, while most of it will be left to future generations and contribute to future GDP. The high energy consumption intensity at present is a necessary precondition for the low energy consumption intensity in the future. As a matter of fact, this is the simple principle of "previous generations planting trees and later generations enjoying their shade".

This involves route selection to reduce energy consumption intensity. One thing is certain, that is, when we have completed the accumulation of capital, become rich, and the structure of industries has developed to an advanced stage, energy consumption intensity will naturally drop.

Moreover, because we enjoy the advantage of backwardness, energy consumption intensity is no doubt lower than that of developed countries at the same stage of development. To realize low energy consumption intensity, there are at least two options.

One option is to have a temporary slow decrease of energy consumption intensity, and correspondingly fast capital accumulation (for which the high savings rate of China provides conditions). On the premise of high investment efficiency, primitive accumulation will be achieved at a quick pace. This means that energy consumption intensity will eventually reach the level of developed countries quickly, and then it will be greatly reduced.

Another option is to ask for a great decrease in energy consumption intensity within a short period of time, which will surely affect the speed of primitive accumulation. It will delay the further decrease in energy consumption intensity, that is, delay the time to reach the level of developed countries. The process of industrialization of China will also be lengthened as a result.

In view of the long-term trend of global resource supply, the supply of energy and raw materials is getting shorter, and the increasing trend of their prices will not change for a long period of time. It should be noted that any delay in the path of capital accumulation will increase the cost of industrialization. By the end of the 20th century, developing countries with a population of nearly 5 billion had entered the stage of industrialization. Under the situation that most developing countries have not yet embarked on the stage of rapid economic growth, that the developed countries have not yet completely stepped out of the economic crisis, and that the prices of energy and raw materials are relatively low, under the premise of ensuring the effectiveness of investment, it is undoubtedly beneficial to the long-term development of China to strive to maintain the momentum of high-speed capital accumulation so that the construction of energy-intensive and resource-intensive infrastructure can be properly advanced ahead of the times. China is now at the end of the period when it enjoys rich labor force. It is thus also necessary to do it from the perspective of drawing on the demographic dividend, which will soon become history. Opportunities are valuable, and once lost these will not come back again. We often emphasize the importance of opportunity, and this is an important opportunity.

In short, the primitive accumulation of China is far from complete. With the view of seizing the opportunity, as well as of fast realization in the long run of the primitive accumulation, realizing industrialization, and decreasing energy consumption intensity, we should not excessively pursue a sharp drop in energy consumption intensity within a short period of time. In fact, if we turn our eyes to India and take a look at the gap in infrastructure between the two countries, we will not single-mindedly admire its low energy consumption intensity.

2.3. *From the perspective of greenhouse gas emission reduction, we should not excessively pursue a sharp drop in energy consumption intensity within a short period of time*

According to the Kyoto Protocol, developing countries are not obliged to assume the responsibilities for greenhouse gas emission reduction for the time being. The regulation actually takes into account the actual situation of developed countries and some of the above-mentioned reasons. The US Senate bill does not require China to immediately begin to assume such responsibilities either. This shows that Americans also understand the situation.

Obviously, we should take advantage of this period of time, seizing the opportunity to do those things which are highly energy-consuming and can be done in advance, and actively prepare for the low energy consumption in the future. Because the adoption of energy-conserving technologies and the realization of low energy consumption require input at an early stage, including energy input, the temporary high energy consumption intensity is for the sake of low intensity later on, while its temporary slow decrease is for the sake of fast decrease in the long run. It is unwise to slam the brakes and bind oneself.

In the long run, the fundamental solution to the energy problem lies in the development of new energy. Conservation alone cannot fundamentally resolve the problem, because the traditional resources of coal and oil will run out sooner or later, and it is already a very realistic problem. As the bottom line, mandatory energy conservation lengthens the use of remaining traditional energy, and thus wins time for human beings to complete the transition from traditional energy systems to new energy systems.

By energy conservation, we refer to the conservation of fossil energy. It can be imagined that if all our energy sources are green and sustainable, then energy conservation may simply refer to lowering production costs, which can be left to market mechanism. In such a case, energy conservation will have no significance for greenhouse gas emission reduction. Therefore, as the proportion of new energy, renewable energy and green energy in energy consumption continue to increase, the government's efforts to control total energy consumption will undoubtedly relax, and there will be less attention paid to energy consumption indicators (including energy consumption intensity indicators).

The world energy system is at the primary stage of transforming from traditional energy to non-fossil energy. Currently, the development of new energy technologies in the world has achieved initial results. With the current trend, the international community is generally optimistic about a substantial growth of new energy within 20–30 years. In a forecast report by the United Nations, "the most ambitious idea" is that renewable energy will account for 3/4 of energy consumption by 2050.[6] Throughout the world, actions on energy conservation do not seem as active as being claimed, which may be attributed to this optimistic attitude toward the prospect of new energy. In the long run, with the development of new energy, there will be less pressure on energy conservation and greenhouse gas emission reduction.

2.4. We should not blindly pursue the traditional road of developed countries to lower energy consumption intensity

In China, because people often non-discriminatingly identify energy consumption intensity with energy efficiency, and lowering energy

---

[6] See "Renewable energy will become a leading part of the world's energy source in 2050", 2011, *Scientific Research Current Express: A Special Issue on the Science of Climate Change*, No. 11, p. 9, National Science Library of the Chinese Academy of Sciences.

consumption intensity with energy conservation, it seems quite natural to look to developed countries with low energy consumption intensity for methods. But there are misunderstandings and misjudgments.

2.4.1. *The traditional development path of developed countries is unsustainable*

Admittedly, the energy consumption intensity of developed countries is much lower than that of developing countries. But from the perspective of resource conservation, the lifestyle of developed countries is far less green than that of developing countries. The US National Geographic Society has conducted surveys of green consumption in 14 countries since 2008 and released the Global Green Consumption Index 2009.[7] In the report for three consecutive years from 2008 to 2010, the green index of China's consumption kept third rank (with India and Brazil as the first in 2008 and India alone in 2010), while the US ranked last, even though the energy consumption intensity of the US was far lower than these countries. Clearly, low energy consumption intensity is not equivalent to effective and reasonable energy consumption. The survey also shows that the consumption pattern of China is far from being Americanized, and that China still has a lot of room to choose its consumption pattern.

The main reason why the energy consumption intensity of developed countries is far lower than that of developing countries is that developed countries have completed energy-intensive primitive accumulation. Along with technological progress and the improvement of income level, they have achieved industry upgrading. A high energy efficiency certainly contributes to the low energy consumption intensity of developed countries, but it is not much higher than that of developing countries. For example, if calculated on the basis of physical quantity, the energy consumption per unit of product for major industrial products of China is at most 10–25% higher than the advanced international level, while the energy consumption intensity of China was 4.3 times that of the US and 9 times that of Japan (in 2006). This means that we must also see the other side of the low

---

[7] China ranks the third: US National Geographic Society announces Green Index, http://news.sina.com.cn/w/2010-06-06/141920421744.shtml.

energy consumption intensity of developed countries, that is, developed countries enjoy huge assets and corresponding high incomes that have long been accumulated by relying on a large amount of resource consumption (including energy). High income enables developed countries to have much higher purchasing power than developing countries to consume products with high added value (i.e., low energy consumption intensity). Consumerism leads to the prevailing of luxury, ostentatious, comparative, and wasteful consumption in developed countries. Developing countries, due to their low income level, can only consume products that meet their basic needs and have low added value (i.e., high energy consumption intensity). This is a major cause of the huge gap between developing countries and developed countries in energy consumption intensity.

In the process of development, human beings have increasingly realized that with the limited resources of the earth, the modes of production and consumption in developed countries and the development paths derived therefrom are not sustainable. No other economic system has been found to replace them so far. Developing countries with a huge population are still following the old path of developed countries, which puts a strain on to the earth's resources and environmental capacity. This is the root cause of the increasingly acute global resource and environment problems and the most important conflict of interest between developed and developing countries. The world today is not peaceful, and military conflicts break out from time to time, which are deeply related to resources. As the biggest developing country in the world, China's industrialization will be difficult to realize without sufficient resources and corresponding strategic guarantee.

2.4.2. *Energy conservation and emission reduction of China are still following the old path of developed countries*

Energy conservation and emission reduction are a part of China's efforts to change its mode of development. An analysis of these efforts to achieve the goals of energy conservation and emission reduction will show that they are basically following the path of developed countries. On the one hand, the work of energy conservation and emission reduction is mainly focused on the production field, including eliminating backward production capacity, "starting big (projects) and suppressing small (projects)", raising the threshold of technology access, improving energy efficiency, and inhibiting the development of high energy-consuming industries. On the other hand, in the field of consumption, the lifestyle of developed countries has been blindly imitated. In China, although people admit that the consumption mode and lifestyle in developed countries should not be the direction of China, they still move toward it recklessly. The lifestyle with high energy consumption is now popular, and even more luxurious than that in developed countries. However, our overall income level is far lower than that of developed countries, and the consumption scale is relatively small.

Speaking of the energy-conserving goal pursued by China, China can surely make its energy consumption intensity reach the level of developed countries in the way of developed countries. Moreover, as a developing country, China's energy consumption intensity will be lower than that of developed countries at the same level of development. However, it does nothing to change the fact that this is a development path of high energy consumption and high waste. To catch up with developed countries by following this path cannot prevent the difficulties in energy that the US and other developed countries have encountered.

In fact, we have already learned a lesson in this respect. The development of China's automobile industry is a case in point. Along with suburbanization, almost every family in the United States has a car. Under the control of interest groups, in order to develop the automobile industry, public transportation in the US declined greatly in comparison with the period before World War II. The United States has become a country highly kidnapped by oil, and wars have been launched for it. This road has come to an end. As a matter of fact, China is different from the US. It should have been possible for China to pursue a different route so as to avoid the detours that the US has taken. Yet in order to pursue short-term rapid growth, on the one hand, we have initiated energy conservation and emission reduction in the production field. On the other, despite the shortage of oil and increasing oil price, we have strongly encouraged car consumption, vigorously promoting the wishful thinking of "market for technology", suppressing national brands, actively introducing foreign capital in order to achieve blowout growth. In a few years, China became the biggest manufacturer of cars in the world. As a result, China has rapidly encountered the difficulty of overdependence on oil and urban traffic congestion, while the automobile market is basically dominated by foreign investment, and most Chinese automobile enterprises are assembly workshops for foreign automobiles. It can be said that there are too many blindfold actions in the development of China's automobile industry.

2.4.3. *Consumption modes should become more important areas for energy conservation and emission reduction*

Under the condition of economic globalization, to weaken the continuous and endless influence of developed countries on the consumption behaviors of China's middle-income and high-income groups is the biggest challenge for China to deal with the severe energy environment situation and build a conservation-oriented society. In order to achieve sustainable development, it is necessary to change the situation of strong economy and weak culture, treating the field of consumption as an important part of energy conservation and emission reduction and taking more effective measures.

It is not advisable for China to treat consumption as individual rights and leave it alone, though there is reasonable room for energy consumption to rise. It is absolutely necessary to strengthen demand management and give proper guidance and control to consumption. We should vigorously advocate energy-conserving and low-carbon consumption behavior, encourage legitimate consumption, suppress irrational consumption, and resolutely fight against waste. In particular, we should inhibit government privileges and suppress the governmental behaviors of ostentation and extravagance, and overcome the recurring disease of lacking effective supervision over the use of public resources by public power. We should encourage a simple material life and a rich spiritual life, formulate consumption guide policies, and guard against being caught in the path of consumerism.

3. Concluding Remarks

As can be seen from the above discussions, energy consumption intensity is an indicator that reflects only the degree of dependence of economic activities on current energy consumption. It cannot fully reflect the efficiency of energy consumption, and there is a lack of comparability between different regions and different countries. It is thus flawed in theory and deficient in practice to take energy consumption intensity as an indicator for the energy efficiency of different regions and sectors.

For assessment and management of energy efficiency and energy consumption in various regions, we must change the practice of decomposing energy consumption intensity into different regions, and conduct it on the basis of physical quantity energy consumption indicators at the product and the industry level. Only in this way can the precious energy resources in China be effectively and reasonably used and energy conservation and emission reduction be carried out in an orderly and healthy manner.

In order to carry out energy management at the product and industry level with physical quantity energy consumption indicators, it is necessary to change the traditional extensive management and implement scientific, standardized, and refined management, in addition to a series of improved industry standards and product standards. The key to China's transformation of development mode is to change the extensive management that has been formed for a long time. If the management mode does not change, the unreasonable structure will be difficult to change, and the result of total amount control will make structural contradictions more prominent.

In order to successfully achieve the goal of energy conservation and emission reduction in our country, we must deepen our understanding of energy consumption intensity and the law of its fluctuations. Due to the uncertainty of the short-term trend of energy consumption intensity, we should refrain from setting binding short-term energy consumption targets. While setting long-term energy conservation and emission reduction targets, short-term fluctuations should be given a full account. The brake-slamming-like practice of excessive pursuit of a sharp drop in energy consumption intensity within a short period of time has various drawbacks and is harmful to the long-term decline of energy consumption intensity and the long-term development of China.

In order to truly and effectively relieve the pressure on resources and environment, China should think more strategically about energy conservation and emission reduction. From the perspective of implementing the

Scientific Outlook on Development and realizing sustainable development, energy conservation and emission reduction of China should be greatly expanded from production field to consumption field. For the establishment of a long-term mechanism for energy conservation and emission reduction, more solid efforts should be made in the broad context of building a resource-saving and environment-friendly society. Under the background of globalization, China should give full play to the advantages of the socialist system and actively explore an innovative mode of development so as to form a materially simple and spiritually rich lifestyle.

Part II
Green Development Path

This part discusses the path of green development and includes Chapters 4–7.

Chapter 4 analyzes the ways to reduce per capita carbon emissions in China with regard to economic development and technological progress. The analysis shows that from 1980 to 2012, the per capita carbon emissions of China have greatly increased and showed a phased feature. This growth is largely brought about by the continuous improvement of labor productivity (per capita output). In the meantime, China has been committed to improving its technical level since the Reform and Opening Up, which has greatly improved the energy efficiency of the country and effectively reduced the per capita carbon emissions. Generally speaking, the building of a moderately prosperous society in all respects in the next 20–30 years cannot be achieved at the cost of economic development, but also requires an enhanced ability to reduce carbon emissions and adapt to global climate change. Thus, the strategy of "energy-conserving first and efficiency-oriented" is of a great significance. At the same time, the potential of adjusting industry structure and energy structure to reduce carbon emissions needs to be further explored.

Chapter 5 discusses the influence of agricultural production modes on the environment, and takes the United States as a case for empirical analysis. The research done shows that the mode of agricultural production influences ecological environment through two channels: means of production or production technologies, and relations of production. New technological instruments have improved the ability of human beings to transform the natural environment, expanded the scale and intensity of agricultural production, and eventually widened the scope of agricultural production and intensified the influence of agriculture on the environment. The established relations of production determine the behavior of farmers. Developing countries have inherited the extremely unequal land ownership of the old colonial system, and poverty and environmental deterioration interactively form a vicious circle. In developed countries, commercialized agriculture is dominant, depriving farm owners of the chance to play their role in environmental management. In order to obtain maximum profits, agricultural producers continue to increase agricultural output, making agriculture a high-risk system with high input and high output, and increasingly high degree of manual manipulation.

Chapter 6 discusses the development path of low-carbon trade through a quantitative analysis of embodied carbon in the trade of China. Based on the latest data available and on the input–output table of non-competitive import, the chapter estimates the embodied carbon in the trade of China from 1987 to 2011 and its distribution among sectors and countries (or regions), examining six major factors through structural decomposition. The results show that China has become a net exporter of carbon since 2005. The rapid increase of embodied carbon in trade is mainly brought about by the growth of trade scale, while the decreasing energy consumption intensity of sectors is the main factor inhibiting its increase. The changes in the product structure of import and export, input structure, energy structure, and carbon emission coefficient have little effect on it. However, regulating the exported embodied carbon does not mean that China should blindly control the export scale. A desirable practice should be to change the export growth pattern, optimize the export product structure, and control the increase of export embodied carbon through changes in the export product structure.

Chapter 7 analyzes the development model of water-conserving trade based on the calculation of virtual water in the foreign trade of China. This chapter applies the method of input–output analysis to study the outflow and inflow of virtual water resources in view of China's increasing trade volume, so as to scientifically evaluate the cost of water resources for the foreign trade volume of China. The model estimates that the direct and total net virtual water exports (exports–imports) of China have grown steadily as reflected by the years 1995, 2002, and 2005. Particularly, the total net virtual water exports have doubled, exceeding the growth of the proportion of net exports in current-year GDP in the same period. In 2005, China directly imported 8 billion cubic meters of net virtual water and exported 43.3 billion cubic meters, with a large amount of precious water resources being exported by way of being embodied in trade. For a "water-poor" country like China, the export policy should fully consider the constraints of water resources and the strategic utilization of world resources in order to facilitate the sustainable utilization and development of national resources.

Chapter 4

Ways to Reduce Per Capita Carbon Emissions in China: Economic Development and Technological Progress

Youguo Zhang

Institute of Quantitative & Technical Economics,
Chinese Academy of Social Sciences

1. Introduction

Developing countries are endowed with rights to the pursuit of modernization, and in order to achieve such a pursuit, per capita carbon emissions will inevitably increase. After all, economic development cannot currently be realized without energy consumption, and among all types of energy, fossil energy is relatively cheap. Although technological progress will weaken the dependence of economic development on fossil energy, generally speaking, its consumption will increase in tune with economic development, and thus carbon emissions will also correspondingly increase. For developing countries, a moderate increase in carbon emissions is reasonably demanded to maintain people's basic needs of life and realize economic development.

As the biggest developing country, China also has the above-mentioned demand of carbon emissions. Nevertheless, China attaches great importance to climate change, has adopted a series of policies and measures to deal with it, has positively contributed to the issue,[1] and will "make new

---

[1] See the National Plan to Deal with Climate Change, the National Development and Reform Commission, printed in June 2007.

contributions to protect global climate."[2] Since carbon in energy consumption is the major component of greenhouse gases produced by human activities,[3] identifying the driving factors of changes in carbon emission is not only helpful to correctly understand the changes in the carbon emissions of China but also of great significance to decision-making concerning future emission reduction.

Based on the relevant literature, the driving factors for carbon emissions are diverse. Different researchers have reached different conclusions via the study of different regions. But most studies show that changes in carbon emissions are mainly related with economic growth. For example, Karakaya & Öznçag (2005) examined the driving factors of carbon emissions in the five Central Asian countries from 1992 to 2001, arguing that the decline of carbon emissions in these countries is mainly caused by their economic contraction after the disintegration of the Soviet Union. Lynn *et al.* (1996) conducted an empirical study of nine OECD countries and found that traffic activities constitute the main reason for their increase in carbon emissions.

Many other studies lay emphasis on the positive influence of technological factors on carbon emission reduction. For example, Hoffert *et al.* (1998) hold that even if we do not take into account increasing productivity, to stabilize carbon emissions, it is necessary to innovate cost-effective and carbon-free energy technologies to meet the additional demand of primary energy. Assuming that energy intensity is constant, about 40 terawatts of carbon-free energy will be needed by 2050. It is therefore necessary to invest significantly in technological innovation in the future. The study of Liaskas *et al.* (2000) on industrial carbon emissions of EU countries also shows that it is possible to reduce carbon emissions in the future through technological progress while leaving the economic growth rate unaffected.

In addition, some scholars also estimate the effect of population on carbon emissions. Their results show that the effect of the population on carbon emissions is limited. For example, Birdsall (1992) argued that the

---

[2] Report of the 17th National Congress of the Communist Party of China, and the National Plan to Deal with Climate Change issued by the State Council, June 2007.

[3] According to the Initial National Information on Climate Change, the People's Republic of China, the proportion of CO_2 emissions in total greenhouse gas emissions increased from 76% in 1994 to 83% in 2004 in China.

decline in population growth rate will be beneficial to carbon emission reduction, but this benefit is not significant. In the next 35 years, a possible decline in population growth rate can only reduce fossil fuel–related carbon emissions by 10%. In yet another example, Shi (2003) suggests that for every 1% increase in population, carbon emissions will increase by an average of 1.28%.

In recent years, an increasing number of studies have been conducted on the driving factors of carbon emissions in China. Some of them are focused on the relationship between carbon emissions and a particular factor, such as Xu Yugao's *et al.*'s (1999) assessment of the relationship between economic growth and carbon emissions, and Zhang Lei's (2006) analysis of the relationship between changes in the structure of primary energy consumption and regional carbon emissions. Most studies (Zhang, 2006; Wang *et al.*, 2005; Wu *et al.*, 2005, 2006; Xu *et al.*, 2006; Liu *et al.*, 2007; Fan *et al.*, 2007; Zhang *et al.*, 2009; Zhang, 2009) examined the influence of several factors on carbon emissions.

In terms of methodology, the IPAT mathematical identity proposed by Ehrlich and Holdren in the early 1970s is a very frequently used method in the analysis of environmental degradation (York *et al.*, 2003). This identity defines environmental impact (I) as the product of population (P), affluence (A, e.g., GDP per capita), and technological level (T, e.g., pollution emission intensity per unit of GDP). The IPAT identity has been continuously improved and extended in practice. For example, Dietz & Rosa (1994) expanded it into a random model STIRPAT; Waggoner & Ausubel (2002) decomposed T into consumption ratio per unit of GDP and pollution emission intensity of consumption, and thus extended the IPAT identity into the ImPACT identity. Kaya identity was obtained by Kaya (1990) by extending IPAT and it has been widely used in studies of greenhouse gas emission (e.g., Hoffert *et al.*, 1998; Liaskas *et al.*, 2000; Raupach *et al.*, 2007).

The most common empirical analysis is the decomposition analysis of influencing factors of carbon emissions. This type of analyses (e.g., Xu *et al.*, 1999), breaking through the limitations of econometric methods which identify only the statistical relationship between carbon emissions and driving factors, can accurately measure the contribution of different factors to changes in carbon emission. Current methods of carbon emission decomposition, according to Hoekstra & van den

Bergh (2003), can be summarized into index decomposition analysis (IDA) based on industry aggregate data and structure decomposition analysis (SDA) based on input–output table. With easy accessibility to the data required, IDA is more frequently utilized. SDA, however, has its unique advantages such as the fact that it can take into account the interaction between industries; thus, there are also many studies (e.g., Zhang, 2009, 2010) adopting this method.

In general, studies by both Chinese and foreign scholars on the driving factors of carbon emissions are mainly focused on the influence of various factors on total carbon emissions, and there are only a few researches on the decomposition analysis of per capita carbon emission. In terms of development rights, per capita carbon emissions is a more equitable indicator, and so the study of its driving factors should be strengthened. In addition, previous studies have generally regarded carbon emissions from the angle of energy consumption for production, somewhat neglecting carbon emissions from energy consumption for living. This limits the analysis of some driving factors, such as the impact of urbanization on carbon emissions, and thus this chapter attempts to address these gaps.

2. Methods and Data

2.1. *Relationship model for per capita carbon emissions and its influencing factors*

The analysis model of per capita carbon emissions proposed in this chapter is also derived from the extension of the IPAT identity. The sources of per capita carbon emissions are divided into two categories here: carbon emissions from energy consumption for production and carbon emissions from energy consumption for living. Just as energy consumption includes both the production and life sectors, total carbon emissions, which are related to energy consumption, come from both the sectors. With regard to the availability of data, the production sector is divided into the following six subsectors of industries: agriculture, forestry, animal husbandry, fishery, and water conservancy; industry; construction; transportation and post and telecommunications; commerce, catering, material supply and marketing, and warehousing; and other industries. There are two ways of population categorization: one is to divide the population into employed and unemployed; the other is to divide it into urban and rural. Terminal energy is decomposed into clean energy (hydropower and nuclear power) and non-clean energy. The latter is further decomposed into six kinds, i.e., of coal, coking products, oil, natural gas, heating power, and thermal power.

Thus, carbon emissions related to energy consumption can be expressed as follows (see the Appendix for specific derivations):

$$C = C_I + C_L = \sum_{ij} PWGS_i I_i R_i M_{ij} H_{ij} + \sum_{ij} PU_l A_l R_l M_{lj} H_{lj} \qquad (4.1)$$

In the above expression, C stands for total carbon emissions related to energy consumption, C_I for carbon emissions from energy consumption in the production sector, and C_L for carbon emissions from energy consumption in the living sector.

The first item to the right of the second equal sign in (4.1) represents the decomposition of the driving factors of carbon emissions in production. In the expression, P stands for total population; W for the proportion of employed population, that is, the ratio of employed population to total population; G for labor productivity, i.e., the ratio of GDP to employed population; S_i for the proportion of the GDP of sector i in national GDP, which is used to indicate the industry structure; I_i for the energy intensity of the sector i, i.e., the proportion of its total energy consumption in GDP; R_i for the proportion of non-clean energy consumed by sector i in its total energy consumption, which measures the overall structure of energy consumption in the production sector; M_{ij} for the proportion of non-clean energy j consumed by sector i in its consumption of non-clean energy, which measures the structure of non-clean energy consumption in the production sector; and H_{ij} for the carbon emission coefficient of non-clean energy j consumed by sector i.

The second item to the right of the second equal sign in (4.1) represents the decomposition of the driving factors of carbon emissions in the living sector. Among them, U_l stands for the proportion of population l (categorized by urban and rural population) in the total population, which measures the urban and rural population structure; A_l for the energy consumption per capita for the living of population l; R_l for the proportion of non-clean energy consumed by population l in total energy consumption, which measures the overall structure of energy consumption in the living sector; M_{lj} for the proportion of non-clean energy j consumed by population l in non-clean energy consumption; and H_{lj} for the carbon emission coefficient of non-clean energy j consumed by population l.

Dividing the items in (4.1) by the number of people will give rise to the following expression of per capita carbon emission:

$$c = c_I + c_L = \sum_{ij} c_{ij} + \sum_{lj} c_{lj} = \sum_{ij} WGS_i I_i R_i M_{ij} H_{ij} + \sum_{lj} U_l A_l R_l M_{lj} H_{lj} \quad (4.2)$$

In the expression, $c = C/P$, $c_I = C_I/P$, $c_L = C_L/P$, $c_{ij} = \sum_{ij} C_{ij}/P$, and $c_{lj} = \sum_{lj} C_{lj}/P$, respectively, stand for per capita carbon emission, per capita carbon emissions in the production sector, per capita carbon emissions in the living sector, per capita carbon emissions from energy j consumption in sector i, and per capita carbon emissions from energy j consumption by population l.

Expression (4.2) shows that per capita carbon emissions can be decomposed into per capita carbon emissions in the production sector and per capita carbon emissions in the living sector (see Fig. 4.1). What drives the changes in per capita carbon emissions are mainly economic factors and technological factors. Among them, economic factors that drive changes in per capita carbon emissions in the production sector are proportion of employed population, labor productivity, and industry structure, while those that drive changes in per capita carbon emissions in the living sector include the urban–rural population structure (or urbanization rate) and energy consumption per capita for living. It can be seen that there is a significant difference between the economic factors that drive changes in the two types of per capita carbon emission. Distinguishing them can help accurately identify the influence of different economic factors on per capita carbon emission.

In addition, the technical factors driving changes in per capita carbon emissions in the production sector are basically similar to those driving the changes in per capita carbon emissions in the living sector. One slight difference is that the former includes energy intensity while the latter does

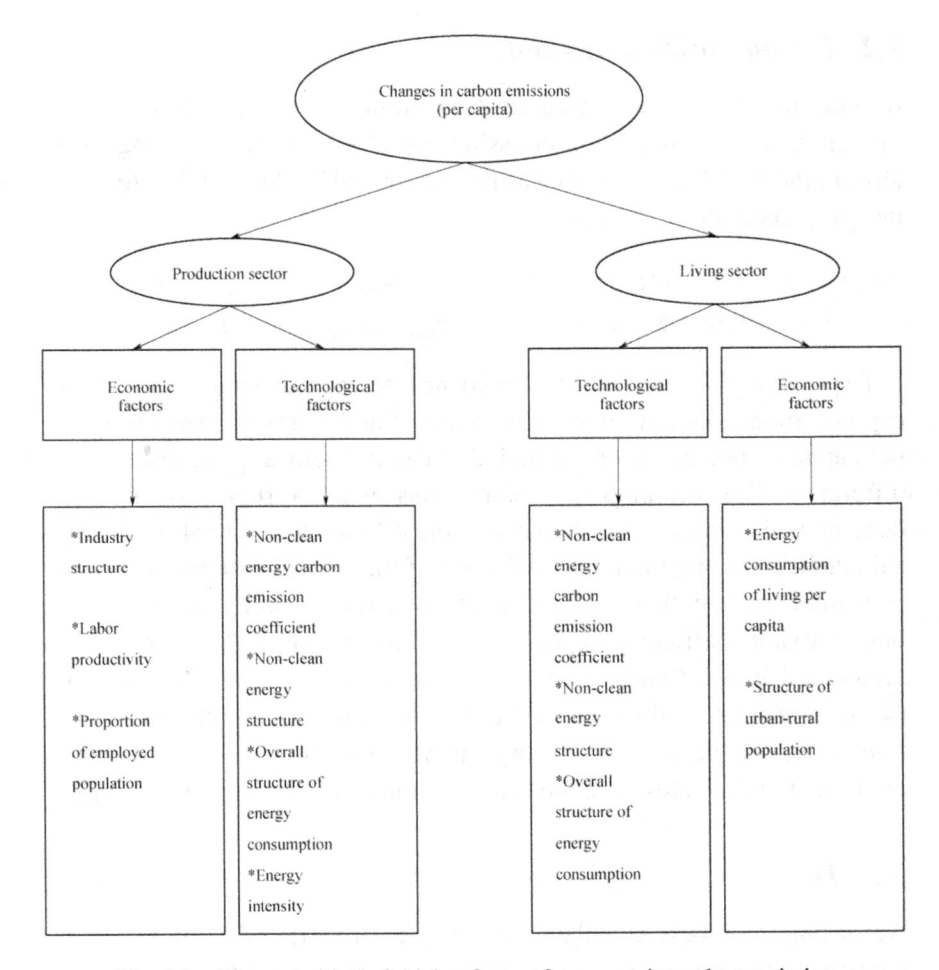

Fig. 4.1 Decomposition of driving factors for per capita carbon emission

not. Overall structure of energy consumption, non-clean energy structure, and non-clean energy carbon emission coefficient are the technological factors common to both types of per capita carbon emission.[4]

---

[4] It should be noted that technological evolution can directly change energy intensity and the carbon emission coefficient of non-clean energy (mainly heating power and thermal power). The two factors measure the changes of energy technology from different angles, and they can thus be classified as technological factors. The reason why this chapter classifies overall structure of energy consumption and fossil energy structure as technological

2.2. Decomposition method

In order to obtain a more accurate estimation of the influence of various factors on per capita carbon emissions of China, we use the Log-Mean Divisia Index (LMDI), which was recommended by Ang (2004), to incrementally decompose (4.2) as

$$\Delta c_{tot} = c^T - c^0 = (c_I^T - c_I^0) + (c_L^T - c_L^0) = (\Delta c_{Iemp} + \Delta c_{Iact} + \Delta c_{Istr} + \Delta c_{Iint} + \Delta c_{Iren}$$
$$+ \Delta c_{Imix} + \Delta c_{Iemf}) + (\Delta c_{Lurb} + \Delta c_{Laff} + \Delta c_{Lren} + \Delta c_{Lmix} + \Delta c_{Lemf}) \qquad (4.3)$$

Expression (4.3) reflects the influence of each driving factor on per capita carbon emission. In the expression, c^T and c^0, respectively, stand for per capita carbon emissions at period T and at 0, and Δc_{tot} represents their difference. The meanings and expressions of the variables obtained by decomposition in (4.3) are shown in Table 4.1 (see Ang, (2004) for technical details). Among them, the influence of the overall structure of energy consumption, non-clean energy structure, and the non-clean energy carbon emission coefficient on per capita carbon emissions in the production sector and in the living sector can be separately aggregated. By using (4.3), an accurate estimation of the driving factors of and their contributions to carbon emissions in history can be obtained, which can be used as the basis to key routes to reduce carbon emission identity in the future.

2.3. Data

According to (4.3), to calculate the influence of various driving factors on the per capita carbon emissions of China requires such data as population, employed population, proportion of urban and rural population, GDP (calculated at the constant price of 1978) and GDP of various industries and sectors (calculated at the constant price of 1978), and energy consumption and its composition over the years, which can be obtained

---

factors is that technology can be understood as a combination of capital, labor, energy, raw materials, information, and other factors in the process of production or service. In fact, the sense of technology can be understood in an even broader sense. Nanduri (1998) pointed out that social organizations, institutions, culture, and factors other than population and wealth that can affect the effects of human activities on the environment can all be regarded as technologies.

Table 4.1 Incremental decomposition of per capita carbon emission

Carbon emissions from the production sector		Carbon emissions from the living sector	
Driving factors	**Expressions for factorial influence**	**Driving factors**	**Expressions for factorial influence**
Employment rate	$DC_{Iemp} = \Sigma_{ij} w_{ij} \ln(W^T/W^0)$	Urbanization rate	$\Delta c_{Lurb} = \Sigma_{ij} w_{ij} \ln(U_i^T/U_i^0)$
Labor productivity	$DC_{Iact} = \Sigma_{ij} w_{ij} \ln(G^T/G^0)$	Energy consumption per capita for living	$\Delta c_{Laff} = \Sigma_{ij} w_{ij} \ln(A_i^T/A_i^0)$
Industry structure	$\Delta c_{Istr} = \Sigma_{ij} w_{ij} \ln(S_i^T/S_i^0)$		
Energy intensity	$\Delta c_{Iint} = \Sigma_{ij} w_{ij} \ln(I_i^T/I_i^0)$		
Overall structure of energy consumption	$\Delta c_{Iren} = \Sigma_{ij} w_{ij} \ln(R_i^T/R_i^0)$	Overall structure of energy consumption	$\Delta c_{Lren} = \Sigma_{ij} w_{ij} \ln(R_i^T/R_i^0)$
Non-clean energy structure	$\Delta c_{Imix} = \Sigma_{ij} w_{ij} \ln(M_{ij}^T/M_{ij}^0)$	Non-clean energy structure	$\Delta c_{Lmix} = \Sigma_{ij} w_{ij} \ln(M_{ij}^T/M_{ij}^0)$
Non-clean energy carbon emission coefficient	$\Delta c_{Iemf} = \Sigma_{ij} w_{ij} \ln(H_{ij}^T/H_{ij}^0)$	Non-clean energy carbon emission coefficient	$\Delta c_{Lemf} = \Sigma_{ij} w_{ij} \ln(H_{ij}^T/H_{ij}^0)$

directly by consulting *China Statistical Yearbook* and *China Energy Statistical Yearbook* of different years, or by simple processing. The specific methods and relevant carbon emission coefficients used to estimate the carbon emissions of various industries and sectors and of resident energy consumption are mainly taken from IPCC (1996).

3. An Empirical Analysis of Changes in the Per Capita Carbon Emissions of China

Figure 4.2 shows the course of change in the per capita carbon emissions of China from 1980 to 2012, and it can be roughly divided into three

Per capita carbon emissions (kg)

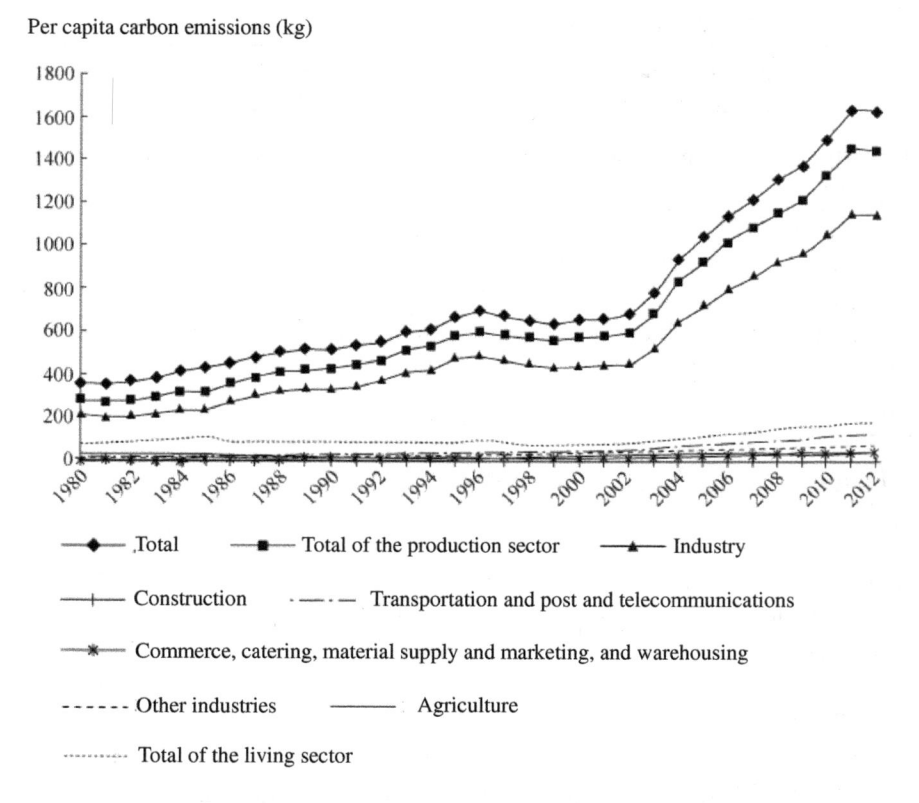

Fig. 4.2   Energy-related per capita carbon emissions and its composition

stages. The first stage (1980–1996) was a period of continuous increase. The per capita carbon emissions grew by 333 kg, with an average annual growth rate of 4.18%. The second stage (1997–2002) saw stable development, and the per capita carbon emissions displayed V-shaped changes. In this stage, the period from 1997 to 1999 was special in that the per capita carbon emissions underwent a downward trend, going against the overall trend of the entire research period. Then from 2000 to 2002, it began to grow slowly. Compared with 1996, it grew by only 8 kg in 2002, with a total change of less than 2%. The third stage (2003–2012) was one of fast growth. In comparison with 2002, the per capita carbon emissions in 2012 increased by 1005 kg, with an average annual growth rate of 9.1%. Its increase at this stage exceeded the total increase of the first 22 years.

Figure 4.2 also shows the sources of per capita carbon emission. As can be seen, it is obvious that the per capita carbon emissions of China come mainly from the production sector, with the industrial sector as the biggest contributor. From 1980 to 2012, the proportion of the industrial sector in per capita carbon emissions increased from 59% to 70%, which meant that carbon emissions of the industrial sector dominated China's per capita carbon emission. During this period, the overall share of other production sectors fluctuated within the range of 15%–20%. The proportion carbon emissions from the living sector decreased from 22% to 11%. In addition, since the mid- and late 1980s, carbon emissions from direct energy consumption by urban residents occupied a major part of the emissions from the living sector (59% in 2012).

Table 4.2 shows the influence of each driving factor on the carbon emissions per capita in China. From 1980 to 2012, all economic factors, including labor productivity, employment rate, industrial structure, urbanization, and energy consumption per capita for living led to an increase in per capita carbon emission. Among technical factors, energy intensity, overall structure of energy consumption, and non-clean energy structure have inhibited per capita carbon emission, but the changes in non-clean energy carbon emission coefficient have since led to an increase.

3.1. *Impact of economic development*

Over either the entire research period or separate stages, labor productivity is the most important factor that contributes to the increase of per capita carbon emission. Since the 1980s, the transfer of the rural labor surplus force to secondary and tertiary industries as well as the continuous flow of labor force from state-owned enterprises to other enterprises have improved the allocation efficiency of the labor force (Liu Shucheng, 2007). As a result, the labor productivity of China has also continued to rise, and the growth rate has shown an overall increasing trend (see Fig. 4.3). The increase in per capita carbon emissions brought about by the continuous increase in labor productivity from 1980 to 2012 is equivalent to about 1.3 times the actual increase in carbon emissions per capita. In terms of separate stages, labor productivity resulted in an annual increase of 30 kg of per capita carbon emissions from 1980 to 1996, 42 kg from 1997 to

Table 4.2 Factor decomposition of changes of the per capita carbon emissions in China (kg carbon)

Period (year)	Economic development						Technological progress			
	Total	Labor productivity	Employment rate	Industry structure	Urbanization	Energy consumption per capita of living	Energy intensity	Overall structure of energy consumption	Non-clean energy consumption structure	Non-clean energy carbon emission coefficient
1980–1996	333.12	474.99	112.30	46.81	10.67	11.97	−324.69	−3.91	2.45	2.52
1996–2002	−14.32	261.90	7.38	11.24	7.95	−12.38	−266.22	−17.33	−8.95	2.10
2002–2003	96.49	62.09	0.12	3.79	1.04	7.80	12.40	7.11	1.22	0.90
2003–2004	157.09	70.08	0.95	2.80	0.95	8.68	76.31	−1.22	−1.66	0.21
2004–2005	104.51	85.36	−0.65	2.30	0.96	9.63	6.64	−0.79	0.57	0.49
2005–2006	96.56	102.97	−0.82	3.78	0.74	8.80	−20.16	0.55	−1.12	1.82
2006–2007	79.18	118.99	−0.63	3.06	0.87	5.00	−46.11	−2.26	−0.70	0.96
2007–2008	94.82	97.70	−2.07	0.51	1.66	20.97	−17.34	0.94	1.53	−9.08
2008–2009	59.26	99.58	−1.63	−6.89	1.01	7.91	−40.80	0.50	1.27	−1.69
2009–2010	127.32	127.40	−1.45	5.54	1.09	8.38	5.17	−1.41	−9.55	−7.85
2010–2011	135.75	120.80	−0.92	5.79	0.80	13.74	−3.06	−1.24	−0.38	0.21
2011–2012	54.21	102.42	−1.83	−0.51	0.74	11.02	−54.63	−0.31	−4.39	1.70
2002–2012	1005.19	902.62	−6.76	21.74	9.12	99.28	−19.55	5.45	1.82	−8.54
1980–2012	1323.99	1639.51	112.92	79.79	27.74	98.87	−610.46	−15.79	−4.68	−3.92

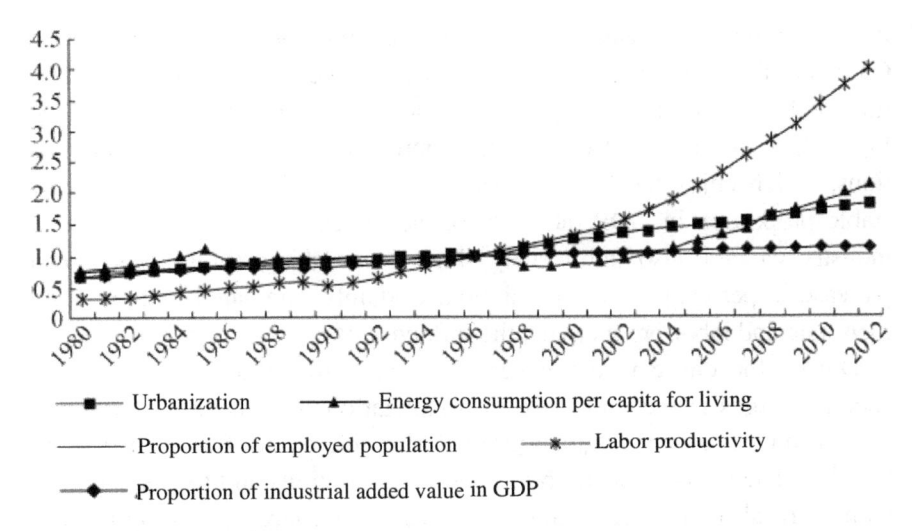

Fig. 4.3 Changes in economic factors

Notes: All indices in the figure have been standardized, i.e., assuming their values in 1996 to be 1, and those for other years are taken to be the relative value between their actual values and the actual values in 1996.

2002, and 89 kg from 2003 to 2012. Thus, the influence of labor productivity on per capita carbon emissions is increasing.

During the entire research period, employment rate served as the second most influential factor contributing to the increase of per capita carbon emission. The employment rate in China increased dramatically in the 1980s; after entering the 1990s, however, its changes were more stable (see Fig. 4.3). In view of this, the increase in employment rate increased the per capita carbon emissions annually by about 7 kg from 1980 to 1996. The relatively stable employment rate period seen next only resulted in an average annual increase of about 1kg of per capita carbon emissions from 1997 to 2002. The change in the employment rate even led to a slight drop in per capita carbon emissions from 2003 to 2012. This means that during the entire research period (1980–2012), the increasing effect of employment rate on per capita carbon emissions occurred mainly in the first stage, followed by a significant decline and even a decreasing effect.

From 1980 to 2012, changes in the industry structure contributed to 6% of the total increase in per capita carbon emission. The reason that changes in industry structure increase per capita carbon emissions lies in the fact that China is still in the process of industrialization, and the proportion of industrial added value in GDP generally shows a slight upward trend (see Fig. 4.3). With the added value of transportation, post, and telecommunications, which enjoy the highest energy intensity and maintain a relatively stable proportion in GDP (about 5%), the increase of the added value of industry, which is also highly energy-intensive (ranking second), leads to an increase in per capita carbon emission. Certainly, compared with employment rate and labor productivity, the influence of industry is much smaller.

During the entire research period, another major feature of China's social changes is the rapid rise in urbanization. During this period, the proportion of urban population in China increased from 19.39% to 53.73%. The energy consumption per capita in cities and towns is higher than in rural areas. For example, in 1980, the energy consumption per capita in cities and towns was 3.6 times that of rural areas, and it was 1.5 times in 2012. Thus, as the proportion of urban population increases, the per capita carbon emissions of China increase as well. At the same time, with the improvement of living standards, both urban and rural population will consume more energy in their daily life (see Fig. 4.3), which will also lead to an increase in the per capita carbon emissions of China.

3.2. *Influence of technological changes*

From 1980 to 2012, the main effect of technological changes on per capita carbon emissions of China lies in energy intensity. Since the 1980s, the energy intensity of the production sector of China has sustainably decreased (see Fig. 4.4). Based on the price of 1978, for each 10,000 yuan of added value in the production sector, the energy consumed dropped from 11.85 tons of standard coal in 1980 to 3.36 tons in 2012 — a drop of more than 72%. The decrease in per capita carbon emissions which is caused by the decrease of energy intensity in the production sector is equivalent to 48% of the actual increase in per capita carbon emission. This means that technological progress, which has been achieved through continuous efforts since the Reform and Opening Up, has made great contributions to carbon emission reduction. Many studies (e.g., Ma & Stern, 2008) show that the decline in energy intensity in China since the

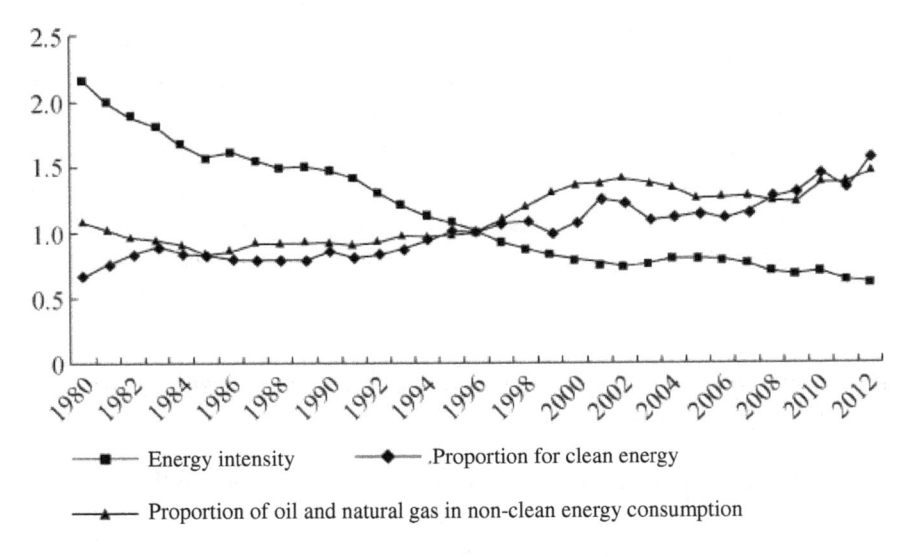

—■— Energy intensity   —◆— .Proportion for clean energy

—▲— Proportion of oil and natural gas in non-clean energy consumption

Fig. 4.4   Changes in technological factors

Note: The indicators in this figure follow the same standardized treatment used in Fig 4.3.

1980s is mainly due to technological progress in various industry sectors. However, due to the rapid expansion of heavy chemical industry, the energy intensity of China was on the rise from 2002 to 2005. This change resulted in an increase in per capita carbon emissions during this period.

During the entire research period, the changes in China's overall structure of energy consumption are generally manifested in the decrease in the proportion of non-clean energy and the increase in the proportion of clean energy (see Fig. 4.4), which has a restraining effect on per capita carbon emission. The overall structure of energy consumption, however, has a limited influence on per capita carbon emission. Its contribution to the decrease of per capita carbon emissions from 1980 to 2012 accounted for less than 5% of the per capita carbon emissions in 1980. This is because the increase in the proportion of clean energy is still very small, from 4.00% in 1980 to 9.38% in 2012.

Changes in the structure of non-clean energy are also conducive to reducing per capita carbon emission. This is mainly because in non-clean energy, the proportion of oil and natural gas with a small carbon emission coefficient has generally increased. The structure of non-clean energy, however, is also limited in influence. This is because oil and natural gas continuously account for over 30% of non-clean energy, and the range of their change is limited. Also, a deeper reason for this lies in the fact that in terms of energy and mineral resources, China is rich only in coal.

In addition, the change in the carbon emission coefficient of non-clean energy causes a slight decrease in per capita carbon emission, which is brought about mainly by the decrease in the carbon emission coefficient of heating power and thermal power.

3.3. *Two special stages in the development of per capita carbon emission*

As has been discussed, there have been two special stages in the development of China's per capita carbon emissions since 1980: one extending from 1996 to 1999 with a decrease in per capita carbon emission, the other from 2002 to 2007 showing a rapid increase. There is an obvious deviation in both stages: what is the reason behind this?

The decrease in per capita carbon emissions from 1996 to 1999 can be attributed to the improvement in energy efficiency. During this period, energy intensity decreased rapidly (see Fig. 4.4), with more contribution to the reduction of per capita carbon emission. In the same period, an obvious decrease in energy consumption per capita for living also contributed to the decrease in per capita carbon emission. The proportion of clean energy increased first (1996–1998) and then decreased (in 1999), with the reduction of carbon emissions per capita as an overall effect. The continuous decline in the proportion of coal over this period (see Fig. 4.4) has also led to per capita carbon emission. And the influence brought about by these factors exceeded other factors, hence the obvious downward trend from 1996 to 1999 for the per capita carbon emissions of China.

There are four reasons for the rapid rise in per capita carbon emissions from 2002 to 2012. First, the labor productivity of China achieved fast development during this period (see Fig. 4.3). It exercised more influence than before on the average annual increase of per capita carbon emissions and on the total increase. Second, the energy efficiency of China unexpectedly deteriorated from 2002 to 2005, and the energy intensity was actually on the rise, which ran counter to the downward trend seen since the 1980s (see Fig. 4.4). The rise in energy intensity led to an increase in per capita carbon emission. From 2003 to 2004 especially, the influence of energy intensity on the average annual per capita carbon emissions even exceeded labor productivity, becoming the leading factor associated with the increase of per capita carbon emission. Third, energy consumption per capita for living also significantly increased during this period. Finally, the increase in per capita carbon emissions brought about by changes in industry structure was also significantly higher than that in other periods.

4. Potential and Ways to Reduce the Per Capita Carbon Emissions of China in the Future

Population is one of the main factors affecting carbon emission. Under the condition that wealth per capita and technological level remain stable, each additional person demands a certain amount of additional energy consumption, and so carbon emissions will naturally increase. Undoubtedly, a country with a large population will have more demands for carbon emissions, which are essential to the basic needs of its population, than a country with a small population. Per capita carbon emission is thus a more reasonable and fairer indicator for the carbon emission level of a country. It would be an unfair practice if the factor of population is ignored in the distribution of carbon emission rights.

The results from empirical analyses show that since the 1980s, five economic factors have led to an increasing trend in the per capita carbon emissions of China, of which labor productivity assumed the dominant role. Among the four technological factors, with the exception of changed carbon emission coefficient of clean energy, all other factors have reduced the per capita carbon emission. The improvement of energy efficiency (GDP energy intensity), in particular, has made a great contribution in this respect. So, how will these factors affect the per capita carbon emissions of China in the future? Which factors will contribute to reducing it? What strategies or measures should be taken to promote these factors in favor of reducing it?

In terms of economic factors, future improvement of labor productivity will still be the main driving factor leading to a rapid rise in carbon emissions per capita in China. The increase in labor productivity means that every worker has created more GDP. In the absence of substantial changes in the mode of economic growth and technology, the rapid growth of GDP means more energy consumption, which will inevitably lead to an increase in carbon emissions. Despite the so-called "environmental Kuznets curve" (EKC) hypothesis — that is, economic growth when reaching a certain level will turn out to be beneficial to reducing pollution emissions — in fact, if the mode of economic growth has not changed (for example, the change of industry structure), technologies have stayed at the old level, and environmental regulations have not been strengthened, it is difficult to imagine what mechanism will automatically lead to the above results.

The Report of the 17th National Congress of the Communist Party of China clearly proposes that the development pattern will be significantly transformed and that the per capita GDP of 2000 will be quadrupled by 2020 through optimizing the economic structure and improving economic returns while reducing the consumption of resources and protecting the environment. Based on the price of 1978, to achieve this goal, the GDP per capita of China must have and maintain a fast growth rate before 2020. This means that per capita GDP will still be the main driving factor for the growth of per capita carbon emissions of China in the future. It is obviously unrealistic and unreasonable to reduce the per capita carbon emissions by reducing the per capita GDP.

Employment rate is a macroeconomic goal that receives much attention. The increase in the employment rate of a country means that more people are employed, thus demanding more means of production. Moreover, in order to produce good economic benefits, we should try our best to reduce the idling of the means of production, i.e., making full use of them. With other conditions remaining unchanged, this will inevitably increase energy consumption in the production sector and lead to an increase in carbon emissions.

To China, a country at the primary stage of socialism, it is even more practically significant to maintain and continuously increase employment rate. Furthermore, expanded employment is one of the "new requirements for attaining the goal of building a moderately prosperous society in all respects" put forward in the Report of the 17th Party Congress, and it is also an important aspect of "accelerating the development of social programs and improving every aspect of the people's well-being". It is thus reasonable and inevitable for China to see per capita carbon emissions increased by efforts to improve employment rate and people's livelihood. This is demanded by the protection of the basic development rights of the Chinese people.

Changes in industry structure can affect per capita carbon emissions in that different industries have different degrees of energy intensity, i.e., there is a difference in the amount of energy consumed for the added value per unit of product. As mentioned above, changes in industry structure usually imply changes in economic growth patterns. Then, along with the changes of a country's industry structure, its energy consumption per unit of GDP (i.e., energy intensity) will generally change. With other conditions staying stable, such changes will lead to variations in per capita carbon emissions in the production sector.

The current industry structure of China lays particular emphasis on industry, especially heavy industry, which is not conducive to decreasing the per capita carbon emission. With the establishment of policies and measures by the central government to obtain macrocontrol of the investment scale, encourage the development of the tertiary industry, as well as further clarify the objective of "accelerating transformation of the mode of economic development and promoting upgrading of the industrial structure" stated in the Report of the 17th Party Congress, there is huge potential for carbon emission reduction in the industrial structure. However, it is unlikely that the proportion of industry will drop dramatically in the next 10–20 years, as China currently needs to deal with the problem of dualistic economic structure and maintain a certain momentum of development for the urbanization process, which necessitates the corresponding industrial products. A possible situation is that the proportion of industry in China's economic system will stay at the current level. Changes in the industry structure may greatly decrease China's per capita carbon emissions in the long run, but there will not be any obvious direct effects within a short term.

The structure of urban and rural population has a role in the per capita carbon emissions because the per capita energy consumption for living of the urban population is much higher than that of the rural population. With other conditions remaining unchanged, changes in population structure will inevitably change per capita energy consumption, thus affecting the per capita carbon emissions in the living sector. As already mentioned, China still needs to deal with the problem of a dualistic economic structure in the future. A notable increase in the proportion of urban residents is also one of the "new requirements for attaining the goal of building a moderately prosperous society in all respects" put forward in the Report of the 17th Party Congress. Thus, the structure of urban and rural population will continue to develop toward increasing per capita carbon emission. But in view of the influence of the population structure on per capita carbon emissions since the Reform and Opening Up, its future influence will be limited.

Per capita energy consumption for living in China seems unlikely to drop. First, as mentioned, there is a requirement for the urbanization level of China to increase significantly, thus leading to an increase in per capita energy consumption for living. Second, the increasingly improved living standards of the people, including the improvement in per capita housing area, the popularization rate, and the utilization rate of electrical appliances and automobiles, will undoubtedly increase the per capita energy consumption for living and the related per capita carbon emission. But we can still expect that the consumption patterns of the people will develop in favor of environmental protection, such as using less high energy-consuming products, driving cars less, reduced usage of air conditioning, and so on, so that the influence of the increased per capita energy consumption on per capita carbon emissions might be reduced.

In addition, in terms of technological factors, improving the energy efficiency will still be a main factor directly affecting future per capita carbon emission reduction in China. Despite the significant decrease of energy intensity in China since the 1980s, the energy consumption per unit of product for China's major energy-consuming products is still about 40% higher than the world's advanced average level. For example, compared with Japan, comparable energy consumption per ton of steel in 2000 was 26% higher — 52% higher than the comprehensive energy consumption of cement, and 25% higher than the coal consumption for thermal power supply (Compilation Committee for the *National Assessment on*

Climate Change, 2007). Moreover, the energy efficiency of China is not only lower than that of developed countries, but also lower than that of many developing countries. It is, however, still possible for China to make full use of backward advantages to introduce and absorb advanced energy-conserving and environmental protection technologies and management methods, thus quickly improving the technological level and energy efficiency. As the Chinese government has incorporated energy conservation and emission reduction as a binding goal in its development plan, corresponding policies and measures will greatly promote the improvement of energy-conserving technologies.

As far as the energy consumption structure of China is concerned, coal will remain the main energy source for the next 10–20 years because of its dominant position in China's energy reserves and the uncertainties in the world oil market, where the competition among various countries is extremely fierce. But with the development of renewable energy and new energy, the proportion of clean energy in the composition of the primary energy will be expected to exceed 30% in 2050 (Compilation Committee for the National Assessment on Climate Change, 2007). If realized, this will not only contribute directly to the reduction of China's per capita carbon emission but also greatly help China to improve its energy efficiency, thus indirectly contributing to the reduction of per capita carbon emission.

On the whole, improving energy efficiency is the main way of reducing per capita carbon emissions in China in the future. There is a great possibility that the energy efficiency of China will improve. In addition to energy-conserving technologies and management levels, such an improvement should also be based on the adjustment of the industry structure and the energy structure, which determines that the reduction of per capita carbon emissions is a long-term and arduous task for China.

5. Concluding Remarks

From 1980 to 2012, the per capita carbon emissions of China increased significantly and showed a phased feature. Such an increase was mainly brought about by the continuous improvement of labor productivity. To maintain a moderate growth rate of labor productivity is the objective need for China, a country at the primary stage of socialism, to achieve the established development goals. The resulting increase in the per capita carbon emissions is thus inevitable. But it should be pointed out that since the Reform and Opening Up, China has been committed to improving its own technological level, which has greatly improved its energy efficiency and effectively reduced the per capita carbon emission.

In recent years, however, the per capita carbon emissions of China has increased rapidly. On the one hand, there has been a rapid, or even accelerated, growth in labor productivity, as well as a continuously increasing employment rate while the industry structure still concentrates on heavy chemical industry; on the other, the improvement of the energy efficiency has stagnated or even slightly deteriorated. Besides, the range of variation for other technological factors, such as energy structure and non-clean energy carbon emission coefficient, is also very small.

On the whole, China should maintain a certain growth rate in the next 20–30 years in order to build a moderately prosperous society in all respects. It is neither realistic nor in line with the condition of China to reduce the growth rate of labor productivity. China should not sacrifice economic development while enhancing its ability to reduce carbon emissions and adapt to global climate change. Thus, the strategy of "energy-conserving first and efficiency-oriented" is of great significance. At the same time, the potential of adjusting the industry structure and the energy structure as a way to reduce carbon emissions needs to be explored further.

Appendix

Suppose $\sum C_i$ represents the total carbon emissions in the production sector and $\sum C_l$ represents the total carbon emissions of different population groups in the living sector, then

$$C = C_I + C_L \tag{A.1}$$

In the expression, C stands for the total carbon emissions from energy consumption, C_I for the carbon emissions from energy consumption in the production sector, and C_L for the carbon emissions from energy consumption in the living sector.

According to the IAPT mathematical identity, the carbon emissions from energy consumption for production can be decomposed as follows:

$$C_I = PAT \qquad (A.2)$$

Taking per capita GDP and carbon emissions per unit of GDP to, respectively, indicate the level of affluence and the level of technology, and decomposing the carbon emissions from energy consumption for production into different industrial sectors, suppose that the carbon emissions of industrial sector i are C_i, we thus obtain

$$C_I = \sum C_i = P \frac{Q}{P} \frac{\sum C_i}{Q} \qquad (A.3)$$

In this expression, Q stands for the GDP calculated at the price of 1978. We divide the production sector into six subsectors of industries: agriculture, forestry, animal husbandry, fishery, and water conservancy; industry; construction; transportation and post and telecommunications; commerce, catering, material supply and marketing, and warehousing; and other industries. We divide population P into employed population P_w and non-employed population, and then obtain

$$C_I = P \frac{P_w}{P} \frac{Q}{P_w} \frac{\sum C_i}{Q} = P \frac{P_w}{P} \frac{Q}{P_w} \sum_i \frac{Q_i}{Q} \frac{C_i}{Q_i} \qquad (A.4)$$

In the above expression, Q_i indicates the GDP of industry i calculated at the price of 1978. Introducing energy intensity into industry sectors, and further decomposing the technology, we obtain the following:

$$C_I = P \frac{P_w}{P} \frac{Q}{P_w} \sum_i \frac{Q_i}{Q} \frac{E_i}{Q_i} \frac{C_i}{E_i} \qquad (A.5)$$

In the expression, E_i represents the total terminal energy consumption of industry i. Since the technology includes not only efficiency factors but also substitution relationships between different inputs, we decompose the terminal energy into clean energy (hydropower and nuclear power) and non-clean energy F_i, and obtain

$$C_I = P \frac{P_w}{P} \frac{Q}{P_w} \sum_i \frac{Q_i}{Q} \frac{E_i}{Q_i} \frac{F_i}{E_i} \frac{C_i}{F_i} \qquad (A.6)$$

Classifying non-clean energy into five categories (coal, coking products, oil, natural gas, and heating power and thermal power) and supposing that C_{ij} indicates the carbon emissions of category j, we have:

$$C_I = \sum_{ij} C_{ij} = P \frac{P_w}{P} \frac{Q}{P_w} \sum_{ij} \frac{Q_i}{Q} \frac{E_i}{Q_i} \frac{F_i}{E_i} \frac{F_{ij}}{F_i} \frac{C_{ij}}{F_{ij}} \qquad (A.7)$$

As a result, we have

$$C_I = \sum_{ij} P \frac{P_w}{P} \frac{Q}{P_w} \frac{Q_i}{Q} \frac{E_i}{Q_i} \frac{F_i}{E_i} \frac{F_{ij}}{F_i} \frac{C_{ij}}{F_{ij}} \qquad (A.8)$$

Suppose $W = P_w/P$, $G = Q/P_w$, $S_i = Q_i/Q$, $I_i = E_i/Q_i$, $R_i = F_i/E_i$, $M_{ij} = F_{ij}/F_i$, and $H_{ij} = C_{ij}/F_{ij}$, we decompose the driving factors of the carbon emissions from energy consumption for production as follows:

$$C_I = \sum_{ij} PWG\, S_i I_i R_i M_{ij} H_{ij} \qquad (A.9)$$

If we divide the population into urban population and rural population and use the per capita energy consumption for living to express the level of affluence, then the carbon emissions from energy consumption for living can be decomposed as follows according to IPAT identity:

$$C_L = \sum_l C_l = P \sum \frac{P_l}{P} \frac{C_l}{P_l} \qquad (A.10)$$

In the expression, C_l represents the total consumption expenditure of population l. Similar to the decomposition of carbon emissions from energy consumption for production, we successively introduce such factors as the structure of urban and rural population, per capita energy consumption for living, energy structure at different levels, and energy conversion efficiency and obtain

$$C_L = P \sum_{ij} \frac{P_l}{P} \frac{E_l}{P_l} \frac{F_l}{E_l} \frac{F_{lj}}{F_l} \frac{C_{lj}}{F_{lj}} \qquad (A.11)$$

Suppose $U_l = P_l/P$, $A_l = E_l/P_l$, $R_l = F_l/E_l$, $M_{lj} = F_{lj}/F_l$, and $H_{lj} = C_{lj}/F_{lj}$, we then decompose the driving factors of carbon emissions from energy consumption for living as follows:

$$C_L = \sum_{lj} PU_l A_l R_l M_{lj} H_{lj} \qquad (A.12)$$

Combining (A.9) and (A.12), i.e., adding carbon emissions from production with carbon emissions from living, we obtain the total carbon emissions as

$$C = C_I + C_L = \sum_{ij} PWG\, S_i\, I_i\, R_i\, M_{ij}\, H_{ij} + \sum_{lj} P\, U_l\, A_l\, R_l\, M_{lj}\, H_{lj} \qquad (A.13)$$

References

Ang, B. W., "Decomposition Analysis for Policymaking in Energy: Which Is the Preferred Model?". *Energy Policy*, No. 32 (2004), pp. 1131–1139.

Birdsall, N., "Another Look at Population and Global Warming", Population, Health and Nutrition Policy Research Working Paper (1992), WPS 1020, World Bank, Washington D.C.

Compilation Committee for the National Assessment on Climate Change. (2007). *National Assessment on Climate Change*. Beijing, China: Science Press.

Dietz, T., & Rosa, E. A., "Rethinking the Environmental Impacts of Population, Affluence and Technology". *Human Ecology Review*, No. 1 (1994), pp. 277–300.

Fan, Y., Liu, L.-C., Wu, G. & Wei, Y.-M., "Changes in Carbon Intensity in China: Empirical Findings from 1980–2003". *Ecological Economics*, No. 62 (2007), pp. 683–691.

Hoekstra, R., & van den Bergh., J. C. J. M., Comparing Structural and Index Decomposition Analysis. *Energy Economics* No. 25 (2003), pp. 39–64.

Hoffert, M. I. *et al.*, "Energy Implications of Future Stabilization of Atmospheric CO_2 Content". *Nature*, Vol. 395 (October 1998), pp. 881–884.

IPCC, Revised 1996 IPCC Guidelines for National Greenhouse Gas Inventories: Workbook (Volume2) (1996); http://www.ipcc-nggip.iges.or.jp/public/gl/invs5a.html.

Karakaya, E., & Mustafa, Ö. "Driving Forces of CO_2 Emissions in Central Asia: A Decomposition Analysis of Air Pollution from Fossil Fuel Combustion". *Arid Ecosystems Journal*, Vol. 11, Nos. 26–27 (2005), pp. 49–57.

Kaya, Y., Impact of Carbon Dioxide Emission Control on GNP Growth: Interpretation of Proposed Scenarios. Paper Presented at the *IPCC Energy and Industry Subgroup*, Reponse Strategies Working Group (1990), Paris, France.

Liaskas, K., Mavrotas, G., Mandaraka, M. & Diakoulaki, D., "Decomposition of industrial CO_2 emissions: The case of European Union". *Energy Economics*, No. 22 (2000), pp. 383–394.

Liu S., "Continue to extend the Moderate High-Level Operation of Current Economic Cycle: An Analysis of the Benign and Large Deformation of Cyclic Fluctuation of the Chinese Economy". *Economic Perspectives*, No. 8 (2007), pp.11–14.

Liu, L.-C.I., Fan, Y., Wu. G. & Wei, Y.-M. "Using LMDI Method to Analyze the Change of China's Industrial CO_2 Emissions from Final Fuel Use: An Empirical Analysis". *Energy Policy*, No. 35 (2007), pp. 5892–5900.

Lynn, S., Lee, S. & Nancy, K., "CO_2 Emissions from Passenger Transport". *Energy Policy*, No. 24 (1996), pp. 17–30.

Ma, C., & Stern, D. J., China's Changing Energy Intensity Trend: A Decomposition Analysis. *Energy Economics*, No. 30 (2008), pp. 1037–1053.

Nanduri, M. An Assessment of Energy Intensity Indicators and Their Role as Policy-Making Tools, Concordia University School of Resource and Environmental Management Report (1998), No. 2232.

Raupach, M. R., Marland, G., Ciais, P., Le Quéré, C., Canadell, J. G., Klepper, G. & Field, C. B., "Global and Regional Drivers of Accelerating CO_2 Emissions". *Proceedings of the National Academy of Science* (2007), http://www.pnas.org/cgi/content/abstract/0700609104v1.

Shi, A., "The Impact of Population Pressure on Global Carbon Dioxide Emissions, 1975–1996: Evidence from Pooled Cross-Country Data". *Ecological Economics*, No. 44 (2003), pp. 29–42.

Waggoner, P. E., & Ausubel, J. H., "A Framework for Sustainability Science: A Renovated IPAT Identity". *Proceedings of the National Academy of Sciences*, Vol. 99, No. 12 (2002), pp. 7860–7865.

Wang, C., Chen, J. & Zou, J., "Decomposition of Energy-Related CO_2 Emissions in China: 1957–2000". *Energy*, No. 30 (2005), pp. 73–83.

Wu, L., Kaneko, S. & Matsuoka, S., "Driving Forces Behind the Stagnancy of China's Energy-Related CO_2 Emissions, Intensity Change and Scale Change". *Energy Policy*, No. 33 (2005), pp. 319–335.

Wu, L., Kaneko, S. & Matsuoka, S., "Dynamics of Energy-Related CO_2 Emissions in China During 1980 to 2002: The Relative Importance of Energy Supply-Side and Demand-Side Effects". *Energy Policy*, No. 34 (2006), pp. 3549–3572.

Xu G., Liu Z. & Jiang Z., "Factor Decomposition Model and Empirical Analysis of Carbon Emissions in China: 1995–2004". *China Population, Resources and Environment*, Vol. 16, No. 6 (2006), pp. 158–161.

Xu Y., Guo Y. & Wu Z., "Economic Development, Carbon Emissions, and Economic Evolution". *Progress in Environmental Science*, Vol. 7, No. 2 (1999), pp. 54–64.

York, R., Rosa, E. & Dietz, T., "STIRPAT, IPAT and ImPACT: Analytical Tools for Unpacking the Driving Forces of Environmental Impacts". *Ecological Economics*, No. 46 (2003), pp. 351–365.

Zhang L., "Changes in the Regional Pattern of Carbon Emissions from China's Primary Energy Consumption". *Geographic Research*, Vol. 25, No. 1 (2006), pp. 629–637.

Zhang Y., "The Influence of Changes in Economic Development Patterns on the Intensity of China's Carbon Emissions". *Economic Research Journal*, No. 4 (2010), pp. 120–133.

Zhang, M., Mu, H., Ning, Y. & Song, Y., "Decomposition of Energy-Related CO_2 Emission over 1991–2006 in China." *Ecological Economics*, No. 68 (2009), pp. 2122–2128.

Zhang, Y., "Structural Decomposition Analysis of Sources of Decarbonizing Economic Development in China: 1992–2006." *Ecological Economics*, No. 68 (2009), pp. 2399–2405.

Chapter 5

Agricultural Production Mode and Its Environmental Impact

Yuhong Li

Institute of Quantitative & Technical Economics,
Chinese Academy of Social Sciences

1. Introduction

The environmental impact of agriculture is mainly manifested in the removal and destruction of the original ecological system, such as forest land, grassland, and wetlands. An artificial open system for input and output according to human needs is to be formed, with the original natural material cycle broken. Historically, agricultural production exercised environmental impact only in the long term and as a slow process, but now this is moving at an accelerated rate.

This chapter points out that the mode of agricultural production determines its environmental impact. The production mode mainly consists of production tools and production relations. After the industrial revolution, agricultural mechanization greatly expanded the area and intensity of agricultural production and objectively intensified its impact on the ecological environment. Either the old and new colonial system or the inequality of land occupation will lead to a vicious circle of environmental deterioration and poverty in some developing countries. With the concentration of land and the decrease of rural population in developed countries, the distance between farmers' residence and production locations becomes wider, and the traditional mechanism for farmers to manage the environment has gradually failed. In order to gain advantages in domestic and international competition, farms, with the purpose of maximizing profits, continuously increase agricultural output, making agriculture a high-risk system with high input–output and an increasingly high degree of manual manipulation.

This chapter takes the environmental impact of agriculture in the United States as an example, attempting to show that the mode of agricultural production determines the environmental impact of agriculture. Since the New World was discovered by Columbus in 1492 and started to receive immigrants from Europe, the history of agriculture has extended less than 500 years, which is quite a short period of time compared with that of Eurasia. But it was during this period that the industrial revolution and the rapid development of capitalism in modern times took place. An examination of this period will clearly show the causes and process of the impact of agricultural production on the environment. In the southern plains of the United States in particular, a 50-year-long agricultural production gave rise to dust storms spreading over 400,000 square kilometers of land for 10 years in the 1930s. This is the epitome of the success and failure of human beings in transforming nature.

2. The Production Mode Determining the Environmental Impact of Agriculture

There are different viewpoints as to the causes and solutions to the environmental impacts of agricultural production. Mainstream economics shows that, like other external problems, environmental problems caused by agricultures lie in an area of unclear definition of property rights of environmental resources, which leads to a lack of prices and markets, and ultimately market failure (Lichtenberg, 2002). However, for many external problems, clear property right is in itself an untenable premise, especially owing to the externality of agriculture. Some environmental historians attribute them to the capitalist mode of production, by which capitalists overexploit natural resources just as they overexploit labor (Worster, 2004). But it cannot be denied that the development of Siberia by the Soviet Union, a socialist country, has also caused serious ecological problems (Ponting, 2007). Thus, the social system itself cannot fully explain the causes of environmental impacts.

Apparently, the environmental impact becomes conspicuous with the development of human society and economy, with the environmental issues a by-product of development. Development is, however, too broad a concept that cannot characterize the essence of human society. In essence, the main body that influences the environment is human beings, who possess not only biological attributes but also social attributes. The latter distinguish human beings from other creatures. In addition to the number of human beings, which affects the environment, the social attributes of human beings are also important influencing factors. The social attributes of human beings lie in the mode of production, which consists of productive forces and production relations. The way human beings conduct agricultural production directly determines the environmental impact of agriculture.

The main factor that determines productivity is production tools or technology. There is an enormous difference between the slash-and-burn farming method and fossil fuel-driven agricultural machinery in terms of the intensity and breadth of transformation of nature. During the hunting and gathering stage, human beings did not have the consciousness to protect the environment. But they were limited by the production tools to transform the environment, and so they had little influence on the environment. After the industrial revolutions, the use of machinery and energy has greatly improved the ability of human beings to transform nature. Places that seemed to be in bad natural condition and that human beings could not reach can now be easily transformed by machinery and energy. The extent of human beings' exploitation of natural resources and their impact on the environment has continuously been expanding and deepening along with the industrial revolution. From 1750 to 1850, forests were cut down in the English villages where the industrial revolution was first realized. Just before 1790, most of the forests in eastern England had been eradicated, and by the end of the 18th century, there were very few forests in southwest England. According to the report of the government committee, the forest area in England and Wales at that time was no more than 2 million acres (12 million *mu*) (Finberg, 1989). The starting point for Brazil to industrialize in the mid-20th century was also the starting point when the virgin forests of the Amazon began to decrease on a large scale. Although it is not the intention of human beings to destroy the environment, their influence on the ecological environment is getting more significant.

In addition, the impact of production relations on the environment is enormous. Under the old colonial system, European countries conquered the world by navigation technology and military force, occupied areas outside Eurasia, and established colonial control. The lands were held in the hands of colonizers, and a set of agricultural systems was formed in favor of colonist countries. Most of the good farmlands in Caribbean countries, South America, and several colonies in Africa were farmed for the growth of cash crops, such as coffee, sugar, and cotton, which were exported to colonist countries, instead of planting food crops to meet the basic needs of the colonial people (Ponting, 2007). Even after World War II, fertile lands were still controlled by a small number of large farm owners and used for producing cash crops as most developing countries kept their old system of land ownership. The poor people, in order to maintain their livelihood, reclaimed land that was not suitable for agriculture, or obtained lands by destroying forests or filling lakes. Developing countries in areas with tropical rainforest, such as Brazil and Indonesia, cut down virgin forests to reclaim farmland for livelihood, which eventually led to soil erosion, leading to the formation of a vicious circle between environmental deterioration and deepening poverty (López & Niklitscheck, 1991).

In developed countries, the impact of agricultural production relations on the environment is shown in another form.

First, the escrow mechanism ceases working. By escrow mechanism we mean that the subjects of economic activities that affect the environment jointly assume responsibility for environmental protection. The rationale behind this mechanism lies in the fact that the subjects of economic activities bear the externality caused by such activities. These subjects have the motivation to protect the environment and reduce environmental pollution. In the early days of the industrial revolution and the rise of the city, cities were noisy and dirty, while rural areas served as beautiful idyllic leisure places for gentlemen and ladies to relax and as a place where they enjoyed walking, hunting, fishing, and other social activities amid the pastoral scenery. Men were both the providers and the consumers of environmental quality. This consistency of demand and supply for environmental quality is an important condition for the escrow mechanism to play its role. However, with the improvement of the city's economic status and environmental quality, more and more people have transferred their social life to the city. The landowner's residence was separated from his land, and he did not have the motivation to protect the environment. As regards tenants, managers, partners, and agricultural workers, they were in the pursuit of the maximization of short-term economic benefits and did not have a sense of responsibility to take care of the environment. Moreover, they were generally poorly paid and had smaller demand for environmental quality than the rich landowners.

Second, there is a conflict between farmers' pursuit of increasing agricultural output and limited environmental capacity. Theoretically, when externality cannot be internalized, goods with positive externality will be in short supply, while goods with negative externality will be oversupplied. Thus, the output of agricultural products that will cause pollution will also exceed the social optimum. In reality, the agricultural product market is nearly fully competitive. Farmers are the recipients not makers of agricultural product prices, and they cannot monopolize the market and control output. On the contrary, for many individual farmers, the objective is to obtain the highest income instead of the highest profit. Once there is surplus labor, they will put it into use to increase the output. To make things worse, the government subsidies on agricultural materials such as chemical fertilizers and pesticides would stimulate farmers to increase the use of these agent. In addition, in order to increase output, farmers often endorse uncertain new technologies, such as genetically modified crops, and new technologies usually have a negative impact on the environment or possess potential negative externalities.

3. An Overview of the Environmental Impact of Agriculture

In the 4 billion years of history of the earth, human beings appeared 2 or 3 million years ago. The use of bronzeware started around 4000–6000 years ago, and before that, stones were used as tools. The history of agriculture can be traced back to the Neolithic Age, which was about 10,000 years ago. Before the first industrial revolution, agricultural production was dominated by manpower, supplemented by simple animal power, and production tools were mainly made of iron. The biggest impact of agriculture on the environment is nothing more than soil degradation and soil erosion. Agricultural production cannot be separated from soil and water. Early irrigated agriculture was distributed near rivers, such as the Tigris and the Euphrates, and the Nile and the Yellow River. Planting involved continuously turning over the earth, and the loosened soil was easily eroded by flowing water and wind, and tiny particles get transported to other places by external forces, thus changing the structure of the soil. As a result, the riverbed gets heightened and become silted up. This is the cause of the soil erosion in the Loess Plateau of China and the formation of the Yellow River. In the period before the industrial revolution, the impact of agriculture on the ecological environment was rather slow.

The industrial revolution that began in the mid-18th century was less than 300 years ago. With the development of metallurgy and the use of fossil fuels such as coal, oil, and natural gas, human beings have rapidly entered into the era of mechanical force, and the importance of human and animal power in agriculture has decreased. The use of mechanical force in agriculture, its impact on the environment, and its reliance on resources have rapidly exceeded any other period in history. The mechanical force greatly expanded the area of agricultural production. Virgin lands, mountains, wetlands, and tropical forests decreased dramatically in area, during this period.

Since the 20th century, chemicals started to contribute to the impact of agriculture on the environment. They have changed the original nutrition cycle of traditional agriculture and have become one of the important characteristics of modern agriculture. Take fertilizer as an example. The history of human use of fertilizer can be roughly divided into three stages.

The first stage features local organic fertilizer. For most of history, agricultural input relied on local organic waste. People, agriculture, and nature formed a closed local cycle. Animal and human excreta are used as organic fertilizers in agricultural production, which is a common practice in East Asian countries such as China and Japan. In ancient Chinese cities and towns which did not have drainage facilities, there were people collecting swill and waste in the early morning for agricultural production.

The second stage saw the use of foreign organic fertilizer. The development of ocean transportation made it possible to circulate organic fertilizer across borders and oceans. In the 19th century, richer countries, such as Great Britain, imported a large amount of seabird excrement from Peru and Chile to supplement their declining soil fertility (McNeill, 2000).

In the third stage, chemical fertilizers appeared and dominated, which changed the past history of relying on organic substances as fertilizers in agriculture. In 1842, Lawes, an Englishman, discovered that the reaction between phosphate rock and sulfuric acid could produce a highly concentrated phosphate fertilizer. In 1909, Haber of Germany separated nitrogen from the air through ammonia nitrogen synthesis, producing nitrogen fertilizer which is necessary for crops. In 1940, the world's fertilizer usage amounted to 4 million tons, rising to 40 million in 1965 and approaching 0.15 billion tons in 1990 (McNeill, 2000).

The popularization and extensive use of chemical fertilizers, combined with the use of mechanical force, have increased agricultural output, which provided the capacity to feed an additional 2 billion people; otherwise, 30% more cultivated land would be needed (McNeill, 2000). On the other hand, with the use of other chemicals, such as pesticides, hormones, antibiotics, and so on, the relationship between agriculture and the ecological environment system has been affected and has changed in a relatively short period of time.

First of all, agriculture has become a highly energy-consuming industry. Modern agriculture not only relies on solar energy for photosynthesis, but also needs energy to drive machinery, produce fertilizer, ensure long-distance transport, store food, and keep the produce fresh.

Second, agricultural production pollutes water and soil. Although relevant estimates tend to vary, it is generally believed that more than half of the chemical fertilizers flow to water bodies (McNeill, 2000), resulting in eutrophication of rivers, lakes, and offshore waters, as well as leading to an increase in nitrate concentration in groundwater. Long-term application of chemical fertilizers will lead to soil hardening and destroy the microcirculation of organisms in the soil, while the decline of soil fertility will lead to an increasing dependence on chemical fertilizers. The use of pesticides, such as DDT, has directly destroyed the ecological chain of the nature and endangered human health. At present, the harmful effects of hormones and antibiotics used in agriculture on human health have been confirmed, and large-scale production has been carried out before the long-term effects of transgenic technology on the ecological environment and human body have been confirmed.

Third, agricultural consumption of groundwater resources outpaces its natural renewal. Agriculture has gradually freed itself from the restriction of certain natural conditions. The exploitation of groundwater for irrigation is a case in point, which makes it possible to carry out agricultural production in extremely dry and arid areas, which would otherwise be unsuitable for such production. Yet groundwater is called fossil water, which is usually formed in a long geological process. Even if there is renewal mechanism for it, its speed is far lower than that of surface water.

Finally, the variety of crops being cultivated has undergone a trend of being narrowed, the ecosystem becomes fragile, and the dependence on pesticides is enhanced. The use of chemical fertilizers in combination with mechanical power produces a screening mechanism for crop varieties: the varieties that are more suitable for chemical fertilizers and mechanical operation have been widely promoted, that is, a situation of monoculture is formed. Single cropping and the use of chemical fertilizers and mechanical forces are mutually reinforcing. In terms of the stability of the ecosystem, a diversified system is relatively stable, while the system of cultivating a single crop is the most unstable and has the weakest resistance to diseases, insect, and pests, which results in a high dependence on pesticides, thus giving rise to more environmental and health problems.

4. Concluding Remarks

The mode of agricultural production has an impact on the ecological environment through two channels: first, production tools or production technologies, and second, production relations. New technologies and advanced production tools have strengthened the ability of human beings to transform the natural environment, expanded the scale and intensity of agricultural production, and ultimately expanded the area and productivity of agricultural production. The existing production relations under the new colonial system has put the poor population in conflict with environmental protection in developing countries, forming a vicious circle between them. On the other hand, the commercialization of agricultural production in developed countries shows that farmers are intent on maximizing profits, either by reclaiming land in an extensive manner or by increasing investment in machinery, chemical fertilizers, or pesticides in an intensive manner, thus greatly transforming the surrounding environment. Capitalist agricultural production, with exchange as its purpose, has brought agriculture closer to industrial production. In order to pursue high output, investment is continuously increased and profound changes have been made to the original ecological system. The agricultural structure in which large farms are dominant has rendered the traditional escrow mechanism ineffective.

As a country with a short history of agriculture, rich resources, and small population pressure, the US has created dust storms — one of the world's three major environmental natural disasters, within half a century — thus embodying the huge impact of its particular production mode on the environment and serves as the epitome of the impact of agricultural activities on the environment. Although the current threat of dust storms has diminished, environmental risks have not been eliminated. Overexploitation of groundwater in the southern plains has increased the risk of unsustainable agricultural development in the future. Currently, American agriculture is highly mechanized and commercialized, which makes some new features formed by modern agriculture aggravate the negative impact on the environment. Monoculture, which is closely linked to mechanization, relies even more on chemical synthesis products, making the agricultural system more fragile.

References

Finberg, H. P. R., *The Agrarian History of England and Wales*, Volume 6, 1750–1850, 1989. Cambridge University Press, Cambridge.

Lichtenberg, E., "Agriculture and the Environment." In *Handbook of Agricultural Economics*, Volume 2, B. Gardner and G. Rausser (eds.). 2002. Elsevier Science, The Netherlands 1249–1313.

López, R., & Niklitscheck, M., "Dual Economic Growth in Poor Tropical Areas." *Journal of Development Economics*, No. 36 (1991), 189–211.

McNeill, J. R., *Something New under the Sun, an Environmental History of the Twentieth-Century World.* 2000. W. W. Norton & Company, New York.

Ponting, C., *A New Green History of the World: The Environment and the Collapse of Great Civilizations,* rev. ed., 2007. Penguin Books, London.

Worster, D., *Dust Bowl: The Southern Plains in the 1930s.* 2004. Oxford University Press, New York.

Chapter 6

Impact of Trade on China's Carbon Emissions (1987–2011)[1]

Youguo Zhang

Institute of Quantitative & Technical Economics,
Chinese Academy of Social Sciences

1. Introduction

Currently, climate change has become an environmental issue of widespread concern to all sectors of society. Wyckoff & Roop (1994) point out that with the signing of the Kyoto Protocol, countries with responsibilities for greenhouse gas emission reduction may carry out their tasks by increasing imports of goods from countries that do not have such obligations and reducing their own production. Thus, the increase in trade may cause carbon leakage and lead to a continuous increase in global greenhouse gas emissions. This problem has attracted the attention of many researchers. Since the mid-1990s, there has also been a rapid increase in empirical analysis on carbon implied in trade. For example, Wyckoff & Roop (1994) and Ahmed & Wyckoff (2003) have studied the carbon implied in trade in several countries; Machado *et al.* (2001) has estimated the carbon implied in trade in Brazil; and Rhee & Chung (2006) have analyzed the carbon implied in bilateral trade between south Korea and Japan.

The input–output model served as the most important analytical tool in previous studies on trade-embodied carbon, because it can effectively combine carbon emissions with final demand, including exports, and can

---

[1] A brief version of the present chapter has been published in *China Economic Quarterly*, No. 4, 2010. Here a longer period has been studied, and new data are added.

fully depict the correlation between industries in the economic system. At the same time, most of the studies are based on the single-region rather than the multi-region input–output model. This may be because most of the analyses are focused on the trade-embodied carbon in a single region, and the single-region model is more suitable for describing the impact of trade on the carbon emissions in a single specific region, while the multi-region model is more suitable for describing that in multiple regions. Thus, the present chapter also applies the single-region input–output model to study the embodied carbon in the trade of China.

Due to the rapid economic development of China in recent years, the accompanying energy consumption and CO_2 emissions have also risen sharply. In the meantime, China's economic growth pattern has assumed obvious export-oriented characteristics, which has made China a recognized "world factory". In recent years, there has been a rapid increase in the empirical analysis of the trade-embodied carbon of China. Most research results[2] show that China has become a "net exporter of carbon", that is, carbon embodied in exports is much more than carbon embodied in imports, or carbon avoided by imports.

Based either on the assumption that imported products involve the same technology as those domestically produced or on the estimation of carbon emission intensity of various countries, the estimates of Ahmed & Wyckoff (2003) show that carbon embodied in exports was significantly higher than that in imports in 1997. Wang & Watson (2007) find that the net export of CO_2 for China in 2004 was 1,109 million tons (MT). According to Pan *et al.* (2008), China's net export of CO_2 in 2002 amounted to 623 MT. Yao *et al.* (2008) estimated that China's embodied carbon in exports exceeded that in imports by 664 MT of CO_2 in 2005. Both the conservative and the optimistic estimates by Qi *et al.* (2008) show that China was a net exporter of carbon from 1997 to 2006. Recently, Yan & Yang (2010) estimate that China's carbon embodied in exports accounted for 10.03–26.54% of China's total carbon emissions in the period 1997–2007, while that embodied in imports took up only 4.04%

---

[2] Among the existing literature, only Weber *et al.* (2008) reaches a conclusion that carbon embodied in exports for China is significantly less than that in imports in the period of 1987–2005.

(1997) and 9.05% (2007). Estimates by Lin & Sun (2010) show that China's carbon embodied in exports was 3,357 MT of CO_2 in 2005, which was significantly more than 2,333 MT of CO_2, the amount of carbon avoided by imports.

Existing literature shows that China is also a net exporter of carbon in bilateral trade with major trading partners. Estimates by Shui & Harriss (2006) show that China's CO_2 exports to the US increased from 213 MT in 1997 to 497 MT in 2003, while little CO_2 was imported from the US. Li & Hewitt (2008) find that in Sino-British trade of 2004, the carbon embodied in exports of China was 186 MT of CO_2, while that of the UK was only 23 MT of CO_2. Wang & Cheng (2006) and Liu *et al.* (2010) find that in the bilateral trade between China and Japan, China's carbon embodied in exports is also far higher than that of Japan.

It is worth pointing out that most of the studies on the estimation of embodied carbon in China's trade are based on (import) competitive input–output table, i.e., an input–output table that differentiates intermediate input, and domestic product and imported product in the final demand (see Table 6.1). This means that most empirical studies have neglected the impact of imports on the results of intermediate inputs. But a few studies such as Weber *et al.* (2008), Yao *et al.* (2008), and Lin & Sun (2010) used

Table 6.1   (Import) non-competitive economy–energy–environment input–output

| | Intermediate use | Final use | | | | |
		Domestic demand	Export	Total	Import	Total output
Intermediate input of domestic products	$A_d X$	Y_{dd}	Y_{ed}	Y_d		X
Intermediate input of imported products	$A_m X$	Y_{dm}	Y_{em}	Y_m	X_m	
Value added	V					
Total input	X					
Energy consumption	FEX					
Carbon emission	CFEX					

(import) non-competitive input–output tables to estimate the embodied carbon in China's trade.

Like Weber *et al.* (2008), Yao *et al.* (2008), and Lin & Sun (2010), this chapter applies (import) non-competitive input–output tables to estimate the embodied carbon in China's trade. But unlike Weber *et al.* (2008) and Lin & Sun (2010), the uses of imported products under different trade methods are differentiated here. And unlike Yao *et al.* (2008) and Lin & Sun (2010), the research period in this chapter is 1987–2007 — these earlier studies were focused only on 2005.

It should also be pointed out that in the above-mentioned studies, only Yan & Yang (2010) have conducted structural decomposition on the changes of carbon embodied in China's trade. However, Yan & Yang (2010) apply only the input–output table and relevant consumer price indices of 1997 of China to estimate the carbon emission multipliers and corresponding trade-embodied carbon in various sectors from 1997 to 2007. They do not make full use of the input–output tables of other years (including 2002, 2005, and 2007). They only distinguish the three factors of trade scale, trade structure, and carbon emission multipliers, studying their respective impact on China's trade-embodied carbon, and could not further subdivide the carbon emission multipliers into important policy variables such as energy intensity, energy structure, and intermediate input–output technology, whose identification provides valuable reference for understanding the changes of embodied carbon in China's trade and establishing related policies. To this end, this chapter compiles comparable price (import) non-competitive input–output tables for the period 1987–2010 for China, drawing on the input–output tables published by the National Bureau of Statistics. Based on these tables, the impact of trade on carbon emissions has been estimated and its changes structurally decomposed.

2. Methods and Data

The input–output model is the mainstream analysis tool in the research on the environmental impact of trade. Limited by data, most studies are based on the single-region input–output model. There are certainly some researchers compiling multi-region input–output models to estimate trade-embodied carbon (e.g., Peters & Hertwich, 2006). The single-region input–output model generally assumes that imported products involve the same technology as local products, so the model is suitable for estimating the local carbon avoided by imports for the region of the importing country. As regards the multi-region input–output model, the carbon emission of imports is estimated based on the technology of the country of origin. What is estimated in this model is the carbon emission produced by these products in the country of origin (carbon embodied imports). Therefore, the imported carbon emissions calculated by the two models have different meanings. In general, the multi-region input–output model can more accurately estimate the impact of trade on global and multi-region carbon emissions, while the single-region input–output model is more suitable for evaluating the impact of trade on single-region carbon emissions. Like most studies of this type, the research in this chapter is also based on a single-region input–output model.

2.1. *Measurement model of embodied carbon in trade*

The core of the input–output model is the input–output coefficient matrix A, each column of which represents the input–output "technology" of an economic sector. In the (import) non-competitive input–output model (see Table 6.1), A is divided into A_d and A_m, which, respectively, represent the technical coefficients of domestic products and imported products in the intersectoral product input demand, i.e., $A = A_d + A_m$. Assuming that the entire economic system consists of n sectors, that the energy consumed at the end of each sector can be divided into g types, and that the energy consumption is in direct proportion to the output (Copeland *et al.*, 2004), then the relationship between the final demand for domestic products and the total carbon emissions Q of the production sector can be expressed as follows:

$$Q = Q(C,F,E,L,Y_d) = CFELY_d \qquad (6.1)$$

In the expression, C denotes $1 \times g$ order row vector, and its element c_k denotes the carbon emission coefficient of the k-th energy; F denotes a $g \times n$ matrix of energy structure, and its element f_{rj} denotes the proportion of the r-th energy consumed by sector j in the total energy consumed by sector j; E denotes an $n \times n$ order diagonal matrix, and its diagonal element e_{ii} denotes the direct energy intensity of sector i; the Leontief inverse matrix, $L = (I - A_d)^{-1}$, reflects the complete consumption of products from other sectors by each sector; Y_d represents the final demand vector of domestic products. Also, Y_d can be further decomposed as follows:

$$Y_d = Y_{dd} + Y_{ed} \tag{6.2}$$

In this expression, Y_{dd} stands for the domestic demand vector of domestic products, including consumption and fixed capital formation; Y_{ed} stands for the export vector.

This chapter defines carbon emissions caused by exports as carbon embodied in exports. According to (6.1), carbon embodied in exports can be expressed as follows:

$$Q_e = Q_e(C,F,E,L,Y_{ed}) = CFELY_{ed} \tag{6.3}$$

Suppose that Q_e represents the $n \times 1$ order matrix of product structure, its element s_{ej} represents the proportion of domestic products of sector j in the final demand, and Y_{ed} indicates the total exports of domestic products, then the estimation of carbon embodied in exports can be expressed as

$$Q_e = Q_e(C,F,E,L,S_e,y_{ed}) = CFELS_e y_{ed} \tag{6.4}$$

Imported products and domestic products are different in terms of carbon intensity in that the consumption of imported products occurs abroad, and the industry structure and technological level of various countries are different. Owing to a lack of data, studies generally assume that imported products are produced by the same technology as the importing country, which is obviously not the actual case. But such treatment is reasonable if the environmental impact of imports is understood as saving domestic energy consumption and reducing domestic pollution emissions. Suppose that the total import volume of China is X_m and that the structure vector of imported products is S_m, then we can obtain the carbon avoided by imports (carbon emission saved due to imports) as

$$Q_m = Q_m(C,F,E,L,S_m, x_m) = CFELS_m x_m \tag{6.5}$$

Expression (6.5) reflects the environmental cost of producing these products in countries other than China.

On the basis of the above discussions, this chapter defines net carbon embodied in trade as the difference between carbon embodied in exports and carbon avoided by imports, i.e.,

$$Q_n = Q_e - Q_m \qquad (6.6)$$

In addition, according to this method, we can also estimate the carbon embodied in the trade of various sectors and that in the bilateral trade between China and specific countries (regions).

2.2. *Structural decomposition of the change in carbon embodied in trade*

Suppose that carbon embodied in exports for period t is $Q_{e,t}$, that total carbon emission for period $t-1$ is $Q_{e,t-1}$, and that the changes in carbon embodied in exports of the two periods are $\Delta Q_e = Q_{e,t} - Q_{e,t-1}$, then ΔQ_e can be incrementally decomposed according to (6.4) as follows:

$$\Delta Q_e = Q_e(\Delta C) + Q_e(\Delta F) + Q_e(\Delta E) + Q_e(\Delta L) + Q_e(\Delta S_e) + Q_e(\Delta y_{ed}) \quad (6.7)$$

Similarly, ΔQ_m of the changes in carbon avoided by imports between the two periods can be incrementally decomposed according to (6.5) as follows:

$$\Delta Q_m = Q_m(\Delta C) + Q_m(\Delta F) + Q_m(\Delta E) + Q_m(\Delta L) + Q_m(\Delta S_m) + Q_m(\Delta x_m) \quad (6.8)$$

In this expression, Δ represents the change of a factor. Expressions (6.7) and (6.8) can be used to identify the influence of various factors on the changes of carbon embodied in exports and imports. It should be pointed out that the specific forms of (6.7) and (6.8) are not unique. Dietzenbacher & Los (1998) proved that if the change of a variable is determined by n factors, then different decompositions will be obtained by starting from different factors, which means that the number of change decompositions for the variable will be $n!$. They hold that it is reasonable to use the average value of dependent variable in the $n!$ change decompositions for a factor to measure the influence of the factor on the dependent variable (for a detailed description of this method, see Dietzenbacher & Los, 1998). This chapter calculates, according to their method, all the above possible influence of each factor on dependent variables and takes their average values as a measure for such influence.

2.3. *Data processing*

2.3.1. *Sequence of comparable price input–output tables*

The comparable price input–output tables are processed here in a similar manner to Zhang (2009a, 2009b, 2010), with the following three aspects included:

(1) The input–output tables of 1987–2007 compiled by the National Bureau of Statistics[3] are converted to comparable price input–output tables. Considering the matching between economic data and energy data, this chapter first converts these input–output tables into input–output table sequences of 26 sectors by merging some sectors,[4] and then uses the Double Deflation method (United Nations, 1999) to convert these tables into comparable price input–output tables based on the price of 2002. The price indices are mainly taken from those in *China Statistical Yearbook* over the years and *China's External Trade Indices* compiled by the General Administration of Customs of China.

(2) The above comparable price input–output tables are converted into (import) non-competitive input–output tables. In the input–output tables published by the National Bureau of Statistics over the years, the intermediate and final uses actually refer to composite products of

---

[3] The input–output tables of 2000 are not adopted, for they include only 17 sectors.

[4] It should be pointed out that the final demand in the input–output tables of 1987–1995 released by the National Bureau of Statistics does not include columns of exports and imports but only net exports. This chapter estimates the ratios of exports to total output based on the comparable input–output tables compiled by Li & Xue (1998), and uses these ratios to estimate the exports and imports of various sectors of agriculture and the secondary industry from 1987 to 1995. At the same time, the export and import of various services are estimated based on the relevant data on service trade in the "China's balance of international payments" in the *China Statistical Yearbook* over the years and the service trade data of China released by the World Trade Organization.

domestic and imported products. In order to avoid exaggerating the environmental impact of various final uses, it is necessary to use (import) non-competitive input–output tables that differentiate domestic products and imported products. Unlike Weber *et al.* (2008), this chapter does not directly separate in proportion imports from intermediate input and final demand. Instead, the chapter adopts the following method: First, the value of imported products in exports is differentiated, that is, the value of products which have not entered into the cycle of domestic production and are exported by way of bonded warehouse entry–exit goods and bonded warehouse reexport trade. Second, the value of imported equipment for processing trade, equipment, and articles imported by foreign-invested enterprises as investments, and imported equipment for export processing zones is mainly calculated into fixed capital formation. Finally, the value of the remaining imported products, after deducting the value of the above bonded imported products and imported products of equipment type, will be proportionally decomposed into intermediate use and final uses (excluding exports). In addition, this chapter deducts the value of products imported in bonded manner from imports so as not to exaggerate the impact of imports on China's carbon emissions. For specific details, see Zhang (2009a).

(3) Carbon emissions of each sector are estimated. This estimate is based on the energy consumption of various industries published in the *China Energy Statistical Yearbook* over the years, with 19 types of energy involved. The average calorific values of various fuels used in the estimation come from the *China Energy Statistical Yearbook 2008*; carbon emission coefficients mainly come from IPCC (1996) and Hu & Jiang (2001).

2.3.2. *Estimation of sectoral trade volume and trade carbon emission multiplier in recent years*

In 2008, 2009, and 2011, the imports and exports of different sectors are estimated according to the following method:

(1) On the basis of weighted average, we obtain the annual import and export quantity indices of different sectors by using the monthly quantity indices of agricultural and industrial sectors in *China's External*

Trade Indices. Then, the imports and exports of different sectors over the years are estimated on the basis of the imports and exports of different sectors in the comparison price input–output tables of 2010.[5]

(2) Due to a lack of prices and quantity indices for service sectors, their corresponding GDP deflators are used as proxy variables for trade price indices. Then, the trade volume of each service sector is estimated on the basis of *China Statistics of Trade in Services 2011* released by the Chinese Ministry of Commerce, and the GDP deflator is estimated on the basis of the current-year-price GDP and GDP indices of each tertiary sector published in the *China Statistical Yearbook 2012*. There are ready-to-hand statistics on the current-year-price trade volume of the construction sector over the years, which can be directly used to estimate comparable price imports and exports in combination with GDP deflators. There is no available statistics on other service sectors treated in this chapter. We use the trade volume of transportation service and its corresponding GDP deflator in *China Statistics of Trade in Services* to estimate the trade indices over the years, and take them for the trade indices of transportation, warehousing, and postal services. At the same time, the trade index estimated based on the total imports and exports of service industry is taken to be the trade volume index of wholesale, retail, accommodation, catering, and non-material production sectors.

In addition, in order to measure the carbon embodied in trade in 2008, 2009, and 2011, we also need to know the carbon emission multipliers of various sectors in these years. Since there are no corresponding input–output tables in these years, we first calculate the short-term trend of carbon emission multipliers of various sectors on basis of the comparable price input–output tables of 2007 and 2010, and then estimate the sectoral carbon emission multiplier for these years. The carbon embodied in trade of these years can thus be calculated by applying these multipliers and the sectoral trade volume estimated above.

---

[5] Since 2009 and 2011 are close to 2010, it is fairly reasonable to choose the trade volume of different sectors of 2010 as the basis for estimation. In order to unify the basis, the trade volume of different sectors of 2008 is also calculated based on the trade volume of different sectors and corresponding trade quantity indices of 2010.

3. An Empirical Analysis

This chapter reports on China's total trade-embodied carbon, trade-embodied carbon in different sectors, major country (region) flows of trade-embodied carbon, and the influence of six factors on trade-embodied carbon from 1987 to 2011, and makes a comparison with existing studies. Unless indicated otherwise, all the data in this chapter are estimated by the authors, and the tables and figures are drawn up based on these data.

3.1. *Carbon embodied in trade and its general trend*

Table 6.2 shows China's trade volume and trade-embodied carbon in the major years of the period from 1987 to 2011 (see Appendix A). Figure 6.1 shows the ratio of trade to total demand over the years and the ratio of

Table 6.2   Trade volume and carbon embodied in trade of China

Year	Export (billion RMB)	Import (billion RMB)	Carbon embodied in exports (MTC)	Carbon avoided in imports (MTC)	Net carbon embodied in trade (MTC)
1987	422	417	66	104	−38
1990	580	428	97	103	−6
1992	763	770	119	149	−30
1995	1,035	1,399	156	256	−99
1997	1,407	1,442	169	222	−53
2002	3,056	2,538	206	208	−2
2005	6,521	4,613	422	340	82
2007	8,805	4,856	478	278	200
2008	8,867	5,124	451	288	163
2009	8,016	5,075	388	300	88
2010	10,603	6,473	491	340	151
2011	11,402	7,163	550	376	174

Notes: The data in the table are calculated according to expressions (6.4) and (6.5). The trade volume is calculated on the basis of the method given in Section 2 at the price of 2002. The figures in the brackets in the 2nd and the 3rd columns are the ratios of trade volume to total demand. The figures in the brackets in 4th and 5th columns are the ratios of all kinds of embodied carbon to the total carbon emissions in the production sector.

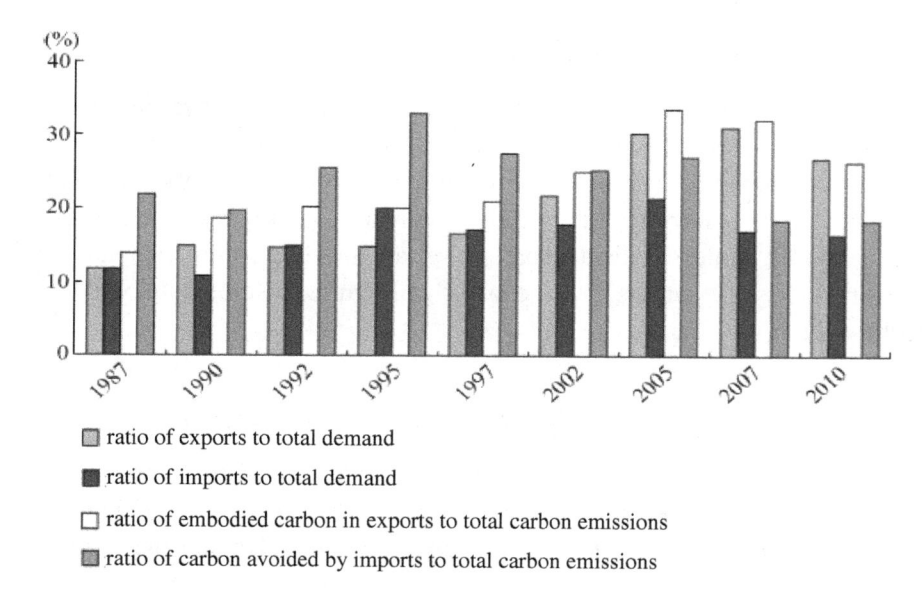

☐ ratio of exports to total demand

■ ratio of imports to total demand

☐ ratio of embodied carbon in exports to total carbon emissions

▨ ratio of carbon avoided by imports to total carbon emissions

Fig. 6.1 The ratio of trade volume to total demand and the ratio of trade-embodied carbon to total carbon emissions

trade-embodied carbon to total carbon emissions in the production sector. With the rapid growth of exports, the carbon embodied in exports has undergone a sustained and rapid growth from 1987 to 2011. According to the growth rate of carbon embodied in exports, the period can be roughly divided into the following three stages: (1) From 1987 to 2002, the carbon embodied in exports achieved an increase equivalent to 140 million tons of carbon (MTC), with an average annual growth rate of 7.9%. It was a stage of long-term rapid and stable growth. (2) From 2002 to 2005, the carbon embodied in exports increased 216 MTC, with an average annual growth rate of 27.0%. It was a stage of short-term high-speed growth. (3) From 2005 to 2011, the carbon embodied in exports increased by 128 MTC, but the average annual growth rate was only 4.5%. It was a stage of slow growth. At this stage, due to the influence of the international financial crisis of 2008, the carbon embodied in exports experienced a brief decline from 2007 to 2009.

In terms of the proportion of export-embodied carbon in the total carbon emission of the national production sector, export-embodied carbon increased continuously from 1987 to 2002, and the proportion increased from 14% in 1987 to 25% in 2002. From 2002 to 2005, it reached an all-time high of 34%. Since then, it has gradually declined, but still accounted for 25% in 2011. This shows that neither the absolute nor the relative influence of exports on China's carbon emissions can be ignored.

While the carbon embodied in exports continues to increase, China's carbon avoided by imports has also increased significantly along with the increase in imports, which means that imports have reduced a lot of carbon emissions for China. The amount of carbon avoided by imports increased by 104 MTC from 1987 to 2002, with an average annual increase of 4.7%, which was also at a stage of stable growth. From 2002 to 2005, its growth rate increased significantly, with an annual average of 17.8%. However, from 2005 to 2007, it decreased by 62 MTC, with an annual average of 9.51%. Since then, it has gone back to the increasing trend, with an increase of 98 MTC from 2007 to 2011, with the average annual growth rate being 7.8%.

In the meantime, the ratio of import-embodied carbon to the total carbon emissions of the national production sector increased from 22% in 1987 to the all-time high of 33% in 1995. Since then, it declined and remained at the stable level of between 25% and 28% from 1997 to 2005. After 2005, it has started a round of significant decrease, falling to about 18% in 2010. Thus, although the absolute impact of imports on China's carbon emissions has been increasing, the relative impact has decreased.

Comparing the carbon embodied in exports with that in imports, we can see that from 1987 to 2002 China's carbon embodied in exports was always lower than that in imports, and the net carbon embodied in trade was negative. This means that China's trade-embodied carbon has been in a state of certain "deficit" in recent years, or that China has in general reduced carbon emissions through trade. The "deficit" reached its peak of 99 MTC in 1995, close to 13% of the carbon emissions in the production sector. However, with a faster growth of carbon embodied in exports than that in imports, the "deficit" has gradually narrowed since 1995. In 2002, a balance was basically achieved between the carbon embodied in exports and that in imports. In 2005, the situation turned from "deficit" to "surplus". Moreover, the "surplus" value increased dramatically, reaching 200 MTC in 2007, exceeding 13% of the total carbon emissions of the national production sector. Since then, the net carbon embodied in trade has decreased, reaching at 88 MTC in 2009, and then rebounded to 174 MTC in 2011.

3.2. *Sectoral distribution and changes of carbon embodied in trade*

Table 6.3 displays the carbon embodied in exports of three industries from 1987 to 2011 (see Appendix B). Throughout the research period, the carbon embodied in the exports of the secondary industry has consistently far exceeded that of the primary industry and the tertiary industry. In 1987, the carbon embodied in exports of the secondary industry reached 57 MTC, accounting for 86% of the carbon embodied in exports of that year. In 2011, it reached at 504 MTC, and its share further increased to 92%. The carbon embodied in exports of the tertiary industry also showed an upward trend from 1987 to 2005, with the amount increasing from 6 MTC to 44 MTC, and remained thereafter within the range between 44 and 50 MTC (except for 2009). Its share, however, has changed little, standing at around 10%. Relatively speaking, the carbon embodied in exports of the primary industry (agriculture) is always very small, and its current share is only about 0.4%.

During the entire research period, the carbon embodied in exports of the secondary industry is mainly contributed by the manufacturing industry. From 1987 to 2011, the carbon embodied in exports of manufacture increased from 52 to 495 MTC. Its share in the carbon embodied in exports of the secondary industry rose from 91% in 1987 to 97% in 2002, and has remained at around 98% since then. Due to the impact of the international financial crisis, it experienced a period of decline from 2007 to 2009, and then gradually rebounded. Compared with that of the manufacturing industry, the embodied carbon in electricity and heat production and supply industry and exports of the construction industry can almost be ignored, and their total share in the carbon embodied in exports of the secondary industry has decreased from 9% in 1987 to about 1% in 2007.

Figure 6.2 reflects the extent of changes in carbon embodied in exports of various sectors. Within the manufacturing industry, the carbon embodied in exports of the manufacturing of communication equipment, computers, and other electronic equipment rose from less than 2 MTC in 1987 to 74 MTC in 2011, with an increase of 72 MTC, the highest increase in the 26 subsectors. The second place goes to the chemical industry, with the carbon embodied in its exports increasing from about 8 MTC in 1987

Table 6.3   Carbon embodied in exports of different sectors (1987–2011) (MTC)

Year	1987	1990	1992	1995	1997	2002	2005	2007	2008	2009	2010	2011
Primary industry	3	4	3	2	2	2	2	2	2	2	2	2
Total for the secondary industry	57	86	105	144	148	176	376	430	400	351	442	504
Total for manufacturing industries	52	80	101	136	142	170	369	424	393	345	434	495
Electric and thermal power	0	0	0	1	1	1	0	0	0	0	0	0
Construction	0	0	0	1	0	1	1	3	4	3	5	4
Total for the tertiary industry	6	8	11	10	19	28	44	46	49	36	48	44
Total	66	97	119	156	169	206	422	478	451	388	491	550

Note: The results in the table are calculated according to expression (6.4).

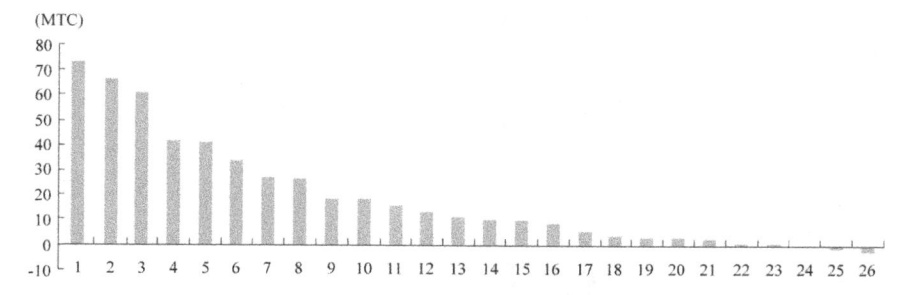

Fig. 6.2 Changes in export-embodied carbon of different sectors (1987–2011)

Notes: 1: Manufacturing of communication equipment, computers, and other electronic equipment
2: Chemical industry
3: Manufacturing of electrical appliances, machines, and equipment
4: Metal smelting, rolling, and processing
5: Manufacturing of general and special equipment
6: Textile industry
7: Metal products
8: Manufacturing of transportation equipment
9: Transportation, warehousing, and posts
10: Non-metal mineral products
11: Clothing, leather, down, and their products
12: Manufacturing of instruments, meters, and machines for culture and office articles
13: Wood processing and furniture manufacturing
14: Wholesale and retail trade/accommodation and catering
15: Non-material production sector
16: Papermaking, printing, and stationary manufacturing
17: Other manufacturing industries
18: Construction
19: Food production and tobacco processing
20: Metal mineral mining and dressing
21: Oil processing, coking, nuclear fuel, and gas processing
22: Electric and thermal power production and supply
23: Non-metal mineral mining and dressing
24: Coal mining and dressing
25: Agriculture
26: Oil and natural gas exploiting

to about 74 MTC in 2011. Ranking third is the manufacturing of electrical appliances, machines, and equipment, enjoying an increase of about 60 MTC in the carbon embodied in its exports. Moreover, in 2011, the export-embodied carbon of the above three sectors also ranked as the top three among the 26 subsectors, together accounting for about 38% of the total carbon embodied in exports. In the entire research period, other sectors also enjoy rapid growth in export-embodied carbon, such as metal smelting, rolling, and processing (42 MTC); manufacturing of general and special equipment (40 MTC); textile industry (33 MTC); metal products (26 MTC); and manufacturing of transportation equipment (26 MTC).

During the entire research period, the sector composition of carbon avoided by imports is very similar to that of carbon embodied in exports, which mainly comes from the secondary industry with the manufacturing industry as a major part (see Table 6.4). Among the manufacturing industries, chemical industries; metal smelting, rolling, and processing; manufacturing of general and special equipment; manufacturing of transportation equipment; manufacturing of electrical appliances, machines, and equipment; and manufacturing of communication equipment, computers, and other electronic equipment have consistently ranked among the top of the 26 subsectors in terms of carbon avoided by imports throughout the research period, and have seen an increase to varying degrees (see Appendix C). The situation is also similar to the sectoral composition of carbon embodied in exports.

However, the carbon avoided by imports of the manufacturing industry changes differently from the carbon embodied in exports of the same industry. As mentioned earlier, the latter continuously increased throughout the research period with the exception of a slight decline in the period 2007–2009. In contrast, after experiencing a continuous increase from 1987 to 2005, the former decreased significantly from 2005 to 2007, which directly resulted in a significant decrease in the carbon avoided by imports of the secondary industry and even the total carbon avoided by imports during this period. Moreover, from 1987 to 2002, the carbon avoided by imports of the manufacturing industry remained higher than the carbon embodied in exports of the same industry, but the relation was reversed since 2005. This may provide a preliminary explanation for the turn of China's trade-embodied carbon from a previous "deficit" to a "surplus" later.

3.3. *Major countries (regions) receiving carbon embodied in the trade of China*

In order to have a thorough understanding of China's trade-embodied carbon, this chapter also estimates, in line with the method introduced in Section 2, the impact of China's cargo trade with major trading partners

Table 6.4 Carbon avoided by imports of different sectors (1987–2011)

Year	1987	1990	1992	1995	1997	2002	2005	2007	2008	2009	2010	2011
Primary industry	1	1	1	3	2	3	5	5	6	6	7	8
Total for the secondary industry	103	102	139	244	216	197	310	254	263	275	312	342
Total for mining and quarrying	1	2	3	7	9	14	16	35	32	36	41	45
Total for manufacturing industries	101	99	136	237	206	182	292	217	229	237	269	296
Electric and thermal power	0	0	0	0	0	0	0	0	0	0	0	0
Construction	0	0	0	1	1	1	1	1	2	2	2	1
Total for the tertiary industry	0	1	9	8	5	8	25	19	19	18	21	26
Total	104	103	149	256	222	208	340	278	288	300	340	376

Note: The results in the table are calculated according to expression (6.5).

(regions) on carbon emissions from 2002 to 2007,[6] so as to reveal the major countries (regions) receiving China's trade-embodied carbon. This chapter selects the top ten countries (regions) with respect to imports and exports of China in recent years mainly on the basis of "the total imports and exports between China and other countries (regions)" in *China Statistical Yearbook* over the years. Generally speaking, from 2002 to 2007, the major exporting countries (regions) and importing countries (regions) have overlapped to a great degree, most of which are located in the Asia-Pacific region or are adjacent to China (see Table 6.5). In the past few years, China's exports to the top 10 countries (regions) of export, respectively, accounted for 74%, 70%, and 64% of the total exports, showing a decreasing trend year by year. China's imports from the top

Table 6.5 Carbon embodied in cargo trade between China and its major trading partners (regions) (2002–2007) (MTC)

Places of export	Carbon emissions embodied in exports to major countries/ regions of export (MTC)		
	2002	2005	2007
The US	29.29 (14.22%)	60.58 (14.36%)	84.39 (17.67%)
Hong Kong (China)	26.61 (12.92%)	42.16 (9.99%)	47.04 (9.85%)
Japan	23.26 (11.29%)	34.89 (8.27%)	35.98 (7.53%)
South Korea	8.13 (3.95%)	17.10 (4.05%)	23.08 (4.83%)
Germany	4.99 (2.42%)	11.23 (2.66%)	15.72 (3.29%)
The Netherlands	3.84 (1.86%)	9.10 (2.16%)	11.97 (2.51%)
The UK	3.94 (1.91%)	7.66 (1.82%)	12.69 (2.66%)
Singapore	3.20 (1.55%)	6.15 (1.46%)	8.85 (1.85%)
Taiwan (China)	3.45 (1.68%)	7.64 (1.81%)	8.53 (1.79%)
Malaysia	1.97 (0.96%)	3.98 (0.94%)	5.47 (1.14%)
Russia	1.37 (0.66%)	4.70 (1.11%)	10.59 (2.22%)
India	1.69 (0.82%)	4.46 (1.06%)	9.42 (1.97%)
Total	111.74 (54.24%)	209.65 (49.69%)	273.73 (57.31%)

(Continued)

---

[6] Owing to a lack of data on service trade between China and different countries, the estimation by country and region for the carbon embodied in service trade has not been done.

Table 6.5 *(Continued)*

Places of import	Carbon emissions avoided by imports from major countries/regions of import (MTC)		
	2002	**2005**	**2007**
Japan	32.46 (15.63%)	45.56 (13.42%)	41.08 (14.77%)
Taiwan (China)	24.29 (11.70%)	33.63 (9.90%)	26.72 (9.61%)
South Korea	18.72 (9.01%)	35.37 (10.42)	26.77 (9.63%)
The US	15.08 (7.26%)	21.47 (6.32%)	20.36 (7.32%)
Germany	8.94 (4.30%)	12.87 (3.79%)	15.51 (5.58%)
Malaysia	4.56 (2.19%)	6.15 (1.81%)	5.83 (2.10%)
Russia	6.70 (3.22%)	8.86 (2.61%)	5.13 (1.85%)
Australia	4.73 (2.28%)	9.08 (2.67%)	7.72 (2.78%)
Hong Kong (China)	5.64 (2.71%)	5.29 (1.56%)	5.04 (1.81%)
Singapore	4.37 (2.10%)	6.09 (1.79%)	4.13 (1.49%)
Thailand	3.48 (1.67%)	5.20 (1.53%)	5.26 (1.89%)
Philippines	1.27 (0.61%)	3.43 (1.01%)	5.21 (1.87%)
Total	130.24 (62.68%)	193.00 (56.83%)	168.76 (60.70%)

Notes: The results in the table are calculated according to expressions (6.4) and (6.5). The figures in brackets represent the share of export-embodied carbon (carbon avoided by imports) in China's bilateral cargo trade with major partners in the total export-embodied carbon (carbon avoided by imports) of the year. It accounts for a higher share in the total carbon embodied in cargo exports (carbon avoided by imports), i.e., the total carbon embodied in exports (carbon avoided by imports) of the primary industry and the secondary industry. For example, from 2002 to 2005, China's carbon emissions embodied in cargo exports to major countries (regions) of export accounted for 62.91%, 55.44%, and 63.44% of the total carbon embodied in cargo exports. The carbon avoided by cargo imports from major countries (regions) of import accounted for 65.14%, 61.31%, and 65.08% of the total carbon avoided by cargo imports.

10 countries (regions) of import, respectively, accounted for 70%, 63%, and 60% of the total imports, again decreasing year by year. This means that the destination countries (regions) for China's exports and countries (regions) of import are being scattered. This is the result of China's trade diversification strategy and is conducive to reducing trade risks.

Table 6.5 shows the carbon embodied in cargo trade between China and its major trading partners (regions) from 2002 to 2007. During this period, the US has remained the biggest recipient of carbon embodied in Chinese exports, whose average annual growth rate reached 24%, and its share of total carbon embodied in China's exports rose from 14.22% to 17.67%. Other important recipients include Hong Kong (China), Japan, South Korea, Germany, the Netherlands, and the UK. 2007 saw the fastest growth of carbon embodied in Chinese exports to Russia and India; the amount that they imported exceeded Singapore, Taiwan (China), and Malaysia. From 2002 to 2007, the carbon embodied in the exports for China to the above 11 major trading partners (regions) increase from 111.74 to 273.73 MTC, while their combined share of carbon embodied in China's exports increased from 54.24% to 57.31%.

In addition, from 2002 to 2007, the carbon avoided by cargo imports from 11 major countries (regions) of import increased from 130.24 to 168.76 MTC, but its share in the total carbon avoided by imports slightly decreased from 62.68% to 60.70%. Among these countries (regions), Japan has consistently been the biggest country of origin for China's cargo imports, and the corresponding carbon avoided by the trade has also been the highest throughout the years, with a stable share of about 14% in the total carbon avoided by imports of China. The carbon avoided by cargo imports from Taiwan, South Korea, the US, and Germany also accounted for a significant share in the total carbon avoided by imports, all being above 5.5% in 2007. Cargo imports from the remaining major trading partners (regions) made a relatively small contribution to the total carbon avoided by imports. The share of carbon avoided by cargo imports from Malaysia, Russia, Hong Kong (China), and Singapore has decreased, while that for Australia, Thailand, and the Philippines has increased.

3.4. *Structural decomposition of changes in carbon embodied in trade*

In order to further understand the changes of carbon embodied in China's trade, this chapter decomposes the changes of embodied carbon in China's exports and carbon avoided by imports in line with expressions (6.7) and (6.8), respectively. It should be noted that the influence of a specific factor obtained by structural decomposition on trade-embodied carbon should be understood under the condition that other factors remain unchanged. In addition, for the sake of reliability, the structural decomposition covers only the years for which there were input–output values in table in the period 1987–2010.

3.4.1. *Structural decomposition of changes of carbon embodied in exports*

Table 6.6 shows the influence of various factors on carbon embodied in exports. During the entire research period and at different stages, the sharp increase of embodied carbon in exports was mainly caused by the rapid growth of total exports (see Table 6.2). At the price of 2002, the total export volume of China was 425.5 billion yuan in 1987, and reached 10,602.8 billion yuan in 2010, increasing by 24 times. The growth of the total export volume increased the embodied carbon in exports by 760.56 MTC during this period, equivalent to 11 times that in 1987.

The rapid growth of total exports follows as an inevitable result of China's long-term export-oriented trade and economic development

Table 6.6   Structural decomposition of changes of embodied carbon in exports (MTC)

| | **Influencing factors** | | | | | | |
Period (years)	Total exports	Structure of exports	Input structure	Energy intensity	Energy structure	Carbon emission coefficient	Total
1987–1990	25.71	8.56	8.77	−13.22	0.65	0.25	30.72
1990–1992	29.77	3.18	3.09	−14.56	−0.03	0.10	21.54
1992–1995	41.89	3.25	−2.75	−3.93	−0.57	−0.12	37.78
1995–1997	50.71	−3.59	−6.19	−28.04	0.00	−0.17	12.71
1997–2002	155.29	−8.88	−13.08	−94.97	−1.74	0.31	36.92
2002–2005	230.16	3.80	1.36	−21.00	1.43	0.25	216.01
2005–2007	136.43	22.88	−2.75	−101.50	0.12	0.38	55.57
2007–2010	90.58	−38.01	−5.92	−22.93	−5.02	−5.15	13.55
1987–2010	760.56	−8.81	−17.46	−300.16	−5.16	−4.14	424.82

Notes: The decomposition results by stages are estimated in accordance with expression (6.7). The decomposition results of the entire research period are accumulated from the results for different stages. They can certainly be obtained using (6.7), but the results will be different, and the method is not adopted here.

strategy. At the beginning of the Reform and Opening Up, China's economic construction was facing the difficult situation of shortage of capital and backward technology, and its domestic consumption capacity was also limited. In order to deal with these difficulties, China has fully implemented a strategy of making use of the international and domestic markets, and has issued a series of policies and measures to encourage foreign exchange earnings through export. Against the background of globalization, China actively participates in the international division of labor mainly by relying on its large number of cheap labor and natural resources, and has gradually earned the title of "world factory". This development strategy of export-oriented economy and export trade of labor-intensive products is similar to that of Japan and the "Four Asian Tigers"[7] during their economic boom.

Especially after acceding to the World Trade Organization (at the end of 2001), the export environment of China has greatly improved and its export potential has rapidly been released. As a result, China's exports accelerated in the early days of its accession (2002–2005), which lies at the root for the large growth margin and the high growth rate of embodied carbon in China's exports during this period. But along with the rapid release of most export potentials, further growth in exports became difficult. From 2005 to 2007, the growth rate of export somewhat fell, and accordingly that of export-embodied carbon also decreased considerably. It can thus be seen that the impact of China's accession to the WTO on carbon embodied in exports seems also to have a marginal effect. In addition, due to the international financial crisis, the export growth further slowed down from 2007 to 2010, and the impact of the total export volume on the carbon embodied in exports also decreased accordingly.

Changes in the structure of export products have reduced the embodied carbon in the entire research period. From 1987 to 2010, the shares of exports of 13 sectors increased, with the most prominent increase going to the manufacturing of communication equipment, computers, and other electronic equipment, and the manufacturing of electrical appliances, machines, and equipment. The shares of some energy-intensive sectors (such as chemical industry, non-metal mineral products, and metal

---

[7] They are South Korea, Singapore, Hong Kong (China), and Taiwan (China).

smelting, rolling, and processing) have also increased in general. The shares of the remaining 13 sectors decreased to varying degrees, among which the shares of traditional labor-intensive products (mainly including agricultural products, food manufacturing and tobacco, clothing, leather, and down and their products) and resource-intensive products (all kinds of mineral products, especially oil and natural gas, and petroleum processing, coking, nuclear fuel, and gas processing products) decreased significantly (see Fig. 6.3). In short, the above changes in the export structure have reduced China's carbon embodied in exports by about 9 MTC. In terms of stages, only in the three periods of 1995–1997, 1997–2002 and 2007–2010 were changes in the export structure conducive to reducing the carbon embodied in exports. Among them, the period from 2007 to 2010 has seen the most obvious effect of structural change on inhibiting the export-embodied carbon, which might be related to China's trade policy of strictly controlling the export of high energy-consuming, high environment-polluting, and resource-intensive products.

Changes in the input structure have also contributed to the reduction of the carbon embodied in exports during the entire research period. The share of agricultural products in intermediate inputs dropped most significantly, and the shares of petroleum processing, coking, nuclear fuel and gas processing, and oil and natural gas mining decreased significantly, while the shares of various mechanical products and chemical products also saw an increase. Such changes have reflected the transformation of the Chinese economy from agriculture to industry, and ultimately reduced the carbon embodied in exports by 17 MTC. In terms of stages, in 1987–1990, 1990–1992, and 2002–2005, changes in input structure resulted in an increase in carbon embodied in exports.

The significant decrease in the energy intensity of the production sector (see Fig. 6.4) is another important factor in inhibiting the increase in carbon embodied in exports, leading to a drop of 300 MTC during the entire research period, equivalent to 39% of the impact of the growth in export scale. This means that China's long-term efforts to improve energy efficiency have already made contributions to reducing carbon emissions. In terms of stages, changes in energy intensity in the production sector are not always effective at offsetting the impact of export growth. For example, its impact during 1992–1995 and 2002–2005 was less than 1/10 that

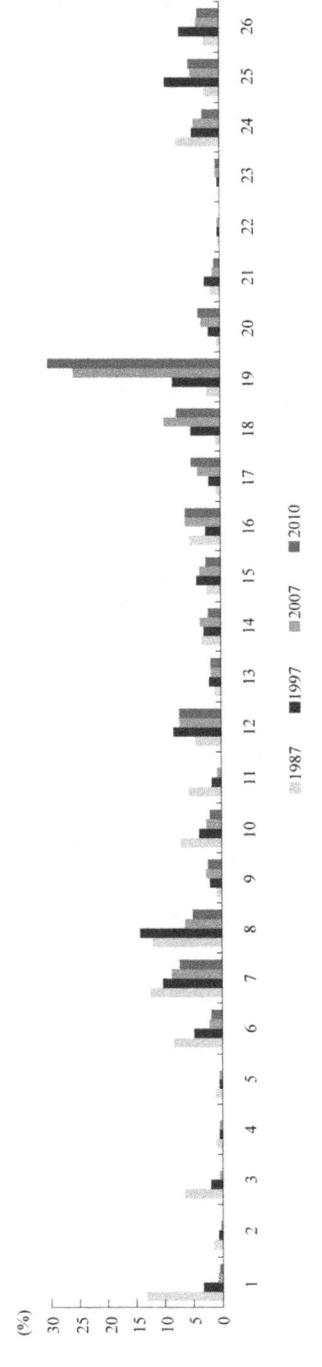

Fig. 6.3   Shares of various export products for China (1987–2010) (%)

Notes: 1. Agriculture 2. Coal mining and dressing 3. Oil and natural gas mining 4. Metal mineral mining and dressing 5. Non-metal mineral mining and dressing 6. Food production and tobacco processing 7. Textile industry 8. Clothing, leather, down and their products 9. Wood processing and furniture manufacturing 10. Papermaking, printing, and stationary manufacturing 11. Oil processing, coking, nuclear fuel and gas processing 12. Chemical industry 13. Non-metal mineral products 14. Metal smelting, rolling, and processing 15. Metal products 16. Manufacturing of general and special equipment 17. Manufacturing of transportation equipment 18. Manufacturing of electrical appliances, machines, and equipment 19. Manufacturing of communication equipment, computers, and other electronic equipment 20. Manufacturing of instruments, meters, and machines for culture and office articles 21. Other industries 22. Electric and thermal power production and supply 23. Construction 24. Transportation, warehousing, and posts 25. Wholesale and retail trade/accommodation and catering 26. Non-material production sector

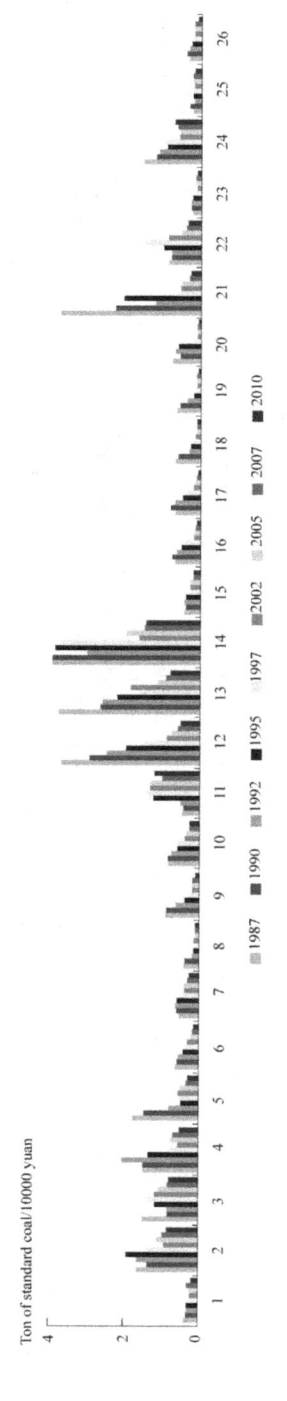

Fig. 6.4 Energy intensity for different industries (1987–2010)

Notes: 1. Agriculture 2. Coal mining and dressing 3. Oil and natural gas mining 4. Metal mineral mining and dressing 5. Non-metal mineral mining and dressing 6. Food production and tobacco processing 7. Textile industry 8. Clothing, leather, down and their products 9. Wood processing and furniture manufacturing 10. Papermaking, printing, and stationary manufacturing 11. Oil processing, coking, nuclear fuel, and gas processing 12. Chemical industry 13. Non-metal mineral products 14. Metal smelting, rolling, and processing 15. Metal products 16. Manufacturing of general and special equipment 17. Manufacturing of transportation equipment 18. Manufacturing of electrical appliances, machines, and equipment 19. Manufacturing of communication equipment, computers, and other electronic equipment 20. Manufacturing of instruments, meters, and machines for culture and office articles 21. Other industries 22. Electric and thermal power production and supply 23. Construction 24. Transportation, warehousing, and posts 25. Wholesale and retail trade/accommodation and catering 26. Non-material production sector of the latter. It is worth noting that it reduced the carbon embodied in exports by 102 MTC from 2005 to 2007, equivalent to 74% of the impact of export growth, far exceeding other stages in both absolute and relative terms. However, the decline in energy intensity slowed down in 2007–2010, and its inhibiting effect on the carbon embodied in exports also declined significantly. This shows that the energy conservation and emission reduction policy vigorously implemented by China since 2006 has played a very active role in the initial stage, but its effect is continuously weakening.

Changes in the energy structure of the production sector in general are also conducive to reducing the carbon embodied in exports, but the impact is small, with a reduction of only 5 MTC. During the entire research period, the changes in the terminal energy consumption structure of the production sector are mainly reflected in the substitution of electricity for raw coal (see Fig. 6.5). The share of raw coal dropped from 40.12% in 1987 to 15.82% in 2007, with an absolute drop of 24.30%. The share of electricity increased correspondingly from 22.53% to 39.04%. In addition, there was also a significant increase for the share of coke and diesel oil, while the share of crude oil and fuel oil has significantly decreased. However, the carbon emission coefficients of these energy sources (see IPCC, 1996) are relatively close to each other, so the impact of changes in energy structure on the carbon embodied in exports is relatively limited.

The change of carbon emission coefficient resulted in the decrease of 4 MTC in export-embodied carbon during the entire research period. The change of carbon emission coefficient was mainly brought about by the change of energy structure for power and heat generation, which led to the change of the carbon emission coefficient of electric power, and thermal energy.[8] From 1987 to 2007, raw coal consistently accounted for a major part of the energy consumed by power and heat generation, and its share continued to rise, while the share of fuel oil with low carbon emission coefficient and that of hydropower, wind power, and nuclear power, which do not produce carbon emission, continued to fall. Such changes in energy structure have resulted in an increase in carbon emission coefficients for electric and thermal power (see Table 6.7), which in

---

[8] We assume that the carbon emission coefficient of other energy sources remains constant.

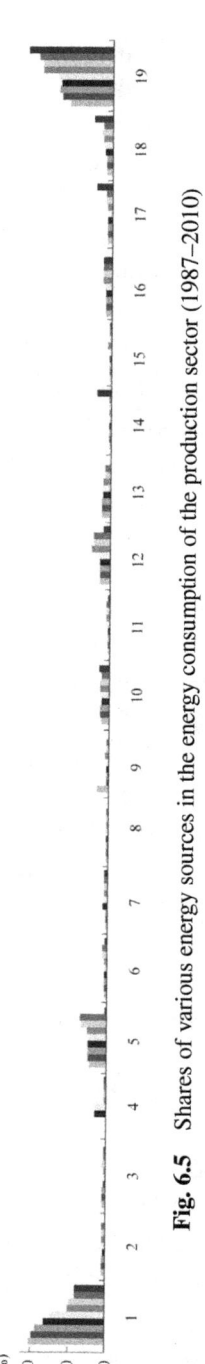

Fig. 6.5 Shares of various energy sources in the energy consumption of the production sector (1987–2010)

Notes: 1. Raw coal 2. Cleaned coal 3. Other washed coal 4. Briquette coal 5. Coke 6. Coke oven gas 7. Other gases 8. Other coking products 9. Crude oil 10. Gasoline 11. Kerosene 12. Diesel oil 13. Fuel oil 14. Liquefied petroleum gas 15. Refinery off-gas 16. Other oil products 17. Natural gas 18. Thermal power 19. Electric power

Table 6.7 Carbon emission coefficient for power and heat generation (%)

Year	1987	1990	1992	1995	1997	2002	2005	2007	2010
Heat generation	0.684	0.705	0.717	0.719	0.719	0.714	0.714	0.722	0.676
Power generation	0.720	0.729	0.729	0.727	0.724	0.735	0.730	0.730	0.718

turn led to an increase in the carbon embodied in exports. During 2007–2010, there was a significant decrease in the carbon emission coefficient of power and heat generation and in the embodied carbon in exports. Since the influence of the carbon emission coefficient at the last stage was much greater than that in the previous stages, its overall influence seems helpful for reduction of the embodied carbon in exports during the entire research period.

3.4.2. *Structural decomposition of the changes of carbon avoided by imports*

The results of structural decomposition of the changes of carbon avoided by imports (see Table 6.8) are similar to those for carbon embodied in exports. The growth of total imports (see Table 6.2) is also the most important factor affecting the change of carbon embodied in imports, while the change of energy intensity is the main factor inhibiting its increase. The changes in input structure, energy structure, and carbon emission coefficient have a similar effect on carbon avoided by imports to that on carbon embodied in exports. Changes in the structure of imports, however, have an opposite effect to that of changes in the structure of exports. Therefore, the following analysis is focused on the impact of the total import volume and the structure of imports on carbon avoided by imports.

The continuous increase in the total import volume is because since the Reform and Opening Up, China has not only attached importance to both international and domestic markets, but also insisted on developing its economy by making use of the international and domestic resources. As a result, with the development of China's economy, China's imports and the corresponding carbon avoided by imports have increased considerably. In

Table 6.8   Structural decomposition of carbon avoided by imports (MTC)

Period (years)	Total exports	Structure of imports	Input structure	Energy intensity	Energy structure	Carbon emission coefficient	Total
1987–1990	2.55	−4.07	12.83	−12.90	0.63	0.31	−0.65
1990–1992	74.43	−0.87	−5.75	−22.60	0.06	0.12	45.38
1992–1995	118.99	−1.15	−8.91	−0.49	−1.46	−0.18	106.79
1995–1997	7.27	4.22	−9.09	−36.11	0.31	−0.24	−33.64
1997–2002	129.52	−6.33	−15.01	−120.93	−1.85	0.33	−14.27
2002–2005	162.65	−29.60	9.20	−12.04	1.41	0.22	131.84
2005–2007	15.89	−5.43	−1.92	−70.13	−0.16	0.25	−61.50
2007–2010	88.89	1.31	−5.87	−15.41	−3.58	−3.16	62.18
1987–2010	600.20	−41.94	−24.53	−290.62	−4.64	−2.35	236.13

Notes: The decomposition results by stages are estimated according to expression (6.8). The decomposition results of the whole research period are accumulated from the results of different stages. They can certainly be obtained using (6.8), but the results will be different, and the method is not adopted here.

the meantime, processing trade with the characteristics of "enormous imports and enormous exports" has become one of China's main trade modes. Under this trade mode, the rapid growth of exports will lead to a corresponding growth of imports. At the price of 2002, China's total import volume was 417.4 billion yuan in 1987, reaching 6473.4 billion yuan in 2010, which is an increase of about 14 times. The increase resulted in an increase of 600 MTC in carbon avoided by imports over the entire research period, which was equivalent to 6 times that of 1987.

In contrast with the total export volume, the growth of the total import volume is smaller, and its impact on the carbon avoided by imports is also lower than that of the total export volume on the carbon embodied in exports. Especially in the three periods of 1987–1990, 1995–1997, and 2005–2007, the growth of the total import volume was very small, 2.5%, 3.1%, and 5.3%, respectively, and consequently its influence on the carbon avoided by imports was limited. As a result, under the combined influence of other factors, especially changes in energy intensity, the amount of carbon avoided by imports decreased in these periods. From

1997 to 2002, although the growth of total imports and its influence on the carbon avoided by imports were relatively significant, most other factors, especially the changes in energy intensity, brought about a decrease in the carbon avoided by imports more than the increase brought about by the growth of total imports, thus the carbon avoided by imports also decreased in this period.

On the whole, the changes in the structure of imports have reduced the carbon avoided by imports by 42 MTC, which is in line with the influence of the structure of exports on the carbon embodied in exports. During the entire research period, the increase in the share of communication equipment, computers, and other electronic equipment in imports was the most prominent (see Fig. 6.6), while their share in exports also increased the most. This provides an adequate case for the characteristic, "enormous imports and enormous exports", of processing trade, and also shows that China still relies heavily on such technology-intensive imports. In addition, the service of the non-material production sector, manufacturing of instruments, meters, and machines for culture and office articles, and oil and natural gas accounted for a larger share in imports, while the share of other mechanical equipment such as general and special equipment decreased the most in imports. The situation seems to indicate that the above-mentioned communication equipment, computers, and other electronic equipment with their high technology have started to take the place of those low-tech mechanical products. Products that have experienced a notable decrease in their share in imports also include clothing, leather, down and down products; metal smelting, rolling, and processing industries; and transportation equipment. On the whole, the changes in the structure of the above-mentioned imports led to a decrease in the carbon avoided by imports during the entire research period. But in the two periods of 1995–1997 and 2007–2010, they brought about an increase.

3.5. *Comparison with previous studies*

There are some important differences in data processing between this chapter and similar studies in the past: (1) This chapter uses (import) non-competitive input–output tables, while previous studies employed (import) competitive input–output tables except for Weber *et al.* (2008), Yao *et al.*

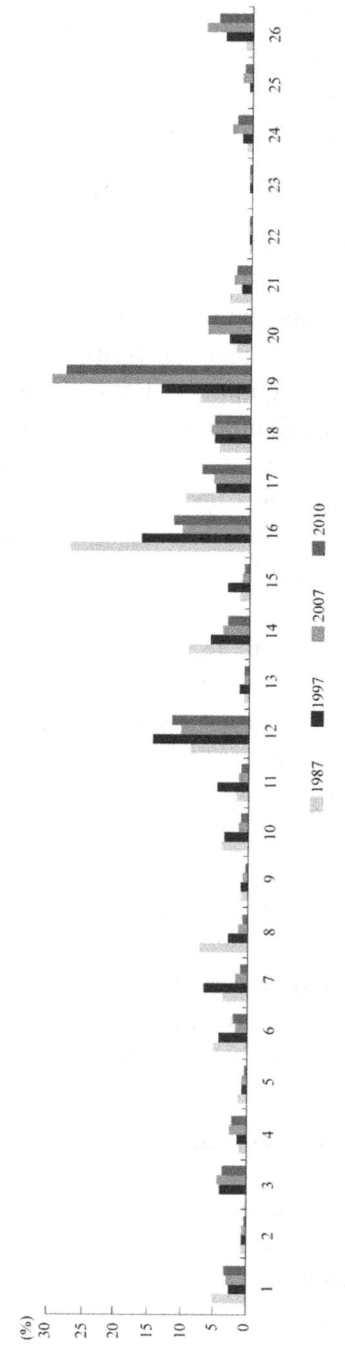

Fig. 6.6 Shares of various import products for China (1987–2010) (%)

Notes: 1. Agriculture 2. Coal mining and dressing 3. Oil and natural gas mining 4. Metal mineral mining and dressing 5. Non-metal mineral mining and dressing 6. Food production and tobacco processing 7. Textile industry 8. Clothing, leather, down and their products 9. Wood processing and furniture manufacturing 10. Papermaking, printing, and stationary manufacturing 11. Oil processing, coking, nuclear fuel, and gas processing 12. Chemical industry 13. Non-metal mineral products 14. Metal smelting, rolling, and processing 15. Metal products 16. Manufacturing of general and special equipment 17. Manufacturing of transportation equipment 18. Manufacturing of electrical appliances, machines, and equipment 19. Manufacturing of communication equipment, computers, and other electronic equipment 20. Manufacturing of instruments, meters, and machines for culture and office articles 21. Other industries 22. Electric and thermal power production and supply 23. Construction 24. Transportation, warehousing, and posts 25. Wholesale and retail trade/accommodation and catering 26. Non-material production sector

(2008), and Lin & Sun (2010), that is, taking into consideration imports with intermediate inputs deducted. (2) This chapter uses various price indices to adjust the input–output tables over the years to the input–output table on the basis of the price of 2002, while other studies are based on the input–output tables of the current price except for Qi *et al.* (2008), which makes price adjustments to the carbon consumption coefficient. (3) In addition, this chapter is also different in the detailed differentiation of sectors, in its methods of trade data processing, in the estimation of carbon emission data, and so on. The differences in data processing lead to different estimations. Table 6.9 lists the methods and results of the existing literature.

Table 6.9 Comparison with previous studies

	Method	Results	
Studies	Input–output table (price)	Carbon embodied in exports (MTCO$_2$)	Carbon embodied in imports (MTCO$_2$)
Ahmed & Wyckoff (2003)	Competitive (current price)	463 (1997[a]); 533 (1997[b])	102 (1997[a]); 486 (1997[b])
Weber *et al.* (2008)	Non-competitive (the price of 1990 and current price)	230 (1987); 360 (1990); 420 (1992); 570 (1995); 580 (1997); 760 (2002); 1670 (2005)	390 (1987); 420 (1990); 569 (1992); 710 (1995); 700 (1997); 1170 (2002); 2200 (2005)
Yao *et al.* (2008)	Non-competitive (current price)	1460 (2005)	796 (2005)
Pan *et al.* (2008)	Competitive (current price)	880 (2002)	257 (2002)
Yan & Yang (2010)	Competitive (current price)	314 (1997); 1725 (2007)	137 (1997); 587 (2007)
Lin & Sun (2010)	Non-competitive (current price)	3357 (2005)	2333 (2005)
The present chapter	Non-competitive (the price of 2002)	243 (1987); 356 (1990); 435 (1992); 573 (1995); 620 (1997); 755 (2002); 1547 (2005); 1751 (2007)	382 (1987); 379 (1990); 546 (1992); 937 (1995); 814 (1997); 762 (2002); 1245 (2005); 1020 (2007)

Notes: The number in brackets refers to the year. The results of this chapter are converted from the results in Table 6.2. On the basis of the atomic weight of carbon (12) and oxygen (16), the coefficient of CO$_2$ based on carbon equivalent is 44/12.

In the studies based on the (import) competitive input–output tables, Ahmed & Wyckoff (2003) apply two methods to estimate China's carbon embodied in trade in 1997: (1) It is estimated on the basis of the emission coefficient of the place of the import; (2) It is estimated on the assumption that imports are produced with Chinese technology. Estimates of both methods are significantly lower than the results reached in this chapter based on the (import) non-competitive input–output tables. Pan *et al.* (2008) put forward a higher estimate than this chapter. But their adjusted estimate on the basis of the energy intensity of the place of import is much lower than this chapter. In addition, the upper limits estimated by Qi *et al.* (2008) for the ratio of China's net trade-embodied carbon to China's total carbon emissions in 1997, 2002, and 2005 (assuming that imported products are produced with Japanese technology) were 12.11%, 14.16%, and 24.38%, respectively, and the lower limits (assuming that imported products are produced with Chinese technology) were 2.54%, 1.02%, and 7%, respectively. The results reached in this chapter are –6.58%, –0.21% and 6.56%, respectively, which are in sharp contrast with previous studies. The estimates of Yan & Yang (2010) for export-embodied carbon in 1997 and 2007 are significantly lower than those obtained in this chapter, and the estimates for import-embodied carbon (relative difference) are significantly lower than the values obtained here in this chapter.

The estimation of Weber *et al.* (2008), Yao *et al.* (2008) and Lin & Sun (2010) is based on non-competitive (import) input–output tables. The input–output tables of 1987, 1990, and 1995 employed by Weber *et al.* (2008) are calculated at the price of 1990, while the rest are calculated at current price. Yao *et al.* (2008) and Lin & Sun (2010) use current-price input–output tables. This chapter is based on the price of 2002. The estimates of Weber *et al.* (2008) for China's export-embodied carbon in 1987, 1995, and 1997 were slightly lower than those calculated in this chapter, but those for 1990, 1992, 2002, and 2005 are slightly higher. On the whole, their estimates for the export-embodied carbon are close to those of this chapter, while their estimates for the carbon avoided by imports in 1995 and 1997 are significantly lower than those calculated in this chapter, but those for 1987, 1990, 1992, 2002, and 2005 are higher. The estimates of Yao *et al.* (2008) for both the carbon embodied in exports and carbon avoided by imports in 2005 were significantly lower than the values obtained in this chapter, and even much lower than those obtained by Weber *et al.* (2008). Lin & Sun (2010) put forward an estimate for the carbon embodied in exports and carbon avoided by imports of China in 2005 that was almost twice as much as the values obtained this chapter, and far exceeding those calculated by Weber *et al.* (2008) and Yao *et al.* (2008).

4. Conclusion and Discussions

Based on the (import) non-competitive input–output model, this chapter estimates China's trade-embodied carbon from 1987 to 2007, analyzes its sectoral distribution and country (region) flow, and examines by way of structural decomposition six factors influencing it, that is, the scale of import and export, the structure of import and export, input structure, sectoral energy intensity, energy structure, and carbon emission coefficient (energy structure for electricity and heat generation). Because of the methods employed here, the results obtained concerning the carbon embodied in the trade of China are significantly different from previous studies. Though the estimation here is preliminary, the authors believe that the results objectively reflect the real situation.

4.1. *Embodied carbon in trade has a great influence on China's carbon emissions*

A practical issue closely related to carbon embodied in trade is the global distribution of rights to carbon emissions. The results here show that in recent years, China's export-embodied carbon has increased rapidly and in huge amounts, accounting for about one-third of the total carbon emissions in the production sector of the country from 2005 to 2007. Though the ratio has declined since then, it still reached one-fourth in 2011. This shows that exports are an important factor leading to an increase in China's carbon emissions, and that a considerable portion of carbon emissions are consumed by other countries through trade. Thus, in the global distribution of rights to carbon emissions, trade is indeed a factor concerning fairness that calls for attention, at least for China.

With the relationship between trade and the fair distribution of carbon emission rights being considered, it is now a controversial issue as to how to calculate a country's carbon emissions. Currently, there are two opposing principles for carbon emission accounting: the production accounting principle and the consumption accounting principle. The principle of production accounting refers to the accounting of a country's total CO_2 emissions on the basis of the actual CO_2 emissions generated in the production process. The principle of consumption accounting refers to the accounting of CO_2 emissions based on the final consumption (including importation) of various products or services (Munksgaard & Pedersen, 2001).

Obviously, the two principles will produce different results concerning carbon emission, and the difference lies in net trade-embodied carbon. As far as China is concerned, it was basically negative before acceding to the WTO, which shows that China's carbon emissions under the consumption accounting principle are slightly higher than those under the production accounting principle. Since 2005, it has turned positive and grown rapidly, which means that China's carbon emissions under the consumption accounting principle have become lower than those under the production accounting principle in recent years, and the gap between the two has rapidly widened and currently is seen as being quite considerable.

Moreover, this chapter assumes that imported products are produced with Chinese technology, which is likely to overestimate their carbon emissions. That is to say, the net trade-embodied carbon of China estimated here may be lower than the actual case, because most of China's imports come from developed countries (regions), and the energy consumption and carbon emissions for the production of these imports are far less in these countries (regions) than China. For example, Japan, the biggest supplier of imports for China, has the highest energy efficiency in the world. Therefore, it is worthwhile to use the multi-country input–output model to estimate China's carbon embodied in imports.

4.2. The composition of carbon embodied in trade reflects the trade growth pattern and the trade pattern of China

The results here show that the rapid increase of embodied carbon in China's trade is closely related to the export-oriented economic growth pattern gradually formed since the Reform and Opening Up. Under this model, the growth rate of exports far exceeds domestic demand such as consumption and fixed capital formation. The embodied carbon in exports thus generated and its share in the total carbon emissions in the production sector also increase rapidly. In addition, with the deepening of opening up to the outside world, China has further integrated into the global division of labor. Cheap and abundant labor and natural resources provide the main advantages for China to participate in the international division of labor, which gradually turns the processing trade into the main trade mode of China. The trade mode has increased China's demand for imports along with the growth in exports, and has caused a substantial increase in the carbon avoided by imports.

In the meantime, the trade mode also makes labor-intensive and resource-intensive manufacturing products become China's advantageous export products. As a result, manufacturing products account for an overwhelming part of China's exports, and their shares are continuously increasing. The share of carbon embodied in the manufacturing industry far exceeds that of other products and services taken together, and continues to increase year by year. Similarly, with manufacturing products dominating the export structure, China shows a greater demand for manufacturing imports than other imports and services. As a result, the carbon avoided by manufacturing imports also dominates the total carbon avoided by imports in China.

In terms of the countries (regions) receiving China's carbon embodied in trade from 2002 to 2007, China's cargo trade with its major trading partners has had a significant impact on the carbon embodied in exports and the carbon avoided by imports. Except Germany, the Netherlands, and the UK, the major trading partners of China are all in the Asia-Pacific region or adjacent to China (Russia). This shows to a certain extent that apart from economic scale and comparative advantages, geographic closeness is also an important factor in determining whether a country can become a major trading partner of China. The geographical relationship is not only an important factor influencing China's trade pattern but also an important factor that determines the embodied carbon flow in China's trade.

Certainly, the trade growth pattern and the trade pattern of China are closely related to international industry transfer and the outsourcing strategy of multinational corporations. For example, since the 1960s and

1970s, Japan has vigorously promoted the "flying-geese model" of Asian development, shifting its labor-intensive industries to the "Four Asian Tigers". Later on, with the Reform and Opening Up of China, these labor-intensive industries were further transferred to China's coastal areas which enjoy labor advantages. China imported key components from these countries (regions) for processing and assembly, and then exported them mainly to these countries (regions) and other developed countries (regions) such as the US. It is precisely this international division of labor that brings about the above-mentioned sectoral distribution and countries (regions) receiving China's trade-embodied carbon.

4.3. *Controlling carbon embodied in trade and even total carbon emissions must rely on the transformation of the pattern of trade and economic growth*

The results of structural decomposition in this chapter show that the rapid growth of China's carbon embodied in trade is mainly caused by the rapid growth of the trade scale of China, but it cannot be taken to mean that China should blindly control the growth of export to reduce carbon embodied in exports. Exports have made great contributions to the economic development of China and its integration into the world economic system. For the present and the future, exports are still an important driving force for China's economic growth and an important way to expand its international political and economic influence. The current development strategy of expanding domestic demand is not to suppress exports, but to promote the coordination of consumption, investment, and exports to drive economic growth.

In addition, balancing export-embodied carbon or slowing down the country's carbon emissions by expanding the import scale also faces great challenges: First, it is difficult for China to find another country with a large amount of cheap and high-quality labor force, a complete industrial system, and geographical advantages to provide manufactured goods demanded by its economic development; second, oil and other mineral resources are limited, and there is fierce competition for these resources in the international market; and third, once the consumption principle for carbon emission accounting mentioned above is established, it will have a negative impact on China.

Thus, as far as trade is concerned, the desirable way to control China's carbon embodied in exports should be to transform the growth pattern of exports and gradually optimize the structure of export products, thereby controlling the increase in export-embodied carbon. During the entire research period, the impact of export structural change is still weak, despite the reduction caused by such change, for China currently occupies the lower processing end of the chain of the international division of labor. Moreover, in terms of periods, only in the three periods of 1995–1997, 1997–2002, and 2007–2010 were changes in the export structure conducive to reducing the carbon embodied in exports. It is, however, worth noting that changes in the export structure from 2007 to 2010 displayed a prominent effect on inhibiting export-embodied carbon, which may be related to China's trade policy of strictly controlling the export of high energy-consuming, high environment-polluting, and resource-intensive products during this period. We should, therefore, continue to encourage the export of products or services with high added value and low energy intensity, such as communication equipment, computers, and other electronic equipment; wholesale and retail trade; accommodation; catering; and other services (see Fig. 6.3), while products with high energy intensity, such as chemical products, and metal and non-metal mineral products, should be restricted by appropriate economic, legal, and administrative means.

The sharp decline in energy intensity in the production sector is the most important factor to restrain the increase of China's carbon embodied in trade during the entire research period. This means that China's long-term efforts to improve energy efficiency have made great contributions to the protection of the global climate. China has identified energy conservation and emission reduction as a binding target of the 11th Five-Year Plan, and will further take the reduction of carbon emission intensity for GDP as a binding target for future development plans, which is beneficial to the reduction of China's carbon emission intensity.

Constrained by the country's natural endowment of energy resources, the energy structure of China was dominated by coal and electricity during the entire research period, while electricity was mainly generated through coal-fired power. Thus, changes in the energy structure and carbon emission coefficient have consistently had little influence on the carbon embodied in exports. However, this also means that China has a great potential to reduce the carbon embodied in exports by changing its energy structure. With this in mind, it is meaningful for China to encourage the production and consumption of clean energy. At the same time, it is also helpful to cultivate new economic growth points for China.

However, it is not easy for China, a developing country, to improve energy efficiency completely through its own technological innovation. Some developed countries, such as the US, Japan, South Korea, Germany, and the Netherlands, which are China's major trading partners, have the world's most advanced energy-conserving and clean production technologies. These countries should export their technologies of clean production or provide technological assistance to China, which will help China to improve its energy efficiency and reduce carbon emissions. It will also help these countries reduce their trade deficit with China (Shui & Harriss, 2006). This will be an important area of cooperation between China and developed countries.

Appendix A: Trade Volume for Various Industries (Based on 2002 Price)

Table A.1   Exports for various industries (billion yuan)

Years	1987	1990	1992	1995	1997	2002
Agriculture	55.2	66.3	48.7	37.6	39.7	46.5
Coal mining and dressing	6.0	8.8	11.6	12.3	7.4	15.2
Oil and natural gas mining	26.4	32.9	21.2	25.6	24.1	11.7
Metal mineral mining and dressing	2.6	1.9	1.7	1.7	0.7	1.8
Non-metal mineral mining and dressing	4.0	5.6	4.7	5.6	6.5	14.6
Food production and tobacco processing	34.2	42.6	54.0	52.4	64.8	88.9
Textile industry	51.5	65.3	98.3	115.5	138.3	270.6
Clothing, leather, down and their products	49.4	67.8	145.6	195.6	192.8	275.8

Table A.1 (*Continued*)

Years	1987	1990	1992	1995	1997	2002
Wood processing and furniture manufacturing	1.8	1.5	12.9	23.6	26.0	66.5
Papermaking, printing, and cultural, educational, and sporting goods manufacturing	28.3	44.9	54.2	66.8	54.2	97.5
Petroleum processing, coking, nuclear fuel, and gas processing	23.5	32.5	18.9	35.3	22.0	25.3
Chemical industry	18.4	43.6	51.8	66.3	114.1	213.6
Non-metal mineral products	4.1	15.1	24.2	25.0	26.9	41.7
Metal smelting, rolling, and processing	12.2	16.2	15.7	34.3	38.9	45.6
Metal products	9.5	14.7	24.0	30.2	54.0	105.4
Manufacturing of general and special equipment	22.1	11.9	32.6	59.0	34.0	127.8
Manufacturing of transportation equipment	1.6	3.2	8.8	16.0	24.3	63.0
Manufacturing of electrical appliances, machines, and equipment	3.1	8.7	21.2	39.0	69.3	198.8
Manufacturing of communication equipment, computers, and other electronic equipment	8.6	17.9	27.8	56.5	113.0	485.8
Manufacturing of instruments, meters, and machines for culture and office articles	0.3	5.8	1.7	1.7	24.9	145.1
Other industries	6.5	14.1	3.2	2.5	34.8	42.7
Electric and thermal power production and supply	0.0	0.1	0.1	4.0	4.3	5.1
Construction	0.0	0.0	0.0	7.0	2.4	10.5
Transportation, warehousing, and posts	30.6	46.1	54.1	55.2	65.7	158.1
Wholesale and retail trade/ accommodation and catering	11.8	0.4	7.7	14.6	129.3	288.8
Non-material production sector	10.8	12.0	18.8	51.6	94.3	209.9
Total	422.5	579.8	763.4	1035.1	1406.8	3056.2

(*Continued*)

Table A.1   (*Continued*)

Years	2005	2007	2008	2009	2010	2011
Agriculture	49.7	46.1	40.9	42.1	47.7	52.1
Coal mining and dressing	15.8	11.5	11.5	6.3	6.0	5.2
Oil and natural gas mining	4.2	6.0	5.5	7.8	6.2	6.1
Metal mineral mining and dressing	5.3	3.2	0.8	1.1	3.4	31.8
Non-metal mineral mining and dressing	20.5	9.8	13.6	8.9	11.2	12.5
Food production and tobacco processing	147.1	169.9	165.5	160.9	179.4	202.8
Textile industry	494.2	740.6	665.1	630.2	756.1	778.2
Clothing, leather, down and their products	446.1	536.6	554.0	456.7	538.7	540.9
Wood processing and furniture manufacturing	152.8	220.0	238.2	205.1	239.5	257.9
Papermaking, printing, and cultural, educational, and sporting goods manufacturing	188.3	216.2	206.2	188.8	214.3	245.6
Petroleum processing, coking, nuclear fuel, and gas processing	50.1	33.1	28.3	27.3	33.5	32.4
Chemical industry	436.9	607.5	647.8	596.2	774.6	918.8
Non-metal mineral products	87.0	139.2	143.3	126.6	162.4	188.2
Metal smelting, rolling, and processing	132.4	301.3	217.9	134.1	216.8	262.2
Metal products	254.7	290.6	282.6	209.3	282.9	354.1
Manufacturing of general and special equipment	317.7	524.1	587.3	482.9	648.5	806.1
Manufacturing of transportation equipment	177.7	339.5	410.2	369.4	529.3	622.6
Manufacturing of electrical appliances, machines, and equipment	481.1	828.1	680.9	592.5	803.7	962.8

Table A.1   (*Continued*)

Years	2005	2007	2008	2009	2010	2011
Manufacturing of communication equipment, computers, and other electronic equipment	1573.3	2233.6	2268.3	2387.5	3263.9	3362.1
Manufacturing of instruments, meters, and machines for culture and office articles	352.6	261.8	342.0	321.6	395.4	445.9
Other industries	59.2	103.3	104.7	94.6	123.2	149.1
Electric and thermal power production and supply	5.1	5.8	5.7	6.0	6.6	6.8
Construction	18.5	32.9	50.6	45.9	79.9	59.3
Transportation, warehousing, and posts	309.9	379.9	408.9	253.8	299.3	331.0
Wholesale and retail trade/ accommodation and catering	510.0	429.9	442.4	371.4	585.2	431.2
Non-material production sector	231.0	335.0	344.8	289.5	395.1	336.1
Total	6521.0	8805.3	8866.8	8016.3	10602.8	11401.7

Table A.2   Imports for various industries (billion yuan)

Years	1987	1990	1992	1995	1997	2002
Agriculture	20.7	23.9	21.2	52.9	35.4	64.6
Coal mining and dressing	0.6	0.5	0.7	1.6	0.7	2.8
Oil and natural gas mining	0.0	2.9	11.0	25.7	54.5	105.1
Metal mineral mining and dressing	2.7	4.6	4.9	12.2	14.6	33.4
Non-metal mineral mining and dressing	3.8	4.6	4.9	6.0	8.5	17.1
Food production and tobacco processing	19.4	15.4	19.2	52.7	53.4	50.8

(*Continued*)

Table A.2 (*Continued*)

Years	1987	1990	1992	1995	1997	2002
Textile industry	13.7	13.7	44.5	89.2	87.9	116.2
Clothing, leather, down and their products	28.6	32.4	17.0	24.9	36.8	42.1
Wood processing and furniture manufacturing	3.3	4.2	7.1	29.9	11.1	19.0
Papermaking, printing, and cultural, educational, and sporting goods manufacturing	15.8	16.9	19.2	15.5	46.0	55.3
Petroleum processing, coking, nuclear fuel, and gas processing	6.1	8.6	17.9	69.7	61.3	50.0
Chemical industry	34.9	41.3	74.9	137.6	202.3	331.1
Non-metal mineral products	2.5	2.4	7.2	16.2	12.9	19.1
Metal smelting, rolling, and processing	36.3	22.0	37.8	77.8	76.8	166.4
Metal products	4.8	7.2	12.0	23.1	42.3	52.1
Manufacturing of general and special equipment	111.4	97.5	178.7	343.4	232.3	293.7
Manufacturing of transportation equipment	38.9	36.0	94.1	81.1	71.5	78.7
Manufacturing of electrical appliances, machines, and equipment	18.5	22.2	32.7	65.7	75.1	156.0
Manufacturing of communication equipment, computers, and other electronic equipment	30.0	30.0	58.4	134.1	188.2	521.6
Manufacturing of instruments, meters, and machines for culture and office articles	8.3	12.3	9.0	19.9	40.2	151.0
Other industries	12.4	19.1	10.4	4.1	14.1	13.0
Electric and thermal power production and supply	1.4	2.3	4.7	0.4	0.0	1.1
Construction	0.0	0.0	0.0	7.5	5.0	8.0
Transportation, warehousing, and posts	0.5	1.4	32.4	31.1	12.5	40.5

Table A.2 (*Continued*)

Years	1987	1990	1992	1995	1997	2002
Wholesale and retail trade/ accommodation and catering	0.0	0.0	48.3	2.9	4.3	0.4
Non-material production sector	3.1	6.1	1.3	73.6	53.8	149.2
Total	417.4	427.7	769.7	1398.7	1441.7	2538.0

Years	2005	2007	2008	2009	2010	2011
Agriculture	123.4	113.4	129.4	136.4	153.7	204.1
Coal mining and dressing	7.2	8.5	11.3	6.1	22.2	38.2
Oil and natural gas mining	41.7	192.4	193.6	166.9	184.5	223.2
Metal mineral mining and dressing	73.3	93.5	119.1	115.5	127.9	139.7
Non-metal mineral mining and dressing	26.0	30.1	20.7	20.3	14.5	22.1
Food production and tobacco processing	71.5	70.5	84.2	99.9	109.4	142.0
Textile industry	120.8	137.5	65.0	69.7	63.4	68.7
Clothing, leather, down and their products	48.7	53.4	42.6	39.3	32.3	40.9
Wood processing and furniture manufacturing	20.6	21.7	18.7	16.6	20.3	30.2
Papermaking, printing, and cultural, educational, and sporting goods manufacturing	79.7	65.1	53.3	54.4	59.5	64.5
Petroleum processing, coking, nuclear fuel, and gas processing	211.2	69.0	53.6	49.6	48.2	56.7
Chemical industry	467.4	463.0	486.3	495.1	565.0	731.3
Non-metal mineral products	21.9	26.3	25.4	28.7	28.0	41.2
Metal smelting, rolling, and processing	174.4	199.3	178.2	166.2	216.8	212.2
Metal products	63.2	68.6	35.0	38.4	34.0	41.5
Manufacturing of general and special equipment	389.6	422.2	483.1	580.2	515.1	731.7
Manufacturing of transportation equipment	125.3	203.2	246.9	294.2	304.7	457.8

(*Continued*)

Table A.2   (*Continued*)

Years	2005	2007	2008	2009	2010	2011
Manufacturing of electrical appliances, machines, and equipment	259.3	389.6	269.8	290.1	272.8	346.3
Manufacturing of communication equipment, computers, and other electronic equipment	1307.5	1466.9	1431.5	1467.3	1364.2	1782.3
Manufacturing of instruments, meters, and machines for culture and office articles	371.1	429.3	292.2	323.8	303.3	411.4
Other industries	62.4	13.6	107.3	133.8	121.6	144.5
Electric and thermal power production and supply	2.0	2.1	1.6	1.0	2.0	1.9
Construction	11.6	13.5	17.8	21.4	28.5	28.0
Transportation, warehousing, and posts	206.2	82.4	127.5	130.3	120.4	138.4
Wholesale and retail trade/ accommodation and catering	97.5	0.5	47.4	49.6	47.4	56.7
Non-material production sector	229.7	280.5	314.9	329.1	314.9	317.9
Total	4613.2	4916.0	4856.4	5123.9	5074.6	6473.4

Appendix B: Carbon Embodied in Various Industries

Table B.1   Carbon embodied in exports of various industries (MTC)

Years	1987	1990	1992	1995	1997	2002
Primary industry	3.33	3.64	2.64	2.14	2.03	1.90
Secondary industry	56.82	85.75	105.18	143.93	147.69	175.72
Mining	5.01	5.35	4.40	6.37	4.77	3.94
Manufacturing	51.81	80.39	100.77	136.10	141.89	170.47
Tertiary industry	6.16	7.64	10.76	10.28	19.35	28.37
Agriculture	3.33	3.64	2.64	2.14	2.03	1.90
Coal mining and dressing	0.99	1.34	2.06	2.45	1.20	1.54
Oil and natural gas mining	2.77	2.58	1.21	2.89	2.75	1.08

Table B.1 (*Continued*)

Years	1987	1990	1992	1995	1997	2002
Metal mineral mining and dressing	0.48	0.38	0.44	0.35	0.11	0.15
Non-metal mineral mining and dressing	0.77	1.04	0.70	0.67	0.71	1.16
Food production and tobacco processing	4.00	4.37	5.66	4.63	4.89	4.74
Textile industry	7.35	9.95	15.12	17.30	13.23	19.13
Clothing, leather, down and their products	5.18	7.21	14.25	17.56	12.64	14.04
Wood processing and furniture manufacturing	0.46	0.35	2.42	3.19	2.51	3.49
Papermaking, printing, and cultural, educational, and sporting goods manufacturing	4.84	7.75	8.08	9.51	6.74	7.19
Petroleum processing, coking, nuclear fuel, and gas processing	1.61	1.85	1.72	5.20	3.40	3.59
Chemical industry	7.88	16.52	16.52	19.28	24.59	25.65
Non-metal mineral products	1.68	4.97	7.50	7.16	6.03	7.98
Metal smelting, rolling, and processing	5.48	7.77	6.00	15.94	17.21	9.27
Metal products	1.89	3.17	5.15	7.11	11.48	11.33
Manufacturing of general and special equipment	5.62	3.32	6.92	11.59	5.33	9.99
Manufacturing of transportation equipment	0.41	0.89	1.74	2.75	3.69	4.67
Manufacturing of electrical appliances, machines, and equipment	0.95	2.62	4.60	7.56	12.36	16.45
Manufacturing of communication equipment, computers, and other electronic equipment	1.67	3.53	4.09	6.32	10.78	21.61
Manufacturing of instruments, meters, and machines for culture and office articles	0.07	1.28	0.29	0.31	2.93	8.13

(*Continued*)

Table B.1   (*Continued*)

Years	1987	1990	1992	1995	1997	2002
Other industries	2.73	4.82	0.71	0.69	4.10	3.22
Electric and thermal power production and supply	0.01	0.01	0.01	0.51	0.73	0.50
Construction	0.00	0.00	0.00	0.95	0.30	0.81
Transportation, warehousing, and posts	4.67	6.80	8.91	6.19	6.80	10.91
Wholesale and retail trade/ accommodation and catering	0.76	0.02	0.55	0.86	7.32	10.47
Non-material production sector	0.73	0.82	1.30	3.24	5.23	6.99
Total	66.31	97.03	118.58	156.35	169.07	205.99

Years	2005	2007	2008	2009	2010	2011
Primary industry	2.02	1.92	1.59	1.63	1.71	1.86
Secondary industry	376.16	429.54	399.86	351.01	441.88	503.97
Mining	5.06	2.95	2.87	2.20	2.38	5.15
Manufacturing	369.24	423.56	392.95	345.10	433.88	494.54
Tertiary industry	43.83	46.11	49.20	35.51	47.55	43.98
Agriculture	2.02	1.92	1.59	1.63	1.71	1.86
Coal mining and dressing	2.24	1.37	1.37	0.75	0.72	0.63
Oil and natural gas mining	0.43	0.59	0.53	0.76	0.60	0.59
Metal mineral mining and dressing	0.64	0.37	0.08	0.11	0.33	3.11
Non-metal mineral mining and dressing	1.75	0.63	0.88	0.58	0.73	0.82
Food production and tobacco processing	6.46	6.66	6.06	5.88	6.09	6.89
Textile industry	34.87	44.35	37.33	35.37	39.60	40.75
Clothing, leather, down and their products	19.91	23.40	22.61	18.64	20.47	20.55
Wood processing and furniture manufacturing	8.61	9.54	10.29	8.86	10.30	11.09
Papermaking, printing, and cultural, educational, and sporting goods manufacturing	13.61	12.48	11.41	10.45	11.35	13.01

Table B.1 (*Continued*)

Years	2005	2007	2008	2009	2010	2011
Petroleum processing, coking, nuclear fuel, and gas processing	7.63	3.73	3.34	3.23	4.14	4.01
Chemical industry	49.29	56.09	55.88	51.42	62.10	73.66
Non-metal mineral products	12.42	15.44	15.39	13.59	16.88	19.56
Metal smelting, rolling, and processing	33.23	58.88	40.82	25.12	38.85	46.99
Metal products	29.38	24.57	23.27	17.24	22.66	28.37
Manufacturing of general and special equipments	25.84	31.10	34.22	28.13	37.08	46.09
Manufacturing of transportation equipment	12.12	17.16	19.22	17.31	22.85	26.88
Manufacturing of electrical appliances, machines, and equipment	31.26	40.87	38.50	33.50	51.22	61.37
Manufacturing of communication equipment, computers, and other electronic equipment	61.67	63.02	57.02	60.02	72.02	74.19
Manufacturing of instruments, meters, and machines for culture and office articles	18.26	10.28	11.74	11.05	11.64	13.12
Other industries	4.69	5.99	5.85	5.29	6.63	8.02
Electric and thermal power production and supply	0.43	0.40	0.37	0.39	0.41	0.42
Construction	1.43	2.63	3.67	3.33	5.21	3.87
Transportation, warehousing, and posts	19.99	23.27	26.47	16.43	20.42	22.58
Wholesale and retail trade/ accommodation and catering	15.25	12.69	12.09	10.15	14.72	10.85
Non-material production sector	8.60	10.15	10.64	8.93	12.40	10.55
Total	422.01	477.58	450.64	388.15	491.13	549.82

Appendix C: Carbon Avoided by Imports of Various Industries

Table C.1   Carbon avoided by imports of various industries (MTC)

Years	1987	1990	1992	1995	1997	2002
Primary industry	1.25	1.32	1.15	3.01	1.81	2.64
Secondary industry	102.59	101.52	138.82	244.35	215.67	197.31
Mining	1.32	2.11	2.75	6.53	9.42	14.22
Manufacturing	101.11	99.18	135.60	236.78	205.62	182.36
Tertiary industry	0.28	0.63	8.88	8.28	4.52	7.78
Agriculture	1.25	1.32	1.15	3.01	1.81	2.64
Coal mining and dressing	0.10	0.08	0.12	0.31	0.11	0.28
Oil and natural gas mining	0.00	0.23	0.63	2.91	6.21	9.75
Metal mineral mining and dressing	0.49	0.94	1.27	2.59	2.17	2.84
Non-metal mineral mining and dressing	0.73	0.85	0.73	0.71	0.93	1.36
Food production and tobacco processing	2.27	1.58	2.01	4.66	4.03	2.71
Textile industry	1.95	2.10	6.85	13.36	8.41	8.22
Clothing, leather, down and their products	3.00	3.44	1.66	2.23	2.41	2.14
Wood processing and furniture manufacturing	0.86	0.95	1.33	4.04	1.07	1.00
Papermaking, printing, and cultural, educational, and sporting goods manufacturing	2.70	2.92	2.87	2.21	5.72	4.08
Petroleum processing, coking, nuclear fuel, and gas processing	0.42	0.49	1.63	10.27	9.47	7.07
Chemical industry	14.93	15.65	23.91	40.03	43.61	39.76
Non-metal mineral products	1.01	0.80	2.24	4.62	2.89	3.66
Metal smelting, rolling, and processing	16.34	10.54	14.44	36.12	33.99	33.80
Metal products	0.96	1.54	2.58	5.43	9.00	5.60

Table C.1 (*Continued*)

Years	1987	1990	1992	1995	1997	2002
Manufacturing of general and special equipment	28.35	27.31	37.90	67.38	36.43	22.95
Manufacturing of transportation equipment	9.81	9.91	18.56	13.96	10.84	5.83
Manufacturing of electrical appliances, machines, and equipment	5.70	6.72	7.12	12.73	13.40	12.91
Manufacturing of communication equipment, computers, and other electronic equipment	5.82	5.94	8.58	15.01	17.96	23.20
Manufacturing of instruments, meters, and machines for culture and office articles	1.77	2.75	1.60	3.58	4.74	8.46
Other industries	5.24	6.55	2.30	1.14	1.66	0.98
Electric and thermal power production and supply	0.16	0.24	0.47	0.04	0.00	0.10
Construction	0.00	0.00	0.00	1.00	0.62	0.62
Transportation, warehousing, and posts	0.07	0.21	5.33	3.48	1.29	2.80
Wholesale and retail trade/ accommodation and catering	0.00	0.00	3.46	0.17	0.25	0.01
Non-material production sector	0.21	0.42	0.09	4.62	2.98	4.97
Total	104.12	103.47	148.85	255.64	222.00	207.73

Years	2005	2007	2008	2009	2010	2011
Primary industry	5.01	5.41	5.70	6.42	7.31	7.79
Secondary industry	309.79	253.91	262.82	275.45	312.09	342.11
Mining	16.38	35.34	31.66	36.39	41.31	45.14
Manufacturing	292.34	217.04	229.38	236.66	268.84	295.83
Tertiary industry	24.77	18.75	19.42	18.32	20.85	25.77
Agriculture	5.01	5.41	5.70	6.42	7.31	7.79
Coal mining and dressing	1.03	1.35	0.73	2.65	4.55	4.96

(*Continued*)

Table C.1 (*Continued*)

Years	2005	2007	2008	2009	2010	2011
Oil and natural gas mining	4.24	18.90	16.29	18.02	21.65	23.54
Metal mineral mining and dressing	8.89	13.77	13.35	14.79	13.65	14.94
Non-metal mineral mining and dressing	2.22	1.32	1.29	0.92	1.45	1.70
Food production and tobacco processing	3.14	3.30	3.92	4.29	4.82	6.99
Textile industry	8.52	3.89	4.18	3.80	3.60	3.37
Clothing, leather, down and their products	2.17	1.86	1.72	1.41	1.55	1.92
Wood processing and furniture manufacturing	1.16	0.81	0.72	0.88	1.30	1.74
Papermaking, printing, and cultural, educational, and sporting goods manufacturing	5.76	3.08	3.14	3.43	3.42	4.02
Petroleum processing, coking, nuclear fuel, and gas processing	32.18	6.05	5.60	5.44	7.00	7.50
Chemical industry	52.73	44.90	45.71	52.17	58.63	65.12
Non-metal mineral products	3.13	2.82	3.18	3.11	4.29	5.13
Metal smelting, rolling, and processing	43.78	34.82	32.47	42.38	38.04	38.16
Metal products	7.29	2.96	3.25	2.88	3.32	3.58
Manufacturing of general and special equipment	31.68	28.67	34.43	30.57	41.83	48.31
Manufacturing of transportation equipment	8.55	12.48	14.88	15.40	19.76	22.74
Manufacturing of electrical appliances, machines, and equipment	16.85	13.32	14.32	13.46	22.07	24.09
Manufacturing of communication equipment, computers, and other electronic equipment	51.25	40.39	41.40	38.49	39.33	40.53

Table C.1 (*Continued*)

Years	2005	2007	2008	2009	2010	2011
Manufacturing of instruments, meters, and machines for culture and office articles	19.21	11.47	12.71	11.91	12.11	14.12
Other industries	4.94	6.23	7.76	7.05	7.77	8.52
Electric and thermal power production and supply	0.17	0.11	0.07	0.13	0.12	0.15
Construction	0.89	1.42	1.71	2.27	1.82	0.98
Transportation, warehousing, and posts	13.30	7.81	7.98	7.38	9.44	12.15
Wholesale and retail trade/accommodation and catering	2.91	1.40	1.46	1.40	1.43	1.47
Non-material production sector	8.55	9.54	9.97	9.54	9.98	12.15
Total	339.57	278.07	287.94	300.19	340.25	375.66

References

Ahmed, N., & Wyckoff, A., Carbon Dioxide Emissions Embodied in International Trade, OECD DSTI/DOC (2003) 15, 2003.

Copeland, B. R., & Taylor, M. S., "Trade, Growth, and the Environment". *Journal of Economic Literature*, Vol. XLII (2004), 7–71.

Dietzenbacher, E., & Bart, L., "Structural Decomposition Techniques: Sense and Sensitivity". *Economic System Research*, Vol. 10, No. 4 (1998), 307–323.G

Hu, X., Jiang, K. *et al.*, *An Evaluation of Technology Selection for the Greenhouse Gas Emission Reduction and Countermeasures of China*. 2001. China Environmental Science Press, Beijing.

IPCC, *Revised 1996 IPCC Guidelines for National Greenhouse Gas Inventories: Workbook* (Volume 2), 1996, http://www.ipcc-nggip.iges.or.jp/public/gl/invs5a.html.

Jim Watson and Tao Wang, Who Owns China's Carbon Emissions. 2007. Tyndall Briefing Note No. 23.

Li, Q., & Xue, T., *A Sector Analysis of the Economic Development of China: A New List of Comparable Input–output Series*. 1998. China Statistics Press, Beijing.

Li, Y., & Hewitt, N., "The Effect of Trade Between China and the UK on National Global Carbon Dioxide Emissions". *Energy Policy*, Vol. 36, No. 6 (2008), 1907–1914.

Lin, B., & Sun, C., "Evaluating Carbon Dioxide Emissions in International Trade of China". *Energy Policy*, Vol. 38, No. 3 (2010), 1389–1397.

Liu, X., Ishikawa, M., Wang, C., Dong, Y. & Liu, W., "Analyses of CO_2 Emissions Embodied in Japan-China Trade". *Energy Policy*, Vol. 38, No. 1 (2010), 613–621.

Machado, G., Schaeffer, R. & Worrel, E., "Energy and Carbon Embodied in the International Trade of Brazil: An Input–output Approach". *Ecological Economics*, Vol. 39, No. 3 (2001), 409–424.

Munksgaard, J., & Pedersen, K. A., "CO_2 Accounts for Open Economies: Producer or Consumer Responsibility?". *Energy Policy*, Vol. 29 (2001), 327–334.

Nadim Ahmad, & Andrew Wyckoff, Carbon Dioxide Emissions Embodied in International Trade, OECD DSTI/DOC (2003) 15, 2003.

Pan, J., Phillips, J., & Chen, Y., "China's Balance of Emissions Embodied in Trade: Approaches to Measurement and Allocating International Responsibility". *Oxford Review of Economic Policy*, Vol. 24, No. 2 (2008), 354–376.

Peters, G. P., & Hertwich, E. G., "Pollution Embodied in Trade: The Norwegian Case". *Global Environmental Change*, Vol. 16, No. 4 (2006), 379–387.

Qi, Y., Li, H. & Xu, M., "Estimation of Embodied Carbon in China's Import and Export". *China Population, Resources and Environment*, No. 3 (2008).

Rhee, H. C., & Chung, H. S., "Change in CO_2 Emission and Its Transmissions between Korea and Japan Using International Input–output Analysis". *Ecological Economics*, Vol. 58, No. 4 (2006), 788–800.

Shui, B., & Harriss, R. C., "The Role of CO_2 Embodiment in US-China Trade". *Energy Policy*, Vol. 34 (2006), 4063–4068.

United Nations, Handbook of Input–output Table Compilation and Analysis, *Studies in Methods Series F*, No. 74, Handbook of National Accounting, United Nations, 1999.

Wang, T., & Watson, J., Who Owns China's Carbon Emissions. 2007. Tyndall Briefing Note No. 23.

Wang, W., & Cheng, Y., "Global Warming and Greenhouse Gas Emissions: CO_2 Emissions in Sino-Japanese Trade". Ecological Economy, No. 7 (2006).

Weber, C. L., Peters, G. P., Guan, D. & Hubacek, K., "The Contribution of Chinese Exports to Climate Change". *Energy Policy*, Vol. 36 (2008), 3572–3577.

Wyckoff, A. W., & Roop, J. M., "The Embodiment of Carbon in Imports of Manufactured Products: Implications for International Agreements on Greenhouse Gas Emissions. *Energy Policy*, Vol. 22 (1994), 187–194.

Yan, Y., & Yang, L., "China's Foreign Trade and Climate Change: A Case Study of CO_2 Emissions". *Energy Policy*, Vol. 38, No. 1 (2010), 350–356.

Yao, Y., Qi, S. & Liu, Q., "A Research on the Relationship and Countermeasures of China's Import and Export and Economy, Employment, and Energy". *Journal of Quantitative & Technical Economics*, No. 10 (2008).

Zhang, Y., "The Energy and Environmental Costs for the Trade Growth of China". *Journal of Quantitative & Technical Economics*, No. 1 (2009a).

Zhang, Y., "Structural Decomposition Analysis of Sources of Decarbonizing Economic Development in China: 1992–2006". *Ecological Economics*, Vol. 68, Nos. 8–9 (2009), 2399–2405.

Zhang, Y., "Supply Side Structural Effect on Carbon Emissions in China". *Energy Economics*, Vol. 32, No. 1 (2010), 186–193.

Chapter 7

Virtual Water in the Foreign Trade of China and Its Policy Implications[1]

Xiao Zhang

Institute of Quantitative & Technical Economics,
Chinese Academy of Social Sciences

1. Introduction

As a natural resource, water plays a role in the production process of various substances like oil, natural gas, and coal. Besides, water, as an element vital to life, supports the survival of all creatures on earth. Although in a general sense the total stock of water in nature is more than that of other natural resources, there are still problems concerning lack of water (water shortage) and low-quality water (water pollution) in some places. The problems of water shortage and water pollution have become and will continue to be major problems hindering China's development.

If we consider water not only as a general natural resource but also as a resource to support human society and all living creatures as well as a strategic resource for national development, then the study of water resources will involve different disciplines such as politics, sociology, anthropology, economics, environmental science, and meteorology, so that an interdisciplinary research can be conducted on water resources and a profound understanding can be obtained.

During the more than 30 years since the Reform and Opening Up, foreign trade has been an important "engine" and pillar of the economic

---

[1] This chapter was drafted in 2009.

Table 7.1   Share of China's foreign trade in GDP over the years since the Reform and Opening Up

Year	Export (billion RMB)	Import (billion RMB)	GDP (billion RMB)	Export/GDP (%)	Import/GDP (%)
1978	16.76	18.74	364.52	4.60	5.14
1980	27.12	29.88	454.56	5.97	6.57
1985	80.89	125.78	901.60	8.97	13.95
1990	298.58	257.43	1866.78	15.99	13.79
1991	382.71	339.87	2178.15	17.57	15.60
1992	467.63	444.33	2692.35	17.37	16.50
1993	528.48	598.62	3533.39	14.96	16.94
1994	1042.18	996.01	4819.79	21.62	20.67
1995	1245.18	1104.81	6079.37	20.48	18.17
1996	1257.64	1155.74	7117.66	17.67	16.24
1997	1516.07	1180.65	7897.30	19.20	14.95
1998	1522.36	1162.61	8440.23	18.04	13.77
1999	1615.98	1373.64	8967.71	18.02	15.32
2000	2063.44	1863.88	9921.46	20.80	18.79
2001	2202.44	2015.92	10965.52	20.09	18.38
2002	2694.79	2443.03	12033.27	22.39	20.30
2003	3628.79	3419.56	13582.28	26.72	25.18
2004	4910.33	4643.58	15987.83	30.71	29.04
2005	6264.81	5427.37	18321.74	34.19	29.62
2006	7759.46	6337.69	21192.35	36.61	29.91
2007	9345.56	7328.46	24952.99	37.45	29.37

Source: *China Statistical Yearbook* 2008, www.stats.gov.cn/tjsj/ndsj.

growth in China. Table 7.1 and Fig. 7.1 show the trend of the proportion of foreign trade in GDP in the past 30 years. The data show that in the past 30 years, the proportion has seen an increasing trend. When it comes to the 21st century, the share grows even faster, accounting for 20–40% of GDP.

The trade scale, especially export scale, has undoubtedly increased domestic employment and national income as well as leading to huge economic benefits. It should, however, be noted that exports are

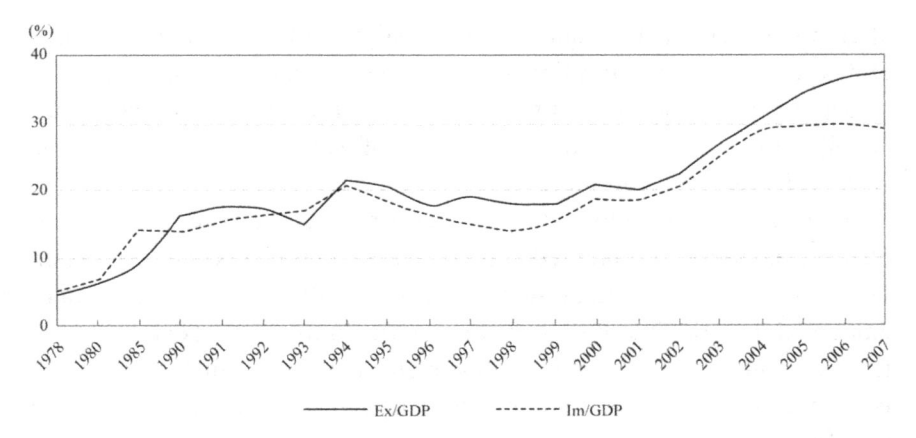

Fig. 7.1   Trend of the share of China's foreign trade in GDP over the years since the Reform and Opening Up

Source: Based on the data given in Table 7.1.

accompanied by resource consumption and environmental pollution. The impact of trade on resources and environment has increasingly become the focus of researchers and decision-makers. Kando *et al.* (1998) analyze and discuss the impact of CO_2 emissions on Japan's import and export. Hayami *et al.* (2002) focus on the impact of CO_2 emission reduction technologies on trade between Japan and Canada. Ackerman *et al.* (2007) discuss the issue of CO_2 embodied in trade between Japan and the US. Shui and Harriss (2006) discuss the role of CO_2 embodied in trade between China and the US, while Muradin *et al.* (2002), Qi *et al.* (2008), Zhang (2009), Machado *et al.* (2001), Sánchez-Chóliz and Duarte (2004), and Peters and Hertwich (2006) provide cases of developed countries (industrialized countries), China, Brazil, Norway, and Spain as regards the impact of trade on environment. Other scholars analyze and discuss the impact of food trade on regional or global water resource security and food security (Hoekstra and Hung, 2002; Ma and Chen, 2006; Velázquze, 2007; Novo *et al.*, 2009), as well as water resources embodied in trade (Zhao *et al.*, 2009; Zhu *et al.*, 2009).

In the national economic system, agricultural production consumes water resources the most. Industrial production also involves the consumption of water resources. Thus, the structure and quantity of exports determine water resource embodied in exports. The present chapter attempts to conduct a quantitative analysis of the water resource embodied in China's foreign trade in recent years, so as to gain an in-depth understanding of its trend along with the export trade, thus enabling further understanding of the cost of water resources paid by the scale of China's foreign trade.

In terms of methodology, this chapter estimates the total virtual water quantity embodied in imported and exported commodities and services on the basis of the input–output model, that is, in addition to the virtual water embodied in agricultural products, non-agricultural products and services is also counted in. Besides, it also estimates the total virtual water which is embodied in products and services through intermediate use (input) transfer.

2. Water Crisis of Human Society and the Concepts of "Water Footprint" and "Virtual Water"

Nowadays, in at least one-third of areas in the world, water, instead of land, has become the main factor restricting the development of productive forces. With the "green revolution" in agriculture, global food growth has exceeded population growth. However, along with the doubling of food production compared with the previous generation, the amount of water extracted from rivers and underground sources has more than tripled. Groundwater is actually a non-renewable resource: rainwater can only replenish 1‰ of the world's groundwater reserves every year. In some dry countries, such as Egypt, Mexico, Pakistan, Australia, and Central Asia, over 90% of the water obtained from the natural environment is used for irrigation,[2] and their water consumption per capita is several times higher than that of some European countries. For example, the per capita water withdrawal in Pakistan is five times that of Ireland, Egypt is five times that of the UK, and Mexico is five times that of Denmark. It can be said that the doubling of growth in grain output achieved by the "green revolution" in agriculture is likely to be lost as rivers dry up, groundwater runs out, and the soil is salinized and hardened (Pearce, 2009).

---

[2] In the dry areas of North China, 75%–90% of water resources have been used for agriculture. See Table 7.3.

It has become a fact that human society gets into conflicts over water resources. In the 1960s, Israel fought with its Arabian neighbors. After the war, a simple fact emerged that Israel's water consumption had become far greater than its rainfall, which was due to its occupation of the West Bank, allowing it to control the underground water there. Its occupation of Golan Heights allowed it to control the Jordan River, and almost the entire Jordan River valley was controlled by the Israelis. In essence, Israel launched the first modern war over water resources in human society (Pearce, 2009).

For a long time, China has been a "water-poor" country, especially current issues of North China. With the climate change, ecological and environmental problems such as drought and desertification, and water shortages have become important factors affecting regional industrial and agricultural production and the survival of the local people. Table 7.2 shows the changes in the total amount of water resources in China in recent years. Table 7.3 displays the structure of water resource utilization in North and South China. The data show that, from 1999 to 2007 with the exception

Table 7.2   Changes in total water resources in China (1999–2007)

| Year | Total volume (billion m³) | Year-on-year change[a] based on multi-year average[b] | |
		Absolute volume (billion m³)	Percentage (%)
1999	2819.6	+71.6	+0.25
2000	2770.1	−42.34	−1.51
2001	2686.8	−125.64	−4.46
2002	2825.5	+13.06	+0.46
2003	2746.0	−66.44	−2.36
2004	2413.0	−399.44	−14.2
2005	2805.31	−7.13	−0.25
2006	2525.5	−286.94	−10.2
2007	2533.0	−279.44	−9.9

Notes: [a]The plus symbol "+" indicates increase, while the minus symbol "−" indicates decrease. [b]The multi-year average of water resources is 2812.44 billion m³ (the Compilation Committee for the Chinese Natural Resources Book Series).

Source: *China Water Resources Bulletin* 1999–2007, www.mwr.gov.cn.

Table 7.3   Structural changes of water resource utilization in North and South China (%)

Year	Region	Agriculture	Industry	Daily life
1980[a]	South	80.1	12.1	7.8
	North	86.7	8.5	4.8
1993[a]	South	68.1	22.0	9.9
	North	79.3	12.4	8.3
1997[a]	South	63.1	25.6	11.3
	North	78.7	13.9	7.4
2000	South	62.4	25.5	12.0
	North	76.3	15.1	8.6
2001	South	61.3	26.2	12.6
	North	77.4	13.9	8.7
2002	South	59.4	27.5	13.2
	North	78.0	13.0	9.0
2003	South	56.5	28.8	13.2
	North	74.7	13.7	10.1
2004	South	55.8	29.5	13.3
	North	75.8	12.9	9.8
2005	South	54.8	30.3	13.7
	North	74.6	13.4	9.9

Note: [a]The data come from Liu and Chen (2001).

Source: Calculations on basis of *China Water Resources Bulletin* over the years.

of 1999 and 2002, the total amount of water resources of China was less than the multi-year average (see Table 7.2). The data further show that the industrial and domestic water consumption in North China is lower than that in South China (see Table 7.3). It is estimated (Liu and Chen, 2001) that the per capita water resources in China are 2220 m^3 — 747 m^3 for North China and 3481 m^3 for South China — while the world average is 6981 m^3 (Guan and Hubacek, 2007). Based on these figures, it can be concluded that the per capita water resources of China account for only 31.8% of the world average, and for North China, the figure is only 10.7%, less than 11%. Thus, water shortage in North China is already serious.

How to measure the demand and consumption of water resources in human society? What is the situation of water resources per capita in different regions of the earth? Modelling on the concept of "ecological footprint"[3] in the 1990s, scholars proposed the concept of "water footprint" in 2002 (Hoekstra and Hung, 2002; Hoekstra and Chapagain, 2007). Water footprint refers to the amount of water resources used and consumed by individuals or communities in the production of products and services. Some scholars have calculated the water footprints of cotton (Chapagain *et al.*, 2006), and coffee and tea (Chapagain and Hoekstra, 2007). Other scholars have calculated the annual water footprint of China, and its provinces and municipalities (Wang *et al.*, 2005). In fact, both the concept of water footprint and the concept of virtual water as put forward by Allan in the 1990s are to reveal the amount of water resources embodied in products and services. The virtual water proposed by Allan (1993, 1994, 1998) refers to the water used and consumed in a product. Allan (1996, 2002, 2003), with his many-year study of the water resources and the conflicts over water resources of the Middle East, also proposed to export virtual water or virtual water trade as one of the ways to solve the regional water shortage and conflicts over water resources.

The concepts of water footprint and virtual water, as well as virtual water trade, have had a profound impact on deepening the understanding of the function of water resources and revealing the influence of water resources on the production and life of human society.

It is estimated (Pearce, 2009) that the global virtual water trade is close to 1 trillion m^3 (986.7 billion m^3) every year, of which 2/3 are stored in crops, 1/4 in meat and dairy products, and 1/10 in industrial products. Table 7.4 shows the world's top 5 countries for virtual water import and export. The data show that the US is the biggest virtual water exporter and Japan is the biggest virtual water importer.

---

[3] Ecological footprint is an indicator for the sustainable development of human society (Rees, 1992, 1996; Rees and Wackernagel, 1994). It refers to the average "biological productive space" owned by individuals or communities (which can be villages, cities, and countries), which is measured with the unit hectare. The total ecological footprint consists of six parts: arable land, grassland, forest land, construction land, productive marine area, and forest areas absorbing carbon dioxide emitted by human beings (Hoekstra, 2009).

Table 7.4 Top 5 countries for virtual water import and export in the world (1995–1999)

Rank	Country	Net import (billion m³/year)	Country	Net export (billion m³/year)
1	Japan	59	US	152
2	The Netherlands	30	Canada	55
3	South Korea	23	Thailand	47
4	China	20	Argentina	45
5	Indonesia	20	India	32

Source: Hoekstra and Hung (2005).

In international trade, invisible water is being transferred between countries in huge and shocking quantities. We should pay close attention to and strengthen the monitoring of the flow of water resources, which are scarce, essential for human survival, and strategically important to national development.

In terms of methodology, this chapter uses the input–output model to estimate the total virtual water volume embodied in the products and services of foreign trade. It estimates not only the virtual water embodied in agricultural products but also that in non-agricultural products and services. In addition, it also estimates the virtual water which is embodied in products and services through intermediate use (input) transfer.

3. Analysis Model and Data Processing

3.1. *Model for analysis*

This chapter attempts to estimate the amount of water resources embodied in China's foreign trade. Some previous studies have already made some basic estimates. They are limited to the estimation and calculation of virtual water in physical agricultural products, such as Liu and Wu (2005), Hoekstra and Hung (2005), Ma and Chen (2006), Velázquez (2007), Novo *et al.* (2009), and Chapagain and Orr (2009). In fact, non-agricultural products, such as industrial products and services, also involve the use or consumption of a large amount of water resources in their production processes. Xiang *et al.* (2006) undertook a calculation of the virtual water in oil products, concluding that in China, 1 ton of oil products imported is at least equivalent to over 5 tons of water imported.

In particular, in the process of producing products and services, besides the direct use and consumption of water resources, there is also indirect use, that is, the use through the intermediate input of materials and equipment between various sectors of the national economy, with water resources transferred in the process. Kondo (2005) put forward the concept of "total water consumption", which refers to the sum of direct and indirect water consumption.

The present chapter estimates not only the virtual water embodied in agricultural products but also that in non-agricultural products and services and that which is embodied in products and services through intermediate use (input) transfer. The input–output model provides a suitable analytical framework and method for such a research.

For the standard input–output model, as shown in (7.1), we further define the direct water consumption vector $\omega(n \times 1)$ of each sector, which indicates the water consumption per unit of output (x). This idea is adopted from Miller and Blair (1985).

$$x = (I - A)^{-1} f \qquad (7.1)$$

Then, we define the water multiplier $[\omega(n \times 1)]$ for each sector as (7.2), which indicates the total water intensity (direct plus indirect) of each sector.

$$w' = \omega' (I - A)^{-1} \qquad (7.2)$$

In (7.2), suppose that the inverse matrix of Leontief is $L = (I - A)^{-1} (n \times n)$, and the vector w includes not only direct water consumption of each sector, but also the water consumption indirectly used in the intermediate input of other sectors. Vector ω is expressed in physical units: cubic meters or 100 million cubic meters. ω' is the transpose vector of ω, $(1 \times n)$.

We define (7.3) and (7.4) to calculate the direct export volume (*DVWE*) and import volume (*DVWI*) of virtual water for each sector.

$$DVWE' = \omega'\hat{\varepsilon} \qquad (7.3)$$

$$DVWI' = \omega'\hat{\lambda} \qquad (7.4)$$

In (7.3) and (7.4), $\hat{\varepsilon}$ and $\hat{\lambda}$, respectively, represent the diagonal matrix $(n \times n)$ of export volume and import volume of each sector.

Suppose that the ratio of water consumption to output of each sector remains constant, we can further define the total water consumption (W) of each sector as (7.5) via (7.1) and (7.2) (Mill and Blair, 1985).

$$W' = \omega'Lf = \omega'L(f^{do} + f^{ex}) \tag{7.5}$$

In (7.5), f^{do} and f^{ex}, respectively, represent the domestic final demand and export vector.

Then, the total virtual water volume embodied in the exports of each sector (*TVWE*) and the total virtual water volume embodied in the imports of each sector (*TVWI*) can, respectively, be expressed as follows:

$$TVWE' = \omega'L\hat{\varepsilon} \tag{7.6}$$

$$TVWI' = \omega'L\hat{\lambda} \tag{7.7}$$

Finally, the total net direct virtual water (*NDVW*) and the total net virtual water (*NTVW*) can be expressed as follows:

$$NDVW = \Sigma DVWE - \Sigma DVWI \tag{7.8}$$

$$NTVW = \Sigma TVWE - \Sigma TVWI \tag{7.9}$$

3.2. Data

3.2.1. *Input–output tables with 17 industry sectors in China*

This chapter focuses on three time points (1995, 2002, and 2005) in the empirical analysis, applying the input–output tables of 17 industry sectors for the three years. See Table 7.5 for the 17 sectors. Table 7.5 also lists the direct water consumption per unit of value-added (sectoral water consumption quota) in 2002. The differentiation of 17 sectors may be too coarse, with some sectors integrated into a bigger one, thus failing to provide a deep analysis of foreign trade and water use for some special sectors. For example, the sector of papermaking is integrated into "other manufacturing industries", while power generation (especially thermal power generation, a major water consumer) is merged into "electric

Table 7.5 Sector list of the input–output tables.

Industry sectors	Direct water consumption of 2002[a] (m³/10⁴ *yuan* value added)
Agriculture	2246.588
Mining	45.943
Food manufacturing	53.343
Textile, sewing, and leather products manufacturing	35.133
Other manufacturing industries	61.514
Electric power, steam, and hot water production and supply	1470.990
Coking, gas, coal products, and petroleum processing	545.378
Chemical industry	308.840
Construction materials and other non-metal mineral products	47.528
Metal products manufacturing	292.319
Manufacturing of mechanical equipment	14.895
Construction	8.643
Transportation and posts	112.820
Commercial and catering industry	297.694
Public utilities and resident services	188.550
Finance and insurance	16.691
Other services	44.768

Note: [a]The direct water consumption of a sector is also called the "sectoral water consumption quota".
Source: National Bureau of Statistics, http://www.stats.gov.cn.

power, steam, and hot water production and supply", and so on. Questions of this kind can be solved by using input–output tables with more finely differentiated industry sectors.

3.2.2. *Estimation of sectoral water consumption quota*

We have the data of actual water consumption of various sectors only for the year 2002 (the Chinese Input–Output Association, 2005). On the basis of these data, we estimate the water consumption quota for various sectors. The water use in industrial sectors for other years is estimated on the

Table 7.6   Sectoral industrial sewage discharge (2005)[a]

Industry sectors	Sewage discharge (10^4 ton)
Agriculture	—[b]
Mining	116,741
Food manufacturing	86,234
Textile, sewing, and leather products manufacturing	199,755
Other manufacturing industries	501,436
Electric power, steam, and hot water production and supply	274,063
Coking, gas, coal products, and petroleum processing	68,122
Chemical industry	436,024
Construction materials and other non-metal mineral products	48,248
Metal products manufacturing	224,725
Manufacturing of mechanical equipment	85,723
Construction	118,708
Transportation and posts	—
Commercial and catering industry	—
Public utilities and resident services	—
Finance and insurance	—
Other services	—

Note: [a]The authors integrate and process the data of 40 sectors into 17 sectors. [b]A lack of data, the same below.
Source: *China Statistical Yearbook* (1996, 2003 and 2006), http://www.stats.gov.cn.

basis of sewage discharge data. Table 7.6 lists the industrial sewage discharge of various sectors in 2005. The data for the water use in the agricultural sector are adopted from the *China Water Resources Bulletin* over the years. The water consumption quota for the service sector is adjusted and estimated based on the 2002 data.

3.2.3. *Data of the import and export trade of China*

Data regarding the import and export trade of China are adopted from *China Foreign Economic Statistical Yearbook* and *China Trade and External Economic Statistical Yearbook*. The original data are listed according to 22 categories of import and export products. Upon sorting and merging, we obtained import and export trade data for 17 sectors, as shown in Table 7.7.

Table 7.7 Import and export trade volume for China (billion RMB)

Industry sectors	1995[a]		2002		2005	
	Export	Import	Export	Import	Export	Import
Agriculture	250922.556	9311.904	239039.76	10263.48	281876.397	17530.238
Mining	214755.786	22282.056	179693.67	39232.98	287282.919	120909.492
Food manufacturing	154477.836	7482.78	228941.82	7449.3	359287.962	10075.791
Textile, sewing, and leather products manufacturing	940585.446	280770.534	1247095.59	271899.45	1637275.079	316281.537
Other manufacturing industries	82144.296	31344.534	111325.65	54710.97	167192.597	103379.254
Electric power, steam, and hot water production and supply	—	—	—	—	—	—
Coking, gas, coal products, and petroleum processing	—	—	—	—	—	—
Chemical industry	134690.04	296484.372	205683.45	611090.91	456933.026	1230147.589
Construction materials and other non-metal mineral products	54042.3	24028.038	70520.04	53883.27	103461.171	87323.522
Metal products manufacturing	119724.48	294655.248	161980.89	495543.99	450215.832	956299.058
Manufacturing of mechanical equipment	527535.99	1439437.446	1402372.11	2863759.23	2834082.449	5317560.138
Construction	—	—	—	—	—	—
Transportation and posts	—	—	—	—	—	—
Commercial and catering industry	88047.378	20619.216	162477.51	17961.09	302437.564	65615.517
Public utilities and resident services	—	—	—	—	—	—
Finance and insurance	—	—	—	—	—	—
Other services	—	—	—	—	—	—
Total	12576.43	11557.43	26947.87	24430.27	62648.09	54273.68

Note: [a]The data are 1996 for.

Source: *China Foreign Economic Statistical Yearbook* (1998, 2004) and *China Trade and External Economic Statistical Yearbook* (2006).

4. Discussion on the Estimates

The model-based estimates for the water resources transferred from China through foreign trade in 1995, 2002, and 2005 are shown in Table 7.8. The results show that China, as a "water-poor" country, is seriously facing a shortage of water resources. However, through foreign trade, China has exported a large amount of virtual water to the world, with its direct net flow reaching billions of cubic meters per year and its total net flow amounting to tens of billions of cubic meters per year (see Table 7.8). This mode of import and export trade obviously does not lead to a comparative advantage in water resources.

According to Hoekstra and Hung (2005), under the condition that only virtual water for grain trade is included, with industrial and total virtual water excluded, the United States will become the biggest exporter of virtual water, and Japan will be the biggest importer, with both of them being "water-rich". This shows that Japan has achieved long-term strategic benefits in the effective use of international water resources, which serves as a lesson for China.

The trend of virtual water volume in China's foreign trade (direct and total) is shown in Fig. 7.2. The results show that from 1995 to 2005, both the net direct volume (excluding indirect transfers between sectors) and the net total volume (including indirect transfers between sector) showed

Table 7.8 Estimation of virtual water volume in China's foreign trade (billion m³)

	1995	2002	2005
DVWE (from China)	19.389	18.875	28.214
DVWI (to China)	13.09	13.752	20.176
Net direct virtual water volume embodied in trade (from China)	6.298	5.122	8.038
TVWE (from China)	78.026	98.735	184.76
TVWI (to China)	66.672	76.186	141.393
Net virtual water volume embodied trade (from China)	11.355	22.549	43.367

Source: The author's estimation.

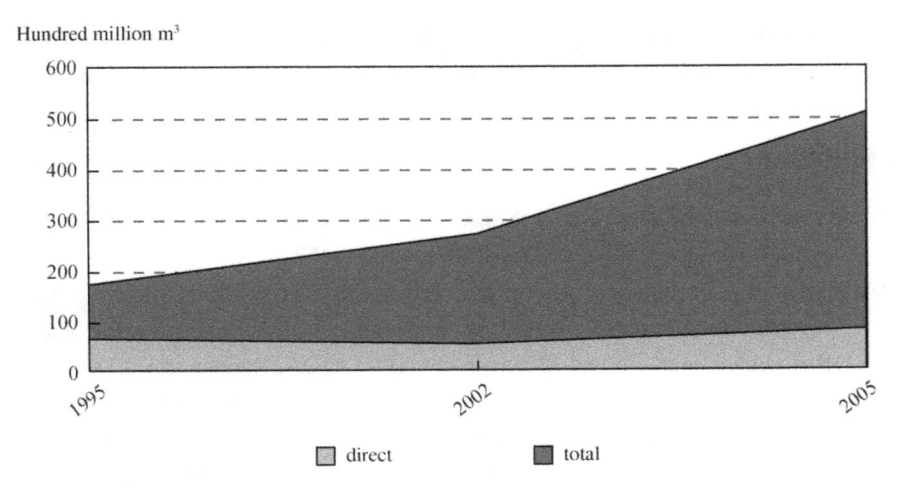

Fig. 7.2 Trend of virtual water volume in China's foreign trade (direct and total)

a gradually increasing trend. The net total export of virtual water, in particular, increased by 74% within 10 years, exceeding the growth rate of the share of net import and export volume in current-year GDP in the same period (49%). This strong growth trend shows that the exports of China in recent years are based on a large amount of water-containing resources, and the amount is still on the rise due to the structure and scale of foreign trade and other factors.

As discussed in section 2 of this chapter, the per capita water resources in China are less than 32% of the world average, and for North China the figure is even less than 11%. With such a natural endowment of water resources, China should consider making more effective use of the world water resources instead of exporting water resources in tangible or intangible ways. Within the framework of free trade, the cost of developing, consuming, and exporting water resources is fairly high for China, regardless of whether it is done in visible or invisible form. Thus, in addition to firmly implementing the policy of saving water resources within the country, the foreign trade policy of China should also fully consider the constraints of water resources. In the reform of the foreign trade pattern, the previous trade structure and scale should be adjusted based on the basic principle of making full use of the complementary advantages of bilateral and multilateral resources (including water resources) in order to benefit the sustainable development of China and the world.

References

Ackerman, F., Ishikawa, M. & Suga, M., The Carbon Content of Japan–US Trade". *Energy Policy*, Vol. 35 (2007), 4455–4462.

Allan, J. A., Fortunately There are Substitutes for Water Otherwise Our Hydropolitical Futures Would be Impossible. ODA, Priorities for Water Resource Allocation and Management. 1993. ODA, London, pp. 13–26.

Allan, J. A., "Overall Perspectives on Countries and Regions". In P. Rogers and P. Lydon (eds.), *Water in the Arab World: Perspectives and Prognoses*. 1994. Harvard University Press, Cambridge, Massachussets, pp. 65–100.

Allan, J. A., *Water, Peace and the Middle East: Negotiating Resources in the Jordan Basin*. 1996. Tauris Academic Publication, London.

Allan, J. A., "Virtual water: Strategic Resource Global Solutions to Regional Deficits". *Groundwater*, Vol. 36, No. 4 (1998), 545–546.

Allan, J. A., *The Middle East Water Question: Hydropolitics and the Global Economy*. 2002. I. B. Tauris Publication, London.

Allan, J. A. "Virtual Water Eliminates Water was a Case Study from the Middle East". In A. Y. Hoekstra (ed.), *Virtual Water Trade-Proceedings of the International Expert Meeting on Virtual Water Trade*. Research Report Series 12, IHE, Delft, pp. 137–145.

Chapagain, A. K., Hoekstra, A. Y., Savenije, H. H. G. & Gautam, R., "The Water Footprint of Cotton Consumption: An Assessment of the Impact Worldwide Consumption of Cotton Products on the Water Resource in the Cotton Producing Countries". *Ecological Economics*, Vol. 60, No. 1 (2006). 186–203.

Chapagain, A. K., & Hoekstra, A. Y. "The Water Footprint of Coffee and Tea Consumption in the Netherlands". *Ecological Economics*, Vol. 64, No. 1 (2007). 109–118.

Chapagain, A. K., & Orr, S. "An Improved Water Footprint Methodology Linking Global Consumption to Local Water Resources: A Case of Spanish Tomatoes". *Journal of Environmental Management*, Vol. 90 (2009), 1219–1228.

Guan, D., & Hubacek, K., "A New and Integrated Hydro-economic Accounting and Analytical Framework for Water Resources: A Case Study for North China". *Journal of Environmental Management*, Vo. 88 (2008), 1300–1313.

Hayami, H., & Nakamura, M., CO_2 Emission of an Alternative Technology and Bilateral Trade Between Japan and Canada: Relocating Production and an Implication for Joint implementation. KEO Discussion Paper No. 075. Keio Economic Observatory (KEO), Keio University, 2002.

Hoekstra, A. Y., & Hung, P. Q. "Virtual Water Trade: A Quantification of Virtual Water Flow Between Nations in Relation to International Crop Trade". *Research Report Series* No. 11 (2002), UNESCO-IHE, Delft.

Hoekstra, A. Y., & Hung, P. Q. "Globalisation of Water Resource: International Virtual Water Flows in Relation to Crop Trade". *Global Environmental Change*, Vol. 15 (2005), 45–56.

Hoekstra, A. Y., & Chapagain, A. K., "Water Footprints of Nations: Water Use by People as a Function of Their Consumption Pattern". *Water Resource Management*, Vol. 21, No. 1 (2007), 35–48.

Hoekstra, A. Y., Human Appropriation of Natural Capital: A Comparison of Ecological Footprint and Water Footprint Analysis. *Ecological Economics*, Vol. 68 (2009), 1963–1974.

Kondo, K., "Economic Analysis of Water Resources in Japan: Using Factor Decomposition Analysis Based on Input-output Table". *Environmental Economics and Policy Studies*, Vol. 7 (2005), 109–129.

Kondo, Y., Moriguchia, Y. & Shimizu, H. "CO_2 Emission in Japan: Influences of Imports and Exports". *Applied Energy*, Vol. 59, Nos. 2–3 (1998), 163–174.

Liu C., & Chen Z., *An Evaluation of the Current Situation of Water Resources in China and an Analysis of the Development Trend of Supply and Demand.* 2001. China Water & Power Press, Beijing.

Liu X., & Wu G., "An Empirical Research on Virtual Water Trade in China's Agricultural Products Trade". *Journal of International Trade*, No. 9 (2005).

Ma T., & Chen J., "The Role of Virtual Water Trade in Solving Chinese and Global Water Crises". *Ecological Economy*, No. 11 (2006).

Machado, G., Schaeffer, R. & Worrell, E. "Energy and Carbon Embodied in the International Trade of Brazil: An Input-output Approach". *Ecological Economics*, Vol. 39 (2001), 409–424.

Miller, R., & Blair, P., *Input-Output Analysis: Foundations and Extension.* 1985. Prentice Hall, Englewood Cliffs, USA.

Muradian, R., O'Conner M. & Martinez-Alier, J., "Embodied Pollution in Trade: Estimating the "Environment Load Displacement" of Industrialized Countries". *Ecological Economics*, Vol. 41, No. 1 (2002), 51–67.

Novo, P., Garrido, A. & Valera-Ortega, C., "Are Virtual Water "Flow" in Spanish Grain Trade Consistent with Relative Water Scarcity?" *Ecological Economics*, Vol. 68 (2009), 1454–1464.

Pearce, F., *When Rivers Dry up: Water — The Defining Crisis of the Twenty-first Century*, translated by Zhang X., collated by Zheng G. and Liu S. 2009. Intellectual Property Publishing House, Beijing.

Peters, G. P., & Hertwich, E. G., "Pollution Embodied in Trade: The Norwegian Case". *Global Environmental Change*, Vol. 16 (2006), 379–387.

Qi Y., Li H. & Xu M., "An Estimation of Embodied Carbon in China's Import and Export". *China Population, Resources and Environment*, No. 3 (2008).

Rees. W. E., "Ecological Footprint and Appropriated Carry Capacity: What Urban Economics Leaves Out". *Environment and Urbanization*, Vol. 4, No. 2 (1992), 121–130.

Rees. W. E., "Revisiting Carry Capacity: Area-based Indicators of Sustainability". *Population and Environment*, Vol. 17, No. 3 (1996). 195–215.

Rees. W. E., & Wackernagel, M., "Ecological Footprint and Appropriated Capacity: Measuring the Natural Capital Requirements of the Human Economy". In *Investing in Natural Capital: The Ecological Economics Approach to Sustainability*. A. M., Jansson, M. Hammer, C. Folke & R. Costanza (eds.). (1994). ISEE/Island Press, Washington, D.C., pp. 362–390.

Sánchze-Chóliz, J., & Duarte, R., "CO_2 Emissions Embodied in International Trade: Evidence for Spain". *Energy Policy*, Vol. 32, No. 18, (2004), 1999–2005.

Shiu, B., & Harriss, R. C., "The Role of CO_2 Embodiment in US-China Trade". *Energy Policy*, Vol. 34 (2006), 4063–4068.

The Chinese Input–Output Association, *China Water Resources Input-Output Tables of 2002* (2005).

The Compilation Committee for the Chinese Natural Resources Book Series, *Chinese Natural Resources Book Series (Water Resources)*. 1995. China Environmental Science Press, Beijing.

Velázquez, E., "Water Trade in Andalusia Virtual Water: An Alternative Way to Manage Water Use". *Ecological Economics*, Vol. 63 (2007), 201–208.

Wang X., Xu Z. & Long A., "A Preliminary Calculation and Analysis of China's Water Footprint in 2000". *Journal of Glaciology and Geocryology*, No. 10 (2005).

Xiang X., Zhou X. & Zhou J., "A Research on the Calculation Method of Virtual Water in Industrial Products". *Journal of Dalian University of Technology*, No. 2 (2006).

Zhang Y., "A Research on Environmental Cost Assessment and Countermeasures in China's Foreign Trade", Research Report of Key Research Projects Sponsored by the Chinese Academy of Social Sciences (No. 0700000470), March 2009.

Zhao X., Yang Z. & Chen B., "China's Virtual Water Trade and Consumption Research Based on Input-Output Analysis Technology". *Journal of Natural Resources*, Vol. 24, No. 2 (2009).

Zhu Q., & Gao J., "A Research on the Virtual Water of China's Foreign Trade: Analysis Based on Input and Output". *China Soft Science*, No. 5 (2009).

Part III
Several Fundamental Problems Concerning Green Development Policies

This part includes Chapters 8–10 and focuses on several fundamental problems concerning green development policies.

Chapter 8 discusses environment value evaluation methods that we should pay attention to when making green development policies. In order to break away from the extensive mode of economic growth and realize green development, policymakers must fully understand and evaluate the loss and gain of protecting the ecological environment and economic growth so as to make trade-offs and policy choices. Understanding and application of the environment value evaluation methods discussed in this chapter can help policymakers and decision-makers evaluate the following problems in a more scientific way when choosing between protection and growth: (1) comparison between ecological environment benefits and protection costs; (2) the impact of protection strategy (or program) on the society and the poor; and (3) how the ecological environment benefits share the protection costs between relevant interest groups through compensation.

Chapter 9 emphasizes the need to include environment factors into efficiency (productivity) evaluation. In particular, it clarifies the different methods for the theory of distance function and directional distance function to deal with undesirable output. Productivity refers to the rate of output to input. Output and input in the traditional sense are rare resources with a price signal and concern no external problems. As a result, undesirable output like environment pollution was often ignored in previous studies of productivity. With the advancement of industrialization, pollutant emissions have reached or even gone beyond the level that the environment can tolerate. Pollution has affected and even threatened the normal production and life of the people, while fresh air and water have become rare products. However, the externality of pollution emissions makes it really difficult to price the environment quality. The methods discussed in this chapter can help solve the above-mentioned efficiency evaluation problems and provide references to relevant policy-making.

Chapter 10 introduces the established international calculation methods for greenhouse gas emission and reviews previous studies of greenhouse gas emissions in China. Finally, it examines problems that we should note in applying these methods, such as the determination of CO_2 emission factors, the determination of economic activity level in the Chinese society, and other sources of emissions.

Chapter 8

Evaluation of Environmental Value: Assessment of Ecological Environment Benefits

Xiao Zhang

Institute of Quantitative & Technical Economics,
Chinese Academy of Social Sciences

1. Introduction

Protecting the environment and the ecological system featuring global or regional significance and biodiversity and, at the same time, maintaining sustainable and equitable growth is a new development goal for a society that tries to break away from its traditional development patterns (which was simply about GDP growth). To realize such a "win–win" goal, it is necessary to fully understand and evaluate the loss and gain of protection and growth so as to make trade-offs and policy choices, which is a significant area in studies of environmental economics.

When choosing between protection and growth, policymakers and decision-makers often face the following problems: (1) comparison between ecological environment benefits and costs of protection; (2) the impact of the protection strategy (or programs) on the society and the poor; and (3) how the ecological environment benefits share the protection costs through compensation between different interest groups. To deal with these problems, we must first carry out the benefit evaluation of the environmental policies, or the economic value evaluation of changes of the ecological environment quality.

This chapter probes into the economic theory about the environmental value evaluation, namely, welfare economics, methods and application range of environmental value evaluation, and several related cases. First, this chapter introduces several basic concepts and key problems concerning environmental value evaluation. Second, this chapter reviews the consumer welfare theory and discusses how economists develop standard empirical approaches by applying this theory and evaluate the welfare impact of changes of environmental quality, which are similar to those of commodity prices. When discussing the uncertainty of the world, the author first defines the general problems about welfare measures then explores the conceptual relationship between WTP and WTA of individuals before discussing preference, estimability, and estimates of WTP and WTA. Finally, as most non-market value evaluation is about the measurement of the impact of changes of a specific item (for instance, the level of an environment indicator) and the absence of an exchange market for environmental items and services makes it impossible to directly estimate the demand function by means of observing consumer behaviors, an alternative solution is to deduce individual value choices in accordance with some other assumed market information. Therefore, when discussing various methods of environmental value evaluation, much of the discussion is about how to transmit and disclose environmental value by using indirect information or figure out the estimates of the benefits of ecological environment policies.

2. Key Points of the Evaluation of Environmental Value

2.1. *Evaluation of non-market value*

Non-market value is a value concept in contrast to market value. The biggest difference between non-market value and market value lies in the different market conditions for the realization of transactions. Market value refers to the asset value that should be realized on a well-developed and open market, an estimate with support of open markets (the valuation elements required for the evaluation come from the market and the evaluation results are recognized by the market). Non-market value refers to the fair value realized by the asset on private markets. Its transaction does not necessarily meet with the requirements of open markets or require the support from open markets, and most valuation elements to be used in the evaluation process do not come from the open markets either. It does not stress the maximum usage of asset or the asset value that can be realized on the market. Instead, it stresses the utility or possible benefits of the asset under specific conditions. Here, fair value does not refer to fairness on the open market. It refers to fairness for a specific buyer and seller. Given the differences of preference and financial strength between a specific buyer and seller, the prices they are willing to pay for commodities or services or their preference for the commodities or services may be different from those of others. Therefore, non-market value may be said to be the estimation or judgement of specific buyer or seller for the commodities or services they have obtained in a specific economic behavior.

Under the current market economy framework, the difficulty of evaluating the environment, ecological resources, and their service values or monetizing them lies in the lack of observable ecological environment market prices based on the principle of exchange in the current market system. For instance, people may be interested in the monetary value of those protected trees in the urban landscape while such a value may be different from that of the trees that can be directly used by the local farmers. Similarly, generally speaking, large-scale ecological diversity protection may prevent the abuse of ecological resources (including mining and woodcutting in protected zones). In contrast to the benefits from selling the ore or the wood, how should we evaluate the monetary value of protecting the ecological diversity? To answer such questions, the first thing we need is a conceptual framework for people's preference of ecological resources. To use a general model framework of family behavior, it is imperative to define the relative value concept, a concept originating from the welfare theory in neoclassic economics.

The general expression of the neoclassical welfare theory holds that Pareto Optimality can be achieved through levying emissions taxes (which are equal to the marginal damage of pollution) when there's pollution in producing certain item. However, the social optimal tax rate is determined by the structure of individual preference. Therefore, in order to understand the preference of actual collection of emissions taxes, it is necessary to examine people's individual behavior and take it as the basis for the calculation of a proper emissions tax rate. More generally, non-market value also needs an estimation of the behavior function. As behavior function can fully reveal people's choices, it can be used to calculate the marginal monetary value or discrete variation value.

As monetary value plays an important part throughout the following discussion, the starting point of environment value evaluation is the definition of the monetary value. Here, the value concept is an individualized and supreme right based on consumers. Therefore, the preference of the people (such as consumption level, requirements for the environment or physical health) will reveal information of relevant values. Of course, any external influence element may change the selected results. Prices can lead to changes of consumption levels indirectly while policies can directly influence the changes of the environment quality, and thereby the individual welfare levels. The implementation of any policy will cause direct or indirect consequences. To monetize such consequences, we need to (1) define the baseline and target line for the implementation of the policies and (2) calculate the individual Willingness To Pay (WTP) so as to reach the target line and the individual Willingness To Accept (WTA) in giving up the target line. There are two key points here: first, the monetary evaluation here is about specific things. For instance, it is impossible to define a person's monetary evaluation of "clean drinking water" in its general sense. However, we can define the value of the influence of reducing carcinogenic pollutants on health under current conditions. Second, it is closely related to WTP and WTA, which are comparable to the income level, and the preference of the baseline and the target line. For instance, the price drop in a certain commodity will in turn influence consumption, and potentially increase welfare. Here, the starting point is the original price and the target line is the new price. WTP refers to the amount of money a person is willing to pay after giving up the new price (the lower price). For them, giving up the new price means that they can obtain a higher welfare level. WTA refers to the compensation a person needs because of the price drop, and the compensation is equivalent to obtaining greater welfare. As WTP and WTA can transform preference information into equivalent monetary amount, they are important concepts in the environment value evaluation while "preference" has always been considered to be inherent in individuals and unable to be quantized. The choice of alternative elements in individual preference function is the key to the determination of WTP and WTA. Let us take the above price drop as example again, if there are a lot of inexpensive commodities which can act as substitutes for a new and cheap commodity, the commodity will be relatively unique and the price drop will bring down the evaluation. When undertaking monetization evaluation of environment items, it is vital to establish the substitutability between market items and environment items. When measuring an individual's WTP and WTA for environment variable changes (often related to "welfare measurement" and "welfare influence"), much of the work is about non-market value evaluation (Phaneuf & Requate, 2010).

2.2. WTP and WTA

2.2.1. WTP

When a consumer buys a certain item at the market price, the price paid directly reveals the bottom amount of money of his greatest WTP, that is, a consumer's WTP for certain item, at least equates to the price that he pays for it (Markandya *et al.*, 2002), as shown by a simplified Marshallian Demand Curve in Fig. 8.1. For a commodity or service (demand curve *DD*) in Fig. 8.1, P_0 represents the shadow price, Q_0 represents purchase quantity, $P_0 \times Q_0$

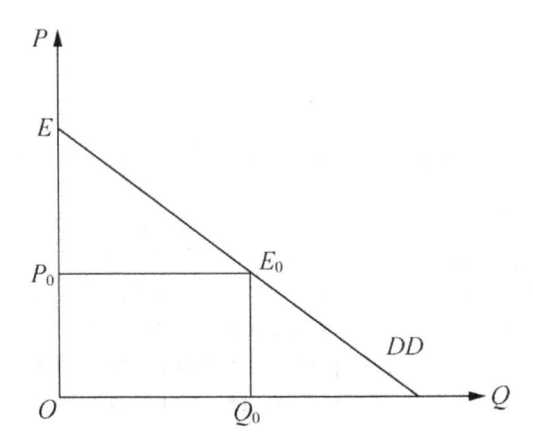

Fig. 8.1   A simple diagram of consumer surplus and WTP

represents actual pay or the area $OP_0E_0Q_0$, the amount that the consumer is willing to pay is the area OEE_0Q_0, while the difference between the consumer's WTP and his actual pay (the area P_0EE_0 in Fig. 8.1) is the consumer surplus. This means: consumer's WTP = consumer surplus + consumer's actual pay. For a relevant exposition, see Yining & Zheng (1995).

We define WTP as the largest monetary amount that an individual is willing to pay for obtaining a certain benefit or avoiding a certain damage. In many cases, WTP reflects the degree of an individual's preference for a certain benefit or damage. Such a preference is based upon an individual's value orientation toward certain items, and the maximum of WPT is an expression of his value judgment.

The WTP for a certain environment policy (or policies) indicates the consumer's paying willingness for improving the environment quality. In essence, it reflects the impact of changes of the environment quality on individual welfare.

2.2.2. *WTA*

Similar to WTP, WTA refers to the minimum monetary compensation an individual considers accepting for giving up a certain benefit or incurring a certain damage. WTA reflects a value expression of benefit or damage. Similarly, when a consumer sells a certain item at an acceptable market price, the amount of money he charges directly indicates the maximum WTA of the consumer for abandoning the use of that item (Markandya *et al.*, 2002).

2.2.3. *Distinction between WTP and WTA*

With clear assumptions about distribution of property rights, WTP and WTA are interchangeable when people account for their choices by using welfare economics analysis. Distinction between WTP and WTA is necessary in discussions of the application of environment problems for it can identify (1) whether those pollution victims have the rights to require reduction of pollution or obtain damage compensation and (2) if a negative answers means they will have to "purchase" pollution reduction. Such a distinction is closely related to the ethical debate about the responsibilities and rights of the polluters and pollution victims. In addition, such a distinction is of much practical significance. For instance, if the willingness of neighbors to accept compensation obviously outweighs the WTP for the prevention of exploitation, a policy that intends to choose exploitation may be more easily accepted or implemented than a policy that favors protection. Therefore, research on the distinction between WTP and WTA and corresponding practice has been an important issue for environmental economics scholars over the past three decades.

Our discussion mainly focuses on the basic behavior model, identification path, and the convergence and separation of estimation of WTP and WTA. Early theoretical work included Willig's (1976) concept of WTP and WTA. Building on Willig (1976), Randall & Stoll (1980) argue that, if commodities can be separated, the market is fully competitive, transaction costs are relatively low, and price flexibility is small; compared with the errors caused by the method of estimation, there are relatively fewer errors if the Marshallian Consumer Surplus is used instead. At this moment, the Compensating Variation (CV) is very close to the Equivalent Variation (EV), while WTP and WTA are almost equal. However, it is noted that, in practice, the estimate of WTA is higher than that of WTP. For instance, the survey of Horowitz & McConnell (2002) finds that, on average, WTA is seven times higher than WTP. That conclusion was based on a stimulation summary of a large amount of research literature, and the methods used in the literature included both neoclassical economics theoretical paradigms and other paradigms. The summary revealed why the estimates of WTP and WTA are so different. Hanemann (1991) believes that the difference between the static neoclassical economics model we used and the people's gut feelings lead to the difference between WTP and WTA.

The separation between WTP and WTA in the first place originated from the budget constraint, namely, WTP is constrained by individual income while WTA is not (Phaneuf & Requate, 2010).

2.2.4. *Information problem regarding the evaluation of WTP and WTA*

The evaluation of environment benefits requires information in the following three aspects:

First, when evaluating the environment benefits of public policies, the benefits must be able to explain the reservation price relative to individual welfare. In particular, if the individual WTP implemented toward certain environment policy is larger than that toward another policy, does it mean the choice of the former policy is better than the choice of the latter policy?

Second, when people are asked about their unconditioned WTP on a certain kind of environmental improvement (caused by the implementation of certain environmental policy) or the WTP according to which an environmental policy is made and the expenditure of the policy is determined, can the existing stimulation which twists WTP considerably influence the authenticity of WTP? If the answer is negative, the expectation to accept the WTP of environmental improvement (or the improvement of other public goods) should be high.

Finally, when taking into consideration the political feasibility, is there any method we can use to figure out the problem design of the presumed WTP which is similar to that of unconditioned WTP while acquiring the WTP estimation of the listener when the question is asked? As assumptions are necessary when evaluating "non-use" value, is there non-use value evaluation which can be made without assumptions? Like the so-called "existence value"?

3. Welfare Economics and Measures of Welfare Changes

3.1. *Part of the theoretical basis for environmental economics: Welfare economics*

Welfare economics is mainly composed of three propositions.

The first theorem of welfare economics states that, supposing each individual and company is a self-interested price maker, the competition equilibrium is Pareto Optimality. Its theory can date back to relevant exposition in Adam Smith's *The Wealth of Nations*, i.e., everyone enables the substantial increase of social income through their labor. Although usually he neither intends to advance public interests nor has an idea of how much he actually helps the increase of public interests, he actually only cares about his own gains. The first theorem answers the following question: in a competitive economic system, an individual only cares about his own utility determined by his consumption; a company only cares about its own profits. Competition equilibrium is about common interests. The so-called "common interests" refer to Pareto Optimality instead of the maximum GDP.[1]

The second theorem of welfare economics states that, supposing each individual and producer is a self-interested price taker, if each individual or company is allowed a proper once-and-for-all taxation and transfer, almost any Pareto Optimality equilibrium can be achieved through the competition mechanism. The second theorem puts forward the problem of fair distribution and answers the following question: in an economic system, as the distribution scheme is made by the ruler, shall we realize the common interests through a somehow flexible market mechanism or simply cancel such a mechanism? The first theorem of welfare economics obviously neglects the preferences of consumers. In practical economic life, the preferences of consumers are constantly changing. Meanwhile, the first theorem assumes that competition works while monopoly is almost everywhere in reality. In addition, the first theorem implicitly assumes the absence of externality or public goods, which is also untrue. Finally, the biggest problem with the first theorem lies in its neglect of distribution for there may be more than one result of Pareto Optimality and one Pareto Optimality cannot guarantee fair distribution of commodities.

The second theorem of welfare economics is built upon market mechanism. Market failure problems like externality and public goods can be solved through certain adjustment of the market mechanism. For instance, Pigou's partial equilibrium analysis framework makes a monetized estimation of the costs and benefits caused by externality, and balances the variation between private benefits and social benefits by imposing an appropriate amount of taxes. Focusing on the reciprocity of externality, Coase argued that compensation should be achieved through negotiation by means of clarifying property rights (pollution rights). However, the

---

[1] Pareto Optimality, or "Pareto Efficiency". See the entry of "Welfare Economics" in *The New Palgrave Dictionary of Economics*, Vol. 4, Economic Science Press, 1996, p. 962.

Coasian Theorem obviously ignores the possibility that the too high transaction costs of the gaining party and the damaged party and the asymmetric information of both parties may make the negotiation impossible may make it fail, let alone the possibility that there is no market entity for the damaged party (Zhang, 2005).

The third theorem of welfare economics states that, there are no Arrow (K. J. Arrow) social welfare functions which satisfy universality, Pareto uniformity, independence, and non-dictatorship. The third theorem answers the following question: is there an alternative wealth-related distribution scheme originating from private interests (real social interests)? It seems that much discussion about the third theorem of welfare economics only leads to a barely optimistic conclusion: there are no reasonable and reliable methods which can aggregate personal preference or there are no reasonable and reliable methods which can solve the distribution problem.[2]

Starting from the ethics of welfare economics, the values of environmental economics comply with the following arguments (James *et al.*, 1986):

(1) Attention must be paid to everyone in the society for social welfare is a function of individual welfare level;
(2) An individual is the best judge of his own welfare and the one who tries to maximize his welfare (Huang, 1991);[3]
(3) If a change increases the welfare of some people without reducing the welfare of any other people, the change shall be regarded as having increased the overall welfare of the society;
(4) More social or individual welfare is more desirable than less social or individual welfare.

---

[2] See the entry of "Welfare Economics" in *The New Palgrave Dictionary of Economics*, Vol. 4, pp. 961–967.

[3] Individual welfare is generally seen as individual happiness or joy. Usually, individual preferences are taken as the indicator of individual welfare. When the condition "an individual is the best judge of his own welfare and the one who tries to maximize his welfare" is recognized and accepted, the measurability of welfare and that of utility is consistent. "Utility" is sometimes used to measure the subjective satisfaction and sometimes indicate objective choices or preferences. In most cases, we assume utility function is in existence and use it as an objective indicator of individual preferences (Huang, 1991).

For an environmental economist, the above basic values of welfare economics are apparently imperfect. For one thing, it has a bias with people as the only center and the social evaluation will ignore the damage of the environment on other species. For another, "the society" does not include considerations for the interests of future generations of humankind. Therefore, environmental economics needs new or other ethics and values so as to complement or replace the values of welfare economics. Apart from the above-mentioned four arguments, some welfare economists put forward that environmental items and services should be included in the public welfare system.

3.2. *Measurement of welfare changes*

According to what principles does a rational consumer pick his favorite commodity out of a commodity pool? That is a typical consumer question. The Marshallian Demand Curve provides an answer to the consumer question. The Marshallian Demand Curve is

$$X_i = x_i\,(P,M) \tag{8.1}$$

The demand of X_i is the function of the price vector P and the income vector M. It is an answer to the following utility maximum problem:

$$\begin{aligned} &max\ U = U(X)\\ &\text{s. t. } \Sigma p_i x_i = M \end{aligned} \tag{8.2}$$

Here, X refers to the commodity quantity vector $(X = x_1, \ldots, x_i, \ldots, x_n)$.

For a given commodity X_2, the budget constraint of the consumer is a straight line: $M = p_1 X_1 + p_2 X_2$ or $X_2 = M/p_2 - p_1/p_2 \cdot X_1$.

Here, X_1 represents all the other commodities and p_1 and p_2 represent corresponding commodity prices. The optimal choice of the consumer is the point of contact of the indifference curve[4] and the budget constraint (Hanley & Spash, 1993).

Studies show there are differences between the price a consumer intends to pay and the price he actually pays when he buys a commodity.

---

[4] If utility function is continuous and strictly concave, the indifference curve is smooth and convex to the origin (Hanley and Spash, 1993).

Consumption is realized only when the price he intends to pay (WTP) is higher than the price he actually pays. Apparently, in the case of consumer surplus, the lowering of the buying price will increase the net benefits of the consumer; in contrast, increasing the price will reduce the net benefits of the consumer (Hanley & Spash, 1993).

3.2.1. *The Marshallian Consumer's Surplus*

A. Marshall found that the monetized consumer welfare equals the "real" utility surplus. In Fig. 8.2, Curve D represents the individual Marshallian Demand Curve,[5] the area P_0PC represents the net benefits of the consumer who purchases Q amount of certain commodity at the price P_0; the area $OPCQ$ represents overall benefits, while the difference between overall benefits and net benefits (the area OP_0CQ) represents the costs of the consumer who purchases q amount of certain commodity at the price of P_0.

Marshallian Consumer's Surplus (MCS) measures the consumer welfare after comparing the two following extreme cases, that is, the consumer can afford to buy a certain commodity (involving purchase) at a given price and the commodity cannot be supplied (involving no purchase). As a matter of fact, as pointed out by Huang (1991), consumer's

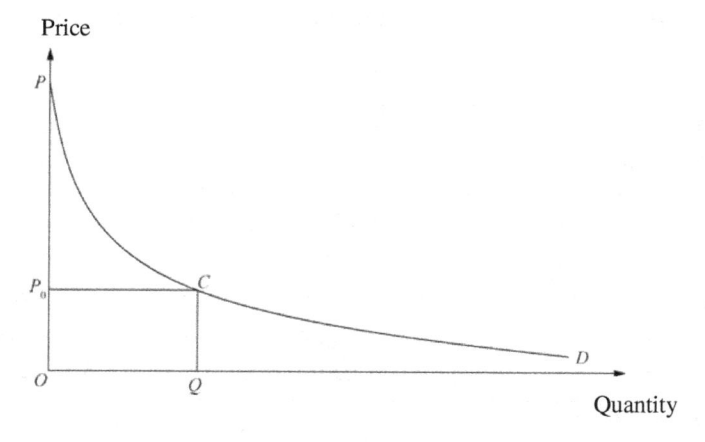

Fig. 8.2   Marshallian Consumer's Surplus

---

[5] Marshallian Demand Curve assumes that income is constant and, given the demand amount of the commodity, utility changes are allowed for different commodity prices.

surplus may not necessarily be limited to the comparison of the two cases of "involving purchase" and "involving no purchase". More often than not, it refers to the welfare measurement with price changes.

3.2.2. *Measurement of Hicks consumer welfare changes*

J.R. Hicks identified four methods for measurement of consumer welfare changes against price changes: Compensating Variation (CV), Compensating Surplus (CS), Equivalent Variation (EV), and Equivalent Surplus (ES) (Hanley & Spash, 1993).

The consumption amount must remain constant if we attempt to measure the welfare changes against price changes by using CS and ES. In contrast, what EV and CV measure are the consumption amount a consumer may freely choose when prices change.

Supposing the price drops, let us have a look at what may happen if we use these methods to measure the consumer welfare changes. What CV measures is the amount of money that can be deducted from consumer income when the consumer maintains his utility level U_0 as that before the price drop (Markandya *et al.*, 2002). What CS measures is the amount of money that can be deducted from consumer income when the consumer still wants to buy the same amount of commodities while maintaining his utility level U_0 as that before the price drop (Hanley & Spash, 1993). What EV measures is the amount of money that should be paid to the consumer when the increase of his income leads him to a new utility level U_1, that is, when the extra income prevents his current income from changing with the changes of his utility levels (Markandya *et al.*, 2002).What ES measures is the extra amount of money that should be paid to the consumer when the consumer still buys the same amount of commodities as that before the price drop and the income increase leads him to a new utility level(U_1) (Hanley & Spash, 1993).

3.2.3. *Choices of different methods for consumer welfare change measurement*

There are many methods for measuring consumer welfare changes through consumer surplus. In actual application, the choice is determined by whether relevant information is adequate and what the problem is about.

The CV approach applies to consumer welfare changes caused by price changes because of taxation, subsidy, or tariff. Besides, it also applies to real compensation for damage (or actual extraction of pay from benefits). If the compensation (or pay) is not actually implemented, the CV approach does not apply to measurement of consumer welfare changes.

The CS approach applies more to the consumer welfare damage (reduction of consumer surplus) caused by rationing, price restriction, or fixed supply for it mainly concerns restriction on commodity quantity but not relative prices.

If we only care for relative damage and benefits but do not make actual compensation (or pay), the Marshallian consumer surplus (MCS) measurement has many advantages over other measures (Huang, 1991).

Willig, (1976) put forward several similarities between consumer welfare change measures (see Fig. 8.3).[6] In Fig. 8.3, the curve D represents the Marshallian Demand Curve and the curves $H(U_0)$ and $H(U_1)$ represent the Hicksian Compensated Demand Curve, HCDC). When the price P_0 drops to P_1, the measurement result of Hicksian CV is the area $x + y$; the

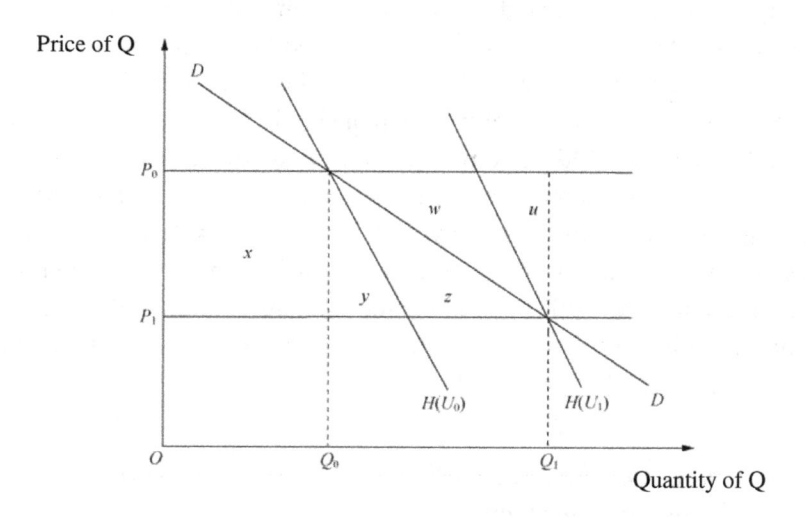

Fig. 8.3   Similarity between Willig Consumer Surplus Measures

---

[6] Hanley and Spash, 1993, Chart 2-6, p. 40. Garrod and Willis, 1999, Chart 2-2, p. 46.

measurement result of Hicksian EV is the area $x + y + z + w$, the measurement result of MCS is the area $x + y + z$, and the change range of consumer surplus shifts from CV to EV.

Freeman (1993) defined Hicksian CV according to the expenditure function. Its calculation equation is as follows:

$$CV = e(p_0, u_0) - e(p_1, u_0) > 0 = M - e(p_0, u_0) \tag{8.3}$$

Here, M represents fixed income value, $M = \Sigma_i p_i q_i$; Q represents the quantity vector $(Q = q_1, \ldots, q_i, \ldots, q_n)$, or $Q = q$; P represents the price vector $(P = p_1, \ldots, p_i, \ldots, p_n)$, or $P = p$; and expenditure function $e = e(P, u_0)$ represents the monetized expenditure amount under specific utility level. As a higher utility level can be achieved if expenditure M is spent on the new price, we can get the following equation:

$$M = e(p_1, u_1)$$

If we substitute it into (8.3), we can get:

$$CV = e(p_1, u_1) - e(p_1, u_0) = \int_{p_1}^{p_0} H(p, u_0) \, dp \tag{8.4}$$

Equation (8.4) indicates that although CV is defined according to the utility level U_0 before the price drop, in practical calculation, CV can be calculated, based on the new price, according to the monetary expenditure needed for the shift from the original utility level to the new utility level.

In the same manner, Freeman (1993) put forward the calculation equation of EV as:

$$EV = e(p_0, u_1) - e(p_0, u_0) > 0 = e(p_0, u_1) - M \tag{8.5}$$

Although EV is defined according to money equivalent during the shift from the original utility level to the new level, EV can also be calculated according to the expenditure changes related to price changes with a given new utility level U_1. That is,

$$EV = e(p_0, u_1) - e(p_1, u_1) = \int_{p_1}^{p_0} H(p, u_1) \, dp \tag{8.6}$$

When we consider the measures of the impact of environmental quality changes on consumer welfare (or utility), Q represents environmental quality, U_1 and U_2 represent the different utility levels related to the environmental quality, and P represents the pollution level. In Fig. 8.3, the Preventative Expenditure (PE) of Q_0 due to the drop of the pollution level is the area x. Bartik (1988) argued that if the changes of Q are really small or the household demand is rigid (lack of flexibility), in contrast to CV measurement, PE is the best similarity estimation of the welfare benefits. In particular, when the demand curve is linear, we get the following simplified equation:

$$[CV - PE(Q_0) / PE(Q_0) = \text{area } y / \text{area } x = \frac{1}{2}(\Delta p / p)(-\varepsilon) \qquad (8.7)$$

Here, ε represents Hicksian Demand Price Elasticity.[7]

3.3. *Relationship between welfare changes and WTP*

The maximum individual WTP and the minimum WTA of a certain environmental asset change level can be estimated by the variation of individual monetary expenditure. Of course, consumers must maintain constancy according to the satisfaction degree (welfare) when the estimation is made. Once the environment changes, the maximum WTP and the minimum WTA may become a monetary signal of individual welfare changes.

In accordance with the basic economics characteristics of products, the changes of environmental items within the specified range will influence individual welfare in different ways. Most environmental items are public items or quasi-public goods. Therefore, as mentioned above, when changes of environmental items influence individual welfare, we cannot control or restrict anyone from using or utilizing environmental items (non-excludability). Generally speaking, with these special items (public items), individuals may obtain or avoid several changes of items through payment or accepting compensation: (1) price drop; (2) price increase; (3) possible improvement of quantity or quality; and (4) possible degradation of quantity or quality. Under the four conditions, the maximum WTP

---

[7] Garrod & Willis, 1999, p. 47.

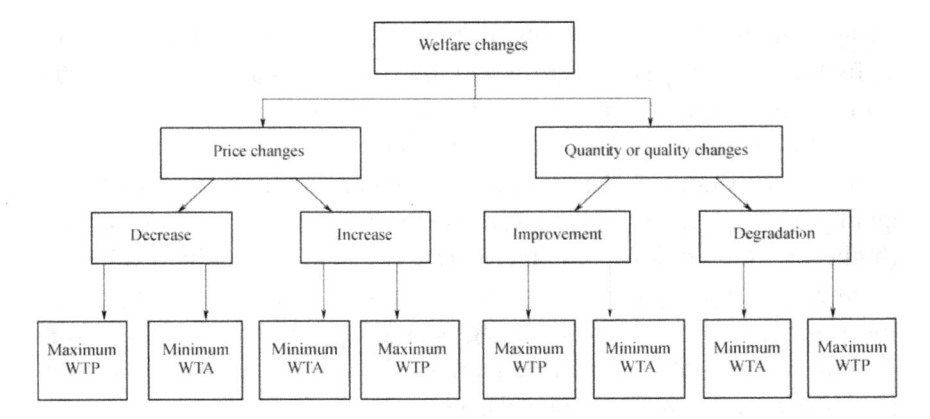

Fig. 8.4   Calculation flowchart of welfare changes.

Source: Markandya *et al.* (2002), p. 298. Fig. 8.2

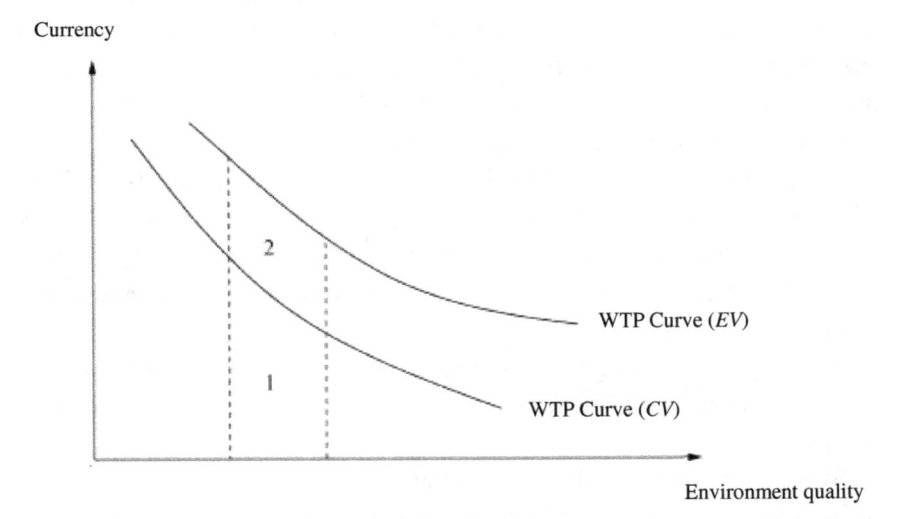

Fig. 8.5   WTP Curve of environment quality

Source: Johansson (2000), Fig. 8.3.

and the minimum WTA are calculated through CV, EV, CS, and ES (Markandya *et al.*, 2002), which can be seen in Fig. 8.4.

In contrast, what the different approaches in Fig. 8.3 measure are the consumer welfare changes caused by price changes, while what the different approaches in Fig. 8.5 measure are the consumer welfare changes caused by changes of environmental quality. In Fig. 8.5, when environmental quality shifts from z_0 to z_1, the consumer welfare (surplus) changes related to the shift are calculated by area 1 (in contrast to the CV curve) or the area (1 + 2) (in contrast to the EV curve) (Johansson, 2000).

A simple example is the air quality issue in a region. Supposing the air quality in this region ranges from 0 (lowest air quality level) to 100 (highest air quality level) and the current regional air quality level is 50. A random sample questionnaire survey on the WTP of the respondents for a minor improvement of the regional air quality (for instance, from the current 50 to 52) is conducted among the local residents. Let us suppose the average WTP among the respondents is 20 yuan. In another survey, the presumed air quality improvement is from 50 to 54, and the average WTP is 30 yuan. Judging from the average WTP differences, it can be inferred when the corresponding utility level at which the air quality of 50 is maintained, the average WTP for the air quality improvement from 52 to 54 is 10 yuan. In Fig. 8.5, there are two points, z_0 and z_1, on the compensated demand curve and the original individual utility level remains constant to the right of z_0. The WTP for the first air quality improvement (from 50 to 52) is larger than that of the other (from 52 to 54), which means the slope of the demand curve is downward. In this way, if we continue to inquire on the air quality improvement from 50 to 56 or 58, we can get other "points" on the compensated demand curve (Johansson, 2000).

If it only takes a program to increase the utility of another person, CV will be a kind of payment while price differences will be a kind of compensation.

Another important problem in welfare economics is the calculation of welfare changes. There are two methods for such a calculation, namely, "preference revealing" and "preference expression". The "preference revealing" approach aims to examine how to reflect and "reveal" a consumer's consumption preference and use such information to calculate the monetized consumer welfare changes by adjusting the actual consumption behaviors of another group of consumers when the consumer faces quantity (quality) changes of prices or environmental items.

The "preference expression" approach directly inquires about the consumer's WTP and WTA for possible price or quantity changes. The basis of such an approach lies in the consumer's account and expression of his preferences when he is directly inquired about his value adaptation (Markandya *et al.*, 2002).

4. Categories of Environmental Values

The lack of a market price of an item means the lack of a market price which can reveal the minimum of a consumer's largest WTP and the maximum of his smallest WTA. In this case, there will be an applicable general criterion and a reference for the evaluation of an individual's value orientation for this item. At this point, in order to assess[8] people's WTP and WTA or obtain an individual's monetary estimates for the value orientation of a non-market item, we need to select and apply other methods (Markandya *et al.*, 2002).

It has been proven that individual welfare is not only determined by a person's consumption of private items and products and services provided by the government but also determined by their enjoyment of the quantity and quality of non-market items and services provided by the resource-environment system. For example, health, visual comfort,[9] outdoor recreation, and so on.

Freeman (1993) defined "economic value" in the resource-environment system as some changes in the resource-environment system and its calculation is the impact of the changes in the resource-environment system on humankind welfare. At the same time, Freeman believed that, even if the economic value which centers on humankind cannot exclude the consideration of the survival and well-being of other species, the reason why human beings make value evaluation of the survival of other species is not only because they are of use (as food or recreation) to humankind but also because of altruistic and ethical considerations. Value evaluation of the "altruistic" and "ethical" function of resources and the environment is defined as "existence value" and "non-use value".

---

[8] "Assessment" and "evaluation" are different in this chapter. Assessment involves both qualitative and quantitative work but not necessarily quantitative studies, while evaluation mainly refers to quantitative work especially economic valuation studies.

[9] Or a "comfortable" environment.

In environmental and resource economics, benefit refers to the value that human society obtains from changes of the environment or the use of certain resource, while cost refers to the value abandoned because of the occupation of resources or its being used as investment elements. Value evaluation of benefits and costs are made according to the different influence on human welfare; therefore, the concepts "economic value" and "welfare change" are interchangeable (Freeman, 1993).

According to Freeman (1993), there are three types of categorization of environmental values.

First, they can be categorized according to the forms or material types of resources and the environment, the atmosphere, such as water, forests, fishery, national parks, to name a few. Generally speaking, pollution control and managerial function divisions in the legislation and administration systems reflect this kind of value categorization of resources and the environment.

Second, they can be categorized according to the types of influence. This type of categorization is mainly made according to whether the environment and resource service flow have an impact on the related system. The influence object system includes the following:

(1) Physical health: To be specific, death and disease risks and environmental comfort (sense of taste, smell, and vision).
(2) Ecological benefits: To be specific, use value of direct markets like food and fuel; direct non-market value like leisure facilities and landscape; indirect ecological value like species diversity and gene banks; and non-use value, like existence value and heritage value.
(3) Agricultural production system, climatic system and material damage, etc. See Fig. 8.6 for specific details.

Third, they can be categorized according to economic types, that is, according to the ways in which the resource and the environmental service flow are realized, that is, realizing their influence by changing the income of the producers and the prices at which the consumers purchase products and services on the market through the market system. These products and services include health and environmental comfort. Specific examples of these are seen in Fig. 8.7.

To put it simply, environmental economists divide all the economic values into (Tietenberg, 2003): (1) Use value, or the present value of the

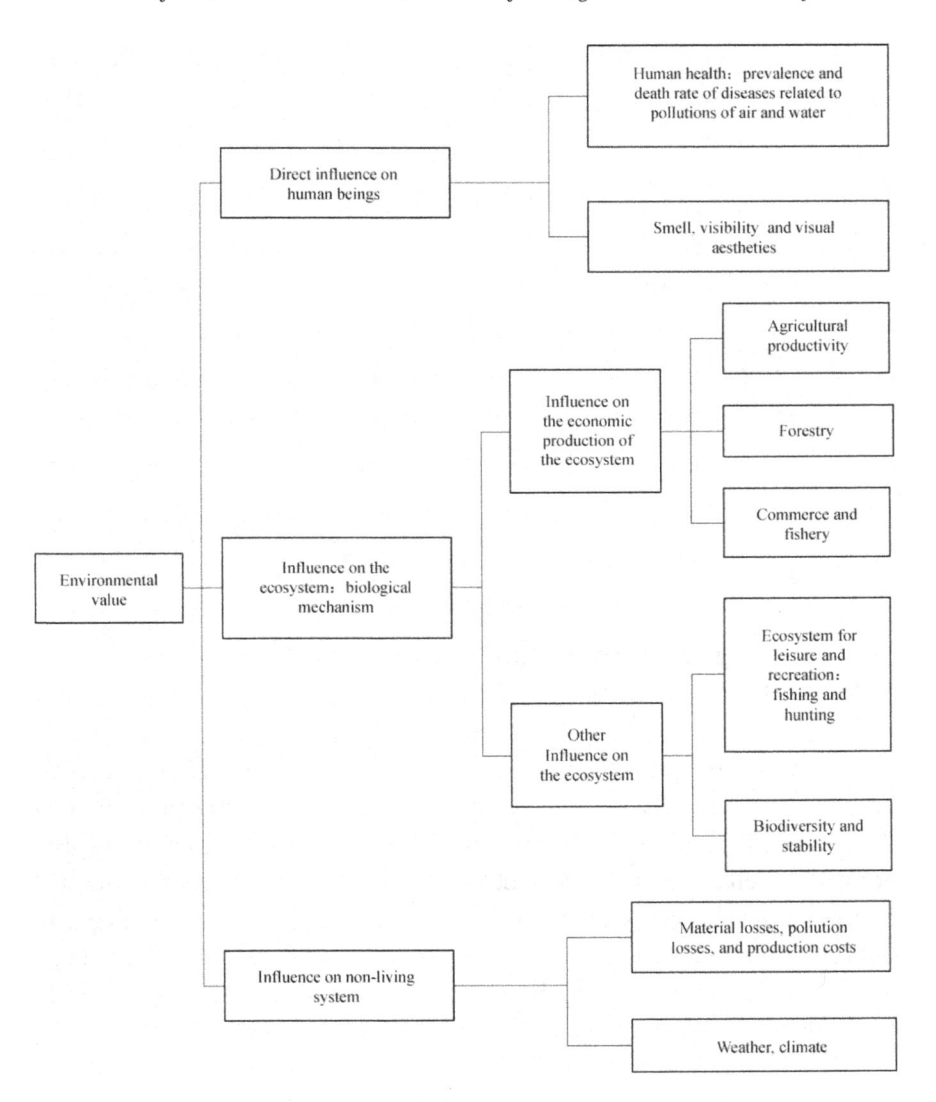

Fig. 8.6 Environmental values categorized according to influence

Source: Freeman (1993), pp. 13–14.

environment, which reflects mankind's direct use of environmental resources. Practical examples include harvest, fishing, woodcutting, irrigation, recreation (angling, hunting, etc.), landscape appreciation, etc. Ecological degradation and pollution may lead to damage of use value like air pollution, water pollution, which can increase prevalence rate and mortality while overcutting

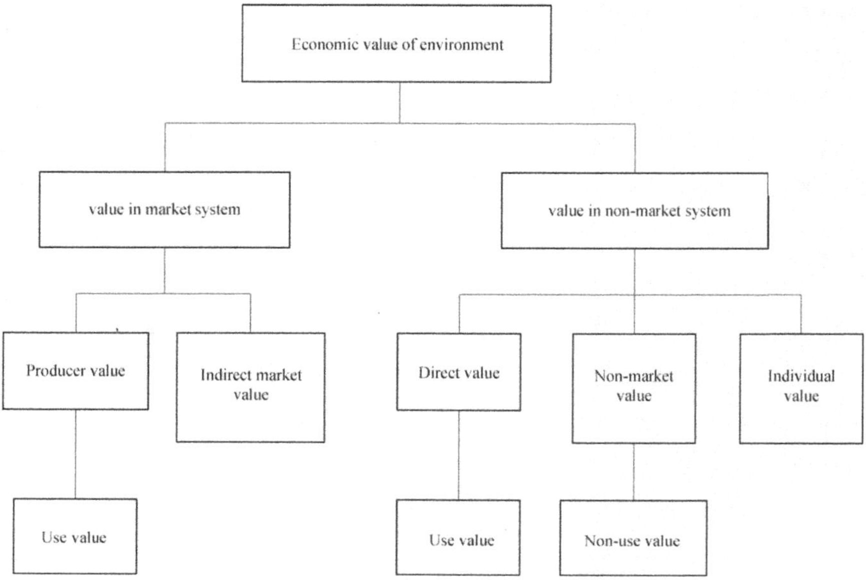

Fig. 8.7   Categorization of environmental economic value
Source: Freeman (1993), pp. 13–14.

may damage landscape harmony. (2) Non-use value, which reflects people's common expectations for paying for the improvement and protection of those unused environmental resources. For instance, the attempt of the government to sell a certain scenic spot to an individual for storage of waste will definitely incur opposition of the majority of the people for ruining and damaging such a unique environmental resource, which will thus cause huge losses. (3) Choice value, which reflects people's wish to save the environment for future use and their wish to choose a future environment.

5. Evaluation Approaches of Environmental Value and Relevant Cases

5.1. *Three types of environmental value evaluation approaches*

There are three types of evaluation approaches related to the value types discussed in Section 4 which are, (1) the market approach; (2) the preference revealing approach; and (3) the preference expression approach.

5.1.1. *The market approach*

The market approach mainly applies to the direct market use value evaluation of ecological benefits. For instance, the calculation of the impact of air quality improvement on agricultural production and the timber industry. In this case, environmental items generally enter market transactions directly as investment factors. Specific market approaches mainly include the cost function and production function approaches and the optimal model approach that imitates market behaviors. The market approach needs relatively detailed market information and data. For relevant application cases, see discussions about pollution management and the American agriculture put forth by (Adams *et al.*, 1986) and discussions about the ozone layer and American agricultural policies put forward by Kopp and Krupnick (1987).

5.1.2. *The preference revealing approach*

When there is no access to market information and data required to use the market approach, the preference revealing approach will play a unique part. Its basic starting point is that those behaviors closely related to the market can reveal the improvement of the environment of the region they live in. For instance, the water quality of a lake influences people's angling there, while the atmosphere quality influences house prices. At present, specific approaches of preference revealing widely used by environmental economists include Recreational Demand Model (including Travelling Cost model, TCM), Discrete Choice Model (DCM), Quality Pricing Model (Hedonic Pricing Model),[10] Averting Behavior

---

[10] Hedonic Pricing Model is literally translated into "Enjoyment Pricing Model", which is hard to understand. Li and Zhang (1995) and Zhang (1998) translated it into "Asset Value Approach". Considering that the main characteristic of this approach lies in its use of the quality information of different types of items and services to interpret price changes, this chapter holds that it may be more appropriate to translate it into "Quality Pricing Model". The "different types" here refer to the various non-monolithic items and services, such as opportunities, houses, cars, and computers. Different houses are constituted by a set of quality factors including building age, size, location, internal layout, overall quality, and community environment. Different cars are constituted by many quality factors such as age, make, color, engine status, and driving reliability.

Model (ABM), and Disease Cost Approach. Common approaches are the following:

(1) Travelling Cost Model: It is a recreational travel demand model for a single or multiple scenic spots mainly used for the direct use value evaluation of non-markets. It first estimates the demand function at the individual level then adds up these before estimating the overall value of the scenic spots (the value that consumers are willing to pay) by using the demand function and consumer surplus. Individual demand function assumes that individual utility is determined by the time spent in the scenic spots, travelling cost, travelling distance, income, and so on. For an application case of TCM, see relevant exposition of Freeman (1993).

(2) Hedonic Wage Studies (HWS) or Risk Wage Studies: Such studies are sometimes called Subsidy Wage Studies, the basic starting point behind which is the trade-off between high wages and the increase of casualty risks. Generally speaking, higher job risks mean higher wages. Risk Wage Studies analyze the wage increase with the increase of job risks through statistical regression of the labor market data. Such models are usually used to estimate the value changes against rather small changes of death risks and disease risks, or the value evaluation of physical health. For successful application cases of Risk Wage Studies, see the series of achievements of Viscusi (1992, 1993) and his coauthors.

(3) Asset Quality Value Studies: The "asset" here most commonly refers to houses. Such studies estimate an individual's perception of the house caused by a set of quality factors and the different utilities caused by the different combinations of that set of quality factors. Asset Quality Value Studies estimate the increase of estate value of different quality combinations through statistical regression of real estate market data. In decision-making, an individual needs to weigh in between price and quality, which reveals the marginal value of quality factors. For one thing, it describes the house price as a function of various quality factors. For another, we can get the marginal value of various quality factors through examination of specific quality factors. Among all the quality factors of houses, Asset Quality

Value Studies especially care about the environmental quality factor. Once we turn the marginal value of environmental factors (individual WTP of the improvement of environmental quality) into a function of factors such as income and environmental quality, we can get the benefit estimated value of the improvement of the environmental quality.

(4) Disease Cost Studies: It is usually used for the value estimation of the changes of the morbidity caused by environmental pollution. It should be noted that Disease Cost Studies do not estimate WTP; they estimate the changes of the market cost of diseases. Disease Cost Studies estimate two types of costs: (1) direct costs such as diagnosis expenses, disposal expenses, and boarding expenses; and (2) indirect costs such as the working hours lost because of diseases. For an application of Disease Cost Studies in China, see the works of Zheng (1999).

5.1.3. *The preference expression approach*

The preference expression approach attempts to directly calculate an individual's WTA for the improvement of the environmental quality. Unlike the preference revealing approach, the value of environmental items and services does not lie in deduction through observed behavior, instead it obtains answers about preferences by directly asking the interviewees relevant questions about value preferences and then calculates the value estimates of environmental items and services. Such approaches include Contingent Valuation (CV) Approach, Choice Expression Approach, or Conjoint Analysis (CA) Approach. At present, the approach used more often is the Contingent Valuation Approach.

The CV Approach inquires about the interviewees' largest WTP for assumed purchases through questionnaires. At present, the CV Approach is widely used in benefit valuation of the impact of the environment on physical health, valuation of non-use value (existence value) in ecological benefits, landscape value valuation in ecological benefits, valuation of changes of surface water quality, etc. Let us take the reduction of the mortality valuation caused by environmental pollution for example, in which case the respondents are asked about the amount or range they are willing to pay for the risk reduction (risk changes) after informing them of the risk baseline. Then the overall average WTP will be estimated. If we divide the overall average WTP by risk changes, we will get the estimate of the value of statistical life (VSL). For economic valuation application cases on the reduction of mortality, see the research report *Economic Valuation of Mortality Risk Reduction: Assessing the State of the Art for Policy Applications* of Alberini *et al.* (2002) and relevant articles by Cropper (1999). For application cases in China, see research reports by Wang (2003) and Zhang (2002). The application advantages of the CV Approach in ecological benefit valuation mainly lie in the valuation of non-use value. In this kind of evaluation, in terms of the different prospects (such as those of a national park or heritage site) (for example, Scene 1: To maintain the *status quo* or turn a blind eye to more resource damage; Scene 2: A management program is launched so as to terminate the ecological degradation) of a certain protected area, the respondent is usually asked about the amount or range of money he/she is willing to pay for the improvement of the ecological environment of that protected area. Or the respondents may be asked whether they are willing to spend some time and work as volunteers at an information center, as game rangers in a national park, or as tour guides so as to secure that protected area, as well as the length of time they are willing to spare. For applied examples of ecological benefit evaluation or protected area benefit evaluation, see the research of Stevens (Stevens *et al.*, 1991) and Hadker (Hadker *et al.*, 1997).

There have always been controversies and arguments about the reliability of the calculation of CV Approach. In particular, as the respondents need not make an actual monetary payment in the investigation of the CV Approach and they simply express their will under hypothetical conditions, deviations of WTP in their expression caused by deviations in description of the hypothetical conditions, accuracy of information, starting point of payment, or the "free rider" mentality are possible (Venkatachalam, 2004). Experts from NOAA argued that the solutions they had put forward, if guided by relevant investigation, would bring about sound results in evaluation of natural resource damages while no significant deviations would occur in such evaluations (NOAA, 1993).

5.2. Case studies

As regards case studies on environmental value evaluation, most published literature focus on two aspects, namely, the impact of the environment on health and service value evaluation of the ecological environment or species diversity.

5.2.1. Evaluation of the impact of environmental quality changes

Typically, changes in environmental quality will directly or indirectly influence our health, and the job of environmental economists is to estimate the value of changes of our health.

Environmental pollution sources affect our health. Along with a gradual cumulative process of influence, there is also a process of changes: good health, disease (acute or chronic), and death (Strand, 2006). Therefore, much of the literature on environmental economics focuses on evaluation of mortality and morbidity in their analysis of the influence of environmental pollution on health.

In studies of environmental economics, value evaluation of the impact of environmental pollution on health is built on effect evaluation of population health in epidemiology. By using economic methods and tools, it transforms the physical quantity of environmental pollution's impact on health into an economic quantity, the key point in which is the assessment of the value of a statistical life (against mortality) or average medical expenses (against morbidity) (Zhang, 2011).

(1) Mortality: Mortality caused by environmental pollution refers to changes of mortality rate caused by changes of environmental quality; it affects changes of individual welfare levels. An individual's evaluation of mortality changes caused by changes of the environmental quality is actually about present (or recent) but not future changes of the environmental quality.

Scholars like Krupnick (Krupnick *et al.*, 2000) hold that, between death and disease risks, the reduction of the former is taken to be the most important social benefit, which is fully revealed in the legislation of laws like the *Safe Drinking Water Act*, the *Resource Conservation and Recovery*

Act, and the *Clean Air Act* in the USA and the *Canadian Environmental Protection Act*. For instance, in the cost–benefit analysis of the *Clean Air Act*, 80% of the benefits that can be calculated by money come from the lowering of premature mortality rate.

When evaluating the impact of mortality, most Chinese scholars choose the HC approach, which takes average income or GDP per capita as alternative indicators of life value. According to an evaluation of Zheng Yisheng, which adopts average wages as indicators, the losses caused by air pollution amount to about 23.9 billion yuan (in 1998).

After massive criticism of the HC approach, some scholars have chosen the WTP approach, which first estimates people's WTP against changes of mortality risks and then obtains the value of a statistical life by dividing that WTP by risk changes (Markandya & Pavan, 1999). Table 8.1 shows the general results of the value of statistical lives estimated in Europe and the USA during the mid-1990s.

After estimating the WTP on the basis of a survey carried out in Beijing, Zhang (2011, 2002) worked out the value of a statistical life ranging from 545,000 yuan to 1.7 million yuan (in 1999), or about 66,000 US dollars to 205,000 US dollars,[11] or about 57,000 Euros to 17,6000 Euros (in 1999[12]). China's estimated value of a statistical life was only about 1–6% that of Europe and the USA at the same period (See Table 8.1).

Table 8.1 Estimated value of a statistical life (million ECU, 1995)

	Europe	**USA**
Risk Wage Approach	3.4–4.2	4.3–6.6
Contingent Valuation Approach	4.9–7.6	1.7–3.0
Market Approach	0.8–4.1	1.2–1.3
Average	3.0–5.3	2.4–3.6

Source: Markandya & Pavan. (1999), p. 45.

---

[11]At a US dollar to Chinese yuan exchange rate of 1: 8.2796, see *China Statistical Yearbook 2000*.

[12]At a US dollar to Euro exchange rate of 1:1.1665 stipulated by the European Central Bank on January 4, 1999.

(2) Morbidity's Morbidity caused by environmental pollution refers to changes of morbidity rate caused by changes of the environmental quality, which also measures changes of direct individual welfare level. When an individual makes an evaluation of changes of the morbidity rate caused by changes of the environmental quality, such evaluation is oriented toward the long-term effect of reduction of the morbidity rate and increase of the health level caused by the environmental quality improvement due to investment in relevant environmental policies or the environment.

Many early disease influence evaluation methods focused on the disease expense approach aimed at preference revealing (Zheng *et al.*, 1999). According to a recent estimate of Zheng (2011), the average medical expense of each additional Chinese COPD[13] patient was 3,000 yuan and the total economic damage of China caused by additional diseases was 5.6 billion yuan (in 1998).

In recent years, the amount of literature that evaluates the impact on health by the CV approach of preference revealing has been on the rise. They mainly probe into respiratory diseases closely related to environmental pollution (Brandt *et al.*, 2012). For instance, at the end of the 20th century and the beginning of the 21st century in Shanghai, the average individual WTP of patients for respiratory diseases (median results) was 100–5,000 yuan, of which the WTP for outpatient expenditure was 100–400 yuan and for inpatient expenditure was 3,000–5,000 yuan (Peng & Tian, 2003).

(3) Evaluation application of the estimates: As studies concerned in this section have their own evaluation results which obviously vary from one to another, it has been an important problem in environmental economics in terms of how to evaluate and use such results.

(A) Evaluation of the reasonability and effectiveness (logic) of methods of evaluating the value of a statistical life. The human capital approach uses the contribution share of an individual in the gross social production to

---

[13] Chronic Obstructive Pulmonary Diseases (COPD) include breathing difficulty, chronic cough, and mucus production (2012 Global Initiative for Chronic Obstructive Lung Disease, Inc., www.csrd.org.cn/cn/COPD/).

represent his individual value. What is problematic about it lies in the fact that it is impossible to reflect the value of a statistical life of the elderly, children, and non–wage-earners in the human capital approach (Johansson, *et al.* 1995).

Krupnick *et al.* (2000) think that, theoretically, the preference expression approach can estimate whether an individual is able to feel risks like death and their changes through investigation. However, many studies are unable to figure out whether the WTP for risk reduction changes in the same direction of the changes of risks. Therefore, the reasonability and effectiveness of the estimated value of a statistical life calculated by WTP is doubtful.

(B) Distinction between voluntary risks and involuntary risks. Apparently, an individual's attitude toward voluntary risks is different from that toward involuntary risks. In terms of WTA, the WTA for voluntary risks is far lower than that of involuntary risks.

(C) How to integrate various estimates when evaluating macro-benefits (total damage of pollution). When evaluating the impact of environmental pollution on health, a large-N survey is necessary in order to get an experience estimate for a region or the whole country. However, given the limitation of expenditure, human resources, and experience, almost all the current studies only concern small sample surveys and the estimates can only reflect characteristics of part of the population instead of the whole population. In addition, the differences between the estimates are usually rather large. In this case, we may adopt a method of "reevaluation" on the basis of multiple estimates so as to obtain an average or median result of various estimates and take that as a macro-estimate (Nijkampa *et al.*, 2008).

5.2.2. *Evaluation of service value of the ecological environment or species diversity*

Although over 80% of the environmental benefits originate from the reduction of premature death and additional diseases, most of the literature on environmental value evaluation take various ecological systems, or service values such as forests (Hou, 2002; Markandya *et al.*, 2008), grassland, mixed ecological systems (López-Mosquera & Sánchez, 2011) and species diversity (Nijkampa *et al.*, 2008) as their evaluation objects. The author thinks that the evaluation object of the value evaluation of the impact of the environment on health is "people"; except in market approaches (such as the "human capital approach"), where the preference revealing approach and where the preference expression approach both have difficulty in accessing data. In particular, when it concerns subjects such as sensitive diseases, death, hypothetical expenditure, or willingness, the psychological pressure of the respondents will lead to information distortion, and thus estimation deviations. In contrast, the evaluation object of the evaluation of service value of the ecological environment and species diversity is "things", and relevant data is relatively easier to obtain because generally there will not be information distortion in the process of the evaluation.

The economic evaluation of the ecological environment refers to that of natural resources: in a special sense, it refers to that of species diversity. It is one of the most challenging jobs faced by environmental economists today. When analyzing the cost benefits of protection schemes, we can directly make comparisons between the economic value evaluation results of multiple schemes. In addition, the monetary value of species diversity is also the basis for the damage evaluation of environmental accounts and natural resources and benefit evaluation. The value of species diversity is also of significance in studies of consumer behaviors as it can reveal an individual consumer's attitude toward specific species diversity management objects and identify his/her initiative for species diversity protection (Nijkampa *et al.*, 2008).

Generally, protected areas featuring species diversity and historical cultural characteristics are called natural and cultural heritage resources. Let us take China as an example, such resources include natural reserves, scenic spots, forest parks, geoparks, wetland parks, and water recreation areas. In particular, those heritage sites with world "outstanding universal value" are protected as world heritage. The *UNESCO World Heritage List* specifies the heritage resources with outstanding universal value, admits them openly, and requires the governments of the member states to give them special protection. These typical heritage resources around the world represent the diversity of world heritage and have important educational significance. The natural and cultural heritage not only preserves the species diversity and the local ecological resources but also carries on the Chinese civilization and traditional culture. The establishment of protected areas of natural and cultural heritage guarantees that the people can enjoy the heritage resources in the long run in light of institutions.

Generally, methods used to evaluate the service value of ecological environment and ecological diversity include Travelling Cost Studies (the Preference Revealing Model), Contingent Valuation Model (CVM, the Preference Expression Model), and the Discrete Choice Model (the Preference Expression Model).

(1) The Contingent Valuation Model evaluates benefits of conservation works near the world heritage sites. Stonehenge, a British World Heritage Site, stands on the Salisbury Plain in Wiltshire, England, about 100 km southwest of London. Built from 5000 BC to 3500 BC, it is a famous heritage site of a prehistoric temple. Some gigantic rocks standing in a circle on the Salisbury Plain, the Stonehenge, the most well-known and most mysterious prehistoric site on the British Isles. It is a scared place in the eyes of the British people. Since about 80 years ago, the British government has been restoring Stonehenge. Since then, Stonehenge has become one of the hottest scenic spots in England, welcoming about one million tourists every year.

In the late 1990s, the quality of the Stonehenge was damaged by the noise of the nearby Highway A303. Therefore, the management institute of the Stonehenge, English Heritage, together with the UN Trust Fund, proposed building a tunnel under Highway A303 so as to reduce the impact of the noise caused by the heavy traffic on the Stonehenge. The budget of that project was about 125 million pounds. The question is, what benefits can the project bring about? According to the research of Mourato & Maddison (2000), the investigation of the WTP of the general public and tourists (including non-use value) found that the most strict protection benefits realized due to this project was 150 million pounds, which was larger than the cost of building the underground tunnel (Hanley & Spash, 1993).

(2) Evaluation of Summer Palace by the Discrete Choice Model. The Discrete Choice Model is a value evaluation method which acquires the indirect utility function of the respondents on the basis of environmental characteristics by observing their choices in hypothetical choice situations and then deducts their benefits from the improvement of environmental characteristics. Here, the choice situation is a problem about respondents' selecting one option out of a set of options. The option set should meet three standards: first, the number of options to be selected is limited; second, the options are mutually exclusive; third, the option set is self-contained (Train, 1993).

We first choose an option set with an experimental configuration composed of different attribute states. Then we assume the respondent chooses his favorite alternative situation out of the option set. With the utility function model chosen by the configuration, we turn the choice issue into a utility comparison issue and use the maximum utility to represent the respondent's choice of optimal scheme in the alternative situation set so as to evaluate the overall model parameters.

According to Louviere (2001), a choice model usually consists of the following elements: First, options. An option may be a name with a specific identification (such as "enhancing water quality") or a name without such an identification (such as "Option 1"). Second, option attributes to describe the characteristics of options. Third, attribute levels to describe the difference between options. The levels may be qualitative or quantitative. Fourth, respondents. The respondents will assess some or all the options in the option set and select a favorite option out of the multiple option set (Gao, 2011).

In 2005, we carried out value evaluation for Summer Palace, a world heritage site, by using the choice model (Gao & Zhang, 2011). After experimental questionnaire survey, data statistics analysis and indirect utility function analysis expressed by models, we came to the following conclusions:

First, WTP for tickets. Statistics show that the highest ticket prices that most respondents (90.15%) were willing to pay were 10–50 yuan, the highest ticket price that 50% of those respondents were willing to pay was

20 yuan or the ticket price at that time, the highest ticket price that 8.33% of those respondents were willing to pay was 10 yuan, lower than the ticket price at that time, the highest ticket price that 31.82% of those respondents were willing to pay was 50 yuan, higher than the ticket price at that time. In addition, the highest ticket price that 2.27% of the respondents were willing to pay was 0 yuan. Statistics show that, given the resource situation of Summer Palace at that time, the highest ticket price that most respondents were willing to pay was no higher than 50 yuan.

Second, the compensated respondent surplus (WTP) in different situations. The respondents' WTP for the improvement from "keeping the exterior basically maintenance and the interior partly open" to "keeping regular maintenance and displaying the interior as in history free of charge" was 48.35 yuan; the WTP for the improvement from "displaying in the open free of charge" to "restoring as they were in history and opening free of charge" was 42.14 yuan; the WTP for the improvement of the water surface landscape of the Summer Palace from "allowing the lake water to be somewhat turbid and the ornamental plants to be not abundant enough" to "crystal clear lake water, no weeds and abundant spectacular ornamental plants" was 49.06 yuan; the willingness to accept compensation for the degradation of water surface landscape from "crystal clear lake water, no weeds and abundant spectacular ornamental plants" to "turbid lake water, weeds everywhere and no ornamental plants" was 72.04 yuan.

Third, total yearly benefits. Supposing all the respondents stay only half a day in the Summer Palace during the off-season, the average compensated surplus for them caused by the improvement from the current situation to "regular maintenance and displaying the interior of the ancient buildings as they were in history free of charge", "restoring the historical sites as they were in history and opening free of charge," and "crystal clear lake water, no weeds and abundant spectacular ornamental plants" in terms of water surface landscape will be 139.55 yuan.

Let us suppose again the total number of tourist to the Summer Palace in 2005 was 6 million. If the sample can represent the tourists throughout the year, the survey in the off-season can represent the yearly survey and each tourist only stays in the Summer Palace for half a day, the total benefits that this improvement can bring about to all the tourists throughout the year will be 837 million yuan.

5.2.3. *Evaluation of the Temple of Heaven by using the Travel Cost Model*

The Travel Cost Model (TCM) is an "ancient" environmental value evaluation method initiated in the USA. In the beginning, it was used to calculate the total economic benefits created by tourists' recreational activities in the national park (Hotelling, 1949).

As the consumer surplus of environmental items and services goes beyond the scale of consumers' "psychological benefits" and reveals part of their "actual benefits", consumer surplus can express the economic value of environmental items and services.

The Travel Cost Model is a preference revealing evaluation method which measures consumers' WTP by consumer surplus and evaluates environmental items or services. Its basic thinking is: with a certain resource site, it establishes the travel cost function model through a survey of the money and the time a tourist spends, estimates the travel demand curve (in place of the demand curve between the number of tourists and the prices of scenic spots) according to changes of the travel cost and the number of tourists, calculates the consumer surplus, and finally obtains the estimate of resource values (Wang & Zhang, 2011a).

In 2005, we carried out value evaluation of the Temple of Heaven, a world heritage site, by using the Travel Cost Model. After experimental survey, data treatment, fitting and selection of the demand curve, and calculation of the consumer surplus, our findings were as follows: First, the evaluation result of the individual travel cost model was 12.5 yuan per capita (in 2005). Second, through two methods of calculation, the integral method and the trapezoid area accumulation method, the regional travel cost model estimated the economic value of the Temple of Heaven in 2005 to be 11.4 billion yuan and 13.8 billion yuan, respectively (Wang & Zhang, 2011b).

References

Adams, R. M., Hamilton, S. A. & McCarl, B. A., The Benefit of Pollution Control: The Case of Ozone and U.S. Agriculture. *American Journal of Agricultural Economics*, Vol. 68, No. 4 (1986), pp. 886–893.

Alberini, A. *et al.*, Economic Valuation of Mortality Risk Reduction: Assessing the States of the Art or Policy Applicy Applications. National Center for Environmental Economics. U. S. Environmental Protection Agency, 2002.

Bartik, T. J., Evaluating the Benefits of Non-Marginal Reductions in Pollution Using Information on Defensive Expenditure. *Journal of Environmental Economics and Management*, Vol. 15 (1988), pp. 111–127.

Brandt, S., Lavin, F. V. & Hanemann, M., Contingent Valuation Scenarios for Chronic Illnesses: The Case of Childhood Asthma. *Value in Health*, Vol. 15 (2012), pp. 1077–1083.

Cropper, M., *Valuing Environmental Benefit — Selected Essays of Maureen Cropper*. 1999. Edward Elgar Publishing Limited, Cheltenham, UK.

Freeman III, A. M., *The Measurement of Environmental and Resource Value: Theory and Method*. 1993. Resources for the Future, Washington, D.C.

Gao, J., & Zhang X., "The Value Evaluation of the Summer Palace as a World Cultural Heritage". In *Environmental Value Evaluation: Methods and Case Studies*, a key research projects sponsored by the Chinese Academy of Social Sciences (Class B), August 2011.

Gao, J., "Discrete Choice Model and Choice Experiment". In *Environmental Value Evaluation: Methods and Case Studies*, a key research projects sponsored by the Chinese Academy of Social Sciences (Class B), August 2011.

Garrod, G., & Willis, K. G., *Economic Valuation of the Environment: Method and Case Studies*. 1999. Edward Elgar Publishing Limited, Cheltenham, UK.

Hadker, N., Sharma, S., David A., & Muraleedharan, T. R., Willingness-to-pay for Borivli National Park: Evidence from a Contingent Valuation. *Ecological Economics* (1997), pp. 105–122.

Hanemann, W. M., Willing to Pay and Willing to Accept: How Much Can They Differ? *American Economic Review*, Vol. 81 (1991), pp. 635–647.

Hanley, N., & Spash, C. L., *Cost-Benefit Analysis and the Environment*. 1993. Edward Elgar Publishing Limited, Cheltenham, UK.

Horowitz, J. K., & McConnell, K. E., A Review of WTA/WTP studies. *Journal of Environmental Economics and Management*, Vol. 44 (2002) pp. 426–447.

Hotelling, H., An Economic Study of the Monetary Valuation of Recreation in the National Parks. U. S. Department of the Interior, National Park Service and Recreational Planning Division, 1949. Washington, D. C.

Hou Y., *Forest Environmental Value Accounting*. 2002. China Science and Technology Press, Beijing, China.

Huang, Y., *Welfare Eonomics*, translated by Zhou J. *et al.*, 1991. China Friendship Publishing Company, Beijing, China.

James, D., Jason, H. & Opscole, H. *Applied Environmental Economics: Techniques and Results of Economic Analysis*, translated by W. Yanxiang *et al.*, Collated by Wang Tiesheng. 1986. Commercial Press, Beijing, China.

Johansson, M., Johansson, P-O., Jonsson, B. & Soderqvist, T., "Valuing changes in Health: Theoretical and Empirical Issues". In P-O., Johansson, K. Bengt, and Karl-Goran Maler (eds.), *Current Issues in Environmental Economics*. 1995. Manchester University Press, UK, pp. 78–97.

Johansson, P.-O., Microeconomics of Valuation. In H. Folmer and H. Landis Gobel (eds.), *Principles of Environmental and Resource Economics: A Guide for Students and Decision-Makers* (Second Edition). 2000. Edward Elgar Publishing Limited, Cheltenham, UK.

Kopp, R. J., & Krupnick, A. J., "Agricultural Policy and the Benefits of Ozone Control". *American Journal of Agricultural Economics*. Vol. 69, No. 5 (1987), pp. 956–962.

Krupnick, A., Alberini, A., Cropper, M., Simon, N., O'Brien, B., Goeree, R. & Heintzelman, M., "Age, Health, and the Willingness to Pay for Mortality Risk Reductions: A Contingent Valuation Survey of Ontario Residents". Resources for the Future Discussion, Washington, D. C. Paper, 00–37, 2002.

Li, Y., & Zhang Z., *Environmental Economics*. 1995. China Planning Press, Beijing, China.

López-Mosquera, N., & Sánchez, M., "Emotional and Satisfaction Benefits to Visitors as Explanatory Factors in the Monetary Valuation of Environmental Goods. An application to Periurban Green Spaces". *Land Use Policy*, Vol. 28 (2011), pp.151–166.

Louviere, J., "Choice Experiments: An Overview of Concepts and Issues". In J. Bennett and R. Blamey (eds.), *The Choice Modelling Approach to Environmental Valuation*. 2001. Edward Elgar, Northampton, pp. 13–36.

Markandya, A., & Pavan M., *Green Accounting in Europe — Four Case Studies*. 1999. Kluwer Academic Publishers, the Netherlands.

Markandya, A., Chiabai, A., Ding, H., Travisi, C. & Nunes, P. A. L. D., Economic Valuation of Forest Ecosystem Services: Methodology and Monetary Estimates. In Final Report "The Cost of Policy Inaction (COPI): The Case of not Meeting 2010 Biodiversity Target". 2008. European Commission Call on ENV. G. 1/ETU/2007/0044, Brussels, Belgium.

Markandya, A., Harou, P., Belland, L. G. & Cistulli, V., *Environmental Economics for Sustainable Growth — A Handbook for Practitioners*. 2002. Edward Elgar Publishing Limited, Cheltenham, UK.

Mourato, S., & Maddison, D., "Valuing Different Road Options for Stonehenge." In S. Navrud and R. Ready (eds.), *Valuing Cultural Heritage*. 2000. Edward Elgar Publishing Limited, Cheltenham, UK.

National Oceanic and Atmospheric Administration (NOAA), Report of the NOAA Panel on Contingent Valuation. *Federal Register*, Vol. 58, No. 10 (1993), pp. 4602–4614.

Nijkampa, P., Vindignib, G. & Nunesc, P. A. L., "Economic Valuation of Biodiversity: A Comparative Study". *Ecological Economics*, Vol. 67 (2008), pp. 217–231.

Peng, X., & Tian, W., "A Study on Willingness to Pay for Economic Losses Caused by Air Pollution Diseases in Shanghai". *World Economic Papers*, No. 2 (2003).

Phaneuf, D. J., & Requate, T., *A Course in Environmental Economics: Theory, Policy, and Practice*. 2010. http://www.aae.wisc.edu/dphaneuf/Environmental Economics Book.

Randall, A., & Stoll, J. R., "Consumer's Surplus in Commodity Space". *American Economic Review*, Vol. 70 (1980), pp. 449–455.

Stevens, T. H., Echeverria, J., Glass, R. J., Hager, T. & More, T. A., "Measuring the Existence Value of Wildlife: What to CVM Estimates Really Show?" *Land Economics*, Vol. 67 (1991), pp. 390–400.

Strand, J., "Valuation of Environmental Improvements in Continuous Time with Mortality and Morbidity Effects". *Resource and Energy Economics*, Vol. 28 (2006), pp. 229–241.

Tietenberg, T. *Environmental Economics and Policy*, translated by Zhu Q. 2003. Shanghai University of Finance and Economics Press, Shanghai, China.

Train, K., *Qualitative Choice Analysis: Theory, Econometrics, and an Application to Automobile Demand*. 1993. Third Edition, The MIT Press, Cambridge, Massachusetts.

Venkatachalam, L., "The Contingent Valuation Method: A Review". *Environmental Impact Assessment Review*, Vol. 24 (2004), pp. 89–124.

Viscusi, W. K., "The Value of Risks to Life and Health". *Journal of Economic Literature*, Vol. 31, No. 4 (1993), pp. 1912–1946.

Viscusi, W. K., *Fatal Tradeoffs: Public and Private Responsibilities for Risk*. 1992. Oxford University Press, New York.

Wang, X., & Zhang, X., "The Application of Two Basic Models of Travel Cost Method: Evaluation of the Temple of Heaven, Beijing, as a World Cultural Heritage". In *Environmental Value Evaluation: Methods and Case Studies*, a key research projects sponsored by the Chinese Academy of Social Sciences (Class B), August 2011b.

Wang X, & Zhang X., "The Demand Theory and Travel Cost Model". In *Environmental Value Evaluation: Methods and Case Studies*, a key research projects sponsored by the Chinese Academy of Social Sciences (Class B), August 2011a.

Wang, H., Willingness to Pay for Reducing Fatal Risk by Improving Air Quality: A Contingent Valuation Study in Chongqing, China. *Professional Association for China's Environment (PACE)* 2003 Symposium Paper, Oct. 24–25, Renmin University of China, Beijing.

Willig, R. D., "Consumer's Surplus without Apology". *American Economic Review* Vol. 66 (1976), pp. 589–597.

Zhang, F., *Environmental and Natural Resource Economics*. 1998. Shanghai People's Publishing House, Shanghai, China.

Zhang, X., "An Analysis of the Externality of Large-Scale Hydropower Engineering Facilities (Dams)". In Z. Yisheng (ed.), *The Scientific Development Concept and River Development*. 2005. Huaxia Publishing House, Beijing, China.

Zhang, X., "Willingness to Pay for Avoiding Premature Death Caused by Air Pollution and Estimation of the Value of Life Statistics: A Case Study of Beijing". In *Environmental Value Evaluation: Methods and Case Studies*, a key research projects sponsored by the Chinese Academy of Social Sciences (Class B), August 2011.

Zhang, X., Valuing Mortality Risk Reductions Using the Contingent Valuation Method: Evidence from a Survey of Beijing Residents in 1999. Presenting Paper for the *Second World Congress of Environmental and Resource Economists*, June 24–27, 2002, Monterey, California, USA.

Zheng, Y., "Economic Evaluation of Health Damage Caused by Air Pollution in China". In *Environmental Value Evaluation: Methods and Case Studies*, a key research projects sponsored by the Chinese Academy of Social Sciences (Class B), August 2011.

Zheng, Y., Yan L. & Qian Y., "An Estimation of China's Environmental Pollution Economic Losses in the Mid-1990s". *Management World*, No. 2 (1999).

Chapter 9

Disposal of Undesirable Output in Measurement of Productivity: Theory and Methods

Yuhong Li

Institute of Quantitative & Technical Economics,
Chinese Academy of Social Sciences

1. Introduction

Undesirable output, or bad production, usually refers to pollution production with negative externality, which is a by-product of desirable production or good production that occurs with desirable production.

Productivity is the rate of output to input. Input and output in the traditional sense is a rare resource with a price signal. As it does not consider externality, undesirable output is often neglected. In the early phase of industrialization, the environmental capacity seemed to be nearly infinite against pollutant emissions, and fresh air and fresh water, which were considered as limitless supply, did not have a market price. However, with the development of industrialization, pollutant emissions came close to or even surpassed what the environment could stand. Environmental pollution affected and even threatened people's normal production and life. As a result, fresh air and fresh water became rare goods. Nevertheless, the externality of pollutant emissions makes it difficult to price the environmental quality.

If we admit that a good environment is a rare resource or product which should be acquired by changing the established production mode, the reduction or increase of environmental pollution can be seen part of the production process. If output includes only desirable production as part of the measurement of productivity, the productivity thus obtained is simply "productivity of desirable production" instead of productivity of the whole production process. For industries under environmental regulations, the management of pollution means that traditional production elements are used for non-production purposes while the reduction of pollution is not included in the enhancement of productivity. Therefore, the actual increase of productivity before and after environmental regulation might be under-estimated. Before the 1990s, similar to that of Jorgenson and Wilcoxen (1990), most productivity measurements and studies of growth calculation did not take into account undesirable output.

However, the lack of price information in undesirable output means improvement in the productivity measures based on the traditional pro-duction theoretical framework is imperative. Development in this aspect mainly refers to the introduction of directional distance function. The distance function's treatment of undesirable output has some advantages, which are as follows: first of all, the distance function can indicate the production technology of multiple input and multiple output; second, the axiom framework of the distance function can treat undesirable output; and finally, the concept of the distance function is based on efficiency. The Malmquist Index established by the distance function method finds exten-sive application while the use of the directional distance function's enhancement of the distance function lies in its changing of the radial extension into extension with active objects as the starting point. At pre-sent, research and development in this area is occurring rather rapidly and this chapter reviews this. We first compare the similarities and differences between the distance function and Farrell Efficiency (1957) and then explain the way the distance function deals with undesirable output and finally introduce advantages of the directional distance function in its disposal of undesirable output.

2. Efficiency Analysis and Distance Function

2.1. *Origin of the thoughts of efficiency analysis*

The literature of efficiency analysis dates back to Farrell (1957), whose contribution to efficiency research mainly lies in the following three aspects: efficiency measurement is based on the radial contraction or expansion of ineffective observation points against the frontier; the production frontier is defined as the piecewise linear envelope of the observation points; and efficiency measurement is realized by calculating the system of linear equations, with a negative slope but without observation points between the frontier and the origin (Finn and Nikias, 2002).

Ferrell defined cost-efficiency and split it into technical efficiency and price efficiency (or allocative efficiency). Technical efficiency is defined as the rate of the input required to produce the observed output under the best production conditions to that observed in practice, which is *OQ/OP* in Fig. 9.1. Price efficiency is defined as the rate of the cost, when technical efficiency is satisfied, for producing the observed output at the price of given elements to the minimum cost on the frontier, or *OR/OQ* in Fig. 9.1. Cost-efficiency refers to, in case both technical efficiency and price efficiency are valid, the rate of cost for producing the observed output to the actual cost, or *OR/OP* = (*OQ/OP*)(*OR/OQ*).

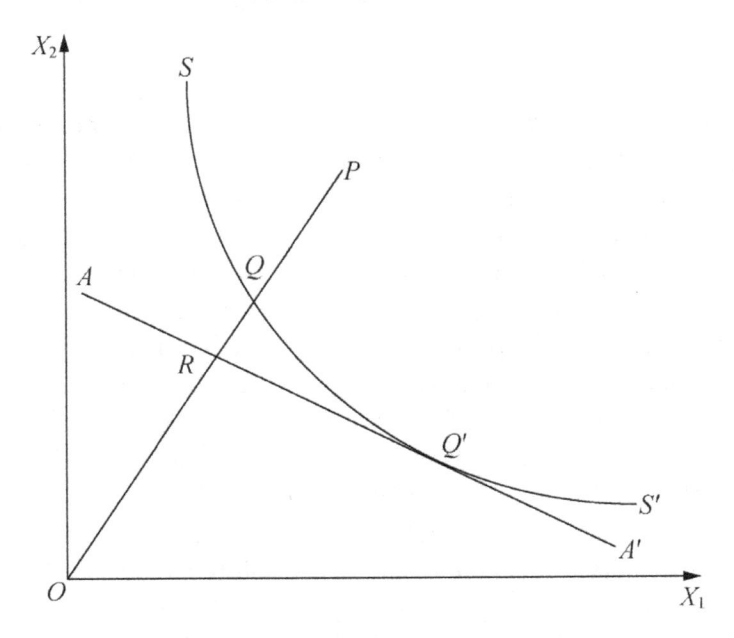

Fig. 9.1 Technical efficiency and price efficiency defined by Farrell

Note: X_1 and X_2 represent input while SS′ represents the unit-value isoquant.

Source: Ferrell (1957).

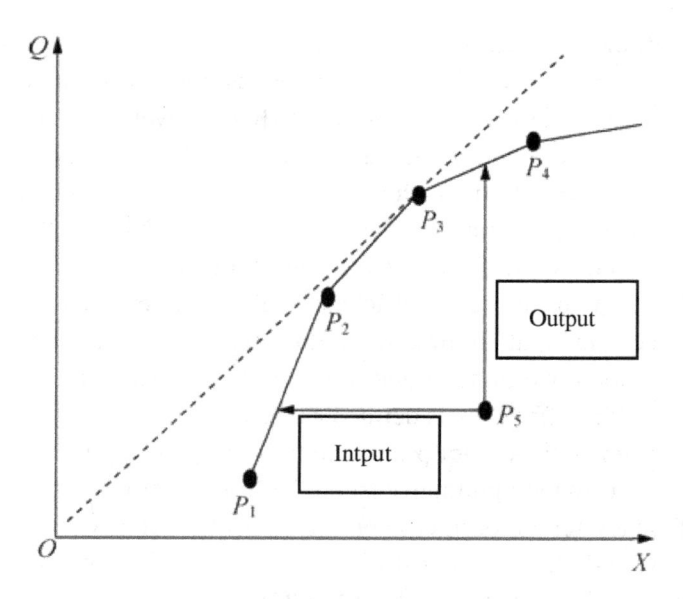

Fig. 9.2   Ferrell's production frontier of single input and single output
Source: Ferrell (1957).

In Fig. 9.2, the distance between each object and the frontier represents its efficiency. In terms of scale benefit, there are two kinds of frontiers: constant scale benefit like the dotted line that passes through the origin in Fig. 9.2, in which case only the efficiency of P_3 is 1 while that of any other point is smaller than 1; and variable scale benefit, in which case the points P_1 to P_4 constitute the production frontier and the efficiency of each point is 1. The efficiency of P_5 is smaller than 1. In terms of input directions, horizontal projection toward Axis Q means reduction of input and increase of efficiency; in terms of output directions, vertical projection toward Axis X means increase of output and improvement of efficiency while the input remains the same.

According to Ferrell, his inspirations came from Debreu and Koopmans. However, Finn and Nikias (2002) argued that Ferrell had neglected Shephard's distance function as the production theory axiom system of the latter can provide appropriate explanation to his radial extension choice. In addition, Ferrell also neglected the contribution of Malmquist, who inspired Caves (Caves *et al.*, 1982a & 1982b) to put forward Malmquist Productivity Index on the basis of Ferrell Efficiency Index.

Inspired by Ferrell's paper, Charnes, Cooper, and Rhodes (CCR, 1978) carried out operational promotion of efficiency measurement. The linear planning model they put forward is of general significance while Ferrell's unit-value isoquant model is a special case in terms of general linear planning problems.

One of CCR's contributions is their associating efficiency index (the rate of the weighting of production to the weighting sum of input) with Ferrell's efficiency measures, which means turning the maximization of certain unit efficiency into a general linear planning problem of maximization of Ferrell's efficiency rating. At the same time, CCR clarified the relationship between Ferrell's technical efficiency measures and the distance function adopted by Shephard.

2.2. Shephard's Distance Function Axiom System

Shephard (1953, 1970) introduced the concept of distance function into the firm production theory and made an axiomatic description of the production theory framework by using the distance function as a basic tool.

2.2.1. Multi-input single-output

Supposing the output of production technology is a non-negative single product or service and y, $x = (x_1, x_2, \ldots, x_n)$ represents the input vector of productive factors. If we substitute it into the non-negative domain D in Euclidean space R^n, we get $D = \{x \mid x \geq 0, x \in R^n \}$.[1] The production input set $L(y)$ of technology is a set of all the input factor vectors which can at least produce non-negative production y.

The input vector x in $L(y)$ is not necessarily efficient. The definition of its subset $E(y)$ is

$$E(y) = \{x \mid x \in L(y), \forall x' \leq x \Rightarrow x' \notin L(y)\}$$

Then, if we divide the domain of definition of x into independent subsets, we get the origin, the edge point set, and the non-edge point set:

---

[1] In terms of the vectors x and y, $x \geq y$ means each component of the vectors $x_i \geq y_i$ but $x \neq y$.

$$D = \begin{cases} \{0\} \\ D_1 = \{x \mid x > 0\} \\ D_2 = \{x \mid x \geq 0, \Pi x_i = 0\} \end{cases}$$

Here, edge point set D_2 includes two subsets

$$D_2 = \begin{cases} D_2' = \{x \mid x \in D_2, \lambda x \in L_\emptyset(y) & \text{for some } u > 0, \lambda > 0\} \\ D_2'' = \{x \mid x \in D_2, \lambda x \notin L_\emptyset(y) & \text{for all } u > 0, \lambda > 0\} \end{cases}$$

D_2 is a point on the coordinate axis. Depending on whether these points have a point of contact with the coordinate axis, they can be divided into two sets: D_2'' is a set in which there are no point of contact between the coordinate axis and any input set of the output, and D_2' is a set in which there are points of contact between the coordinate axis and input sets of the output. All the four subsets are subject to $D = \{0\} \cup D_1 \cup D_2' \cup D_2''$.

The definition of the distance function expressed by input set is[2]

$$\psi(y,x) = \begin{cases} \dfrac{\|x\|}{\|\xi\|} = \dfrac{1}{\min\{\lambda \mid \lambda x \in L_\emptyset(y)\}} & \text{for all } x \in D_1 \cup D_2' \\ y = \begin{cases} (1, +\infty) & x \text{ inside } L_\emptyset(y) \\ 1 & x \text{ on } E_\emptyset(y) \\ (0,1) & x \text{ outside } L_\emptyset(y) \end{cases} \\ 0 & \text{for all } x \in \{0\} \cup D_2'', y > 0 \\ +\infty & \text{for all } x \in D, y = 0 \end{cases}$$

Here, $\xi = \lambda_0 x$, $\lambda_0 = \min\{\lambda \mid \lambda x \in L_\emptyset(y)\}$. This definition equals to *OP/OQ* in Fig. 9.1 and is the reverse of Ferrell's efficiency definition.

With this definition of the distance function, input set and production function can be expressed, respectively, as

$$L_\emptyset(y) = \{x \mid \psi(y,x) \geq 1, x \in D\}$$
$$E_\emptyset(y) = \{x \mid \psi(y,x) = 1, \psi(y,x') < 1, \quad \text{for any } x' \leq x, y > 0\}$$

---

[2] For nature of the distance function, see Appendix A of this chapter.

2.2.2. *Multi-input multi-output*

Supposing there are M kinds of output or services and the products are not necessarily desirable production or of positive economic or social value. For instance, pollution can be taken as a product of joint production. To define the non-negative domain in the Euclidean space R^m, we use $y = (y_1, y_2,...,y_M)$ to represent the output vector in productive technology. $X = \{x \mid x \geq 0\} = R^n_+$ and $Y = \{y \mid y \geq 0\} = R^m_+$ represent non-negative input and output vector set respectively.

Definition. $P: X \to Y$ represents production of the mapping from X to Y. The output set $P(x) \subset Y$ corresponding to $x \in X$ is the mapping from the point set in X to the subset of Y.

Definition. Inverse correspondence $L: Y \to X$ is U's mapping in X, the subset $L(y)$ of X is the input vector set which can at least produce the output y. Input set $L(y) = \{x \mid y \in P(x), x \in X\}$.

If $y = (y(D), y(\bar{D}))$, in which $y(\bar{D})$ represents the component of undesirable output, the former represents the components of desirable production.

Definition. Effective subset of output set $P(x)$, a production function similar to single-output.

$$E_p(x) = \left\{ y \left| \begin{array}{l} y \in P(x); \max\{\theta \mid \theta.y \in P(x), \theta \in [0,+\infty) = 1; \\ v = [v(D), V[\bar{D}]] \notin P(x) \\ \text{if } y(\bar{D}) \text{ is non-empty and} \begin{cases} (a)v(D) \geq y(D), v(\bar{D}) \leq y(\bar{D}) \\ (b)v(D) \geq y(D), \ v(\bar{D}) \leq y(\bar{D}) \end{cases} \end{array} \right. \right\}$$

Definition. The effective subset of the input set $L(y)$ is $E_L(y) = \{x \mid x \in L_{(y)}, x' \notin L_{(y)} \text{ if } x' \leq x, y \in Y\}$.

The two definitions are somewhat similar. The effective subset of the input set is to identify the minimum input required for the production y. The effective subset of the output set is to identify the maximum output of the input x. Nevertheless, the less undesirable output, if any, the better. The reduction of undesirable output without reduction of desirable production and increase of desirable production without increase of undesirable output both mean greater efficiency.

It is not difficult to represent the production technology of multi-input single-output by the production function. It is also easy to represent the production technology of single-input multi-output by the inverse function of the production function. However, we can only represent the production technology of multi-input multi-output by the more abstract transfer functions. In comparison, the distance function has the advantage of simplicity in terms of representation of production technology. Based on output set $P(x)$ and input set $L(y)$, respectively, two types of distance functions can be defined as follows:

Definition. The distance function $\psi(y, x)$ of the input set $L(y)$ is

$$\psi(y, x) = \frac{\|x\|}{\|\xi(y, x)\|} = \frac{1}{\lambda(y, x)}$$

Here, $\xi(y, x) = \lambda(y, x)$ and $\lambda(y, x) = \min\{\lambda \mid (\lambda x) \in L(y), \lambda \geq 0\}$.

Definition. The distance function $\Omega(x, y)$ of the input set $P(x)$ is

$$\Omega(x, y) = \frac{\|y\|}{\|\eta(x, y)\|} = \frac{1}{\theta(x, y)}$$

Here, $\eta(x, y) = \theta(x, y) \cdot y$ and $\theta(x, y) = \max\{\theta \mid (\theta \cdot y) \in P(x), \theta \geq 0\}$.

For an explanation of the nature of the above two types of distance functions, see Appendix B of this chapter. The input set $L(y)$ and the output set $P(x)$ expressed by the distance function are as follows:

$$L(y) = \{x \mid \psi(y, x) \geq 1\}$$
$$P(x) = \{y \mid \Omega(x, y) \leq 1\}$$

As the main characteristic of the input distance function lies in its radial variation or the length of a ray from the origin, the components of the input vector all change in proportion.

Thus, as the distance function value of input is no smaller than 1, the denominator in the distance function is the very efficiency value of Ferrell — each is the inverse of another.

To be consistent with other relevant studies, input distance function and output distance function are expressed as follows:

$$D_1(x,y) = \max\{\rho : (x/\rho) \in L(y)\}$$
$$D_0(x,y) = \min\{\theta : (y/\theta) \in P(x)\}$$

2.3. *Distance Function and Malmquist Productivity Index*

Caves *et al.* (1982a, 1982b) put forward the Malmquist Productivity Index. It was thus named because Malmquist had put forward a concept of reduction, that is, on two different points, to what extent the company can reduce its input while maintaining its target production, or the Malmquist Input Index. Similarly, we can define the output index. The contribution of CCD lies in the fact that they relaxed the assumption that production technology is constant by using the Malmquist input and output indexes and put forward the Malmquist Production Index, which can not only be used to compare various time series but also can be used to compare the production rates of bilateral and multilateral economies.

Supposing there are two time points (or economies), the Malmquist output indexes with *s* and *t* as base periods, respectively, are

$$m_0^s(y_s, y_t, x_s, x_t) = \frac{d_0^s(y_t, x_t)}{d_0^s(y_s, x_s)}$$

$$m_0^t(y_s, y_t, x_s, x_t) = \frac{d_0^t(y_t, x_t)}{d_0^t(y_s, x_s)}$$

Output-oriented Malmquist index is

$$m_0(y_s, y_t, x_s, x_t) = [m_0^t \cdot m_0^s]^{\frac{1}{2}}$$

Similarly, input-oriented Malmquist index is

$$m_i(y_s, y_t, x_s, x_t) = [m_i^t \cdot m_0^s]^{\frac{1}{2}} = \left[\frac{d_i^s(y_t, x_t)d_i^t(y_t, x_t)}{d_i^s(y_s, x_s)d_i^t(y_s, x_s)}\right]^{\frac{1}{2}}$$

Malmquist Production Index is

$$TFPG_m = \frac{m_0}{m_i}$$

There's a saying that goes "All roads lead to Rome". By rights, measures of Ferrell Efficiency, distance and Malmquist Indexes are all results of independent research. However, the three clues coincide in the area of productivity measurement. According to thoughts of Ferrell, CCR (1978) put forward the data envelopment analysis approach. According to thoughts of distance function, Caves *et al.* (1982b) developed the Malmquist Productivity Index, while DEA is one of the major methods used for estimation of the distance function. Their convergence in the productivity area, together with the needs of productivity measurement, enhanced their own research in return.

3. Distance Function's Disposal of Undesirable Output

In Shephard (1970)'s distance function axiom system, the joint production theory paid attention to undesirable production. There are two important properties related to undesirable output: realizability and disposability, which are two important properties of the production correspondence of multi-input and multi-output, $P: X \rightarrow Y$.

3.1. *Realizability*

(1) If $x \geq 0, \bar{y} \geq 0$ and certain scalar $\bar{\lambda} > 0$ subject to $\bar{y} \in (\bar{\lambda}x)$, then for any $\theta > 0$, there exists $\lambda_\theta > 0$ subject to $(\theta\bar{y}) \in P(\lambda_\theta x)$.
(2) If $x > 0$ or $x \geq 0$ and for certain $\bar{y} > 0$ and $\bar{\lambda} > 0$ subject to $\bar{y} \in P(\bar{\lambda}x)$, for any $y \in Y$, there's always $\lambda_y > 0$ subject to $y \in P(\lambda_y x)$.

In the first case, not all output vectors $y \in Y$ can be realized. For instance, some output components are undesirable outputs, which cannot be controlled under a certain minimum level but have to be kept in specific proportion to desirable outputs. The proportionate relationship between the two makes the realizable output set a cone in the space $U = R_+^M$, with its peak at the point $y = 0$. In the second case, as long as there are enough production input, all outputs are realizable. The condition $x \geq 0$ means there can be zero input in terms of input components. The above two cases are the weak realizability and strong realizability of outputs, respectively.

3.2. *Disposability*

(a) $y \in P(x) \Rightarrow \{\theta y \mid \theta \in [0,1]\} \subset P(x)$

(b) $y \in P(x)$ and $y' \leq y \Rightarrow y' \subset P(x)$

The definition of (a) is the weak disposability while that of (b) the strong disposability. If all the output components are desirable, strong disposability applies to any property whose output components are subject to liberal disposal. If there are undesirable outputs in output components like pollutants, some output combinations cannot be realized. For instance, desirable output is positive but the undesirable output is zero. In fact, undesirable output is usually in certain proportion to desirable output. Weak disposability refers to the proportionate changes of output components and the proportionate expansion of undesirable output and desirable output.

Weak realizability and weak disposability are two important properties of undesirable output in productive relations.

For example, in a two-dimensional output space, y_1 represents the undesirable output and y_2 represents desirable output, $P(x)$ represents the bounded closed convex set, and the thick line represents effective points. If undesirable output y_1 and desirable output y_2 are produced in a fixed proportion, feasible set $\overline{P}(x)$ is the triangle area OAA_1 and point A is the only effective point; if y_1 represents desirable output, $\overline{P}(x)$ will be the rectangle area OA_2AA_1 (see Fig. 9.3). For Point A_2, no matter how large the input x is, neither $P(x)$ nor $\overline{P}(x)$ is realizable.

It should be noted that both segments OA and OB (except Points A and B) are invalid. According to the definition of the effective subset of the output set, suppose $y \in P(x)$, the effective subset satisfies $\max\{\theta \mid \theta y \in P(x), \theta \in [0,+\infty)\} = 1$. However, for points on OA and OB

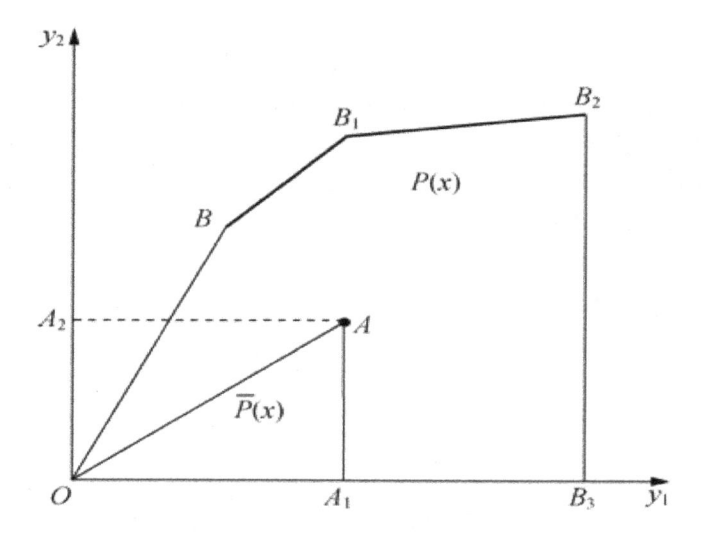

Fig. 9.3   Realizability and disposability of production in production correspondence relations

Source: Shephard (1970), p. 188.

(except Points A and B), $\max\left\{\theta \mid \theta\, y \in P(x), \theta \in [0, +\infty)\right\} > 1$, it is therefore not an effective subset. Those on AA_1 and B_2B_3 (except the upper extreme point) are all invalid subsets. Here, it should be differentiated from the frontier of DEA, and the Shephard edge points are not necessarily the effective frontier in DEA.

Shephard (1970) takes into account the property of undesirable output in his production theory. His contribution to fundamental theory directly influenced the method adopted to consider undesirable output in productivity measurement. Fare (Fare *et al.*, 1989, 1993) was one of the first to apply distance function in the productivity measurement of undesirable output and clarify the output vector.

4. Introduction of Undesirable Output in Productivity Measurement

4.1. *Enhanced multilateral productivity*

Pittman's (1983) enhanced multilateral productivity was one of the earliest researches which introduced undesirable outputs into productivity measurement. On the basis of traditional productivity index, he introduced undesirable outputs, which do not have a market price, in the productivity index.

Suppose there are two firms, k and l. Their input is X, which has N kinds of input components, and their output is Y, which include three components, namely, Y_1, desirable output, and Y_2 and Y_3, two kinds of undesirable outputs. Apparently, if the productivity level and the input do not change, the firms can reduce the three kinds of outputs by the same proportion or reduce Y_1 while proportionately increasing Y_2 and Y_3. The transfer function of Translog is

$$F[\ln(Y_1^k / \delta_k), \ \ln(Y_2^k \delta_k), \ \ln(Y_3^k \delta_k), \ \ln X^l, \ l] = 1$$

Although we can get δ_k and δ_l, it should be noted we will get δ if the proportion of desirable output changes and that of the inverse undesirable output changes are the same.

$$\ln \delta_{kl} = -\sum_i^3 \left[\frac{1}{2} F_i \left(\ln Y^k, \ln X^k, k \right) + \frac{1}{2} F_i (\ln Y^l, \ln X^l, l) \right] \ln \left(\frac{Y_i^k}{Y_i^l} \right)$$

Suppose there is profit maximization, $F_i = -P_i Y_i \sum_j^I P_j Y_j = -R_i$, which can be simplified as

$$\ln \delta_{kl} = \frac{1}{2} \sum_i^3 (R_i^k + R_i^l) \ln \left(\frac{Y_i^k}{Y_i^l} \right)$$

As Y_2 and Y_3 do not have any market value, it is impossible to measure their output shares. One feasible method is to calculate their shadow prices so as to access their output shares. The Lagrangian Function is

$$L = P_1 Y_1 - \sum_n^N r_n X_n - \theta_l \left[F \left(\ln Y_1, \ln Y_2, \ln Y_3, \ln X, k \right) - 1 \right]$$
$$- \theta_2 \left(Y_2 - Y_2^* \right) - \theta_3 (Y_3 - Y_3^*)$$

Here, r_n represents the price of the input X_n, and Y_2^* and Y_3^* are exogenous constraints on the maximum emissions of undesirable outputs. According to first-order condition, we can get[3]

---

[3] For relevant proofs, see Appendices A, B, and C of this chapter.

$$F_1 = \frac{-P_1 Y_1}{P_1 Y_1 - \theta_2 Y_2 - \theta_3 Y_3}$$

$$F_2 = \frac{P_2 Y_2}{P_1 Y_1 - \theta_2 Y_2 - \theta_3 Y_3}$$

$$F_3 = \frac{P_3 Y_3}{P_1 Y_1 - \theta_2 Y_2 - \theta_3 Y_3}$$

Here, θ represents the shadow price of undesirable outputs. It is not difficult to expand the bilateral comparison of outputs to the multilateral comparison of outputs.

$$\ln \delta_{kl}^* = -\frac{1}{2} \sum_i^3 (F_i^k + \overline{F_i}) + \frac{1}{2} \sum_i^3 (F_i^l + \overline{F_i})(\ln Y_i^l - \ln \overline{Y_i})$$

Here, $\ln \overline{Y_i}$ represents the arithmetic mean of s fixed points.

Similarly, the multilateral input index of Translog takes the form of CCD

$$\ln \rho_{kl}^* = -\frac{1}{2} \sum_n^N (W_n^k + \overline{W_n})(\ln X_n^k - \ln \overline{X_n}) + \frac{1}{2} \sum_i^N (W_n^l + \overline{W_n})(\ln X_n^l - \ln \overline{X_n})$$

Here, W_n represents the proportion of nth input value.

Multilateral productivity index of Translog means output index minus input index, given as

$$\ln \lambda_{kl}^* = \ln \delta_{kl}^* - \ln \rho_{kl}^*$$

Enhanced productivity needs the price information of undesirable outputs. With the absence of transaction prices, we must estimate the shadow prices of undesirable outputs.

The weak point of the index studies is whether the value identity is established. In growth accounting, $\sum p_i y_i = \sum w_i x_i$, if we add undesirable outputs to it, we get $\sum p_i y_i < \sum w_i x_i$.

4.2. *Output-oriented enhanced hyperbolic efficiency*

As discussed above, if we put aside whether outputs are of free disposability, the Shephard input distance function is the reciprocal of Ferrell efficiency. That is, distance function is another expression of efficiency. However, if there exist undesirable outputs, distance function is somehow problematic in terms of its expression of efficiency. For instance, in Fig. 9.4, only the segment AB is an effective subset while the contact points of the area behind the radial shadow and the boundary may not be effective points. In addition, the proportionate increase of desirable outputs and undesirable outputs do not conform to Shephard's definition of an effective point. The following two methods are both a correction of this situation.

Ferrell (1989) improved the Ferrell efficiency measures in two aspects: one is by introduction of undesirable outputs in joint outputs; the other is by asymmetrical disposal of desirable and undesirable outputs instead their proportionate contraction or expansion.

If y represents outputs, the output component v represents desirable outputs and w represents undesirable outputs, y satisfies weak disposability, then

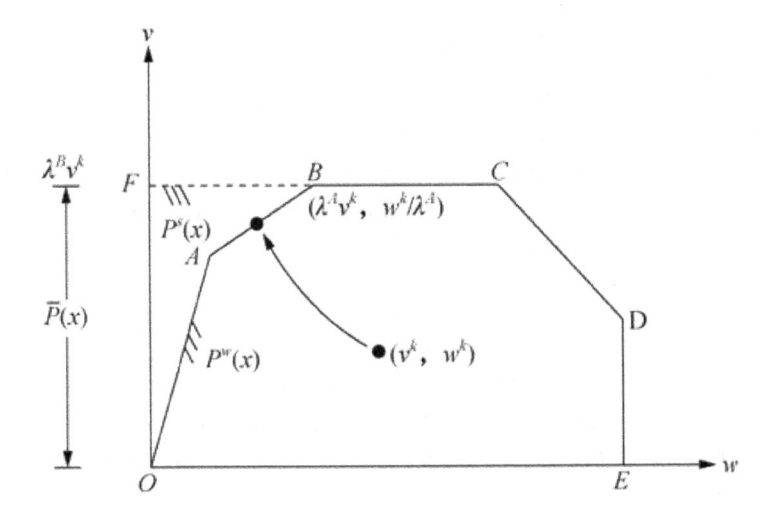

Fig. 9.4   Output subsets of weak disposability

Source: Fare (1989), p. 92.

$$y \in P(x) \Rightarrow \{\theta y \mid \theta \in [0,1]\} \subset P(x)$$

Here, v is at your free disposal, that is,

$$(v, w) \in P(x) \Rightarrow (v', w) \in P(x) \qquad \text{for all } v' \le v$$

Suppose there are K producers, n kinds of inputs, N represents input matrix $n \times K$, $M = (V, W)$, in which V represents desirable output matrix and W undesirable output matrix. A technology output set that satisfies weak disposability is as follows:

$$P^w(x) = \{(v, w) : v \le V_z, w = W_z, N_z \le x, z \in R_+^k\}$$

Here, z is a $K \times 1$ vector used to establish a convex set of output combinations. As shown in Fig. 9.4, *OABCDE* is an output set that satisfies weak disposability while *OFBCDE* is an output set that satisfies strong disposability.

To solve efficiency by *DEA*, we face the problem of the establishment of the frontier. In a traditional output set which only has desirable outputs, the boundary is usually an effective subset and the efficiency of Point A is segment *OA/OB*, or the specific value of the length of a segment that starts from the origin (see Fig. 9.5).

However, in joint production which takes undesirable outputs, the boundary may not be an effective subset. In accordance with Shephard's definition of an effective point, in Fig. 9.4, only the segment AB is effective. The definition of Fare's (1989) output-oriented enhanced hyperbolic efficiency is given as

$$H_o^A(v^k, w^k, x^k) = \max\{\lambda v^k, \lambda^{-1} w^k) \in P^w(x^k)\}$$

The definition of this measurement is: the way in which points (v^k, w^k) in the output set expand toward the boundary are no longer through the origin in the radial direction; instead, it is in an asymmetrical form, that is, if desirable outputs become λ times larger, the undesirable outputs reduces to $1/\lambda$ of its original amount. We can get efficiency H by solving nonlinear programming problems

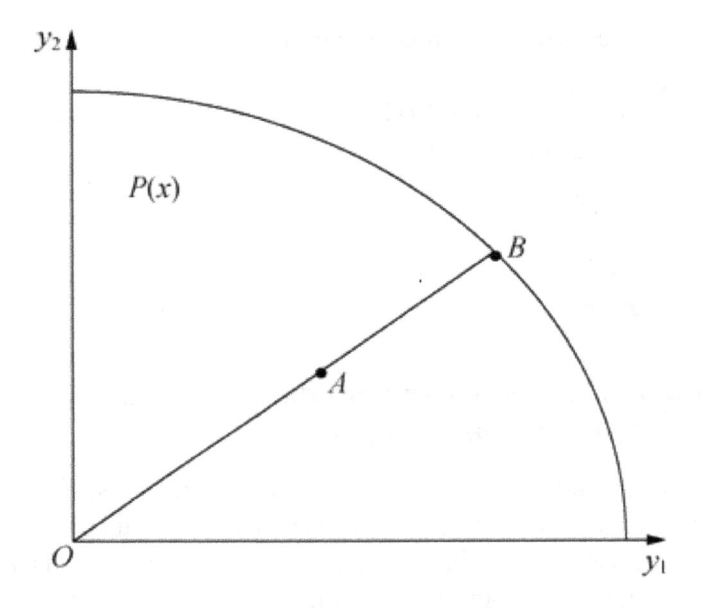

Fig. 9.5   Efficiency measurement in case of desirable outputs

$$H_o(v^k, w^k, x^k) = \max \lambda$$
$$\text{subject to} \quad \lambda v^k \leq V_z$$
$$\lambda^{-1} w^k = W_z$$
$$N_z \leq x^k$$
$$z \in R_+^K$$

If we Taylor-expand the constraint condition $\lambda^{-1} w^k = W_z$ at $\lambda = 1$ for an approximate first derivative, we can get an approximate linear programming problem

$$H_o(v^k, w^k, x^k) = \max \lambda$$
$$\text{subject to} \quad \lambda v^k \leq V_z$$
$$2w^k - \lambda w^k = W_z$$
$$N_z \leq x^k$$
$$z \in R_+^K$$

The enhanced hyperbolic productivity is

$$H_p(v^k, w^k, x^k) = \max\{\lambda : (\lambda v^k, \lambda^{-1} w) \in P^w(\lambda^{-1} x^k)\}$$
$$\text{subject to } \lambda v^k \le V_z$$
$$\lambda^{-1} w^k = W_z$$
$$N_z \le \lambda^{-1} x^k$$
$$z \in R_+^K$$

4.3. *Malmquist–Luenberger productivity index based on directional distance function*

Chambers (Chambers *et al.*, 1996) argued that, in terms of the interest function Shephard put forward in his consumer theory and the generalized form of Shephard (1953) input distance function, the former makes directional formulation of preferences. Suppose $u(x)$ is a utility function, $x \in X \subset R_+^N$, g is a vector in R_+^N, the interest function is given as

$$b(g; u, x) = \sup\{\beta \in R : x - \beta g \in X, u(x - \beta g) \ge u\}$$

If we adopt distance function instead, it becomes

$$D_i(u, x) = \sup\{\lambda : (x / \lambda) \in X, u(x / \lambda) \ge u\}$$

It is obvious that all the variables in the distance function make proportionate radial changes while variables in the interest function may have more than one directional option. As for the latter, if the direction of g is the same as that of x, they make radial changes. Therefore, in terms of mathematical expressions, the distance function is a special case of interest function.

Chung *et al.* (1997) put forward the Malmquist–Luenberger (ML) Productivity Index. It has two strong points: one is, like Malmquist Index, it only needs quantity rather than price information and is able to break productivity index up into technological improvement and efficiency enhancement; the other is that, drawing on advantages of the interest function, it treats desirable outputs and undesirable outputs differently through the directional distance function, taking the reduction of undesirable output as a contributive element for the increase of productivity as shown in the research by Fare (1989). However, theoretically, the directional distance function is more systematic.

Suppose $v \in R_+^M$ represents desirable outputs, $w \in R_+^I$ represents undesirable outputs, and $x \in R_+^R$ represents inputs, then productive technology expressed by outputs is

$$P(x) = \{(v,w) : x \text{ can produce } (v,w)\}$$

It satisfies the following three properties:

(1) undesirable outputs are of weak disposability
   $(v,w) \in P(x), 0 \le \theta \le 1 \Rightarrow (\theta v, \theta w) \in P(x)$
(2) inputs and desirable outputs are of free disposability
   if $x' \ge x$, then $P(x') \ge P(x)$
   $(v,w) \in P(x)$ and $v' \le v \Rightarrow (v',w) \in P(x)$
(3) if the target is zero pollutant emission, the price is zero production or if $w = 0$, then $v = 0$.

As mentioned earlier, with the existence of undesirable outputs, the Shephard boundary points may not be effective points. Therefore, the denominator of the "efficiency" calculated through distance functions is not the distance from the firm to the frontier; the proportionate increase of outputs and pollution means "efficiency improvement", which does not make sense in economics. Thus, the key first lies in the identification of the effective subset on the boundary of distance functions then the fact that non-effective subsets may not necessarily project in the radial direction.

The definition of the directional distance function is

$$\vec{D}_0(x,v,w;g) = \sup\{\beta : (v,w) + \beta g \in P(x)\}$$

Here, g is directional vector defined as $g = (v, -w)$.

Suppose v and w are both one-dimensional variables. As shown in Fig. 9.6, $P(x)$ represents the output set, v represents desirable outputs, and w represents undesirable outputs. Desirable outputs first increase then

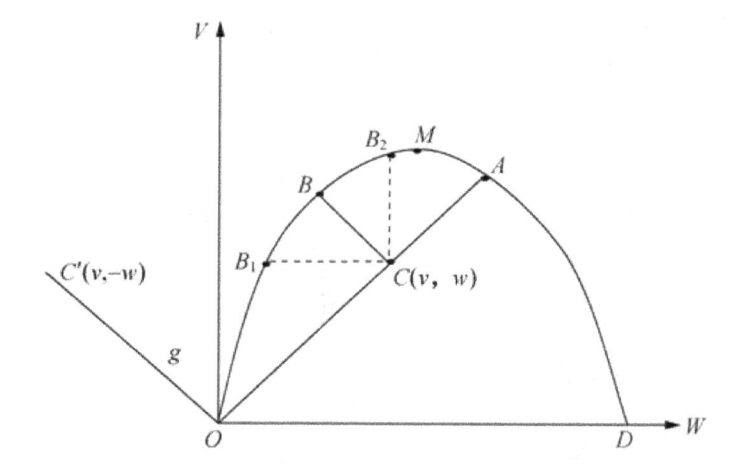

Fig. 9.6 Efficiency measurement with undesirable outputs

decrease, while undesirable outputs keep on increasing until Point D where desirable outputs reduce to zero. Before desirable outputs reach the maximum M, the increase in the speed of v remains lower than that of w. As for non-efficiency point C, if we directly use the definition of Shephard output distance function in efficiency measurement, the efficiency of C will be OC/OA. Such a measurement that is problematic for A may not be an efficiency point, and the proportionate increase of undesirable outputs and desirable outputs will be considered to be more efficient even if A is efficient, which does not make sense in terms of reason. Due to the existence of undesirable outputs, Shephard (1970) believed that the increase (no reduction) of desirable outputs without any increase (reduction) of undesirable outputs means higher efficiency. According to this standard, in contrast to Point C, apparently A does not meet with its requirements while the points between $B1$ and $B2$ do meet with the requirements for desirable outputs, do not reduce, and undesirable outputs do not increase on these points.

In Fig. 9.6, if $g = (v, -w)$, or it matches (v, w) in the second quadrant, and Point C and $B_1 B_2$ intersect at Point B in the direction of g with BC/OC as corresponding efficiency. For the efficient Point B, the value of the directional distance function is zero, and larger directional distance function means lower efficiency.

The relationship between the two types of distance functions is if $g = (v, -w)$ or we project in the radial direction of C,

$$\vec{D}_0(x, v, w; (v, w)) = \sup\{\beta : (v, w) + \beta(v, w) \in P(x)\}$$
$$= \sup\{\beta : (1 + \beta)(v, w) \in P(x)\}$$
$$= \sup\{(\rho^{-1}) : \frac{v, w}{\rho} \in P(x)\}$$
$$= \frac{1}{\inf\{\rho : \frac{v, w}{\rho} \in P(x)\}} - 1$$
$$= D_0(v, w)^{-1} - 1$$

The expressions show that if the direction of g coincides with that of (v, w), then Shephard's output distance function is an exception of directional distance function. To establish ML productivity index according to this relationship, we should first take the traditional M productivity index of undesirable outputs to be

$$M_t^{t+1} = \left[\frac{D_o^t\left(x^{t+1}, v^{t+1}, w^{t+1}\right) \times D_o^{t+1}\left(x^{t+1}, v^{t+1}, w^{t+1}\right)}{D_o^t\left(x^t, v^t, w^t\right) \times D_o^{t+1}\left(x^t, v^t, w^t\right)} \right]^{\frac{1}{2}}$$

If we resolve it into the product of efficiency changes and technology changes, we get:

$$M_t^{t+1} = \frac{D_o^{t+1}(x^{t+1}, v^{t+1}, w^{t+1})}{D_o^t(x^t, v^t, w^t)} \left[\frac{D_o^t(x^{t+1}, v^{t+1}, w^{t+1}) \times D_o^t(x^t, v^t, w^t)}{D_o^{t+1}(x^{t+1}, v^{t+1}, w^{t+1}) \times D_o^{t+1}(x^t, v^t, w^t)} \right]^{\frac{1}{2}}$$

To make sure M productivity index is the same as ML when $g = (v, w)$, we define the output-oriented ML productivity index as

$$\text{ML}_t^{t+1} =$$

$$\left\{ \frac{\left[1 + \vec{D}_o^t(x^t, v^t, w^t; v^t, -w^t) \right] \times \left[1 + \vec{D}_o^{t+1}(x^t, v^t, w^t; v^t, -w^t) \right]}{\left[1 + \vec{D}_o^t(x^{t+1}, v^{t+1}, w^{t+1}; v^{t+1}, -w^{t+1}) \right] \times \left[1 + \vec{D}_o^{t+1}(x^{t+1}, v^{t+1}, w^{t+1}; v^{t+1}, -w^{t+1}) \right]} \right\}^{\frac{1}{2}}$$

Similarly, the ML index can be resolved into product of efficiency changes and technology changes as

$$ML_t^{t+1} = \frac{1 + \overrightarrow{D_o^t}\left(x^t, v^t, w^t; v^t, -w^t\right)}{1 + \overrightarrow{D_o^{t+1}}\left(x^{t+1}, v^{t+1}, w^{t+1}; v^{t+1}, -w^{t+1}\right)}$$

$$\times \left\{ \frac{\left[1 + \overrightarrow{D_o^{t+1}}\left(x^t, v^t, w^t; v^t, -w^t\right)\right] \times \left[1 + \overrightarrow{D_o^{t+1}}(x^{t+1}, v^{t+1}, w^{t+1}; v^{t+1}, -w^{t+1})\right]}{\left[1 + \overrightarrow{D_o^t}\left(x^t, v^t, w^t; v^t, -w^t\right)\right] \times \left[1 + \overrightarrow{D_o^t}(x^{t+1}, v^{t+1}, w^{t+1}; v^{t+1}, -w^{t+1})\right]} \right\}^{\frac{1}{2}}$$

The consequence of such a definition of the directional distance function is: if ML index is larger than 1, it means productivity is improved. Suppose there are T time periods and K producers, input–output is expressed as

$$(x^{t,k}, v^{t,k}, w^{t,k}), \quad k = 1, \ldots, K; t = 1, \ldots, T$$

For each ML index, it is necessary to calculate the following four distance functions to resolve linear planning problems:

$$\overrightarrow{D_o^t}(x^{t,k}, v^{t,k}, w^{t,k}, -w^{t,k}) = max\, \beta$$

$$\text{subject to} \sum_{k=1}^{K} z_k v_{k,m}^t, \quad m = 1, \ldots, M$$

$$\sum_{k=1}^{K} z_k w_{k,i}^t = \left(1 - \beta\right) w_{k,i}^t, \quad i = 1, \ldots, I$$

$$\sum_{k=1}^{K} z_k x_{k,n}^t \leq (1 - \beta) x_{k,n}^t, \quad n = 1, \ldots, N$$

$$z_k \geq 0, \quad k = 1, \ldots, K$$

5. Conclusion

This chapter introduces the disposal of undesirable outputs in productivity measures by focusing on the methods through which the distance function theory and the directional distance functions dispose of undesirable outputs. In order to constitute the production frontier required by DEA when undesirable outputs are concerned, both Fare's (1989) hyperbolic curve productivity indices and Chung *et al.*'s (1997) directional distance functions attempt to change the radial projection manners of no-efficiency points in Shephard's distance functions so as to project toward the frontier by expanding desirable outputs and contracting undesirable outputs.

Appendix A: Properties of Distance Functions

D.1 $\psi(u,x)$ is the homogenous function of x.

D.2 $\psi(u,x+y) \geq \psi(u,x) + \psi(u,y)$ related to non-negative output u.

D.3 $\psi(u,x)$ is the non-monotone decreasing of x.

D.4 $\psi(u,x)$ is the concave function of x.

D.5 $\psi(u,x)$ is the continuous function of x.

D.6 $\psi(u,x)$ is the non-monotone increasing function of u.

D.7 If $x \in D$ and $\{u_n \to +\infty\}$, then $\lim sup_{n \to +\infty} \psi(u_n,x) = 0$.

D.8 If $x \in D$ and $\{u_n \to 0\}$, then $\lim sup_{n \to +\infty} \psi(u_n,x)$ may be finite.

D.9 If $x \in D$, then $\psi(u,x)$ is the upper semi-continuity of u.

Appendix B: Properties of Input Distance Function $\psi(u,x)$

Δ.1 $\psi(0,x) = +\infty$, for any x; $\psi(y,x) = 0$, if $(y,x) \in \Delta^c$.

If outputs are zero, $L(0) = X$, $\lambda(0,x) = 0$, therefore its reciprocal is infinite. If $(y,x) \in \Delta^c$, then $\{\lambda \mid (\lambda x) \in L(y), \lambda \geq 0\}$ is an empty set and λx does not intersect with $L(y)$.

Δ.2 For each $(y,x) \in \Delta, \psi(y,x) > 0$ and is finite.

Δ.3 $\psi(y,x)$ is a homogenous function of x.

$$\psi(y,x) = \frac{\|x\|}{\|\xi(y,x)\|} = \frac{1}{\lambda(y,x)}$$

$$\psi(y,\beta x) = \frac{1}{\lambda(y,\beta x)} = \frac{1}{\min\{\lambda \mid \lambda \beta x \in L(y)\}} = \frac{\beta}{\min\{\lambda \mid \lambda x \in L(y)\}}$$

Δ.4 $\psi(y,x+x') \geq \psi(y,x) + \psi(y,x')$

According to $\Delta.3$, $\psi\left(y,\frac{x}{\psi(y,x)}\right)=\psi\left(y,\frac{x'}{\psi(y,x')}\right)=1$, therefore $x/\psi(y,x)$ and $x'/\psi(y,x')$ both belong to $L(y)$. As $L(y)$ is a convex set, $\theta[x/\psi(y,x)]+(1-\theta)[x'/\psi(y,x')]$ also belongs to $L(y)$. So:

$$\psi\left(y,\ \theta\frac{x}{\psi(y,x)}+(1-\theta)\frac{x'}{\psi(y,x')}\right)\geq 1$$

If $=\frac{\psi(y,x)}{\psi(y,x)+\psi(y,x')}$, the above expression becomes:

$$\psi\left(y,\frac{x}{\psi(y,x)+\psi(y,x')}+\frac{x}{\psi(y,x)+\psi(y,x')}\right)\geq 1$$

According to properties of homogenous functions, the larger the input distance function is, the further it is from the frontier while the lower the efficiency is.

$\Delta.5$ If $x'\geq x$, $\psi(y,x')\geq\psi(y,x)$.

Given the same outputs, the more inputs, the larger the distance function is while the lower the efficiency is.

$\Delta.6$ $\psi(y,x)$ is the concave function of x.

Suppose x and x' both belong to $L(y)$:

$\psi\left(y,\theta x+(1-\theta)x'\right)\geq\psi\left(y,\theta x\right)+\psi\left(y,(1-\theta)x'\right)=\theta\psi\left(y,x\right)+(1-\theta)\psi\left(y,x'\right)$

$\Delta.7$ $\psi(y,x)$ is the continuous function of x.

$\Delta.8$ $\psi(\lambda y,x)\leq\psi(y,x)$, if $\lambda\geq 1$; or/and $\psi(y',x)\leq\psi(y,x)$, *if* $y'\geq y$.

$\psi(y,x)$ is the non-monotone increase function of y, if $y'\geq y$, then $L(y')\subset L(y)$ and a ray that starts from the origin always first intersects with $L(y)$. Its economic significance is, given the same inputs, the more outputs, the smaller the distance function is, the larger the efficiency is. The former shows strong disposability, while the latter weak disposability.

$\Delta.9$ $\psi(y,x)$ is the upper semi-continuity function of y.

$\Delta.10$ $\psi(y,x)$ is the quasi-concave function of y.

The input distance function $\psi(y,x)$ means the input set $L(y)=\{x\,|\,\psi(y,x)\geq 1\}$.

If we define the output set $P(x)$ by the output distance function $\Omega(x,y), P(x)=\{y\,|\,\Omega(x,y)\leq 1\}$. The output distance function has the following properties:

∇.1 $\Omega(x,0) = 0$ for all x; $\Omega(x,y) = +\infty$, if $(y,x) \in \Delta^c$.

∇.2 $\Omega(x,y) > 0$ and is finite.

∇.3 $\Omega(x,y)$ is the homogenous function of y.

$\Omega(x,\lambda y) = \frac{1}{\theta(x,\lambda y)} = \frac{1}{\max\{\theta \,|\, \theta\, \lambda y \in P(x)\}} = \frac{\lambda}{\max\{\rho \,|\, \rho y \in P(x)\}}$. Note: if outputs are multiplied by λ, to guarantee $\theta\, \lambda y \in P(x)$, θ shall be reduced by the same times, multiplying the distance function.

∇.4 $\Omega(x, y+y') \le \Omega(x,y) + \Omega(x,y')$

According to ∇.3, $\Omega\left(x, \frac{y}{\Omega(x,y)}\right) = \Omega\left(x, \frac{y'}{\Omega(x,y')}\right) = 1$, therefore $y/\Omega(x,y)$ and $y'/\Omega(x,y')$ both belong to $P(x)$. As $P(x)$ is a convex set, $\theta[y/\Omega(x,y)] + (1-\theta)[y'/\Omega(x,y')]$ also belongs to $P(x)$, and:

$$\Omega(x, \theta y/\Omega(x,y) + (1-\theta)y'/\Omega(x,y')) \le 1$$

If $= \frac{\Omega(x,y')}{\Omega(x,y) + \Omega(x,yx')}$, the above expression becomes:

$$\Omega\left(x, \frac{y}{\Omega(x,y) + \Omega(x,y')} + \frac{y'}{\Omega(x,y) + \Omega(x,y')}\right) \le 1$$

According to properties of homogenous functions, the smaller the output distance function is, the further it is from the frontier while the lower the efficiency is.

∇.5 $\Omega(x, \theta y) \le \Omega(x,y)$ if $\theta \in [0,1]$; or/and $\Omega(x,y') \le +\Omega(x,y)$ if $y' \le y$.

$\Omega(x,y)$ is the non-monotone decreasing function of y. With given inputs, the more outputs are, the higher the efficiency is. The former refers to the proportionate changes of output components and the latter includes the unproportionate changes of outputs, which is the difference between strong disposability and weak disposability.

∇.6 $\Omega(x,y)$ is the convex function of y.

If y and y' both belong to $P(x)$,

$$\Omega\left(x, \theta y + (1-\theta)y'\right) \le \theta\,\Omega(x,y) + (1-\theta)\Omega(x,y')$$

∇.7 $\Omega(x,y)$ is the continuous function of y.

∇.8 $\Omega(x',y) \le \Omega(x,y)$ if $x' \ge x$.

$\Omega(x,y)$ is the non-monotone increasing function of x. Given the same outputs, the more outputs, the smaller the efficiency is.

$\nabla.9$ $\Omega(x,y)$ is the lower bound semi-continuity function of x.

$\nabla.10$ $\Omega(x,y)$ is the quasi convex function of x.

Appendix C: Proofs

$$F_1 = \frac{-P_1 Y_1}{P_1 Y_1 - \theta_2 Y_2 - \theta_3 Y_3}$$

$$F_2 = \frac{\theta_2 Y_2}{P_1 Y_1 - \theta_2 Y_2 - \theta_3 Y_3}$$

$$F_3 = \frac{P_3 Y_3}{P_1 Y_1 - \theta_2 Y_2 - \theta_3 Y_3}$$

Proofs:

$$L = P_1 Y_1 - \sum_{n}^{N} r_n X_n - \theta_1 [F(\ln Y_1, \ln Y_2, \ln Y_3, \ln X, k) - 1]$$
$$- \theta_2 \left(Y_2 - Y_2^*\right) - \theta_3 (Y_3 - Y_3^*)$$

f.o.c

$$\frac{\partial L}{\partial Y_1} = P_1 - \theta_1 F_1 \frac{1}{Y_1} = 0$$

$$\frac{\partial L}{\partial Y_2} = -\theta_1 F_2 \frac{1}{Y_2} = 0$$

$$\frac{\partial L}{\partial Y_3} = -\theta_1 F_3 \frac{1}{Y_3} - \theta_3 = 0$$

Given $\sum_i F_i = -1$; therefore, $\theta_1 = P_1 Y_1 - \theta_2 Y_2 - \theta_3 Y_3$.
Once the first-order condition is substituted, we can get the result.

References

Caves, D. W., Christensen, L. R. & Diewert, W. E., "Multilateral Comparisons of Output, Input, and Productivity Using Superlative Index Number". *The Economic Journal*, Vol. 92 (1982a), pp. 73–86.

Caves, D. W., Christensen, L. R. & Diewert, W. E., "The Economic Theory of Index Number and the Measurement of Input, Output and Productivity". *Econometrica*, Vol. 50 (1982b), pp. 1393–1414.

Chambers, R. G., Chung, Y. & Fare, R., "Benefit and Distance Functions". *Journal of Economic Theory*, Vol. 70 (1996), pp. 407–419.

Charnes, A., Cooper, W. W. & Rhodes, E. L., "Measuring the Efficiency of Decision Making Units". *European Journal of Operational Research*, Vol. 2 (1978), pp. 429–444.

Chung,Y. H., Fare, R. & Grosskopf, S., "Productivity and Undesirable Outputs: A Directional Distance Function Approach". *Journal of Environmental Management*, Vol. 51 (1997), pp. 229–240.

Färe, R., Grosskopf, S., Noh D. W. & Weber, W., "Characteristics of a Polluting Technology: Theory and Practice". *Journal of Econometrics*, Vol. 126 (2005), pp. 469–492.

Färe, R., Grosskopf, S., Lovell, C. A. K. & Pasurka, C., Multilateral, Productivity Comparisons When Some Outputs Are Undesirable: A Nonparametric Approach. *The Review of Economics and Statistics* (1989), pp. 90–98.

Färe, R., Grosskopf, S, Lovell, C. A. K. & Yaisawarng, S., "Derivation of Shadow Prices for Undesirable Outputs: A Distance Function Approach," *The Review of Economics and Statistics*, Vol. 75 (1993), pp. 374–380.

Farrell, M. J., "The Measurement of Productive Efficiency of Production". *Journal of the Rayal Statistical Society*, Series A, Vol. 120, No. III (1957), pp. 253–281.

Førsund, Finn R., & Sarafoglou, Nikias, "On the Origins of Data Envelopment Analysis". *Journal of Productivity Analysis*, Vol. 17 (2002), pp. 23–40.

Jorgenson, D. W., & Wilcoxen, P. J., "Environmental Regulation and U. S. Economic Growth". *Rand Journal of Economics*, Vol. 21, No. 2 (1990), pp. 314–340.

Pittman, R. W., "Multilateral Productivity Comparisons with Undesirable Outputs". *The Economic Journal* (1983), pp. 883–891.

Shephard, R. W., *Theory of Cost and Production Functions*, 1953. Princeton University Press, Princeton, NJ, USA.

Shephard, R. W., *Theory of Cost and Production Functions*, 1970. Princeton University Press, Princeton, NJ, USA.

Chapter 10

Calculation of Greenhouse Gas Emissions in China: Methods and Practice

Yuhong Li and Yisheng Zheng

Institute of Quantitative & Technical Economics,
Chinese Academy of Social Sciences

Since the Reform and Opening Up, the Chinese economy has been growing at the overwhelming rate of 9.5% a year. Simultaneously, China's resource consumption, mainly coal consumption, has been increasing year in and year out, and its CO_2 emission has repeatedly gone beyond expectations of relevant international institutions, becoming one of the largest concerns in the global efforts to deal with climate change. The 2007 *World Energy Outlook* published by the IEA (IEA, 2007) looks into China and India's energy demand and supply projections as well as their carbon emissions in the future based on different scenarios. At present, China's greenhouse gas emission is not only a research priority of international energy and environmental organizations and relevant institutions in those developed countries in Europe and the USA (UNFCCC, the World Bank, IEA, WRI, EIA, PBL, etc.) but also a research focus in the domestic academic community.

1. Position of Greenhouse Gas Emission Calculation in Studies of Climate Change

The climate change issue differs from traditional ecological environment problems which are regional in essence, emerging as a thorny global issue. Climate talks are at the core of current international political and economic relations, drawing concerns no less than those on the global disarmament, nuclear disarmament, and environment conferences in history.

The climate change issue is a comprehensive project including a series of issues such as greenhouse gas emission, atmospheric concentration, radiative forcing,[1] climate change, and their influence and damage, with a research area going beyond both natural science and social science, ranging from national decision-making to the calculation of the greenhouse gas emission from the rumination of a cow.

Greenhouse gas emission research plays a fundamental role in studies of climate change and acts as a pre-condition for studies related to other problems (Fig. 10.1). For instance, in terms of scenario analysis, we must first estimate the GHG emission so as to calculate its concentration in the atmosphere, and then input it into the global climate model

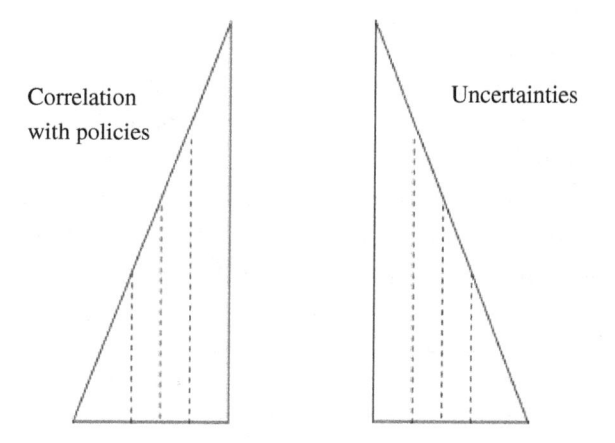

Fig. 10.1   Position of greenhouse gas emission in studies of climate change

---

[1] Energy changes per square meter of the Earth's surface quantified at the top of the atmosphere. According to evaluation reports of IPCC, radiative forcing is a measure of the influence a factor has on altering the balance of incoming and outgoing energy in the Earth–atmosphere system and is an index reflecting the importance of the factor as a potential climate change mechanism. Positive forcing warms the system, while negative forcing cools it. In this report, radiative forcing values are for changes relative to preindustrial conditions defined in 1750 and are expressed in Watts per square meter (W/m^2). See http://en.wikipedia.org/wiki/Radiative_forcing.

as an important parameter. Unlike other issues under discussion, the emission issue has weak correlation with policies and a rather small uncertainty. On the contrary, studies of influence and damage of climate change have rather strong correlation with policies and carry huge uncertainty.

2. Calculation Methods and Principles of Calculation of Greenhouse Gas Emission

Through practice of more than a decade, IPCC has formulated a set of relatively complete calculation methodology of the GHG inventories and successively published and updated its guidelines for national greenhouse gas inventories (1996, 2006). The greenhouse gas emission of a certain unit's social and economic activities within a certain period of time is calculated as

$$E_t = \sum_{it} A_{it} EF_{it} \tag{10.1}$$

Here, E represents emissions, A represents the social and economic activities that emit GHG, EF represents the emission factor, and i represents the category of the social and economic activities. The units may range from a project at the micro-level, such as the CDM project, to the emissions of an area or industry at the medium level or the emission inventories of a country or countries at the macro-level.

The emission factor is the vital element in the calculation formulas. Generally speaking, different methods are adopted for different levels. For the emission factors in CDM, their emissions should be calculated through calculation of the emissions of the project itself according to the specific project. Therefore, different CDMs have different emission factors. In terms of the emission inventory of a certain country, we generally adopt a relatively rough method. The simplest method is implementing the calculation by using the default values in the IPCC guidelines, and then identifying the different regional emission resources by adopting emission factors that correspond with the local characteristics. In actual practice, we should obtain the best calculation results by choosing the most feasible method according to the actual situation.

Calculation methods of GHG emissions must satisfy the following principles[2]:

(1) Transparency: We must clearly define the assumptions and methods for GHG emission calculation so that the objects that use the inventory data can repeat their calculation. That is the most important principle for the calculation of the inventory data.

(2) Consistence: The calculation methods and data caliber must be consistent in time.

(3) Comparativity: The inventory comparison of all parties should adopt a method recognized by the COP such as the IPCC guidelines. That is the unity of horizontal comparison.

(4) Integrity: The calculation boundary should be integral, which means, for one thing, it should include not only the emission resources or sinks identified in IPCC guidelines but also those emission resources or sinks, unique to certain countries, not identified in the IPCC guidelines, and for another, the integrity of the geochart boundaries.

(5) Accuracy: It is a relative index, that is, apart from avoiding systematic overestimation or underestimation in the calculation results, we should also try our best to exclude uncertainty. Appropriate methods and data should be used to increase the accuracy of the results.

The above-mentioned characteristics are generally referred to as principles of TCCCA.

3. Types of Greenhouse Gases and Emission Resources

3.1. *Types of greenhouse gases*

Among all the greenhouse gases, the global warming potential of CO_2 is relatively low, but its lifetime is longer than that of two other important greenhouse gases, methane and hydrofluoro nitride. Table 10.1 lists out several major greenhouse gases.

---

[2] Available at http://www.epa.gov/ttn/chief/conference/ei12/poster/todorova.pdf.

Table 10.1 Types and characteristics of greenhouse gases

Types	Global warming effect (%)	Lifetime (years)	Global warming potential (GWP) (100 years)
CO_2	63	50–200	1
CH_4	15	12–17	23
N_2O	4	120	296
HFC_s	11	13	—
PFC_s		50,000	—
SF_6 and others	7	3200	22,200

Source: Appendix A, *Kyoto Protocol.*

3.2. *Resources of greenhouse gas emissions*

The Guidelines for *National Greenhouse Gas Inventories* identify five types of the resources of greenhouse gas emissions: fossil fuel combustion, industrial processes, agriculture, land use change and forestry (LULUCF), and waste (Table 10.2).

3.2.1. CO_2

Major emission resources of CO_2 include fossil fuel combustion, industrial processes, land use change, forestry, and waste.

3.2.2. CH_4

Major emission resources of CH_4 include industrial processes, agriculture, and waste.

3.2.3. NO_x

Major emission resources of N_2O include fossil fuel combustion (including automobile exhaust), industrial processes (non-ferrous metal production, nitric acid production, synthesis ammonia production, carbamide production), agricultural waste combustion, agricultural soil, land use change, and forests.

Major emission resources of NO_x include fossil fuel combustion, industrial processes (non-ferrous metal production, nitric acid production,

Table 10.2 Major sources of greenhouse gas emissions

National Greenhouse Gas Inventories	Energy	Fossil fuel combustion	Static emission resources	Energy industry
				Manufacturing industry and construction industry
			Mobile emission resources	Highway transportation
				Railway transportation
				Aviation
				Navigation
		Fugitive emission from fuels	Coal	
			Oil and natural gas	
	Industrial processes	Building materials		
		Chemical products		
		Metal products		
		ODS		
	Agriculture	Animal husbandry	Intestinal fermentation	
			Animal waste management	
		Planting industry	Paddy fields	
			Other agricultural lands	
	Land use change and forestry	Forestry carbon sink		
		Land use change		
	Waste	Solid waste management		
		Waste water treatment		

Source: IPCC, Guidelines for National Greenhouse Gas Inventories (2006).

ammoniate production, steel production, ethylene production), agricultural waste combustion, land use change, and forests.

3.2.4. *HFC$_s$*

Major emission resources of HFC$_s$ include:

(1) HFC$_s$ production as a byproduct in the production of HCFC-22; the emission of HFC-23 is about 4% of that of HCFC-22. During the

production of Freon, the estimated leak amount is about 0.5% of the production.

(2) Use and disuse of air conditioners and refrigerators, foamed plastic, solvent, fire extinguishers, aerosol containers.

3.2.5. *PFC$_s$*

Major emission resources of PFC$_s$ include use and disuse of refrigerators, foamed plastic, solvent, fire extinguishers, and aerosol containers.

3.2.6. *SF$_6$*

Major emission resources of SF$_6$ include insulating liquids of high-voltage electrical appliances, fire extinguishers, flame-proof equipment, and casting of aluminum and magnesium. SF$_6$ is used as an isolation gas during the casting of aluminum and magnesium. As SF$_6$ is an inert gas, its emission equals its usage amount during this process. However, the emission inventory investigation carried out in relevant institutes for energy finds that no SF$_6$ is used in China's casting of aluminum and magnesium, which means China's current SF$_6$ emission is zero.

4. Previous Studies of Estimation of China's Greenhouse Gas Emissions

Since the 1990s, relevant organizations of the Chinese government have carried out a series of studies concerning China's greenhouse gas emissions, such as *China's National Countermeasures to Global Climate Change Research* by the State Scientific and Technological Commission (now the Chinese Ministry of Science and Technology) and Asian Development Bank, *Problems and Countermeasures to Greenhouse Gas Control in China* by the National Environmental Protection Agency (now the State Environmental Protection Administration) and the World Bank, Estimations of Sources and Sinks of China's Greenhouse Gases Control in 1990, a sub-report of the Global Environmental Facility program, *National Research of Climate Change* and *Countermeasures for Asian Greenhouse Gases Reduction at the Minimum Cost* by the State Scientific and Technological Commission, and *A Comprehensive Analysis of the*

Research Results of China's Greenhouse Gases Emissions and Sink Absorption and *Current Situation and Future Vision of China's Greenhouse Gases Emissions* by the National Climate Change Coordinating Group Office. Specialists from the Energy Research Institute, National Development and Reform Commission, Qinghua University, the Institute of Atmospheric Physics, Chinese Academy of Sciences, the Chinese Academy of Agricultural Sciences, Beijing Municipal Environmental Monitoring Center, and so on took part in these studies.

China's estimations of greenhouse gases emissions mainly focus on CO_2. It is not only because CO_2 takes up the largest proportion in the greenhouse gases but also because of the difficulty in obtaining data of other greenhouse gases. According to estimations of Gao *et al.* (1994), in the emissions of China's greenhouse gases in 1990, CO_2 was about 2.12 billion tons while the official figure was 2.4 billion tons. The difference was partly because the estimated industrial sector involved only referred to the cement industry. They predicted that China's emission of CO_2 would be 3.96 billion tons by 2010 while that of 2020 would be 4.9 billion tons. Today, such estimations seem to be too conservative.

According to *1996 IPCC Guidelines for National Greenhouse Gas Inventory (Revised)*, Zhang *et al.* (2001) calculated China's emission of CO_2 in 1990 and found that it was 2.22 billion tons, 92.5% of which came from fossil fuel combustion while 47.2% of the industrial emissions resources was from the cement industry. In 1994, the Chinese emission of CO_2 reached 2.79 billion tons, 25.7% higher than that of 1990.

In 2005, UNFCCC declared that China's greenhouse gases emission in 1994 included 4.058 billion tons CO_2 equivalent (not including land use and forestry) (see Table 10.3), 34.6% of all the 122 non-Annex 1 parties.

Table 10.3   China's greenhouse gas emissions (CO_2 equivalent) in 1994

	Energy	Industry	Agriculture	Waste	Total
Emissions (100 million tons)	30.08	2.83	6.05	1.62	40.58
Rate (%)	74.1	7.0	14.9	4.0	100.0

Note: The sixth compilation and synthesis of initial national communications from Parties not included in Annex I to the Convention: Inventories of Anthropogenic Emissions by Sources and Removals of Greenhouse Gases.

Source: UNFCCC, 2005.

The greenhouse gases included CO_2, methane, and nitrous oxide. The emission of CO_2 was 3.073 billion tons, taking up 75.7% of all the three kinds of greenhouse gases. The greenhouse gas emissions from the energy sector were the largest, followed by agriculture and industry. These data were rather authoritative and comprehensive as they were based on the Chinese government's calculation according to *IPCC Guidelines for National Greenhouse Gas Inventory*.

Drawing on data on energy consumption, cement production, and waste gas combustion, the Carbon Dioxide Information Analysis Center of ORNL calculated the CO_2 emissions of various countries since the dawning of the industrial age. According to their calculation, the Chinese emissions of CO_2 in 1990 and 1994 were 2.41 billion tons and 3 billion tons, taking up 10.7% and 13.1% of the global emissions of CO_2, respectively (see Table 10.4). As of 2006, the accumulative total carbon emission of China took up 8.4% of that of the world, about one-third of that of the USA.

Since 2007, IEA reports show China's CO_2 emissions related to fossil fuels were 5.1 billion tons in 2005, 5.645 billion tons in 2006, and 6 billion tons in 2007 (see Table 10.5), 21% of that of the world, 300 million tons more than that of the USA.

In 2007, the Netherlands Environmental Assessment Agency (NEAA) first declared to the whole world that China's CO_2 emission in 2006

Table 10.4 CDIAC's estimation of China's CO_2 emissions

Year	Total emissions (100 million tons)	Annual growth (%)	Global proportion (%)
1990	24.1	—	10.7
1994	30.0	—	13.1
2000	34.1	2.6	13.8
2001	34.9	2.4	13.8
2002	37.0	6.1	14.5
2003	43.5	17.6	16.3
2004	51.0	17.1	18.1
2005	56.3	10.3	19.2
2006	61.0	8.5	20.2

Source: Website of the Carbon Dioxide Information Analysis Center of ORNL, cdiac.ornl.gov/trends/emis/meth_reg.html.

Table 10.5   Summary of research on CO_2 emissions in China (billion tons)

Institute/ author	Publishing time (year)	Calculation range	1990	1994	2004	2005	2006	2007	2008
Gao *et al.*	1994	Fossil fuel, cement	2.12						
Zhang *et al.*	2001	Fossil fuel, industrial processes	2.219	2.788					
UNFCCC	2005	Guidelines for IPCC inventories		3.073					
ORNL	2009	Fossil fuel, cement and waste gas combustion	2.41	3	5.1	5.63	6.1		
IEA	2008 2009	Fossil fuel	2.411		4.761	5.1	5.645	6	
EIA	2009	Fossil fuel	2.262		4.707	5.249	6.018		
NEAA	2007	Fossil fuel, cement				5.89	6.59	7.13	7.57
Guan *et al.*	2008	Fossil fuel, cement, metallurgy and chemical engineering					5.67		

Source: Gao *et al.* (1994); Zhang *et al.* (2001); UNFCCC (2005) The sixth compilation and synthesis of initial national communications from Parties not included in Annex I to the Convention: Inventories of Anthropogenic Emissions by Sources and Removals of Greenhouse Gases); Boden, Marl, & Andres (2009); IEA, (2009); EIA, (2009); Guan *et al.* (2008).

ranked the first in the world. Their calculation showed China's CO_2 in 2006 was 8% more than that of the USA, making China the largest emitter in the world (the updated amount was 6.59 billion tons in 2009, 13% more than that of the USA, and the concerned fields were fossil fuels and cement). In 2009, the EIA report showed that China's carbon emissions had exceeded those of the USA. Some suspicious scholars estimated China's CO_2 emission in 2006 was 5.67 billion tons, lower than that of the USA, which was 5.955 billion tons that year.

5. Identification of CO_2 Emission Resources and Factors in China

Economic activities such as fossil fuel combustion and industrial processes are the main CO_2 emission resources among human activities. The CO_2 emission of the energy sector in developed countries takes up more than 90% of their total CO_2 emission. In 1994, fossil fuel combustion and industrial processes resulted in more than 90% of China's total CO_2 emission. Of course, other human activities such as raw material combustion, garbage combustion, and changes of land use and forest use also emit CO_2. However, compared with fossil fuel combustion and industrial processes, these activities bring about less emissions, and relevant research in these areas are also rather scarce. Therefore, our discussion mainly focuses on emission factors of two emission resources, namely, fossil fuel combustion and industrial processes.

5.1. *The fossil fuel emission resources*

Usually, the energy sector is the most important greenhouse gas emitter. The emission of CO_2 in the energy sector of developed countries often takes up 95% of its total greenhouse gas emission.[3] Stationary source combustion usually produces about 70% of greenhouse gas emissions of the energy sector. About 50% of such emissions are related to the combustion in the energy industry, mainly concerning power plants and oil refineries. Mobile source combustion (roads and other transports) produces about 25% of greenhouse gas emissions of the energy sector. During combustion, the carbon and hydrogen in fossil fuels (not considering sulfur) turned into CO_2 and water.

There are two approaches for the calculation of CO_2 emissions: reference approach and sectoral approach. Generally speaking, the former is a top-down method based on different types of combustion while the latter is a bottom-up method based on different technology. Cross-checking can be done for the results of these two types of methods (IPCC, 2006).

CO_2 emission factors in fuel combustion are mainly determined by the carbon content of the fuels. Combustion conditions (combustion efficiency, the carbon residue in the slag heaps and stove ash) are relatively insignificant. Therefore, we can make a rather accurate calculation based on the total amount of fuels during the combustion and the average carbon content of the fuels.

Due to geological conditions, the calorific value and carbon content of fossil fuels in different countries are different. The 2006 IPCC guidelines provided the CO_2 emission factors per unit of calorific value of various

---

[3] The other two gases are methane and nitrous oxide.

Table 10.6 CO_2 Factors emission of different fuels (per unit standard coal equivalent)

Institute/product	Coal/bunker coal	Oil/bunker oil	Natural gas/fuel gas	Charcoal
ERINDRC	0.651	0.543	0.404	
ORNL	0.733	0.596	0.411	
IPCC	0.785[a]	0.585[b]	0.449	0.856

Notes: [a] represents anthracite, [b] represents crude oil.

Sources: Gao *et al.* (1994); Qian, J. & Yu L. (2003); IPCC, (2006).

types of fossil fuels, which serve as reference values for countries that lack relevant materials in their calculation. After being converted into standard coal equivalent per unit, the emission factor of anthracite was 0.785, that of crude oil was 0.585, of natural gas was 0.449, and of charcoal was 0.856 (see Table 10.6).

The CO_2 emission factors of coal, oil, and natural gas calculated by the Energy Research Institute, National Development and Reform Commission, China (ERINDRC) were 0.651, 0.543, and 0.404, respectively (Gao *et al.*, 1994) (see Table 10.6).

CO_2 emission factors of bunker coal, bunker oil, and fuel gas calculated by ORNL were 0.733, 0.596, and 0.411, respectively (Qian & Yu, 2003) (see Table 10.6).

It is obvious that the emission factors adopted by ERINDRC and were relatively lower, while those adopted by foreign institutes were relatively higher. For instance, the IPCC default emission factor of coal was 20.6% higher than that adopted by ERINDRC, and the IPCC default emission factors of oil and natural gas were 7.4% and 11.1% higher than those adopted by ERINDRC, respectively. That would certainly have an impact on the amount of CO_2 emissions.

5.2. *The industrial processes emission sources*

The industrial emission sources mainly refer to the greenhouse gases emitted during the industrial processes, not including the greenhouse gases generated by the use of fuels during the processes. The main emission sources are released in such industrial processes as chemical or physical conversion of materials. For example, ordinary Portland cement is produced by first grinding and calcinating such main raw materials as limestone and clay and then levigating them together with gypsum and admixture. During the calcinating of the limestone, the heated $CaCO_3$ decomposes and releases CO_2. In addition, the heated limestone, 1% of which is $MgCO_3$, also releases a small amount of CO_2. Judging from the actual situation of China, industrial products such as cement, limestone, iron, aluminum, and manure have been produced at a rather huge scale; therefore, a considerable amount of CO_2 is being released during its industrial processes. That amount is determined by the yield of industrial products and the per unit of CO_2 emission factors.

Let us take the production of cement as an example. According to some domestic scholars, the production process of one ton of cement releases about 0.356 ton of CO_2 (Zhu, 2000), and 0.41 according to some regional research (Wu, 2006) while relevant empirical emission factor of ORNL is about 0.4987. The following two factors determine the emission factor: the first is the proportion of calcium oxide in the clinker, which determines the amount of CO_2 in the emissions of the clinker. The higher the proportion is, the larger the emission factor will be. The second factor is the rate of the conversion of the clinker into cement. The 2006 IPCC Guideline identified the emission factor of the clinker as 0.5071. Suppose it takes 0.75 ton of clinker to produce 1 ton of cement, the CO_2 emission factor of cement will be about 0.3803.

This chapter calculates over six types of products which generate CO_2 during their production. Apart from cement, the other five types of products are limestone, glass, ammonia gas, sodium carbonate, and virgin Aluminum, the CO_2 emission factors per unit yield of which were 0.75, 0.20, 3.273, 0.138, and 1.6, respectively (see Table 10.7). All these factors come from the default values identified by the 2006 IPCC Guideline.

Table 10.7 CO_2 emission factors of major industrial processes

Product	Cement	Limestone	Glass	Ammonia gas	Sodium carbonate	Virgin aluminum
Emission factor	0.3803	0.75	0.20	3.273	0.138	1.6

Source: IPCC Guideline for National Greenhouse Gas Inventories (2006).

6. Determination of Social Economic Activity Levels

Although social economic activity level is a relatively simple variable in (10.1), the acquisition of relevant activity levels is rather difficult. For instance, when calculating CO_2 emissions through the reference approach, coal consumption usually replaces coal combustion as an activity level value for the former is easily accessed from statistical sectors. However, it is rather ambiguous to take the coal consumption as the activity level data of CO_2 for coal is not only used to burn but also to produce raw chemical materials. For example, coal carbonization has been the earliest and most important method, which mainly aims to produce coal carbon for metallurgy. It also produces such by-products as coal gas and such aromatic hydrocarbon as benzene, methylbenzene, xylene, and naphthalene. Apart from coal carbon, the other chemical products all contain carbon molecules, which, however, are not for combustion purpose.

There are an even more considerable amount of chemical products related to oil. China has grown to be one of the largest manufacturers in the international community. In 2009, China's industrial added value was only second to that of the USA. China's outputs of synthetic rubber, synthetic resin (plastic), and synthetic fiber are among the largest in the world. China's outputs of ethylene, plastic, and chemical fiber are all over 10 million tons, with a synthetic rubber output of 2.749 million tons (see Table 10.8). All these chemical raw materials are important materials

Table 10.8   Output of major chemical products in China (10,000 tons)

Year	Ethylene	Primary plastic	Chemical fiber	Synthetic rubber
1978	38.0	67.9	28.5	
1980	49.0	89.8	45.0	
1985	65.2	123.4	94.8	
1990	157.2	227.0	165.4	
1995	240.1	516.9	341.2	58.6
2000	470.0	1087.5	694.0	86.5

Table 10.8   (*Continued*)

Year	Ethylene	Primary plastic	Chemical fiber	Synthetic rubber
2005	755.5	2308.9	1664.8	205.1
2006	940.5	2602.6	2073.2	199.8
2007	1027.8	3184.5	2413.8	228.9
2008	987.6	3680.2	2453.3	296.0
2009	1072.6	3630.0	2747.3	274.9

Source: *China Statistical Yearbooks* over the years.

while the energy their production uses is not combusted. Therefore, they should be deducted from the energy consumption.

At present, much overestimation exists in estimating CO_2 emissions by using only consumption of coal, oil, and natural gas. Given China's status as a large manufacturer, it is imperative to deduct the non-combustion carbon in coal chemical products and oil chemical products.

7. Other Emission Sources Not to Be Overlooked

One last thing to be noted is, apart from fossil fuel combustion and industrial processes, the CO_2 emissions in agriculture, land use changes, forestry, and waste are on the rise, which must not be overlooked.

7.1. *Agriculture*

Greenhouse gas in agriculture mainly refers to methane emitted from paddy fields, enteric fermentation, and animal manure. China's total paddy field size has not gone through considerable changes. However, with the improvement of people's living standard, people's demand for meat is apparently on the rise. The sharp rise in the number of cattle and sheep leads to dramatic increase of social economic activities, which thus bring about new emission sources.

According to the Second National Agricultural Census, both the livestock scale and the poultry scale in rural areas of China have more or less expanded. In particular, the number of cows increased by 10 million, about 350% more (see Table 10.9).

Table 10.9 Amounts of major livestock and poultry on hand and their changes in rural areas of China

	Unit	1996	2006	Amount changes	Increase (%)
Large domestic animal	10,000	13360.6	24091.6	10731.0	80.3
Cow	10,000	332.9	1506.1	1173.2	352.4
Pig	10,000	36283.6	41850.4	5566.8	15.3
Goat	10,000	12315.8	14763.6	2447.8	19.9
Sheep	10,000	11412.5	13134.0	1721.5	15.1
Poultry	10,000	267664.7	483401.1	215736.4	80.6

Source: A Brief Summary of the Second National Agricultural Census.

7.2. Land use changes and forests

7.2.1. Land Use

Land use concerns are as follows:

Forest land, which meets the definition of a forest.

Farmland, including agroforestry systems, which do not meet the standard of the definition of a forest.

Grassland, including unused grassland, grazing land, and silvo-pastoral systems that do not meet the definition of a forest.

Wetland, including permanent or seasonal wetlands such as rivers, lakes, marsh, and reservoirs.

Residential land, including mining sites and transport infrastructure sites.

Other land, including bare land, bare rocks, glaciers, and desert.

Different land use methods have different carbon fixation ability. The soil of wetlands has the strongest capability of all, almost ten times that of farmland, followed by boreal forests and temperate grassland. Among all types of vegetation, forests, and wetlands have high carbon fixation capabilities, while the carbon fixation capability of grassland and farmland is almost zero. In general, the carbon fixation capability of farmlands is rather weak, only stronger than that of deserts and semi-deserts.

With the advancement of urbanization and industrialization, land use develops toward the release of carbon sinks: forests, grassland, and wetlands are being turned into farmlands, which in turn are being turned into construction sites. The contribution of such practice to China's greenhouse gas emissions is increasingly noticeable.

7.2.2. *Forests*

The total carbon reserve in the global terrestrial biosphere is about 2477 billion tons, among which vegetation carbon takes up about 20% and soil carbon takes up about 80% (see Fig. 10.2). In terms of the forests, which take up about 30% of the global land area, the forest carbon reserve takes up about 77% of that of the global vegetation while the soil carbon reserve takes up about 39% of that of the global soil. Therefore, land use and land use changes and forests are important CO_2 emission sources or carbon sinks.

Deforestation[4] is an important emission source of atmospheric CO_2. It not only results in biomass carbon emissions (except that some timber

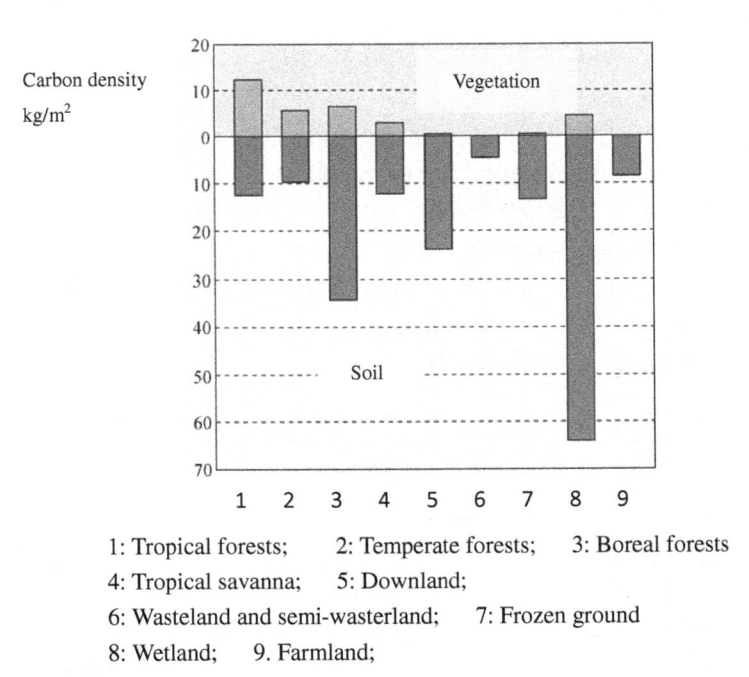

1: Tropical forests;   2: Temperate forests;   3: Boreal forests
4: Tropical savanna;   5: Downland;
6: Wasteland and semi-wasterland;   7: Frozen ground
8: Wetland;   9. Farmland;

Fig. 10.2 Vegetation and soil carbon density of different land uses

---

[4] Deforestation refers to conversion of forests into other land use or forest canopy coverage remaining under a certain threshold for a long time or permanently.

and woodware can be reserved for a relatively long time) but also causes land use changes, which then result in large emissions of forest SOC. Before 1950, deforestation mainly happened in temperate areas such as North America and Europe and tropical areas in Asia and South America. After 1950, deforestation in North America and Europe (except USSR) basically came to a standstill while deforestation increased dramatically in tropical Asia, Latin America, and tropical Africa, which has become a major emission source of atmospheric CO_2.

In the past, the forest coverage rate of China was relatively low because large areas of forests were cut in order to increase grain output. It was only 13% in 1995. Since 1998, China has been implementing the project of converting cultivated land into forests or pastures. China's forest coverage rate reached 20% in 2009, which to a certain degree contributed to the increase of carbon sinks.

7.2.3. *Waste*

Major sources of waste treatment objects include methane emission from waste landfill treatment; methane emission and nitrous oxide from domestic sewage, industrial wastewater and sludge treatment; CO_2 emission from trash burning; and so on.

As both the amount of solid waste and the discharge of wastewater have been on the rise, the greenhouse gas emission from waste treatment will also be on the rise (see Table 10.10).

Table 10.10   Discharge of wastewater and waste in China in recent years

Item / Year	Discharge of wastewater (100 million tons)			Chemical oxygen demand emissions (10,000 tons)			Solid waste (10,000 tons)	
	Total	Industry	Urban life	Total	Industry	Urban life	Industry	Urban life
1998	395.3	200.5	194.8	1495.6	800.6	695.0	80068	
1999	401.1	197.3	203.8	1388.9	691.7	697.2	78442	
2000	415.0	194.0	221.0	1445.0	705.0	740.0	81608	
2005	524.5	243.1	281.4	1414.2	554.8	859.4	134449	15577
2009	589.1	234.4	354.7	1277.6	439.7	837.9	204094	15734

Source: China Statistical Yearbook over the years.

References

2006 IPCC Guidelines for National Greenhouse Gas Inventories. Prepared by the National Greenhouse Gas Inventories Programme, Eggleston, H.S., Buendia, L., Miwa, K., Ngara,T. & Tanabe, K. (eds.), IGES, Japan, 2006.

Boden, T. A., Marl, G. & Andres, R. J., Global, Regional, and National Fossil-Fuel CO_2 Emissions [DB/OL]. Carbon Dioxide Information Analysis Center, Oak Ridge National Laboratory, U. S. Department of Energy, 2009. http://cdiac.ornl.gov/trends/emis/meth_reg.html.

Gao S., Zhang H., Yang L. *et al.*, "A Preliminary Study on Estimation of Greenhouse Gas Emissions in China". *Research of Environmental Sciences*, No. 6 (1994).

Guan, D., Hubacek, K., Weber, C. L. *et al.*, "The Drivers of Chinese CO_2 Emissions from 1980 to 2030." *Global Environmental Change* (2008), pp. 626–634.

International Energy Agency, CO_2 Emissions from Fuel Combustion: Highlights [R/OL]. 2009. http://www.iea.org/CO_2highlights/.

International Energy Agency, World Energy Outlook 2007: China and India Insight [R/OL]. 2007. [2009-12-29]. http://www.iea.org/publications/free_new_Desc.asp?PUBS_ID=1927.

Netherlands Environmental Assessment Agency, China Now No.1 in CO_2 Emissions; USA in Second Position. 2007 [EB/OL]. [2009-12-29]. http://www.pbl.nl/en/dossiers/Climatechange.

Qian, J., & Yu L., "A Research on Carbon Dioxide Contribution from Fossil Fuels in Shanghai", *Shanghai Environmental Sciences*, No. 11 (2003).

UNFCCC, *Inventories of Anthropogenic Emissions by Sources and Removals by Sinks of Greenhouse Gases* [R/OL]. http://unfccc.int.

US Energy Information Administration, International Energy Outlook 2009 [R/OL]. 2009-05-27. [2009-12-29]. http://www.eia.doe.gov/oiaf/ieo/index.html.

Wu X., "A Calculation of Carbon Dioxide Production and Analysis of Utilization Ways in Cement Production". *Environmental Protection Science*, No. 6 (2006).

Zhang R., Wang M., Zheng X. *et al.*, "An Analysis of the Current Situation of China's Carbon Dioxide Emission Sources". *Climatic and Environmental Research*, No. 3 (2001).

Zhu, S., "An Analysis of Greenhouse Gas Emission and Emission Reduction Measures in Cement Industry". *Energy of China*, No. 7 (2000).

Part IV
Review and Evaluation
of Green Development Policy

This part, which includes chapters 11–14, is about the overall review, prospect, and analysis of the two specific policies of China's green development.

Chapter 11 systematically reviews the green development policy of China, and envisages its future. The environmental policies of China have taken form and developed mainly since the Reform and Opening Up. Three principles have been formed before the 1980s, i.e., prevention first, clear responsibility, and strengthening environmental supervision and management, which resulted in a series of systems and policies. The environmental policies during this period were mainly command and control (CAC). Since the 1990s, the environmental policy has made new progresses, with a more complete policy system established. But in its formulation, the government is still dominant, and marketization is still low in degree. Also, the implementation mechanism of environmental policies was imperfect, with little public participation and supervision. Due to the fragile ecological environment and insufficient environmental capacity in recent years, the environmental problem has gradually become a major issue in China's development, and environmental policies have been continuously strengthened. As far as the current situation is concerned, the environment has become an important decision-making factor in the economic and energy planning and policies. China has also been actively carrying out environmental policy innovation so as to explore the positive behavior of using economic means to control polluting industries and polluting products, which is conducive to overcoming the problems brought about by relying too much on CAC methods in the past, opening up a new path for environmental protection. Generally speaking, the economic policies, energy policies, and environmental policies of China are being merged with each other and gradually evolving to an integrated policy system.

Chapter 12 specifically studies the impact of water price adjustment on industrial water use efficiency. In view of the fact that the low efficiency of industrial water use in our country has become a resource "bottleneck" that restricts industrial development, this chapter, based on the panel data of 30 provinces (autonomous regions and municipalities directly under the central government) from 1999 to 2011, conducts an empirical study with the SBM-underlying model and meta-frontier model on industrial water use efficiency and its influencing factors in these provinces under the common front and the group front. The results show that due to the heterogeneity of the technical level of industrial water use in these provinces (autonomous regions and municipalities directly under the central government), there is a great difference in the efficiency of industrial water use under different fronts. With the view of industrial water pollution, the efficiency of water use is generally low and there is much room for improvement. Further investigation shows that the current water price is rather distorted and does not play its due role in improving the effectiveness in the allocation of water resources. The policy implication shows that the efficiency of industrial water use is not only related to the technological heterogeneity of regional industrial development but also to industrial water pollution and its treatment. The current industrial water price should be gradually increased, and the ladder water price can be modelled on that of domestic water use.

Chapter 13 evaluates the structural and macro effects of carbon emission constraints. In this chapter, the dynamic computable general equilibrium model is used to simulate the impact of carbon intensity constraints at the macro- and industrial levels of China. The results show that China needs to speed up the reduction of carbon intensity in the near future in order to achieve the established goals for carbon intensity constraints. Carbon intensity constraints will cause significant price increase for fossil energy products and carbon-intensive products, which will have a certain negative impact on the economic growth and domestic demand, especially investment, and will lead to a slight decline in the average wage, capital rent, and investment return of the whole society. Domestic supply and total output in most sectors will also decline. Decrease in exports occurs mainly in fossil energy supply and carbon-intensive sectors, while the export of many labor-intensive and technology-intensive sectors may increase, resulting in an increase in the total export volume. Most sectors will experience a decline in imports, but some carbon-intensive sectors are likely to rise. In the meantime, the overall energy consumption and carbon emissions will drop dramatically, with most of them contributed by thermal power generation, heating and supply. On the one hand, we can ensure that the targets of carbon intensity constraints, can be achieved through policies such as imposing carbon taxes. On the other hand, some effective measures should be taken, such as accelerating the development of clean energy, actively promoting energy-conserving technologies, and encouraging all sectors, especially the thermal power generation, heating, and supply industries, to improve energy efficiency so as to strengthen the energy-conserving and carbon-reducing effects of carbon intensity constraints and reduce their negative impact on the economy.

Chapter 14 applies the dynamic computable general equilibrium model to analyze the impact of carbon tariffs on China's economy and carbon emissions under different levy standards. When the levy standard changes from embodied carbon coefficient to direct carbon coefficient, from the Chinese carbon coefficient to the US or the EU carbon coefficient, or when the carbon coefficient decreases due to technological progress, the impact of carbon tariffs will be significantly reduced. Only when the United States and the European Union levy carbon tariffs will China's exports to these two regions drop sharply, but exports to other regions will rise significantly. When carbon emission reductions are the same, China's economy is far less affected by its own carbon tax than by carbon tariffs. However, if China reduces its carbon coefficient to the level of the United States by 2020 through carbon tax, its impact will exceed that of all trading partners imposing carbon tariffs. Therefore, China should not only resist carbon tariffs, but also actively implement the innovation-driven development strategy and the progressive low-carbon development strategy, and optimize the trade structure to cope with their potential adverse impacts.

Chapter 11

Review and Prospect of China's Environmental Policy: A Perspective of Environment and Development

Youguo Zhang

Institute of Quantitative & Technical Economics,
Chinese Academy of Social Sciences

1. Evolution of China's Environmental Policy System

1.1. *Environmental policies from pre-Reform and Opening-Up to the 1980s*

Influenced by the international and domestic situation, before the Reform and Opening Up, the economy of China developed basically along a catch-up strategy, i.e., trying to catch up with and surpass Western developed countries in economy, military affairs, and social development (Yao Xiaorong, 2005). The main development goal was to realize industrialization as soon as possible, with the priority going to the development of heavy industry, which in turn had heavy industry as its center.

Due to the adoption of the above-mentioned catch-up development strategy, although China had already formulated relatively detailed environmental planning and policies before the Reform and Opening Up, due to various reasons, the relevant departments regrettably had been unable to fully and successfully implement these environmental policies. Like many political movements, the goal of environmental governance was also mainly achieved by mass movements.

With the changes in the international situation, especially the restoration of China's seat in the UN, environmental protection had received more and more attention in China under the influence of the international trend of environmental protection. "Sending a delegation to the Stockholm UN Conference on Human Environment in 1972 can be regarded as a new starting point for the cause of environmental protection in new China" (Zhang, 1999). At the meeting, the Chinese representative put forward in his speech that the guiding principle of China's environmental policy was "comprehensive planning, rational layout, comprehensive utilization, turning harms into benefits, relying on the masses with all hands on so as to protect the environment and benefit the people". These guidelines were officially established as the basic guidelines for China's environmental protection at the First National Conference for Environmental Protection in 1973, and were fixed in legal form in the *Some Regulations on Environmental Protection and Environmental Improvement (A Draft for Trial Implementation)* and *the Environmental Protection Law of the People's Republic of China (A Draft for Trial Implementation)* issued in 1979.

In 1973, the Environmental Protection Leading Group and its office were instituted under the State Council, and the treatment of industrial "three wastes" (waste water, waste gas, and waste residue) was promoted throughout the country. In 1982, the Ministry of Construction was renamed the Ministry of Urban and Rural Construction and Environmental Protection, and the Bureau of Environmental Protection was set up under it. In 1983, at the Second National Conference for Environmental Protection of the State Council, environmental protection was established as a basic national policy, and it was stipulated that the basic strategic policy of environmental protection should be "three synchronizations and three unifications", that is, the synchronic planning, implementation, and development of economic construction, urban and rural construction, and environmental construction, so as to achieve the unification of economic benefits, social benefits, and environmental benefits. In 1984, the Bureau of Environmental Protection under the Ministry of Urban and Rural Construction and Environmental Protection was upgraded to be the National Bureau of Environmental Protection. In 1988, it was separated from the Ministry of Urban and Rural Construction and Environmental Protection, and became an institution directly under the State Council.

In the 1980s, China gradually established three principles of environmental protection, that is, prevention first, clear responsibility, and strengthening environmental supervision and management, and thus derived a series of systems or policies from them. The principle of prevention first is to stress that environmental policies should focus on the source of environmental problems, preventing their occurrence in the first place. The measures to eliminate pollution and protect the ecological environment should be implemented before or during the process of economic development and construction so as to fundamentally eliminate the root causes of environmental problems and reduce the cost of the treatment thereafter. The details can be summarized as "prevention first, combining of prevention and treatment, and comprehensive treatment". The environmental policies derived from this principle include integrating environmental protection into the plan for national economic and social development to carry out a comprehensive balance, carrying out the comprehensive improvement and treatment of the urban environment, implementing the environmental impact assessment system for construction projects, and implementing the "three synchronizations".

The principle of clear responsibility is to urge relevant subjects to take actions to protect the environment by clarifying the responsibilities of environmental protection, including the principle that local governments are responsible for environmental quality for their prefecture; the principle of environmental protection of "whoever pollutes is responsible for treatment", and "whoever develops is responsible for protection"; the pricinple of natural protection of "paying equal attention to the development, utilization, protection and reproduction of natural resources". Many policies are derived from the principle of "whoever pollutes is responsible for treatment", including the prevention and treatment of industrial pollution through technological transformation, the pollutant discharge permit system and the collection of sewage charges, the deadline control of industrial pollution, the target responsibility system for environmental protection, environmental protection assessment for enterprises, and so on.

There is also the principle of strengthening environmental supervision and management. Developing countries like China can neither follow the principle of "environment first" in environmental protection like Japan, nor can they rely on high investment and high technology like Western countries. They can only focus their policies on strengthening environmental management within a certain period of time. Thus, the most important thing to protect and improve the environment at present is to change the people's behavior through appropriate policy arrangements, especially decision-making behavior in economic development and environmental governance, rather than only increasing investment and improving technology. Specific policies include enhancing legislation for environmental protection and law enforcement; establishing environmental management organizations and national network for environmental protection management; and mobilizing the people and non-governmental organizations to participate in the supervision and management of environmental protection, such as the implementation of the green sign system.

From the above analysis, it is not difficult to see that before the 1980s, the environmental policies of China were mainly mandatory environmental policies or command and control (CAC) policies. The so-called mandatory policy refers to the mandatory and binding environmental policy implemented by the state on the whole society. All economic entities must abide by it unconditionally. For example, the environmental impact assessment system, the "three synchronizations", the environmental protection target responsibility system, the environmental protection planning and programming system, the quantitative assessment system for the comprehensive improvement and treatment of cities, the pollutant discharge permit system and the collection of sewage charges, the centralized control system for pollutants, the deadline control system, the total amount of pollutants control, the regional deadline to meet the standards and to shut down enterprises, and so on. These systems are based on the long-term experience of China in environmental protection, with most of them obtaining a status in environmental legislation, while a small number of systems, such as deadline to meet the standards and to shut down enterprises, appearing in the form of government orders. However, there are few guiding policies, such as the collection of sewage charges, which make use of economic means to provide certain incentives and constraints to economic subjects, so that they can choose behaviors beneficial to the environment from their own interests.

1.2. *Environmental policies since the 1990s*

In the early 1990s, with the gradual formation of the socialist market economy system, China's economic growth accelerated, and the domestic environmental problems became increasingly prominent. In the meantime, international environmental problems also received increasing attention, and the environmental policies of China underwent changes, which reflected the following three features: first, good ecological environment has become an important goal for China's development; second, the environmental system, especially the construction of environmental legal system, has been enhanced; and third, the international environmental cooperation has been strengthened.

1.2.1. *China's environmental protection receives more attention*

In 1992, two months after the Rio de Janeiro Conference, China clearly put "implementing the sustainable development strategy" in the *Ten Major Measures for Environment and Development*. The environmental policy has begun to attach importance to integration with the national development strategy, especially the economic development strategy, thus gradually assuming a higher position in the entire national policy system. In 1994, China issued *China's Agenda for the 21st Century*, which was the first of its kind in the world, providing the guide for China to implement its sustainable development strategy. In 1996, the National People's Congress examined and approved the environmental protection targets for 2000 and 2010 and formulated the *Ninth Five-Year Plan for National Economic and Social Development and the Long-Term Target Outline for 2010*, which, for the first time, established the implementation of the sustainable development strategy and the strategy of rejuvenating the country through science and technology as two major national development strategies in the national long-term and medium-term development plan, and it also issued the *Decision on Several Issues Concerning Environmental Protection*. Subsequently, the new State Environmental Protection Administration (ministerial level) was established in 1998, and its functions and powers were strengthened.

In 2002, the Report of the 16th National Congress of the Communist Party of China put forward the goal of building of a moderately prosperous society in all respects, emphasizing the all-round development of economy, politics, culture, and society (sustainable development). In 2005, the *State Council's Decision on Implementing the Scientific Outlook on*

Development and Strengthening Environmental Protection (the State Council [2005] No. 39) further pointed out that strengthening environmental protection is an important measure to implement the Scientific Outlook on Development, an inherent requirement for building a moderately prosperous society in all respects, a practical action to persist in governing for the people and improve the governing ability, and a strong guarantee for building a harmonious socialist society. In order to fully implement the Scientific Outlook on Development, accelerate the construction of a harmonious socialist society, and realize the goal of building a moderately prosperous society in all respects, environmental protection must be placed in a more important strategic position.

It is proposed, in the *11th Five-Year Plan for National Economic and Social Development* formulated in 2006, to implement the basic national policy of conserving resources and protecting the environment and to build a national economic system that is low in input, high in output, low in consumption and emission, and is recyclable and sustainable, as well as a resource-conserving and environment-friendly society; to lay emphasis on the development of circular economy and the enhancement of energy conservation; to strengthen water-saving policies in various aspects; to conserve land use; to save materials; to strengthen the comprehensive utilization of resources; and to strengthen policies and measures to promote conservation.

The 6th Plenary Session of the 16th CPC Central Committee held in October 2006 examined and approved the *Decision of the CPC Central Committee on Some Major Issues Concerning the Construction of a Harmonious Socialist Society*. The Decision clearly sets out the goals and main tasks of building a harmonious socialist society by 2020, including a marked improvement in the efficiency of resource utilization and in the ecological environment. For this purpose, emphasis is laid on solving environmental problems that endanger the health of the masses and affect sustainable development; speeding up the construction of a resource-conserving and environment-friendly society; optimizing industrial structure, developing circular economy, promoting clean production, conserving energy resources, eliminating backward technology and production capacity according to law, and controlling environmental pollution from the sources; and implementing major projects of ecological construction and environmental improvements, effectively curbing the trend of ecological environment deterioration.

The 17th National Congress of the Communist Party of China held in October 2007 put forward that "promoting ecological civilization" should be regarded as a higher requirement for the goal of building a moderately prosperous society in all respects established at the 16th NCCPC, and "an energy- and resource-efficient and environment-friendly structure of industries, pattern of growth and mode of consumption" will be basically formed. In 2008, according to the "Plan for the Institutional Reform of the State Council" approved by the First Session of the 11th National People's Congress, the State Council organized and established the Ministry of Environmental Protection of the People's Republic of China, making the official environmental protection agency a justified ministerial unit, which reflects the attitude and determination of the supreme decision-makers to implement the spirit of the 17th NCCPC and the Scientific Outlook on Development to strengthen environmental protection.

The 18th NCCPC further promoted the construction of ecological civilization to be an important part of the five-pronged approach to building socialism with Chinese characteristics. The Third Plenary Session of the 18th Central Committee of the Communist Party of China proposed a series of goals for system construction in promoting ecological civilization. The Fifth Plenary Session of the 18th CPC Central Committee put forward the five development concepts of "innovation, coordination, green, openness and sharing".

1.2.2. *The environmental system, especially its legal aspect, has been strengthened*

Since the 1990s, the prevention and control of industrial pollution of China has begun to change from "end treatment" to full-process control, from decentralized control to a combination of decentralized and centralized control; from simple enterprise management to adjustment of industrial structure, clean production, and development of circular economy; from concentration control to a combination of control of total amount and concentration; and from point source control to comprehensive flow and regional management. As a result, a series of very influential policies and measures have been promoted, such as sewage charge reform, implementation of cleaner production, development of ecological industrial parks, and circular economy.

In 2003, the *Regulation on the Collection, Use and Management of Sewage Charges* issued by the State Council stipulated that starting from July 1, 2003, a new method of sewage chargeing would be implemented. Based on the equivalent of pollution, sewage charges were to be collected according to the total amount of pollution discharged by polluters, while those with excessive discharge concentrations would be charged twice. This move has changed the original simplified way of sewage charges based on a certain concentration standard, and has strengthened the incentive effect for emitters.

On October 27, 2005, in order to practice and implement the Scientific Outlook on Development, accelerate the development of circular economy, and promote the transformation of economic growth mode, the National Development and Reform Commission, together with relevant departments such as the State Environmental Protection Administration, the Ministry of Science and Technology, the Ministry of Finance, the Ministry of Commerce, the National Bureau of Statistics, and the governments at the provincial level, organized the first batch of national circular economy pilot projects in key industries, key areas, industrial parks, and provinces and cities in accordance with the *Notice of the State Council on Better Performing Recent Key Tasks in Building a Conservation-Oriented Society* and *Several Suggestions of the State Council on Accelerating the Development of Circular Economy* (the State Council [2005] No. 21 and No. 22).

While paying continuous attention to environmental protection and introducing various environmental protection plans, outlines, and measures, the system of environmental laws and regulations has also improved. Since 1996, environmental laws enacted or revised by the state include environmental protection laws such as water pollution prevention and control, marine environmental protection, air pollution prevention and control, noise pollution prevention and control, solid waste pollution prevention and control, environmental impact assessment, and radioactive pollution prevention, as well as laws closely related to environmental protection such as those related to water, clean production, renewable energy, agriculture, grassland, and animal husbandry.

China has been promoting clean production since 1993, and passed the *Law for Clean Production Promotion of the People's Republic of China* at the 28th Meeting of the Standing Committee of the Ninth National People's Congress, which was formally implemented from January 1, 2003. The law has gained high praise, and its formulation was believed to "mark a historic progress in China's sustainable development and definitely have a positive impact on promoting the further healthy development of China's economy and society and realizing the strategic goal of the third step of economic and social development."[1]

In order to further strengthen the source control of environmental pollution and ecological damage, the *Environmental Impact Assessment Law of the People's Republic of China*, which began to be implemented in 2003, extends the environmental impact assessment system from construction projects to various development and construction plans. The environmental protection administrative regulations formulated or revised by the State Council have numbered more than 50, including *Regulations on Environmental Protection Management of Construction Projects, Detailed Rules for the Implementation of the Water Pollution Prevention Law, Regulations on the Safety Management of Hazardous Chemicals, Regulations on the Collection and Use of Sewage Charges, Measures for the Management of Hazardous Waste Business Licenses, Regulations on the Protection of Wild Plants*, and *Regulations on the Safety Management of Agricultural Genetically Modified Organisms*. In addition, the relevant departments of the State Council, the local people's congress, and the local people's government have formulated and promulgated more than 660 regulations and local regulations in accordance with their functions and powers for the implementation of national environmental protection laws and administrative regulations.

On August 29, 2008, the 4th Meeting of the Standing Committee of the 11th National People's Congress voted to pass the *Circular Economy Promotion Law of the People's Republic of China*, which was promulgated by Decree No. 4 signed by the then President Hu Jintao. The new law came into effect on January 1, 2009. With circular economy as one of

---

[1] "Carrying out Clean Production According to Law and Implementing Sustainable Development Strategy", *People's Daily*, 5th edition, July 5, 2002.

the most important breakthroughs of changing the growth mode, as the main starting point to adjust the economic structure, as the basic means to complete the task of energy conservation and emission reduction, and as the important measure to implement the Scientific Outlook on Development to build a resource-conserving and environment-friendly society, the promulgation and implementation of the *Circular Economy Promotion Law of the People's Republic of China* means that China has laws to follow in vigorously developing circular economy and then promote the transformation of the mode of economic growth. This scientific, strategic, comprehensive, and systematic law has provided a powerful guarantee and booster for the country to implement the Scientific Outlook on Development, vigorously develop circular economy, fully implement the sustainable development strategy, and build a resource-conserving and environment-friendly society.

The newly revised *Environmental Protection Law of the People's Republic of China*, which began to be implemented on January 1, 2015, is regarded as the most stringent environmental protection law in history. The law emphasizes the environmental protection responsibilities of local governments and strengthens the environmental protection accountability system and legal responsibilities. In order to strengthen the functions of local environmental protection agencies, the vertical management system reform of monitoring, supervision, and law enforcement of environmental protection agencies under the provincial level was implemented in 2016. The inspection tour of the central environmental protection inspector that year was also an important institutional arrangement for the construction of ecological civilization and environmental protection.

Since the 1990s, China's environmental information disclosure, environmental protection publicity and education, and efforts to encourage the public to participate in environmental protection have also been strengthened. By the end of 2005, all cities above prefecture level in the country had achieved automatic monitoring of urban air quality, with air quality reported on a daily basis; the monthly report for the water quality of ten major watersheds and the weekly report for automatic monitoring of water quality had been organized and implemented; water quality monitoring work on the eastern route of the South-to-North water diversion project had been regularly conducted; 113 key environmental protection cities had implemented monthly report for centralized drinking water source water quality monitoring; and a quarterly analysis system of environmental quality had been established to release environmental quality information in a timely manner. Governments at all levels and environmental protection departments hold regular or irregular press conferences to promptly report environmental conditions, important policies and measures, environmental emergencies, and cases of law and regulation violation. In February 2006, the state environmental protection department issued the *Interim Measures for Public Participation in Environmental Impact Assessment.*

1.2.3. *International environmental cooperation has been strengthened*

With the deepening of China's opening to the outside world and the worsening of the country's environmental problems, China has acceded to more than 50 international treaties concerning environmental protection, including the *United Nations Framework Convention on Climate Change* and the *Kyoto Protocol*, the *Montreal Protocol on Substances that Deplete the Ozone Layer*, the *Rotterdam Convention on the Prior Informed Consent Procedure for Certain Hazardous Chemicals and Pesticides in International Trade*, the *Stockholm Convention on Persistent Organic Pollutants*, the *Convention on Biological Diversity* (the *Cartagena Protocol on Biosafety*), and the *United Nations Convention to Combat Desertification*, and has actively fulfilled its obligations under these treaties.

What is worth mentioning in particular is that as a responsible developing country, China has attached great importance to the issue of climate change and has established a national coordinating body for climate change countermeasures. And according to the requirements of the national sustainable development strategy, it has adopted a series of policies and measures to cope with climate change, and has made positive contributions to mitigating and adapting to climate change. On June 4, 2007, in response to the *UN Framework Convention on Climate Change*, the Chinese government officially issued *China's National Plan to Deal with Climate Change*, clarifying the specific objectives, basic principles, key areas, and policies and measures to deal with climate change by 2010. This is the first comprehensive policy document for China to deal with climate change, and the first national plan to deal with climate change issued by a developing country. The promulgation and implementation of this plan has demonstrated the attitude of the Chinese government toward being a responsible power.

On November 12, 2014, China and the United States made a *Joint Statement on Climate Change between China and the United States*, which set out China's peak carbon emission target. In 2016, at the G20 summit, China and other member states reached an agreement to play an exemplary role in implementing the *Paris Agreement on Climate Change.*

In addition, in 1992, the Chinese government approved the establishment of the China Council for International Cooperation on Environment and Development (hereinafter referred to as the China Council). The Council is a senior international advisory body, the chairmanship of which is assumed by one of the leaders of the State Council of the People's Republic of China (usually a vice-premier). The main duty of the Council is to provide policy suggestions and make policy demonstrations and project demonstrations on major and urgent key issues in the environment and development of China. The members include ministers or deputy ministers of all relevant ministries and commissions under the State Council, well-known experts and professors in the field of environment and development at home and abroad, as well as ministers of other countries and leaders of international organizations. In the past ten years, the policy recommendations of the Council have played an active role in promoting the sustainable development of China. It has promoted the coordination between environment and development and the perfection of laws and regulations concerning environment and development.

2. Innovation of China's Environmental Policy System: Prospects and Challenges of Economic Means

Economic theorists generally believe that market failure and policy failure characterized by the externality of environmental costs are the fundamental causes of environmental problems. Upon this understanding, in the long-term practice of coordinating economic and ecological development, effective environmental policy tools have been developed, that is, various methods to internalize environmental costs. After many years of innovation and practice, environmental policy tools have been well developed and have become rich and diverse. It is already too simplified to classify today's environmental policy tools only in terms of command and control (CAC) and economic means (Sterner, 2003). Yet, the most widely used environmental policy tools still fall into these two categories.

2.1. *Main characteristics and problems of China's current environmental policy tools*

With more than 20 years of reform and opening up, China has seen an increasingly high level of marketization, and its environmental protection policy system is getting more perfect and effective. On the whole, however, CAC environmental policy tools are still most widely used to achieve environmental goals, and there is a lack of foundation and experience in using economic means. This is because China is at the stage of economic transformation, and the market is still immature in development. At present, China has few economic means to regulate polluting industries and products. The only economic means commonly implemented is the sewage charging system, and tradable emission rights are limited to SO_2 and CO_2 emissions in some areas. Environmental taxes and many other economic means are basically at the stage of theoretical discussion. Even the so-called economic means that have already been used are also directly operated by the government, which takes a lot of force. In this sense, the economic means are actually a part of the administrative means, an administrative means that makes use of economic values such as fees and fines for the purpose of control. And this kind of environmental policy tool system brings many problems in the regulation of polluting industries and products.

First, due to legal development, cultural customs, and other reasons, the final settlement of cases of environmental pollution is rarely found in court in China. Many pollution problems are often solved by bargaining and even bribery between individual government officials and enterprises, and the possibility of actually solving the problems is very low. Owing to the fact that China historically lacks the social basis of "rule by law", the laws and regulations established are often not satisfactorily implemented (Xia, 2001) and cannot be effectively implemented. Although the system of laws and regulations is getting perfect, it is useless.

Second, CAC methods are not suitable for controlling the pollution of the numerous scattered small enterprises. The pollution produced by each small enterprise seems to be little and not worth monitoring, but the total amount of pollution emitted by many small enterprises taken together is surprisingly massive. In China, large-scale enterprises are difficult to start in relevant industries because of policy control, while small enterprises are spreading all over the country, because they are not under any policy control. Small enterprises are unable to install and operate environmental protection equipment due to their limited capital, and they are not easily monitored for pollution; thus, their pollution intensity often exceeds that of large enterprises of the same type. This makes it difficult for CAC methods to work in the control of polluting industries and products.

Third, local protection makes it difficult to implement CAC methods. China is in the process of development and shows unbalanced economic development among different regions. Conflicts between the environmental protection goals of the central government and the development goals of the local government occur from time to time, thus making it difficult for national environmental laws and regulations to be well implemented at the local level. In China, many regions still rely on polluting enterprises of resource development for their fiscal revenue. Local governments are, therefore, apt to turn a blind eye to the environmental problems thereof. In addition, the local environmental protection bureau is generally under the local government instead of belonging to the vertical management system of the State Environmental Protection Administration. The local environmental protection bureau is unable to effectively supervise the pollution prevention and control of local polluting enterprises due to administrative intervention. Recently, a series of environmental emergencies broke out in China (for example, the arsenic content in drinking water in a county seriously exceeded the standard due to pollution by an enterprise, that is specifically protected by the county government).

Fourth, CAC methods cannot do anything about some cross-border pollution. It is difficult to identify the major polluters for some pollution problems, and CAC methods thus lose their targets. For example, many rivers of China are also boundary lines between adjacent areas and are public resources. When serious pollution occurs in these river reaches, neighboring areas often shirk their responsibilities, and it is also difficult for regulators to determine which party to blame, not to mention the problem of effective management.

In addition, CAC methods have some other drawbacks. For example, although the cost of controlling pollution emissions by CAC is eye-catching, it is much higher than economic means. Due to the weak severity of pollution punishment, CAC methods are not sufficient to deter violations of environmental laws and regulations. Moreover, CAC methods are often easy to be taken as a tool by some policymakers to obtain benefits in the name of environmental protection.

Generally speaking, since the 1990s, the environmental policy of China has made new progresses compared with the past, but there are still many problems. Among them, the most prominent is that the environmental protection in China still retains the characteristics of planned economy, in which too much presence and total absence of government coexist in environmental policies. Specifically, in the formulation of environmental policies, the government assumes the dominant role, involving a low level of marketization. This makes mandatory policies occupy the main position in China, and the policies and regulations lack operability or are too rigid. However, due to the insufficient use of market mechanisms, the application of environmental and economic policies with incentives is very limited, and economic entities lack incentives to protect the environment. There is still a big gap between the current environmental protection standard management system on the one hand, and legal provisions, international common practices, and China's commitment to the World Trade Organization on the other. Its scientificity, integrity, systematicness, coordination, and operability need to be improved. In short, though China's environmental policy system is relatively sound and complete, its implementation mechanism and effects are far from satisfactory.

2.2. Theoretical prospect of economic means to control environmental pollution

Economic means indirectly leads to environment-friendly behaviors by changing the cost and benefit of economic entities. Commonly used economic means include environmental taxes and fees, and tradable emission permits. In many cases, economic means are also called market-based means, but strictly speaking, there is still a difference between the two (Barbe, 1994). CAC is a traditional tool in environmental policy, which is used by the government to restrict or prohibit certain activities of economic entities, such as establishing pollution discharge permits and setting up environmental standards. Currently, CAC is a policy tool widely adopted in various countries, while the use of economic means has been on the rise in recent years.

Due to a series of drawbacks in pollution control by means of CAC, countries all over the world have been committed to finding and creating more effective and efficient environmental policy tools. Driven by this motive, economic means have begun to receive attention. Certainly, the abuse of CAC methods cannot be taken as an argument for economic means. The main reason why economic means are increasingly favored by experts, scholars, and policymakers is that economic means have more advantages than CAC according to the mainstream economic theory (neoclassical economics). These advantages are summarized as follows:

(1) Static efficiency (cost effectiveness): Economic means can achieve emission reduction at the lowest cost. The reason is that economic means can effectively distribute sewage discharge among enterprises. Although the CAC method may also achieve static effectiveness in principle, the government must find out an effective sewage distribution scheme and implement it, which requires a large amount of information about the technology and cost of emission reduction of enterprises. But enterprises are generally unwilling to provide such information. Thus, the government had better let the market find such an effective sewage distribution scheme instead of doing it by itself.

(2) Dynamic efficiency: Dijkstra (2000) believes that when economic measures are taken to control pollution emissions, the size and the number of enterprises would be optimal. Whereas, when direct control is adopted, enterprises would be too large or too small, and their number would be too many or too few. Economic means can provide long-term and sustained incentives for enterprises to reduce their emissions, which will urge enterprises to strengthen research and development and adopt more advanced and cost-effective emission reduction technologies or processes. However, when direct control is

adopted, enterprises are rarely willing to raise the emission reduction above the prescribed level.

(3) Flexibility: It is much easier for the relevant departments to adjust the tax rate or rate for relevant fees than making a change to a CAC method. Moreover, enterprises can respond flexibly and reconsider whether to pay fees or reduce emissions based on these adjustments.

(4) Fiscal revenue increase: Economic means are conducive to raising funds for environmental protection. For example, the taxes and fees collected and the tradable permits contribute considerably to financial revenue, which can be used for environmental protection or other government budgets.

(5) Compared with CAC environmental policy tools, economic means are less likely to be exploited in the process of pollution prevention and control, thus being more effective and more just.

It is precisely because of these theoretical advantages that economic means are receiving more attention from government departments and are becoming more popular in environmental policies, such as the tradable emission permit system in the US and the environmental taxes and fees in the European Union. Economic means have not only become a powerful supplement to CAC but also have the momentum to replace CAC as the mainstream environmental policy tools.

2.3. Challenges faced by China in using economic means to control pollution

Obviously, China is in need of environmental policy innovation to overcome the drawbacks of previous pollution control. Theoretical superiority and many successful experiences of developed countries make economic means an ideal choice for China's policy innovation. But we must clearly see that in the actual environmental policies, the overall policy tools are dominated by CAC, and the application of economic methods has a long way to go to meet the suggestions of economists. Apart from political reasons, there is still a big gap between the actual situation and a series of conditions necessary for economic means to make use of their advantages. For example, the market is not fully competitive, featuring incompleteness and asymmetric information, and there are regional characteristics in environmental pollution. These situations exist to varying degrees in China. Thus China still faces many challenges to effectively control polluting industries and products by economic means.

2.3.1. *Incomplete competitive market*

The analyses of economic means in environmental policies always assume that the market is completely competitive, but this is not the case in the real market. It is still a question as to whether economic means can realize the maximization of welfare. For example, at the stage of economic transformation, China still has many market areas that are not completely competitive. Those pollution-intensive enterprises with monopoly can easily transfer environmental costs to downstream enterprises or consumers. In this way, economic means fail to provide incentives in terms of environmental protection to these pollution-intensive enterprises.

2.3.2. *Incomplete information and uncertainties*

Under the condition of complete information, for example, when one can know the marginal damage caused by each economic subject to the environment, or when the policy tool is mainly for the realization of specific political goals and has nothing to do with the marginal loss, the reward and punishment mechanism of economic means can optimize the behavior of the whole society (Russell & Powell, 1998). But information in the real world is often incomplete. There will be uncertainties about the price, quantity, and other variables in pollution control, and the quantitative estimation in pollution control will also become too difficult (Russell & Powell, 1998), and it is thus impossible to determine the pollution control level that minimizes social cost, rendering the economic means ineffective. For example, the sewage charges in China generally cannot reach an efficient level, and, in many industries, are at a level even far lower than the average cost cutting of pollutants. In this way, the sewage charges are bound to fail to promote the improvement of enterprises' behaviors, and even lead to agreement-like implementations of environmental policies (Zhang S., 2004).

2.3.3. *Regional differences in pollution*

There may be significant differences in the environmental pollution in different regions. Due to the different capacities of endurance for environmental pollution, and the differences of difficulties in monitoring and evaluating pollution sources by relevant departments, the environmental damage caused by the same amount of pollutants in some regions may far exceed that in other regions. If we ignore this factor when using economic means, it is very likely that the pollution in some areas will exceed the policy objective. These differences imply that when applying economic means, different standards must be applied to different regions. Only by adopting a whole series of such standards can we ensure the static efficiency of economic means. But it is almost impossible to set a series of effective standards, because we lack full understanding of the marginal cost of pollutant emission reduction and the extent of its impact on the environment.[2] And China is facing the problem of huge regional differences in pollution, thus increasing the technical difficulty in the application of economic means.

2.3.4. *Disconnection between economic incentives and technological development*

Some countries or enterprises mainly depend on the introduction of technology for technological development, owing to lack of awareness and to

---

[2]For example, when sewage tax is used alone, the tax rate is generally required to be uniform. In order to avoid the occurrence of this situation, the tax rate must be unified according to that required by the most pollution-sensitive areas, that is, the highest tax rate must be implemented. This will lead to a sharp rise in the marginal cost of emission reduction or an abnormal production due to a significant reduction in pollution. If different tax rates are adopted for different regions, this will make the sewage tax collection scheme too complicated and difficult to be approved by the current financial policies and regulations. Even if the relevant departments have painstakingly established a set of charging standards that can achieve static effectiveness, bigger troubles will ensue. Any changes in exogenous variables, such as inflation, birth and death rates, and technological progress, require a revision of this set of standards, which is too much work. Although the economic method of tradable permits can "automatically" adapt to changes in exogenous variables, it is not suitable for use because it does not have general static effectiveness.

have the ability to be independent. In this case, economic means are not only difficult to realize static efficiency, but it is also difficult to achieve dynamic efficiency (Russell & Powell, 1998). Due to the weak originality and strong imitation of China's current industrial technology (Jin, 2005), that is, industrial technological progress relies mainly on introduction rather than independent innovation, the incentive effects of economic means (such as environmental taxes and fees) usually encourage enterprises to continuously introduce environment-friendly technologies instead of carrying out research and development themselves. Improper application of economic means may even harm the enthusiasm of enterprises to adopt environmental protection technology. For example, with regard to the allocation of the total amount of SO_2, many places in China have adjusted the base year for the new total amount allocation from 1995 to 2000, thus reducing the quota of enterprises that have adopted advanced environmental protection technologies and performed better in environmental protection, resulting in the phenomenon of "the outstanding getting beaten" in environmental policies (Zhang S., 2004). In addition, without government supervision, the adoption of environmental protection technologies may also lower the market price of the (discharge) permit, which will also affect the application of environmental protection technology.

2.3.5. *Economic means are susceptible to the influence of interest groups*

Policies reflect the distribution of economic benefits, with different economic means leading to different cost distribution among polluters, between polluters and victims of pollution, and society (Sterner, 2003). Generally speaking, there is no policy tool that is "optimal" to all interest groups. In the field of pollution control, some powerful political interest groups may influence policymakers' choice of environmental policy tools (Dijkstra, 2000), making it difficult for economic means to be designed as depicted in theory due to political factors. And the final design and implementation of economic measures will be at the expense of the interests of weak groups or unorganized groups, thus sacrificing efficiency even though they have gained political recognition.

In addition, there is another serious defect in the economic theories that demonstrate the advantages of economic means, and this is the fact that they only consider a part of the social costs, i.e., costs for pollution reduction, and take it as a standard to demonstrate the static efficiency of economic means. The value or utility of many non-market commodities (such as landscapes and biotic populations) and non-market behaviors cannot be expressed or considered in these theoretical models. Because the static effectiveness of policy tools should be evaluated on the basis of total social costs, only considering a part of them probably leads to a partial evaluation.

2.4. *Giving full play to economic means: A line of thought for policymaking*

The above analysis shows that economic means impose high demands on the system. If the gap between reality and theory is ignored, a slight mistake in the application of economic means in pollution control may cause a failure of economic means to display their theoretical advantage, and even cause more serious pollution. But economic means can be attractive policy tools if the market itself is strengthened (Dieter & Pearce, 1991). China should fully understand all kinds of practical problems of economic means in pollution control, and adopt a correct plan to maximize the effectiveness of economic means and promote environmental protection.

First of all, sufficient preparations must be made to create good external conditions for the application of economic means to effectively control polluting industries and products (Cole & Grossman, 2001), including perfecting market mechanisms, improving transparency of environmental information, fully considering regional characteristics, encouraging enterprises to carry out technological innovation, enhancing research on environmental value assessment, and strengthening publicity and training. We will detail these in the following.

(1) Perfecting market mechanisms: China is currently in a period of economic system transition. The market mechanism should be perfected so that economic means can play a normal role. It mainly includes breaking monopoly in various fields as far as possible, defining

property rights, establishing effective markets, treating the public sector and the private sector on the same level, and reducing or eliminating subsidies and other price distortions that are unfavorable to the environment.

(2) Improving the transparency of environmental information: We should further improve the technology of data collection and analysis, disclose information in time, urge enterprises to disclose environmental information, and increase the transparency of economic entities and the effective exchange of information between economic entities. Reliable monitoring requires persuasive data and analytical support.

(3) Fully considering regional characteristics when formulating policies: China is a vast country with great regional differences in environment and economic development. When applying economic measures to control pollution, different policies should be adopted according to the characteristics of different regions, which is indeed very difficult. It is thus necessary to enhance research in this respect and promote environmental control and treatment in regional development. The sewage charging standard of China has already taken a welcome step in this respect, and other economic means should still adhere to this principle.

(4) Encouraging enterprises to carry out technological innovation: Independent innovation of enterprises is an inherent requirement of China's economic development, and a basic requirement for economic means to realize dynamic efficiency in pollution control (as discussed above). Enterprises should be encouraged to conduct innovations while applying economic methods. For example, in order to reduce the cost of enterprise technology and equipment adjustment, new environmental taxes and fees should be levied based on new equipment instead of outdated factories and equipment with higher marginal costs by which higher taxes and fees would be collected. A special part of the environmental tax should also be devoted to accelerating technological progress, such as subsidizing the research and development of enterprises.

(5) Enhancing research on environmental value assessment: When applying economic methods, it is necessary to evaluate the environmental value. Although it is difficult to assess the environmental value, any

reasonable evaluation and assessment would be better than assuming the value of the ecological environment to be zero or infinite (Zhang X., 2004). We must overcome the thought of inaction, enhance research in this field, and incorporate environmental value assessment into key national scientific research projects with the new demands brought about by the *Environmental Impact Assessment Law* (Guo, 2004), so that the design of economic means is based on a relatively comprehensive social cost.

(6) Strengthening publicity and training: In the environmental policy of China, there is a long history of the use of CAC methods. Government officials, administrative personnel, and business people have accumulated a lot of experiences with such tools. In contrast, economic means are new to them, requiring them to spend time and energy to familiarize themselves with the operation rules of economic means and then gradually adapting to them. It is, therefore, necessary to strengthen the publicity of economic means and the training of all kinds of relevant personnel.

Second, the idea of using economic means to control polluting industries and products should be expanded from the partial equilibrium framework to the general equilibrium framework. The main objective of economic means is to encourage economic entities to choose the most appropriate environmental protection measures based on their own costs or benefits. But if only pollution control is considered with economic development and fairness neglected, the application of economic means will encounter economic and political problems, making it difficult to realize their effects in the short term. Thus, when designing and implementing economic means, we should not only consider their operation mechanism and possible pollution control effects under the framework of partial equilibrium, but also consider various problems and consequences that may occur in their operations under the framework of general equilibrium.

We can consider combining the incentive mechanism of economic means with their function of increasing fiscal revenue. For example, earmarking the fiscal revenue generated by economic means for certain specific environmental goals may provide a way to deal with the difficult situation in the period of economic transition. The usages of the fiscal revenue include carrying out various environmental plans, setting up environmental funds, redistributing them to manufacturers or individuals who bear the tax, and paying for various environmental-related services. Environmental tax revenues can also be used to reduce government deficits, increase public expenditures, and reduce or eliminate other (distorting) taxes (corporate income taxes) (Barbe, 1994). At the same time, the government should also incorporate environmental factors into the scope of comprehensive economic decision-making. Decisions on finance, energy, agriculture, transportation, and land use should take full account of the bearing capacity of the environment. It is also necessary to introduce new activities and management methods with higher benefits and less damage to the environment, so as to promote the upgrading of industry structure, thus limiting the various policy conflicts and contradictions encountered in the operation of economic means to the smallest possible extent.

Finally, China should proceed from its own basic national conditions and avoid neglecting the application of CAC methods and other environmental policy tools due to one-sided emphasis on economic means. Indeed, economic instruments have been widely used in developed countries, and governments of various countries do hope to draw upon the role of market in environmental policies. For environmental policies, developed countries still employ a "mixed system", including both economic means such as environmental taxes and fees as well as traditional CAC methods, and the only difference lies in the concrete situation of the mixing of these policy tools. In some countries, economic means constitute the core of environmental policies, such as water pollution fees in France, Germany, and the Netherlands, and air pollution fees in Sweden. In some other countries, economic means are only measures to provide economic incentives, such as product tax. In other countries, economic means are only a cost-saving option, such as the tradable emission permits of the US. China must design and implement economic measures based on its own national conditions, "comprehensively using laws, economy, technology and necessary administrative methods to solve environmental problems, and consciously following economic laws and natural laws, improving the level of environmental protection work."[3]

---

[3] Wen Jiabao, speech at the Sixth National Conference for Environmental Protection, April 2006.

3. Integration of Environmental Policy With Economic Policy and Energy Policy

Since the Reform and Opening-Up, with the sustained and rapid development of China's economy, environmental problems that occurred over different stages of industrialization in developed countries in the period of more than a hundred years have been concentrated in China, and the contradiction between environment and development is getting sharp. The fragile ecological environment and insufficient environmental capacity have gradually become major problems in the development of China, and environmental policies have been continuously strengthened accordingly. Due to the close relation between the environment and economic development and energy use, with the continuous popularization of the concept of sustainable development, the environmental policy economic policy, and energy policy are developing along a trend of gradual integration.

3.1. *Integration of environmental and economic policies*

In the first place, the integration of environmental policy and economic policy is manifested in the gradual promotion of economic means in the field of environmental protection. A typical case in point is the continuously improved environmental charging policy. China introduced the sewage charging policy in the 1980s. In 2003, the reformed sewage charging policy began to be implemented. Compared with the past, the new sewage charging policy has strengthened the collection and management of sewage charges. The collection and use of sewage charges are strictly managed by the "two lines of revenue and expenditure", and the revenue from sewage charges is earmarked for the prevention and treatment of environmental pollution. In the meantime, through the collection of fees for the treatment of urban sewage, garbage, and hazardous waste, social funds will be directed for investment in the construction and operation of environmental protection facilities in various ways to actively promote the marketization and industrialization of pollution control. A franchise system for the treatment of municipal sewage and garbage has been established and implemented. In some places, government construction facilities such as sewage treatment plants and garbage disposal stations are handed over to enterprises for operation by way of contracts through bidding (the Information Office of the State Council, 2006). In recent years, there has been pilot work on carbon emissions trading in seven provinces and municipalities, such as Beijing, which is also a typical case in this respect. At present, China is actively preparing for the establishment of a unified national carbon emission trading market.

Second, the integration of environmental policy and economic policy is increasingly manifested in the rising weight of environmental protection in major economic policies. Industrialization and urbanization are important ways for the current economic development of China. In the process of vigorously promoting industrialization and urbanization, China is paying more attention to environmental quality.

As regards industrialization, the relationship between economic development and environmental protection is mainly coordinated by actively adjusting the industry structure, promoting clean production, and developing circular economy. First, enterprises with backward technology, serious pollution, and waste of resources are being outdated and shut down. Second, eco-industry is developed in industry-concentrated areas, so that waste from upstream enterprises can be used as raw materials for downstream enterprises, with production chains extended, waste generation minimized, and "zero emission" realized. Eco-industrial areas are built to realize the most effective utilization of resources with regions or enterprise groups. Third, circular economy is being vigorously developed. China has selected 82 units in key industries, key fields, industrial parks, and relevant provinces and cities to carry out the first batch of circular economy pilot work (the Information Office of the State Council, 2006). Fourth, more and more attention has been paid to the development of environmental protection industry. In 1990, the General Office of the State Council issued *Several Suggestions on Actively Developing Environmental Protection Industry*, which means that economic decision-makers started to be aware of environmental problems and the potential role of environmental markets in promoting economic development. In 2001, the State Economic and Trade Commission issued the *Tenth Five-Year Plan for the Development of Environmental Protection Industry*, which provides guidance for the production and management of environmental protection products and comprehensive utilization of resources and environmental services.

With respect to urbanization, the Chinese government has taken a series of comprehensive measures to solve urban environmental problems. Currently, many cities in China, when formulating and implementing overall urban planning, will rationally determine their scale and direction of development, adjust the industry structure and the spatial layouts, and gradually optimize their functional division based on their environmental capacity and resources guarantee capacity. Many large and medium-sized cities have implemented the strategy of "retreating from the secondary and entering into the tertiary" in their urban development, that is, withdrawing from the secondary industry and entering into the tertiary industry, shutting down a number of heavily polluting enterprises, transferring some polluting enterprises out of urban areas by means of land price leverage to move, and implementing technological transformation and centralized pollution control in accordance with the principle of "industries into the park and centralized pollution control". Some cities combine the renovation of the old downtown areas with the adjustment of its layout so as to solve the problem of "dirtiness, disorder, and inferiority" and improve the living environment of the residents. The urban energy structure is vigorously adjusted, clean energy and central heating are actively promoted, and coal-fired pollution is reduced (the Information Office of the State Council, 2006).

In addition, in agricultural construction, the Chinese government has carried out the construction of ecological agriculture and ecological demonstration areas in an all-round manner, taking the construction of ecological agriculture as an important measure to promote the overall and coordinated development of rural economy and ecological environment. In order to promote environmental protection, the Chinese government has also established and perfected policies and systems such as price, tax, credit, trade, land, and government procurement that are conducive to environmental protection. For example, enterprises that recycle and comprehensively utilize renewable resources, produce environmental protection industrial equipment, and utilize waste water, waste gas, waste residue, and other wastes as main raw materials for production are given preferential tax relief (the Information Office of the State Council, 2006).

It is worthy of special attention that, with the strengthening of the status of environmental protection, the environment has become an important decision-making factor in economic planning and policymaking. The 16th National Congress of the Communist Party of China in 2002 explicitly proposed that China should take the road of new industrialization, that is, informationization drives industrialization, which will in turn promote informationization, blazing a new trail to industrialization featuring high scientific and technological content, good economic returns, low resources consumption, little environmental pollution, and a full display of advantages in human resources. In 2005, the *State Council's decision on Implementing the Scientific Outlook on Development and Strengthening Environmental Protection* (the State Council [2005] No. 39) demanded that "economic and social development be coordinated with environmental protection". In order to implement this decision, the then-Premier Wen Jiabao stressed at the Sixth National Conference on Environmental Protection convened by the state Council from April 17 to 18, 2006, that the key to environmental protection in the future is to accelerate the realization of three transitions: the first is to shift from emphasizing economic growth over environmental protection to paying equal attention to both environmental protection and economic growth; the second is to transit from the situation of environmental protection lagging behind economic development to that of environmental protection synchronized with economic development; the third is to change from taking administrative means as major tools to protect the environment to comprehensively using laws, economy, technology, and necessary administrative methods to solve environmental problems. These three directional, strategic, and historical transitions serve as a new milestone in the development of China's environmental protection.

3.2. *Environmental considerations in energy policy*

Since energy consumption generally leads directly to air pollution, the formulation of energy policies directly affects environmental quality. It should be recognized that the energy policy of China is mainly designed to meet the needs of economic and social development, and environmental protection is not its focus. However, with the concept of sustainable development gradually popularized, environmental factors have gained more weight in energy policies. For example, the current energy strategy of "energy-conservation first" is highly beneficial to environmental protection, even though its starting point is energy conservation. The policy of energy structure adjustment also reflects the concern of environmental quality in energy policy.

The adjustment of energy structure in cities is mainly manifested in the clean car campaign in some cities, by which cars with clean and low-pollution fuels such as natural gas and liquefied petroleum gas are actively promoted. Since July 2000, China has stopped selling and using leaded petrol, which can reduce the amount of lead discharged by 1,500 tons per year. The state adjusts the energy structure in the "two-control zones", promotes the use of clean fuels and low-sulfur coal, and prohibits the use of bulk coal for civilian stoves in large and medium-sized cities. In rural areas, new energy resources are developed and promoted. During the Tenth Five-Year Plan period, the state successively invested 3.5 billion yuan to promote the ecological energy model linked with biogas construction. By the end of 2005, the number of biogas users nationwide had reached more than 17 million, with the production of biogas amounting to 6.5 billion cubic meters annually. The state has vigorously developed biogas projects for livestock and poultry breeding waste, with more than 2,200 completed and more than 60 million tons of livestock and poultry excrement treated each year. The number of biogas digesters that have been built for domestic sewage purification reaches 137,000, that of centralized gas supply projects for straw gasification comes to more than 500, and 189 million households are now using firewood-saving stoves, with 28.5 million square meters covered by solar water heaters. Also, the state actively promotes the use of renewable energy sources such as solar ovens, wind energy, and geothermal energy (the Information Office of the State Council, 2006). In addition, because of the prominent position of coal in the energy structure of China, the Chinese government set up a clean coal technology promotion planning team in 1994 to carry out the promotion of clean coal technology. In 1997, the State Council approved the *Ninth Five-Year Plan of China's Clean Coal Technology and the 2010 Development Outline.*

In terms of the overall energy development strategy, the adjustment of energy structure is mainly focused on increasing the proportion of renewable energy in future energy composition. Key renewable energy sources include wind energy, biomass energy, and solar energy. Here are the specific development goals: through large-scale development, the total installed capacity of wind energy is to reach 5 million kilowatts in 2010 and 30 million kilowatts in 2020; the annual consumption of biomass briquettes is to reach 1 million tons nationwide in 2010 and 50 million tons in 2020; that of biogas and biomass gasification is to reach 19 billion cubic meters in 2010 and 40.4 billion cubic meters in 2020; biomass liquid fuel is to replace 10 million tons of refined oil by 2020; the annual production of fuel ethanol with sweet sorghum stalks, sugarcane, and cassava as raw materials is to reach 2 million tons in 2010 and 10 million tons in 2020; that of biodiesel is to reach 200,000 tons in 2010 and 2 million tons in 2020; solar power generation (PV) is to reach 300,000 kilowatts in 2010 and 1.8 million kilowatts in 2020; and the number of solar heaters is to cover 150 million square meters (equivalent to 22.5 million tons of standard coal) in 2010 and 300 million square meters (equivalent to 45 million tons of standard coal) in 2020. In order to promote the development of renewable energy, the state promulgated the *Renewable Energy Law* in 2005 and issued a series of specific implementation rules and policies for the law.

In addition, the impact of environmental policies on energy policies is also reflected in the decision-making of energy development. Ecological environmental protection has become an important part subject to approval in water energy development and construction planning. For example, the government has carried out environmental impact assessment in the development and utilization planning of Tarim River basin, the middle and lower reaches of Lancang River, Dadu River (Sichuan), and the upper reaches of Yalong River and Yuan River basin. The environmental impact assessment of Nujiang River basin hydropower development plan has compared the environmental impact of different multistep development plans in the aspects of development layout, scale, mode, and development timing and has provided measures to prevent and mitigate the environmental impact for the implementation of the plan. The environmental impact assessment of the elevator-level water development plan of the Dadu River basin has fully considered the coordination between environment and development and put forward an overall arrangement of environmental protection for the development of the basin resources, reducing gradient inundation by 39 km, and reducing the inundation of cultivated land by 1,867 ha, keeping 2 counties from being inundated, and reducing the number of immigrants by 85,000.

3.3. *It is necessary to establish and perfect the coordination mechanism of economic, energy, and environmental policies*

Although the environmental policy system of China is already full-fledged, including all links from environmental pollution prevention to environmental control, since China is at a special stage of economic development — the rapid advancement of industrialization — it has not adopted the strategy of "environment first" but a strategy of coordination with economic development when formulating its environmental policies. In view of the mutual influence among the economic, energy, and environmental policies of China, it can be said that economic policies have always been absolutely dominant, guiding the formulation and implementation of energy policies and restricting the formulation and implementation of environmental policies. But along with the worsening of energy and environmental problems, energy policy has finally become an important part of economic policy, and the environment has also gradually become an important decision-making factor in the formulation of economic plans and policies. Specific development plans, the establishment of relevant laws and regulations, and measures for policy implementation in different fields are also gradually showing a trend of mutual coordination. Many specific action plans have been implemented, and progress has been made.

China, however, is far from perfect. At present, there is a disconnection between the three types of policies, with the planning and decision-making system lagging behind the economic system reform. Particularly, there is a lack of comprehensive decision-making and planning mechanisms, procedures are not standardized, the boundary between the government and the market is not clear, and their cohesion and coordination are insufficient (Gao *et al.*, 2004). For example, due to the lack of ways to coordinate the development of the energy industry with the sustained and rapid development of the entire economy and society as well as the lack of mechanisms to establish self-coordination, on the one hand, many irrational and non-market-oriented behaviors are driving the rapid growth of energy demand and pushing the disorderly expansion of the energy industry beyond the capacity of resources and environment; on the other hand, the government applies non-market methods to ensure production and increase supply (the Research Group of Macroeconomic Research Institute, National Development and Reform Commission, 2005).

The unified management and coordination mechanism for policy implementation in various fields needs to be further strengthened. For example, some high energy-consuming and high-polluting industries that the central government hopes to control are usually pillar industries in the regions, so the central government's industrial adjustment policies often conflict with local industrial policies and are difficult to implement. Another example is that many cross-sectoral and cross-industry energy policies face major obstacles in the implementation process due to the division of departments and monopoly of industries, the lack of a unified energy management organization, and absence of a comprehensive decision-making mechanism. Some policies are difficult to carry out in an all-round manner, such as construction energy conservation and clean coal technology. Some overlap and cut across each other, causing waste, such as energy research and development. Some derive their origins from too many departments, making it difficult to implement the relevant planning, such as the development and utilization of renewable energy (the Research Group of Macroeconomic Research Institute, National Development and Reform Commission, 2005). As for the environment, the laws and regulations formulated by the State Environmental Protection Administration are often difficult to implement effectively because the local bureau of environmental protection is under the jurisdiction of the local government, not subject to the State Environmental Protection Administration. It is thus difficult for the Administration to independently conduct environmental supervision and management of the development of local economy. Policies within various fields can hardly be unified and coordinated, which seriously affects the formation of coordination mechanism of economic, energy, and environmental policies.

Thus, to truly establish a relatively perfect coordination mechanism of economic, energy, and environmental policies, China faces many realistic challenges. The proportion of heavy and chemical industry in the economic structure is very high, and is still on the rise. It is difficult to change the mode of economic growth. The problem of unbalanced regional development has not been fundamentally solved, with industrialization treated as the leading concept of development for many regions (even some regions which serve as China's ecological barrier). There is also a lack of effective measures and related technology to improve energy efficiency and promote energy conservation. The environmental policy system is becoming complete, while its implementation is very weak. The relation between economic and environmental policies on the whole falls into a "two-skin" situation, with one separated from the other. The current environmental policies have not been able to fundamentally affect the formulation and implementation of economic policies and energy policies, and the situation of "pollution first and treatment afterwards, and destruction alongside treatment" has, in effect, not been changed.

4. Conclusion

The formation and development of China's environmental policies are mainly concentrated in the period after the Reform and Opening-Up. Before the 1980s, China formulated the three principles of prevention first, clear responsibility, and enhancing environmental supervision and management, from which a series of systems and policies were derived. The environmental policies during this period were mainly CAC. Since the 1990s, China has made new progresses in environmental policy compared with the past, and has formed a more complete policy system. Yet the government assumed a dominant role in the formulation of environmental policy, with the level of marketization being fairly low. The implementation mechanism of environmental policies is also imperfect, with low public participation and little supervision.

China's exploration of economic means to control polluting industries and products is an active act of environmental policy innovation, which is conducive to overcoming the problems brought about by relying too much on CAC in the past, opening up a new route for the environmental protection of China. Compared with CAC methods, economic means have a series of theoretical advantages. However, special attention should be paid to the fact that in order to give full play to the advantages of economic means, many external conditions must be satisfied, such as a sound market mechanism and relatively sufficient environmental information. These are the areas about which China has a lot to do. China needs to overcome unfavorable factors and strive to create favorable conditions for the application of economic means in pollution control. When applying economic means to control polluting industries and products, we should break through the thinking pattern of partial equilibrium and consider problems more from the framework of general equilibrium. In addition, one-sided emphasis on economic means should be avoided. Attention should be given to the comprehensive application of economic means and various environmental policy tools. It is believed that with the continuous development of economy and society, economic means will definitely play an important role in solving the environmental problems of China.

As the fragile ecological environment and insufficient environmental capacity have gradually become major problems in the development of China in recent years, environmental policies have accordingly been continuously strengthened. Since environmental problems are closely related to economic development and energy use, environmental policies, which are aimed at environmental problems, have also had a series of positive impacts on economic policies and energy policies. For example, the government has increased its financial investment in environmental protection and formally incorporated environmental protection expenditures into the financial budget system in 2006; the environmental charging policy has been continuously improved; the government is actively adjusting the industry structure; clean production has been promoted and circular economy developed to coordinate the relationship between economic development and environmental protection; a series of special and comprehensive measures have been taken to deal with urban and rural environmental problems, respectively; economic policies conducive to environmental protection have been formulated; the energy structure has been optimized; and the implementation of the energy saving policy has been strengthened. Judging from the current situation, the environment has become an important decision-making factor in China's economic and energy planning and policies. The economic policy, energy policy, and environmental policy are merging with one another and gradually evolving to be an integrated policy system.

References

Barbe, J.-P., *Economic Instruments in Environmental Policy: Lessons from OECD Experince and Their Relevance to Developing Economies*, Paris: OECD Development Center, 1994, Technical Papers, No. 92.

Cole, D. H., & Grossman, P. I., 2001, Toward a Total-Cost Approach to Environmental Instrument Choice, Draft, June 23.

Dieter, H., & Pearce, D., "Economic Policy Towards the Environment: An overview". In *Economic Policy Towards the Environment*, Dieter Helm (eds.),. 1991. OXERA Publishing Ltd., Oxford, pp. 289–320.

Dijkstra, B. R., *The Political Economy of Environmental Policy: A Public Choice Approach to Market Instruments*. 2000. Edward Elgar Publishing Ltd., Cheltenham, UK.

Gao, S., Qu, S. & Geng, Z., "A Review and Evaluation of Energy Strategies and Policies". *Review of Economic Research*, No. 83 (2004).

Guo, X., "Economic Losses Caused by Environmental Pollution and Ecological Destruction". In *China's Environment and Development Review* Vol. 2. 2004. Zheng Y. (ed.), Social Sciences Academic Press.

Information Office of the State Council, *China's Environmental Protection 1996–2005*, June 5, 2006.

Jin, B., "China's Industrial Development under the Constraints of Resources and Environment". *China Industrial Economics*, No. 4 (2005).

Li, K., "South Korea's Environmental Tax System". *Taxation Research*, No. 6 (2003).

Russell, C. S., & Powell, P. T., Rethink Advice on Environment Policy Instrument Choice in Developing Countries. Paper for World Congress of Environmental Economics, Venice, 1998.

Sterner, T., *Policy Instruments for Environmental and National Resource Management*. 2003. Resource for the Future, Washington, D. C., USA.

The Research Group of Macroeconomic Research Institute, National Development and Reform Commission, "Energy Development of the 11th Five-Year Plan: Ideas and Strategic Priorities". *Macroeconomics*, No. 10 (2005).

Xia, G., *Environmental Policy Innovation: Economic Analysis of Environmental Policies*. 2001. Social Sciences Academic Press.

Yao X., "The Scientific View on Development and the Historical Evolution of Development Strategy on Economy". *Academic Exchange*, Vol. 133, No. 4 (2005), pp. 70–73.

Zhang, S., "An Analysis of the Marginalization of Environmental Policy and the Direction of Reform". In *China's Environment and Development Review* Vol. 2, 2004. Zheng Yisheng (ed.), Social Sciences Academic Press.

Zhang, X., "Environmental Value: Measurement of Non-Market Goods and Services". In *China's Environment and Development Review* Vol. 2. 2004. Zheng Y. (ed.), Social Sciences Academic Press.

Zhang, X., "The Overall Evaluation of China's Environmental Policies". *Social Sciences in China*, No. 3 (1999).

Chapter 12

Industrial Water-Use Efficiency Under the Dual Constraints of Resources and Environment: An Empirical Study Based on SBM-Undesirable and Meta-Frontier Models[1]

Jing Li and Xiaocan Ma

Institute of Quantitative & Technical Economics,
Chinese Academy of Social Sciences

1. Introduction

Water is an environmental resource indispensable to life on earth, and also a limited and irreplaceable resource important for human production and human life. Relevant studies have found that on the one hand, China is facing a crisis of water resources, and on the other hand, the water-use efficiency of agriculture, industry, and other industries is at a low level when compared with the rest of the world, far lower than that of developed countries. At the middle stage of industrialization, the development of industry in China demanded more water consumption. At the end of the 11th Five-Year Plan period, industrial water consumption increased by more than 27% compared with the beginning of the 10th Five-Year Plan period, with an average annual growth rate of 2.43%, and the proportion

---

[1] A brief version of the present chapter has been published in *Journal of Natural Resources*, June, 2014.

of water consumption increased from 20.7% to 24.1%. In the same period, the average annual growth rate of China's total water supply was less than 1%. In the meantime, the problem of industrial water pollution in China has not been fundamentally solved. In recent years, although chemical oxygen demand and ammonia nitrogen emissions in industrial waste water have decreased, they are still at relatively high levels. For this reason, the State Council issued *Suggestions on the Implementation of the Most Stringent Water Resources Management System* in January 2012, pointing out that China is now in a terrible situation in terms of water resources, and the problems of water shortage, serious water pollution, and deterioration of water ecological environment are increasingly prominent, which has become the main bottleneck restricting the sustainable development of economy and society. It has also put forward the "red-line", i.e., the bottom line, of water resources: by 2030, the total amount of water used in the country is to be controlled within 700 billion cubic meters; water-use efficiency reaches or approaches the advanced level of the world; and water consumption for industrial added value per 10,000 yuan decreases to less than 40 cubic meters. It can be said that the current and future industrial development in China is facing the dual constraints of water use, that is, on the one hand, it is subject to the control of the total amount of industrial water supply; on the other hand, it must also face the problem of industrial water pollution control. With this background, scientific and efficient utilization of water resources and gradual improvement of industrial water-use efficiency are essential to the medium- and long-term industrial development.

2. Literature Review

In recent years, scholars have made beneficial explorations in the area of water-use efficiency. Qian & He (2011) apply the input-oriented DEA model to estimate China's water-use efficiency from 1998 to 2008, arguing that the water-use efficiency has showed a trend of first decreasing and then increasing over the years, with the eastern, central, and western areas ranging from high to low, and also pointing out that the industry structure, import and export demand, and regional endowment of water resources have a significant influence on the water-use efficiency. The influencing factors on water-use efficiency mainly include water price (Schneider & Whitlatch, 1991; Jia & Kang, 2000; Lei *et al.*, 2005), industry structure (Zhu, 2007; Romano & Guerrini, 2011; Pan *et al.*, 2011; Dong & Liao, 2011), allocation system (Yang *et al.*, 2009), regional economy, or industrial development (Hu *et al.*, 2006; Li *et al.*, 2008; Sun & Liu, 2009). In addition, in terms of industrial water-use efficiency, most of the researches focus on agricultural water-use efficiency (Wang & Zhao, 2008; Wang *et al.*, 2013), while the efficiency of industrial water use has attracted the attention of only a few scholars (Sun *et al.*, 2007; Lu, 2008).

Although existing studies have applied different methods to analyze the use efficiency of water resources at home and abroad from different perspectives, neither of them, except Yue & Zhao (2011), has taken the impact of water pollution on water-use efficiency into account. Based on the data of 13 typical industrial provinces (autonomous regions and municipalities directly under the central government) in China from 2003 to 2009, they apply the directional environmental distance function (DEDF) to estimate the efficiency of industrial water use, arguing that there are differences among different regions in the efficiency, which has shown an increasing trend over time. By applying the Malmquist–Luenberger (ML) exponential decomposition, they come to the conclusion that the main driving factor for its improvement is the rate of change in efficiency, while technological progress has no obvious effect on it. Although the research takes into account the impact of industrial pollution on water-use efficiency, it has the following shortcomings: (1) decision-making unit (DMU) calculated with only 13 provinces (autonomous regions and municipalities directly under the central government) obviously violates the strict rule of thumb of Data Envelopment Analysis (DEA): the DMU number should not be less than twice the product of input and output variables[2] (Dyson *et al.*, 2001); (2) the possible impact of the differences in the industrial development of different regions on industrial water-use efficiency has not been considered; (3) the efficiency measured by the ML index should, in fact, be understood as the

---

[2]This article selects 13 provinces (autonomous regions and municipalities directly under the central government) as DMU. Considering the situation of 3 input and 3 output indicators, the number of DMU is less than twice the product of input and output variables.

growth rate of industry with industrial water use and pollution taken into consideration, not genuine industrial water-use efficiency.

Drawing on the results and shortcoming of previous studies, this chapter conducts an empirical analysis of the industrial water-use efficiency in the industrial development of 30 provinces (autonomous regions and municipalities directly under the central government) of China, which is under the dual constraints of resources and environment, and studies the influence of different factors on it, especially the price of water resources.

3. Methodology and Data

3.1. *Meta-frontier model*

When using DEA to measure the industrial technological efficiency of different provinces (autonomous regions and municipalities directly under the central government), its underlying assumption is that the DMUs under evaluation have the same or similar technological level so as to explore the technological gap and management level behind the technological inefficiency. But there is a big gap, among different provinces (autonomous regions and municipalities directly under the central government) in China, in the level of industrial and technological development, in industry structure, natural resources and urbanization level, and in the production frontier. If we do not consider these differences and continue to use the overall sample to evaluate industrial water-use efficiency, we will not be able to accurately measure the real industrial development efficiency and industrial water-use efficiency of various provinces (autonomous regions and municipalities directly under the central government). In order to solve this problem, Batese and Rao (2002) first put forward the following method: DMU is divided into different groups according to a certain standard, with different group frontiers and meta-frontiers defined by stochastic frontier analysis (SFA), and the technical efficiency of different group frontiers and meta-frontiers estimated, obtaining the technology gap ratio (TGR). SFA assumes that all DMUs have the potential to reach the same technological frontier, which may lead to the meta-frontier failing to envelop group frontiers. In addition, SFA cannot deal with the situation of multi-input and multi-output (Rao *et al.*, 2003). Battese *et al.* (2004) solve the above problems by expanding the research with DEA.

Industrial Water-Use Efficiency Under the Dual Constraints of Resources 309

3.1.1. *Meta-frontier and group frontier*

The meta-frontier involved in the meta-frontier model refers to the potential technical level of all DMUs, while the group frontier refers to the actual technical level of each group of DMU, with the main difference lying in the sets of technologies they refer to. In view of this, 30 provinces (autonomous regions and municipalities directly under the central government) of China are divided into three major groups, eastern, central, and western, according to the homogeneity of industrial development.[3] Although the division is relatively rough, it has always been the main basis for the division of China's regional economic and industrial gradient development. Moreover, the rule of thumb of DEA on the relationship between variables and DMU quantity also requires that the division of groups not be too detailed. In addition, a careful investigation shows that the indicators of water resources per capita, natural resources, urbanization level, industry structure, and industrialization degree in the three groups all display a trend of gradient development, and the differences within the groups are less than the whole. The division of the three groups is thus necessary and reasonable, by which the efficiency of industrial water use under the frontier of their respective groups and under the meta-frontier can be discussed. Based on the single-input and single-output meta-frontier model, the three major groups are taken as research objects. The general positions of the meta-frontier and the group frontiers are shown in Fig. 12.1.

According to the meta-frontier model of Battese *et al.* (2004), the common technology set (T^m) considering undesirable output is

$$T^m = \left\{ \begin{array}{l} (x, y^g, y^b), x \geq 0, y^g \geq 0 \\ y^b \geq 0; x \ can \ produce \ (y^g, y^b) \end{array} \right\} \tag{12.1}$$

wherein x represents an input vector, y^g represents a desirable output vector, and y^b represents an undesirable output vector. That is to say, the input

---

[3]The eastern group includes Beijing, Tianjin, Hebei, Liaoning, Shanghai, Jiangsu, Zhejiang, Fujian, Shandong, Hainan, and Guangdong; the central group includes Shanxi, Jilin, Heilongjiang, Anhui, Jiangxi, Henan, Hubei, and Hunan; the western group includes Inner Mongolia, Guangxi, Chongqing, Sichuan, Guizhou, Yunnan, Shaanxi, Gansu, Qinghai, Ningxia, and Xinjiang.

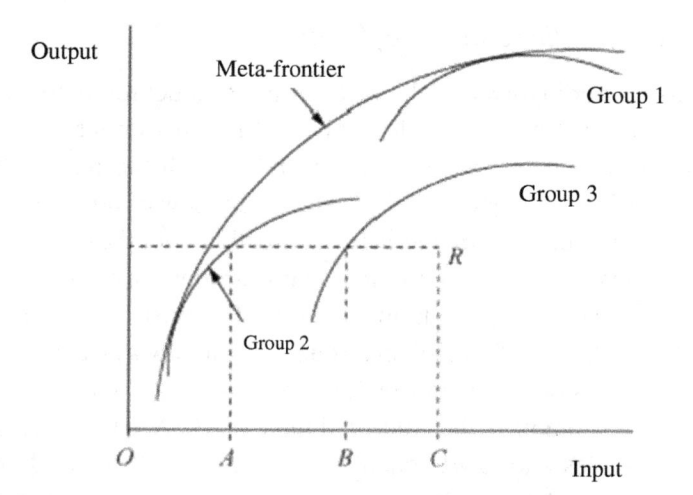

Fig. 12.1　Meta-frontier and group frontier

(x) needed to obtain a certain output (y^g, y^b) meets the conditions under the technology (T^m). The corresponding set of production possibility is

$$P^m(x) = \{(y^g, y^b): (x, y^g, y^b) \in T^m\} \tag{12.2}$$

Therefore, the common distance function of common technical efficiency can be expressed as

$$D^m(x, y^g, y^b) = \sup_\lambda \{\lambda > 0: (x/\lambda) \in P^m(y^g, y^b)\} \tag{12.3}$$

According to different levels of industrial development, the set of group technology for the three groups of eastern, central, and western $(i = 1,2,3)$ is as follows:

$$T^i = \{(x, y^g, y^b): x \geq 0, y^g \geq 0, y^b \geq 0; x \to (y^g, y^b)\}, i = 1, 2, 3 \tag{12.4}$$

The set of production possibility corresponding to the group is

$$P^i(x) = \{(y^g, y^b): (x, y^g, y^b) \in T^i\}, i = 1, 2, 3 \tag{12.5}$$

Then, the group distance function of group technical efficiency is

$$D^i(x, y^g, y^b) = \sup_\lambda \{\lambda > 0 : (x/\lambda) \in P^k(y^g, y^b)\}, i = 1, 2, 3 \quad (12.6)$$

In the expression, $D^i(x, y^g, y^b)$ represents the input distance function at the level of group technology (T^i). If the input vector x is external to the set $P(y^g, y^b)$, $D^i(x, y^g, y^b) > 1$; If input vector x is on the boundary of the set $P(y^g, y^b)$, $D^i(x, y^g, y^b) = 1$.

Since the meta-frontier technology is the envelope curve of the group frontier technology, $T^m = \{T^1 \cup T^2 \cup T^3\}$ is satisfied.

3.1.2. *Technology gap ratio (TGR)*

When the input–output combination is (x, y^g, y^b), the technical efficiency from the input angle for the group $(i = 1,2,3)$ can be expressed as follows:

$$TE^i(x,y) = \frac{1}{D^i(x,y)}, i = 1, 2, 3 \quad (12.7)$$

The TGR from the input angle can be expressed as a common and group distance function

$$TGR^i(x, y^g, y^b) = \frac{D^i(x, y^g, y^b)}{D^m(x, y^g, y^b)} = \frac{TE^m(x, y^g, y^b)}{TE^i(x, y^g, y^b)}, i = 1, 2, 3 \quad (12.8)$$

As shown in Fig. 12.1 for province R (autonomous region, municipality directly under the central government), the calculation process of its corresponding TGR is as follows:

$$TE^m(R) = \frac{OA}{OC}; TE^i(R) = \frac{OB}{OC};$$

$$TGR^i(R) = \frac{TE^m}{TE^i} = \frac{OA/OC}{OB/OC} = \frac{OA}{OB} \quad (12.9)$$

TGR connects the meta-frontier and the group frontier, and measures the technical efficiency difference under different boundaries of the same DMU. The higher the value is, the closer the actual production efficiency is to the potential production efficiency. It can be used to judge the necessity of new group division. When TGR average is less than 1, a division can be considered appropriate and necessary, otherwise, it is not.

3.2. *SBM-Undesirable model*

There are many DEA models available to solve the above groups and meta-frontier distance function including industrial water consumption and pollution (Liu & Wu, 2011). However, models such as input–output transposition, forward attribute transposition, and directional distance function are either against the essence of production or have great limitations. For example, undesirable output may decrease at the same proportion with the growth of desirable output, with the slack of input and output neglected. The SBM model (Tone, 2003) can directly introduce the slack of input and output into the objective function, which solves the slack of input and output and the deviation of radial and angle selection. The current chapter applies this model of undesirable output to solve the problem of industrial water-use efficiency in the provinces (autonomous regions and municipalities directly under the central government) of China. It can be expressed as (12.10).

$$
\rho^* = \min \frac{1 - \dfrac{1}{m}\sum_{i=1}^{m}\dfrac{s_i^-}{x_{i_0}}}{1 + \dfrac{1}{s_1 + s_2}\left(\sum_{r=1}^{s_1}\dfrac{s_r^g}{y_{r_0}^g} + \sum_{r=1}^{s_2}\dfrac{s_r^b}{y_{r_0}^b}\right)}
$$

$$
\begin{aligned}
\text{s.t. } & x_0 = X_\varphi + s^- \\
& y_0^g = Y_\varphi^g - s^g \\
& y_0^b = Y_\varphi^b + s^b \\
& s^- \geq 0, s^g \geq 0, s^b \geq 0, \varphi \geq 0
\end{aligned}
\tag{12.10}
$$

where φ represents the optimal weight variable to be obtained, and s^-, s^g, and s^b, respectively, represent the slack variables of input, desirable output, and undesirable output. The objective function ρ^* is strictly decreasing with respect to $s_i^-(\forall\, i)$, $s_r^g(\forall\, r)$, and $s_r^b(\forall\, r)$, and $0 < \rho^* \leq 1$. When and only when $\rho^* = 1$, that is, $s^- = 0$, $s^g = 0$ and $s^b = 0$, the decision-making unit is valid; when $\rho^* < 1$, that is, the value of s^-, s^g, and s^b are not all zero, the decision-making unit is invalid, i.e., there is a need to improve input and output.

If the industrial water consumption separated from the input variable X and its slack are designated as X_w and S_w^-, the water-use efficiency under the meta-frontier is $TE_w^m = (X_w^m - S_w^{-m}) / X_w^m$, and the water-use efficiency under different groups is $TE_w^i = (X_w^i - S_w^{-i}) / X_w^i$ $(i = 1, 2, 3)$. Similarly, the TGR of industrial water is defined as $TGR_w = TE_w^m / TE_w^i$. If TE_w^m is significantly different from TE_w^i in mean value, or TGR_w is significantly less than 1, the division of the three major regional groups will be considered necessary to study the efficiency of industrial water use.

3.3. *Data sources*

The input factors in this chapter mainly include industrial water consumption, industrial employees, and industrial net assets, while the output indicators include desirable output, i.e., industrial added value, and undesirable output, i.e., chemical oxygen demand and ammonia nitrogen emissions in industrial wastewater. After obtaining the industrial water-use efficiency of different provinces (autonomous regions and municipalities directly under the central government), the influencing factors of industrial water-use efficiency differences are further examined. Relevant data mainly come from *China Statistical Yearbook on Environment* (2000–2012), *China Statistical Yearbook* (2000–2012), and provincial *Statistical Yearbook* (2000–2012), *China Water Resources Bulletin* (1999–2011), *China Compendium of Statistics 1949–2008*, Soshoo (http://www.soshoo.com/index.do), and the statistical database of China Economic Network (http://db.cei.gov.cn/). All price indicators are deflated to the constant price of 1999. The degree of industrialization is expressed by the proportion of industrial GDP in the current-year GDP of the province (autonomous regions and municipalities directly under the central government) under investigation. The prices of industrial water from 1999 to 2010 mainly come from China Water Network (http://price.h2o-china.com/), and the prices of industrial water in different regions are replaced by the average price of the cities at the prefecture level. For the prices of industrial water in 2011, data released by the municipal water supply groups and government websites are first checked, and for the prices in prefecture-level cities that cannot be obtained in such a manner, the economic forum of Renmin University of China (bbs.rdjjlt.org) is searched, from which an average price is adopted. See Table 12.1 for the descriptive statistics of input–output indicators and factors affecting industrial water-use efficiency.

Table 12.1 Descriptive statistics of input–output indicators and factors affecting industrial water-use efficiency

Variable		Variable specification	Sample average	Standard deviation	Min.	Max.	Sample size
Input–output indicators	indu_water	Industrial water consumption (100 million m³)	42.84	40.75	3.00	225.30	390
	labour	Labor (100 thousand)	51.45	48.05	1.98	230.35	390
	net_asset	Net assets (10 billion yuan)	99.83	110.36	4.13	660.78	390
	indu_added	Industrial added value (10 billion yuan)	28.12	32.58	0.59	205.06	390
	cod	Chemical oxygen demand in industrial wastewater (10 thousand tons)	17.52	13.90	0.49	69.35	390
	nh	Ammonia nitrogen emissions in industrial wastewater	12.29	11.05	0.23	50.51	390
Factors affecting industrial water-use efficiency	mee	Meta-frontier industrial water-use efficiency (%)	53.81	36.69	0.55	100	390
	gee	Group-frontier industrial water-use efficiency (%)	78.95	30.22	2.99	100	390
	lnwpc	Water resources per capita (m³ per capita)	7.01	1.27	3.35	9.69	390
	lny	GDP per capita (yuan)	9.99	0.10	9.86	10.31	390
	ind	Degree of industrialization (%)	39.72	8.14	12.61	56.49	390
	tc	Water consumption per 10 thousand yuan of industrial value added (m³)	5.18	1.00	2.34	8.28	390
		Actual price logarithm (yuan/m³)	0.90	0.42	0.13	2.06	390
	lnp	Meta-frontier shadow price logarithm (yuan)	3.11	1.02	−1.78	5.60	390
		Group-frontier shadow price logarithm (yuan)	2.85	1.20	−1.30	5.77	390
	lninvest	Investment in industrial wastewater treatment projects (10 thousand yuan)	10.39	1.177	6.49	12.90	390
	cycle	Reuse rate of industrial water	77.51	16.77	30.80	96.40	390

4. Analysis and Discussion

4.1. *Industrial water-use efficiency*

The mean test of TGR reveals that the average value of TGR is significantly less than 1. By calculation, the average TGR of industrial water use from 1999 to 2011 in the eastern group has been at a high level (close to 1), indicating that the eastern group is closer to the meta-frontier of industrial technology, while the central and western groups are farther away, which reflects the rationality of the division of the three groups according to the level of industrial development.

First, the meta-frontier method is used to measure the meta-frontier and group-frontier industrial water-use efficiency of the eastern, central, and western groups in terms of temporal change. This is shown in Figs. 12.2 and 12.3.

As can be seen from Fig. 12.2, the eastern group and the western group respectively, have the highest and the lowest meta-frontier industrial water-use efficiency during the period 1999–2011, with the central group in the middle. The efficiency of industrial water use in the eastern group is relatively high, but there is a downward trend. The efficiency in both the central and western groups is not high and has seen little change, which shows that the industrial water-use technology in the two groups is farther from the meta-frontier than the eastern group, and there are technological

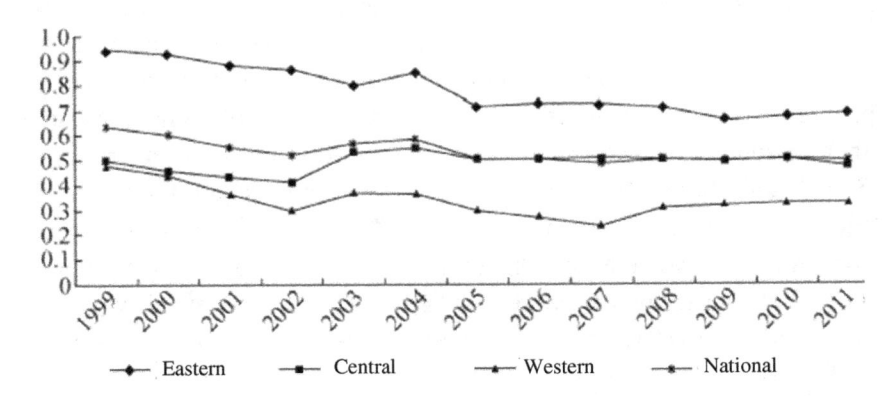

Fig. 12.2 Meta-frontier industrial water-use efficiency of the eastern, central, and western groups (1999–2011)

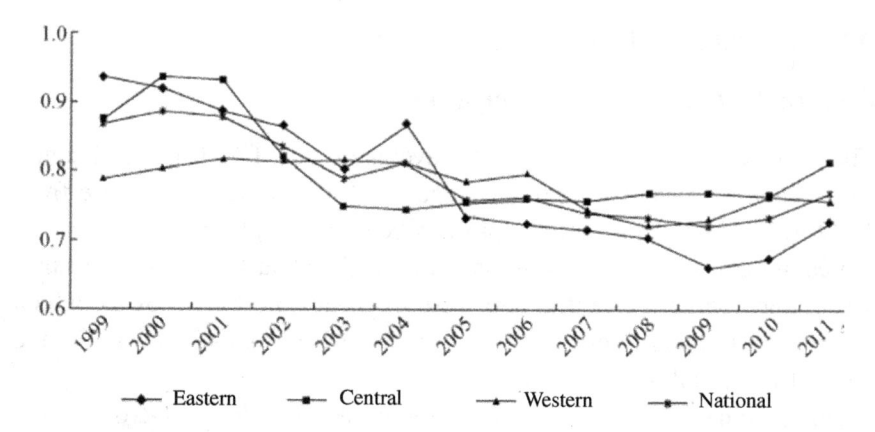

Fig. 12.3 Group-frontier industrial water-use efficiency of the eastern, central, and western groups (1999–2011)

improvements to varying degrees. At the group frontier (see Fig. 12.3), the industrial water-use efficiency of the central and western groups has increased, indicating that they are closer to the respective group frontier than to the meta-frontier. The eastern group has not seen much improvement at its group frontier, but has fallen instead.

Then, the average meta-frontier and group-frontier industrial water-use efficiency of 30 provinces (autonomous regions and municipalities directly under the central government) 1999 to 2011 is discussed, and is shown in Table 12.2.

The average TGR for the eastern group is 0.9901, which indicates that it has reached 99.01% of the meta-frontier industrial water-use technology. This may be due to the relatively high level of economic development, an emphasis on the introduction and diffusion of technology, and other reasons. The average TGR for the central and western groups is 63.20% and 40.05%, respectively. In terms of the average meta-frontier industrial water-use efficiency, there is 22.28%, 51.33%, and 65.35% room for improvement for the eastern, central, and western groups, respectively. In terms of the average group-frontier industrial water-use efficiency, there is 21.25%, 19.60%, and 22.81% room for improvement, respectively, for these groups.

In terms of industrial water-use efficiency, Beijing, Tianjin, Shanghai, Shandong, and Guangdong in the eastern group and Heilongjiang in the

Table 12.2 Average industrial water-use efficiency and TGR at different frontiers in different provinces (autonomous regions and municipalities directly under the central government) of China

Eastern	*mee*	*gee*	*TGR*	Central	*mee*	*gee*	*TGR*	Western	*mee*	*gee*	*TGR*
Beijing	1.0000	1.0000	1.0000	Shanxi	0.3830	1.0000	0.3830	Inner Mongolia	0.6213	1.0000	0.6213
Tianjin	1.0000	1.0000	1.0000	Jilin	0.2439	0.9983	0.2442	Guangxi	0.4419	1.0000	0.4419
Hebei	0.8822	0.8822	1.0000	Heilongjiang	1.0000	1.0000	1.0000	Chongqing	0.0152	0.0436	0.3125
Liaoning	0.5554	0.5639	0.9884	Anhui	0.4035	0.6211	0.7406	Sichuan	0.9768	1.0000	0.9768
Shanghai	1.0000	1.0000	1.0000	Jiangxi	0.4103	0.5467	0.7884	Guizhou	0.1570	1.0000	0.1570
Jiangsu	0.4612	0.4754	0.9835	Henan	0.7664	1.0000	0.7664	Yunnan	0.3841	0.9035	0.4035
Zhejiang	0.5202	0.5202	1.0000	Hubei	0.1678	0.5858	0.2984	Shaanxi	0.4648	1.0000	0.4648
Fujian	0.8887	0.9691	0.9196	Hunan	0.5188	0.6802	0.8350	Gansu	0.1548	0.8630	0.1816
Shandong	1.0000	1.0000	1.0000					Qinghai	0.1218	0.4399	0.2777
Guangdong	1.0000	1.0000	1.0000					Ningxia	0.1734	0.5701	0.3247
Hainan	0.2410	0.2410	1.0000					Xinjiang	0.1903	0.7812	0.2437
Average	0.7772	0.7865	0.9901	Average	0.4867	0.8040	0.6320	Average	0.3365	07819	0.4005

central group have the best performance. The average of both meta-frontier and group-frontier industrial water-use efficiency is 1, while worst performance goes to Hainan and Hubei in the eastern and central groups, respectively. In the western group, in terms of meta-frontier water-use technology, Sichuan performs the best, while Chongqing performs the worst. There is a difference of 2.32% and 98.48% for improvement in the two places, respectively. In terms of group-frontier water-use technology, five provinces (autonomous regions and municipalities directly under the central government) (Inner Mongolia, Guangxi, Sichuan, Guizhou, and Shaanxi) achieve an average of 1, while Chongqing has the worst performance, its average being 0.0436, with 95.64% room for improvement in efficiency.

There is a big difference in the meta-frontier and group-frontier industrial water-use efficiency among the eastern, central, and western groups, which shows that the imbalance of economic development in these three groups leads to a big difference in the level of their industrial water-use technology. However, the efficiency of industrial water use is generally low in the three major groups, indicating that the industrial water use of China is still extensive and the industrial water supply has not been fully and reasonably utilized. This may be the result of a series of factors such as the low technical level of industrial water use, the low price of industrial water, and the unreasonable industry structure.

4.2. Main influencing factors of price distortion and differences in industrial water-use efficiency

According to general economic principles, the efficiency of industrial water use in different regions may be related to the following factors.

First, the abundance of water resources in a region. If a region enjoys an abundance of water resources, the price of water there will be low, and consequently the people there will have a weak sense of water conservation, resulting in a lower efficiency of industrial water use than other regions. The abundance is measured on the basis of total amount of water resources and amount of water resources per capita. The second indicator takes into account the population factor; thus the combination of the two can better measure the effect of the amount of water resources on the efficiency of industrial water use in the province (autonomous region and municipality directly under the central government).

Second, the price of water resources in a region. According to general economic principles, price is the most effective market adjustment means to determine the efficiency of resource utilization. It can be expected that regions with higher prices also have a higher efficiency of industrial water use. However, it must be considered that the pricing of industrial water in China is a non-market behavior, with the government dominating pricing for a long time, which, in fact, cannot reflect the scarcity of water resources. In addition, under the fiscal decentralization system, maximization of local tax revenue is being stimulated. Local governments are competing to attract foreign investment by various preferential policies, such as lower prices for land, water, and electricity, which may also lead to a distortion of the price of industrial water. Thus, this chapter, on the one hand, collects the industrial water prices of prefecture-level cities in different provinces (autonomous regions and municipalities directly under the central government) [which are further processed to obtain the average prices of the provinces (autonomous regions and municipalities directly under the central government)], and on the other hand, estimates the shadow prices of industrial water[4] to reflect the real market prices, making a comparison between them and the current industrial water prices, and, respectively, examining the impact of the two prices on the efficiency of industrial water in various places so as to judge whether there is any price distortion. We predict that the current industrial water price is much lower than the estimated shadow price, and it has not played its due role in improving the efficiency of industrial water use. The price of industrial water replaced by shadow price will show obvious positive incentive to the efficiency of industrial water use.

Third, regional economic development and industrial development. This study mainly examines whether the water-use efficiency increases with the increase of income, or whether it shows an inverted U-shaped relationship that increases first and then decreases, as shown in other researches. In

---

[4]The shadow price of industrial water refers to the industrial economic cost needed to reduce per unit industrial water consumption, which reflects the marginal price of industrial water use.

addition, the degree of industrialization is also an important explanatory variable that affects the efficiency of industrial water use. The level of industrial development directly determines the total amount of industrial water consumption. It affects the efficiency of water use mainly through two channels: income effect and technological effect. When the industry gets more developed and the income becomes higher, the sensitivity to water price will get weaker, that is, a low tendency of marginal consumption water resources, resulting in poor awareness of water saving and low efficiency of water use in enterprises. In addition, industrial development will encourage enterprises to invest more profits in more efficient and more water-saving technologies, leading to an increase in the efficiency of industrial water use. The influence of industrial development on water-use efficiency is manifested in the interaction between the two effects. If the latter is greater than the former, the water-use efficiency will be improved, and vice versa.

Fourth, regional industrial water-saving technology and treatment of industrial water pollution. Industrial water-saving technology can be expressed in terms of water consumption per 10,000 yuan of industrial added value and reuse rate of industrial water. Obviously, the lower the water consumption per unit of output value, the higher the water efficiency; the higher the reuse rate, the higher the water efficiency. In addition, the present study of water-use efficiency also takes environmental quality into consideration. Then, the investment in industrial pollution control of a region may also have a significant impact on the improvement of industrial water-use efficiency.

In order to better explain the technological efficiency of industrial water use and its differences, it is necessary to understand the influencing factors of industrial water-use efficiency. The regression equations of the meta-frontier and group-frontier industrial water-use efficiency and influencing factors such as water price are as follows:

$$mee = \alpha_0 + \alpha_{1t} + \alpha_2 \ln p + \alpha_3 tgc + \alpha_4 \ln wpc + \alpha_{5j} Z_j \qquad (12.11)$$

$$gee = \beta_0 + \beta_{1t} Y_t + \beta_2 \ln p + \beta_3 \ln wpc + \beta_{4j} Z_j \qquad (12.12)$$

wherein, Y_t includes three explanatory variables: the logarithm of GDP per capita (ln y) and the square of the logarithm of GDP per capita, and the degree of industrialization (ln d). Z_j includes three explanatory variables: water consumption per 10,000 yuan of industrial added value (tc), industrial water reuse rate ($cycle$), and the logarithm of project investment of industrial pollution control (ln $invest$), indicating the technology gap ratio between regional groups.

As the value of industrial water-use efficiency is 1 for some provinces (autonomous regions and municipalities directly under the central government), to distinguish them requires a special dependent variable model — Tobit — which can be truncated at both ends. Since the processed efficiency value ranges between 0 and 100, the right end of the Tobit model is taken at 100. In addition, for panel data, the estimation of fixed-effect Tobit model has been proven to be biased (Anderson & Hsiao, 1982), and thus the current effective solution is to choose the stochastic-effect Tobit model

$$
\begin{aligned}
e_{it}^* &= \eta + E_{it}' \delta + v_i + \varepsilon_{it} \\
e_{it} &= e_{it}^* \quad (0 < e_{it}^* \leq 100) \\
e_{it} &= 0 \quad \left(e_{it}^* < 0\right) \\
e_{it} &= 100 \quad \left(e_{it}^* > 100\right)
\end{aligned}
\tag{12.13}
$$

wherein, e_{it}^* represents potential variables and e_{it} represents observed variables; E_{it}' denotes an explanatory variable vector, v_i denotes a random variable that changes with the individual but does not change with time, ε_{it} denotes a random variable that changes independently with time and the individual, and these two random effects are independent and both obey a normal distribution; η denotes a constant and δ denotes a parameter vector.

See Table 12.3 for Tobit regression results of industrial water-use efficiency, actual industrial water use price, and other influencing factors under different frontiers.

As can be seen from Table 12.3, the overall significance test p of the four models are all 0, indicating that the four models are significant. The values of *rho* are all above 0.80, which shows that the change of individual effect mainly explains the change of industrial water-use efficiency.

The logarithm of GDP per capita and its square show that there is a U-shaped relationship, that is, decreasing at first and then increasing,

Table 12.3 Tobit model regression results (actual water price)

Industrial water-use efficiency	Meta-frontier	Eastern group	Central group	Western group
lny	(–6403.85)***	–21118.54	(–20891.03)***	–5917.52
(lny)^2	(318.32)***	1050.08	(1035.38)***	286.87
lnwpc	(–5.81)*	–5.43	–11.09	–3.32
tc	–2.60	28.39	(32.77) *	(31.62)***
tgc	(0.73)***	—	—	—
cycle	(0.57)***	(1.48)**	–0.05	(1.07)*
ind	(0.83)***	0.32	0.55	0.98
lnp	8.96	–48.30	(–28.09)*	(28.58)*
lninvest	–5.82	41.05	–1.11	2.11
_cons	(32352.3)***	107037.6	(105737.7)***	30848.8
Standard deviation of individual effect	(31.43)***	(69.71)**	(31.51)*	(49.88)***
Standard deviation of random interference	(15.05)***	(29.76)***	(13.17)***	(16.52)***
rho	0.81	0.85	0.85	0.90
Wald test	298.91	39.28	43.56	34.10
P	0.0000	0.0000	0.0000	0.0000

Notes: ***significantly below 1%; **significantly below 5%; *significantly below 10%.

between water-use efficiency and the logarithm of GDP per capita, which is different from the inverted U-shape of other studies. All the turning points of the U shape exceed 23155.8. The actual GDP per capita, 21807.3, is less than 23155.8, which means that the GDP per capita of China is still on the left side of the turning point, indicating that the industrial water-use efficiency will fall with the growth of GDP per capita at the current stage of development.

The relationship between water resources per capita and industrial water-use efficiency is all negative under the meta-frontier and the frontier of the three major groups, that is, the higher the water resources per capita, the lower the water-use efficiency. The meta-frontier industrial water-use efficiency is inversely related to the water consumption of per

10,000 yuan of industrial GDP, while under the group frontiers, it is positive, but not statistically significant. The relationship between the meta-frontier industrial water-use efficiency and TGR is significantly positive, with an impact of 73%, which indicates that it is necessary to study industrial water-use efficiency by distinguishing the three groups of eastern, central, and western. It has a significant positive relationship with the reuse rate of industrial water on the whole, which means that the higher the reuse rate is, the higher the industrial water-use efficiency will be, and this is in line with the expectation. Industrial water-use efficiency is in a positive relationship with the degree of industrialization, which shows that the technological effect brought by high industrialization degree is higher than the income effect. There is a positive relationship between the meta-frontier industrial water-use efficiency and the actual water price, but it is not significant. Under the frontier of the eastern group, the relationship is negative, but not significant either. For the central group and the western group, it is statistically significant, with one being positive and the other negative, which indicates that the actual industrial water prices in the eastern, central, and western regions do not reflect the actual situation of water resources. Instead of the expected significantly positive relationship, the efficiency of industrial water use and the amount of investment in pollution control show a negative relation, indicating that the investment does not achieve the desired effects.

In order to reflect the real relationship between the price of industrial water and the efficiency of industrial water use, it is necessary to consider the shadow price of industrial water, because the actual price fails to do the job. While discussing the influence of the actual market price of industrial water on the efficiency of industrial water, the actual price is converted into the shadow price. The difference between the shadow price and the actual price of industrial water is shown in Fig. 12.4.

Comparing the shadow price of industrial water with the actual water price calculated by the meta-frontier SBM dual price (see Appendix for the dual form and shadow price process), we find that there is a big gap between the two. During the research period, the actual price of industrial water was about 27 yuan per cubic meter, while the shadow price was about 363 yuan per cubic meter, more than 12 times of the current industrial water price. Fig. 12.4 clearly shows this huge difference. It is

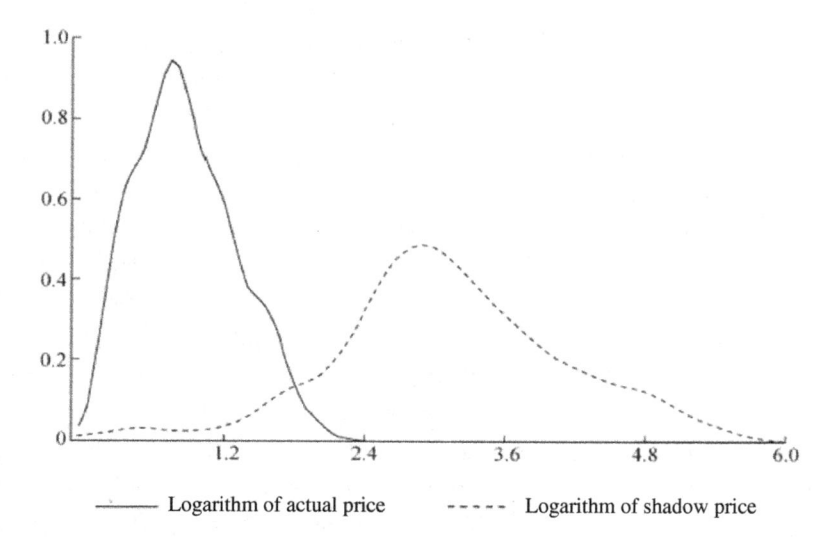

———— Logarithm of actual price   - - - - - Logarithm of shadow price

Fig. 12.4 Distribution of shadow prices and actual prices of industrial water

reasonable to believe that the low price of industrial water has seriously deviated from the real price in a full market, which has also resulted in a negative effect on the improvement of the efficiency of industrial water use. In order to test the above judgment, the actual price of industrial water is replaced by the shadow price of the meta-frontier and group frontier SBM model, and the influence of "real" water price on the efficiency of industrial water use is tested again, while keeping other control variables unchanged.

With "real" water price instead of actual water price, the Tobit model regression results of industrial water-use efficiency, shadow price of industrial water, and other influencing factors under different frontiers are shown in Table 12.4.

As can be seen from Table 12.4, these four models are significant. In comparison with Table 12.3, the relationship between industrial water-use efficiency and GDP per capita is still U-shaped. Except for the meta-frontier, the turning points of the eastern, central, and western groups are all over 24587.7 yuan, that is, the actual GDP per capita is still less than the turning point. The meta-frontier industrial water-use efficiency has a significant positive relationship with the shadow price of industrial water use, while it has no such a relationship with the actual

Table 12.4 Tobit model regression results (shadow water price)

Industrial water-use efficiency	Meta-frontier	Eastern group	Central group	Western group
lny	(−3672.35)**	−20403.15	(−16346.98)***	(−5270.4)*
(lny)²	(183.99)**	1008.85	(805.01)**	(257.42)*
lnwpc	(−6.05)**	−3.46	(−14.54)***	1.65
tc	(18.75)***	(38.14)*	(6.79)***	(3.96)***
tgc	(0.52)***	—	—	—
cycle	−0.20	1.68	−0.01	−0.62
ind	(0.43)*	0.47	0.05	0.63
lnp	(2.63)***	6.41	(2.03)***	(2.29)***
lninvest	−4.65	−38.85	1.60	−3.11
_cons	(18619.39)**	103990.60	(83579.60)**	27391.80
Standard deviation of individual effect	(23.00)***	(68.19)***	(23.66)***	(36.80)***
Standard deviation of random interference	(11.68)***	29.572	(13.57)***	(13.08)***
rho	0.80	0.84	0.75	0.89
Wald test	603.74	40.33	121.86	70.21
P	0.0000	0.0000	0.0000	0.0000

Notes: ***significantly below 1%; **significantly below 5%; *significantly below 10%.

water price, indicating that the shadow price can better reflect the scarcity of water resources, thus affecting the efficiency of industrial water use. Although its influence on the efficiency of industrial water use is not significant in the eastern group, its significance in the central and western regions has changed from 10% to 1% compared with the actual price, that is, the rise in the shadow price of industrial water has a more significant positive effect on improving the efficiency of industrial water use.

5. Conclusion and Policy Implications

The shortage of water resources has become an important "bottleneck" affecting the industrial development of China. Industrial water pollution in turn constrains the supply of industrial water and industrial development. Thus, the study of industrial water-use efficiency must consider the industrial development under the two constraints. This chapter studies the industrial water-use efficiency of 30 provinces (autonomous regions and municipalities directly under the central government) in China under the constraints of industrial water resources and water pollution. The present study adopted DEA-SBM model with undesirable output (industrial water pollution) and, with the meta-frontier model, examines in more detail the industrial water-use efficiency of these provinces (autonomous regions and municipalities directly under the central government) according to the differences in regional industrial development technologies. And finally, the role of industrial water price and its distortion degree in determining the industrial water-use efficiency is investigated. The conclusions of this chapter are as follows:

(1) The results of the meta-frontier model and the TGR show that the TGR of the eastern group is close to 1, while that of the central and western groups is 0.632 and 0.401, respectively, sharply different from that of the eastern group. It is, therefore, impossible to accurately measure the real industrial development technology and water-use efficiency of different provinces (autonomous regions and municipalities directly under the central government) without considering the regional heterogeneity of industrial technology. The problem is solved in this chapter by combining the meta-frontier model and SBM model which can deal with industrial pollution output.

(2) Although the technology of industrial water usage continues to improve, after considering the by-products of industrial water pollution, we find that the overall efficiency of industrial water use has not correspondingly improved over the years, and has even decreased. After controlling the factors such as the regional economic development level, the conditions of industrialization, industrial water-saving technology, and industrial water pollution treatment, the current industrial water price does not show the expected positive impact on water-use efficiency, and even shows the opposite impact instead.

(3) With the "real" market water price reevaluated, we find that there is a big gap between this and the actual price. It can then be argued that the current water price is distorted to a large extent, and has not played its due role in improving the effective allocation of water resources. With the current price substituted by the "real" market price, the new regression shows that the efficiency of industrial water use will increase by 2.63%, when the water price increases by 1%. The results for the three groups are also roughly the same.

The above research results have important policy implications, including the following aspects:

(1) The study of industrial water-use efficiency does not only concern the level of industrial development and the utilization of water resources, but also the water environment. Therefore, the study must pay attention to water resources management. The reasonable way to improve the efficiency of industrial water use should take into account the value of water resources and the sustainability of water resources.

(2) The study of industrial water-use efficiency must also take into account the differences in the technological level of industrial water use in different regions. The industrial water-saving technology in the eastern region is relatively advanced, and thus in the process of industrial transfer, such advanced technology should be effectively used to promote economic development. At the same time, through increasing the technological investment in the central and western regions, the technological level of industrial water use will be improved, with the efficiency of industrial water use improved as a result.

(3) According to the current situation of water resources and water treatment, the price of industrial water should be gradually increased, and the multi-stepped water price can also be applied to industrial water, with the distortion of the current water prices gradually corrected, so that the price of industrial water can truly reflect the value of water resources, which is of great benefit to the suppression of industrial water waste.

Appendix

The dual form of SBM-Undesirable model can be expressed as follows:

$$\max u^g y_0^g - vx_o - u^b y_0^b$$

$$\text{s.t. } u^g Y^g - vX - u^b Y^b \le 0$$

$$u^g \ge \frac{1 + u^g y_0^g - vx_o - u^b y_0^b}{s}(1/y_0^g) \tag{12.14}$$

$$u^b \ge \frac{1 + u^g y_0^g - vx_o - u^b y_0^b}{s}(1/y_0^b)$$

wherein, $s = s_1 + s_2$, the dual variables $v \in R^m, u^g \in R^{s_1}, u^b \in R^{s_2}$ can be interpreted as the virtual prices of inputs, desirable outputs, and undesirable outputs. Similarly, the dual variable v_w of industrial water input is separated from v. Assuming that the absolute shadow price of the desirable output is equal to its market price, the relative shadow price of industrial water relative to industrial output is $p^w = p^{yg} \frac{v_w}{u^g}$, which can be interpreted as the water cost per unit of industrial output produced or the industrial output reduced per unit of water saved (Coggins and Swinton, 1996; Lee, 2005). When water prices are not available or are significantly distorted, it can measure real industrial water prices. This chapter mainly uses the average prices of industrial water in different provinces (autonomous regions and municipalities directly under the central government) to compare with the shadow prices, so as to judge whether the prices of industrial water in different provinces (autonomous regions and municipalities directly under the central government) are distorted, and to examine its impact on the efficiency of industrial water.

References

Anderson, T. W., & Hsiao, C., "Formulation and Estimation of Dynamic Model Using Panel data". *Journal of Econometrics*, Vol. 18, No. 1 (1982), pp. 47–82.

Battese, G. E., & Rao, D. S. P., Technology Gap, Efficiency and a Stochastic Meta-Frontier Function. *International Journal of Business and Economics*, Vol. 1, No. 2 (2002), pp. 87–93.

Battese, G. E., O'Donnell, C. J. & Rao, D. S. P., "A Meta-Frontier Frameworks Production Function for Estimation of Technical Efficiency and Technology Gap for Firms Operating Under Different Technology". *Journal of Productivity Analysis*, Vol. 21, No. 1 (2004), pp. 91–103.

Coggins, J. S., & Swinton, J. R., "The Price of Pollution: A Dual Approach to Valuing SO_2 Allowances". *Journal of Environment Econometrics Manage*, Vol. 30, No. 1 (1996), pp. 58–72.

Dong, Y., & Liao, H., "A Study on Water Resources Utilization Efficiency of Western Provincial Capital Cities Based on DEA". *Bulletin of Soil and Water Conservation*, No. 31 (2011), pp. 134–139.

Dyson, R., Allen, G., Camanho, R., *et al.*, "Pitfalls and Protocols in DEA". *European Journal of Operational Research*, Vol. 132, No. 2 (2001), pp. 245–259.

Hu, J.-L., Wang, S.-C., Yeh, F-Y., "Total-Factor Water Efficiency of Regions in China". *Resources Policy*, Vol. 31 (2006), pp. 217–230.

Jia, S., & Kang, D., "An Analysis of the Impact of Increasing Water Price on Water Resource Demand: A Case Study of North China". *Advances in Water Science*, No. 11 (2000), pp. 49–53.

Lee, M., "The Shadow Price of Substitutable Sulfur in the US Electric Power Plant: A Distance Function Approach". *Journal Environment Manage*, Vol. 77, No. 2 (2005), pp. 104–110.

Lei, X., Qiu, Y., Wang, Z. *et al.*, "The Impact and Analysis of Water Price Increase". *China Water Resources*, No. 13 (2005), pp. 107–112.

Li, S., Cheng, J. & Wu, Q., "An Analysis of the Regional Differences in Water-use Efficiency in China". *China Population, Resources and Environment*, No. 18 (2008), pp. 215–220.

Liu, Y., & Wu, P., "Energy Consumption, Carbon Dioxide Emissions and Economic Growth in APEC Region: An Empirical Study Based on SBM Undesirable and Meta-Frontier Model", *Economic Review*, Vol. 6 (2011), pp. 109–120.

Lu, L., "A Study on Utilization Efficiency of Industrial Water Resources in Zhejiang Province", School of Economics, Zhejiang University, 2008.

Pan, D., Huang, W., Wang, S. *et al.*, "A Research on Water-use Efficiency Based on DEA Model: A Case Study of Yunnan Province". *Journal of Yangtze River Scientific Research Institute*, No. 28 (2011), pp. 15–18.

Qian, W., & He, C., "A Study on Regional Differences and Influencing Factors of Water Resource Utilization Efficiency in China". *China Population, Resources and Environment*, No. 21 (2011), pp. 54–60.

Rao, D. S. P., O'Donnell, C. J. & Battese, G. E., "Meta-Frontier Functions for the Study of Inter-Regional Productivity Differences". Queensland School of Economics, Queensland University, 2003.

Romano, G., & Guerrini, A., "Measuring and Comparing the Efficiency of Water Utility Companies: A Data Envelopment Analysis Approach". *Utilities Policy*, Vol. 19 (2011), pp. 202–209.

Schneider, M. L., & Whitlatch, E. E., "User-specific Water Demand Elasticities". *Water Resources Planning and Management*, Vol.117, No.1 (1991), pp. 52–73.

Sun, A., Dong, Z. & Wang, D., "Industrial Water Consumption Efficiency Estimation and Water Consumption Prediction Based on Temporal Order". *Journal of China University of Mining & Technology*, No. 36 (2007), pp. 547–553.

Sun, C., & Liu, Y., "An Analysis of the Space-Time Pattern of the Relative Efficiency of Water Resource Utilization in China Based on DEA-ESDA". *Resources Science*, No. 31 (2009), pp. 1696–1703.

Tone, K., "Dealing with Undesirable Outputs in DEA: A Slacks-based Measure (SBM) Approach". *GRIPS Research Series*, (2004), pp. 44–45.

Wang, P., Song, X., Yuan, R. *et al.*, "A Study on Water Consumption Law of Summer Maize in North China Based on Stable Isotope of Hydrogen and Oxygen". *Journal of Natural Resources*, No. 28 (2013), pp. 481–491.

Wang, X., & Zhao L., "China's Agricultural Water-use Efficiency and Its Influencing Factors: An SFA Analysis Based on the Provincial Panel Data of 1997–2006". *Issues in Agricultural Economy*, No. 6 (2008), pp. 10–18.

Yang, L., Xu, X. & Jia, X., "A Discussion on Evaluation Index System of Water Resource Efficiency". *Journal of Beijing Normal University* (Natural Science Edition), No. 45 (2009), pp. 642–646.

Yue, L., & Zhao, H., "A Research on China's Industrial Water-use Efficiency under Environmental Constraints Based on the Data of 13 Typical Industrial Provinces in China 2003–2009". *Resources Science*, No. 33 (2011), pp. 2071–2079.

Zhu, Q., "China's Industrial Water Efficiency and Water-Saving Potential: An Empirical Study". *Journal of Industrial Technological Economics*, No. 26 (2007), pp. 48–51.

Chapter 13

Macro and Structural Effects of Carbon Intensity Constraints[1]

Youguo Zhang and Yuxin Zheng

Institute of Quantitative & Technical Economics,
Chinese Academy of Social Sciences

1. Questions Raised

Mitigating and adapting to climate change are two major strategic measures for all countries in the world to deal with climate change. At the Climate Change Conference, Copenhagen 2009, the Chinese government announced to the world that by 2020 its carbon emissions per unit of GDP, i.e., the intensity of carbon emissions, will be cut by 40–45% of the level of 2005. This was the first time that China has proposed a target of climate change mitigation, and this attracted attention worldwide. In 2011, China included a 17% reduction in carbon emissions per unit of GDP from 2010 to 2015 as one of its binding targets in the 12th Five-Year Plan Outline, further highlighting the importance of carbon intensity constraints. So, how will the carbon intensity constraints affect the economic development, energy consumption, and carbon emissions of China, and in particular, what impact at the level of industry will they have on the economy, energy, and environment of China? These are the questions this chapter tries to answer. Analyzing this problem will help China to adopt correct strategies to strengthen the positive impact of carbon intensity constraints

---

[1] A brief version of the present chapter has been published in *China Industrial Economics*, No. 6, 2014.

and mitigate their adverse effects, thus improving the ability of China to mitigate and adapt to climate change.

Many research institutions and scholars at home and abroad have analyzed and commented on the target of China's carbon intensity constraints. Most researches focus on the question of whether it will be difficult for China to achieve this target (Qiu, 2009; Stern & Jotzo, 2010), or what factors may influence this achievement (Zhang, 2010). In recent years, some studies have also explored the impact of carbon intensity constraints on China's economy and carbon emissions, and these studies are mainly based on the computable general equilibrium (CGE) model. The simulation results of Wang *et al.* (2009) show that the implementation of carbon intensity constraints from 2020 to 2050 will have a negative impact on China's total economy. If subsidies are given to technological progress at the same time, the negative effects can be effectively relieved. Dai *et al.* (2011) analyze the impact of carbon intensity constraints on China's total economy and carbon emissions in 2020, on the condition that the proportion of clean energy is increased as planned. Lu *et al.* (2013) compare the impacts of two carbon intensity constraining policies: one is only to achieve the target of carbon intensity constraints in 2020; the other is to realize the target of 2015 as well as that of 2020. Zhang *et al.* (2013) compare the impact of carbon intensity constraints of provinces (autonomous regions and municipalities directly under the central government) and the single national carbon intensity constraints on China's economy. Zhang (2013) conducts a theoretical analysis and numerical simulation of the performance of equivalent carbon intensity constraints and total carbon constraints under uncertainties.

Although the existing studies have made a relatively comprehensive analysis of the economic and environmental impacts of carbon intensity constraints in China, they mainly focus on the macro-impacts, seldom analyzing their impacts at the industry level, and even less combining the macro-effects with the structural effects. Analyzing the impact of carbon intensity constraints at the industry level will not only contribute to the understanding of its macro-impacts, but also help decision-makers to adopt corresponding policies and measures for key industries. Like most previous studies, we use the CGE model for the analysis here.

2. Model, Data and Scenario Design

2.1. *Policy analysis model*

The CGE model we adopt draws on the modeling ideas of Devis *et al.* (1982) and the PRCGEM model (Zheng *et al.*, 1998). On the one hand, the model assumes that the energy synthesis products formed by various fuels combine with capital to form capital-energy synthesis products, which combine with labor to form element-energy synthesis inputs. These inputs then combine with other various intermediate inputs, thus enabling enterprises to produce products demanded by the market. On the other hand, it is assumed that enterprises determine the proportion of domestic sales and exports according to the international and domestic prices of products, and those products for domestic sales together with similar imported products meet various final domestic demands (including resident consumption, government consumption, investment and inventory, etc.) and intermediate input demands. The key behavior equations of the model are listed in the following:

(1) Production behavior. The production behavior of this model can be expressed as follows:

$$X_i = min(\mathrm{A}_{z_{ji}} Z_{ji}, A_{Qi} Q_i) \tag{13.1}$$

$$Q_i = \left[\alpha_{L_i} \left(A_{L_i} L_i \right)^{\frac{\sigma_{Q_i}-1}{\sigma_{Q_i}}} + \left(1 - \alpha_{L_i}\right) \left(A_{N_i} N_i \right)^{\frac{\sigma_{Q_i}-1}{\sigma_{Q_i}}} \right]^{\sigma_{Q_i}/(\sigma_{Q_i}-1)} \tag{13.2}$$

$$N_i = \left[\alpha_{K_i} \left(A_{K_i} K_i \right)^{\frac{\sigma_{N_i}-1}{\sigma_{N_i}}} + \left(1 - \alpha_{K_i}\right) \left(A_{F_i} F_i \right)^{\frac{\sigma_{N_i}-1}{\sigma_{N_i}}} \right]^{\sigma_{N_i}/(\sigma_{N_i}-1)} \tag{13.3}$$

$$F_i = \left\{ \sum_j \left[\alpha_{K_{bk_i}} \left(A_{Z_{bk_i}} Z_{bk_i} \right) \right] \right\}^{\sigma_{F_i}/(\sigma_{F_i}-1)} \tag{13.4}$$

In these equations, Z_{jt} represents the category j intermediate synthesis input (including fossil energy used as raw materials), Q_i represents the labor-capital-energy synthesis input, Z_{bki} represents the category k fossil energy used for power generation, heating, and terminal consumption of various sectors, N_i represents the capital-energy synthesis input, and L_i, K_i, and F_i, respectively, stand for labor input, capital input, and energy synthesis product. A indicates the efficiency of various inputs, and its changes reflect technological progresses; α and σ, respectively represent the share coefficient and the elasticity of substitution. Expressions (13.1) and (13.4) mean that the total output is not only a multi-layer nested constant elasticity of substitution (CES) function of labor, capital, and fossil energy synthesis products but also a Leontief production function of intermediate inputs (including various non-fossil energy products and services, and fossil energy used to produce secondary fossil energy products).

It is easy to know that the intermediate input demand of each sector is in direct proportion to its total output. Moreover, we assume that the producers, i.e., each production sector, want to obtain the established total output at the minimum cost. By solving the first-order conditions of this optimization problem, we can obtain the optimal labor, capital, and energy requirements of each sector, and then obtain the carbon emissions of each sector and the total carbon emissions of the production sector.

(2) Resident consumption. Suppose that residents pursue utility maximization under certain expenditure budget constraints, and the utility is a Klein–Rubin function of various synthesis products or services, which are represented by Z_{H_i}:

$$\max \prod_i \left(Z_{H_i} - z_{H_{subi}} \Psi \right)^{\beta_{luxi}} \tag{13.5}$$

$$\text{s.t.} \ P_{Z_{H_i}} Z_{H_i} \leq (1-s)\left[(1-t_H)\left(wL^s + U_{HP} \right) + U_{HG} + U_{HF} \right] = W_H \tag{13.6}$$

In the expressions, $z_{H_{subi}}$ represents the basic demand per capita for synthesis consumer goods i, Ψ represents the total population, $P_{Z_{H_i}}$ represents the price of synthesis goods consumed by residents, β_{luxi} represents the share coefficient of various goods in total luxury consumption, L^s represents the total supply of labor, w represents the wage rate, U_{HP} represents the property income of residents from enterprises, U_{HG} represents the government transfer payment, U_{HF} represents the net overseas remittance, s represents the savings rate, t_H represents the income tax rate, and W_H represents the total expenditure of residents.

(3) Investment behavior. We assume that the investment Z_{V_i} obtained by each sector is related to their respective capital stock K_i and the rate of static expected relative return. Drawing on the method of Jung & Thorbecke (2003) and making appropriate simplifications, we establish the following equation for the investment of a sector:

$$Z_{V_i} = \alpha_{V_i} \left(R_i / \Omega \right)^{\delta_i} K_i \tag{13.7}$$

wherein, R_i represents the net capital return of sector i, Ω represents the interest rate, Ri/Ω represents the static expected relative return rate of sector i, and α_{V_i} and δ_i, respectively, represent the coefficient of investment scale and the coefficient of investment elasticity. It should be noted that we assume that the investment elasticity coefficient of the public investment sector is 0, that is, their investment is proportional to their capital stock ($Z_{V_i} = \alpha_{V_i} K_i$). Like most studies, we further assume that the share of each sector's demand for various investment products $Z_{V_{ji}}$ is fixed in its total investment demand. At the same time, we assume that each sector's inventory is in proportion to its total output.

(4) Government behavior. The government obtains income through income tax, consumption tax, investment tax, customs duty, environmental tax and other channels, and spends through subsidies to enterprises and residents and purchases of various products. We assume that the government levies a carbon tax on fossil energy to reduce the intensity of carbon emissions. Suppose that $P_{Z_{FO_i}}$ represents the price of fossil energy without carbon tax, ξ_i is the carbon emission coefficient of various fossil energy sources (carbon emissions per unit of fossil energy consumption), and T_c represents the rate of carbon tax, then the price P_{F_i} of fossil energy with carbon tax can be expressed as follows:

$$P_{F_i} = P_{FO_i} + \xi_i T_c \tag{13.8}$$

(5) International trade. We assume that there is a substitution elasticity relationship of Armington (Armington, 1969) between domestic products and imported products, that is, the total domestic demand for a certain product is the CES function of the corresponding domestic products and imported products. After determining the demand of producers, residents, investors, governments, and other various entities for various types of synthesis products, the demand function of category i imported products M_i can be obtained from the first-order condition of cost minimization as

$$M_i = \left(1 - \alpha_{D_i}\right)^{\sigma_i} \left(P_{Z_i} / P_{M_i}\right)^{\sigma_i} Z_i \tag{13.9}$$

Wherein, Z_i represents the total demand of a country for category i synthesis products. P_{Z_i} and P_{M_i} indicate the prices of Z_i and M_i, respectively; α_{D_i} and σ_i ($\sigma_i > 0$), respectively, represent the share coefficient and the coefficient of Armington substitution elasticity. The import price P_{M_i} is determined by the international market, i.e., exogenously given.

In the international trade module, we partially relax the assumption that the price of domestic export products is determined by the supply of domestic export and the demand of the international market. We assume that each sector determines the domestic supply and export volume of its products or services based on their domestic sale price and export price. In this way, the relationship between the total supply of the products and services and their domestic supply and export can be characterized by using a fixed elasticity coefficient of transformation (CET) function. Based on the first-order condition of income maximization, the export supply E_{S_i} of sector i can be expressed as follows:

$$E_{S_i} = \left(1 - \alpha_{S_i}\right)^{\sigma_{s_i}} \left(P_{E_i} / P_{X_i}\right)^{\sigma_{s_i}} X_i \tag{13.10}$$

Wherein, P_{E_i} represents the export price, P_{X_i} represents the comprehensive output price, and α_{S_i} and σ_i ($\sigma_i > 0$), respectively, represent the share coefficient and the transformation elasticity coefficient. Export E_{D_i} of sector i can simply express the decreasing function of export price P_{E_i}, i.e.,

$$E_{D_i} = \beta_i P_{E_i}^{-\theta_i} \tag{13.11}$$

In the expression, β_i and θ_i $(0 < \theta_i < \infty)$ represent the export scale coefficient and the export price elasticity respectively. In an equilibrium state

$$E_{S_i} = E_{D_i} \tag{13.12}$$

(6) Energy and carbon emissions. According to the first-order conditions of minimizing the cost, as expressed by (13.3) and (13.4), the demand F_i for synthesis energy and the demand Z_{bki} for category k fossil energy of sector i can be obtained as follows:

$$F_i = \left(1 - \alpha_{K_i}\right)^{\sigma_{N_i}} \left(P_{F_i}/P_{N_i}\right)^{\sigma_{N_i}} N_i \tag{13.13}$$

$$Z_{bki} = \alpha_{Z_{bki}}^{\sigma_{F_i}} \left(1 - \alpha_{S_i}\right)^{\sigma_{si}} \left(P_{Z_{bki}}/P_{F_i}\right)^{\sigma_{F_i}} F_i \tag{13.14}$$

Wherein, P_{F_i} and P_{N_i}, respectively, represent the synthesis fossil energy input price and the capital-energy synthesis input price. Also, various fossil energy sources consumed by residents can be obtained by minimizing the cost, as expressed by (14.5) and (14.6). On this basis, the total energy consumption, total carbon emission, GDP-based energy intensity, and carbon emission intensity of the whole country can be obtained.

(7) Equilibrium conditions. We assume that the market is in a state of equilibrium, which means that all kinds of economic entities will optimize their objective function under their respective constraints and the market will be clear. The specific equilibrium conditions include the following: producers obtain zero net profit; the demand and the supply for all goods and elements are equal; income and expenditure are in balance for residents and the government, that is, their expenditures are equal to their respective disposable incomes minus their corresponding savings; international payments are in balance, that is, the total imports at international prices are equal to the sum of the total exports at border prices, net foreign transfers, and net foreign capital inflows; and investment and savings are in balance, i.e., the total investment equals the sum of domestic savings and foreign capital inflows.

(8) Macro-closure. We assume that government consumption and resident consumption change in the same proportion, and that government transfer payments (subsidies) and various tax rates are exogenous, which means that government savings and deficits are endogenous. We assume that the rate of household savings is fixed and the exchange rate is chosen as the baseline price, while the net inflow of foreign capital is endogenous. Thus, the adjustment of the net inflow of foreign capital can ensure between balance of investment and savings.

(9) Dynamic model. The model can be made dynamic through accumulation of production factors and technological progress, and by adopting a recursive form. We assume that the total capital supply at the end of the period is equal to the depreciation of the total capital supply at the beginning of the period plus the total amount of fixed capital formation added in the current period.

$$K_i^* = K_i(1-d_i) + Z_{V_i} \tag{13.15}$$

In the expression, K_i^*, K_i, Z_{V_i}, and d, respectively, represent the final capital stock, initial capital stock, new investment, and capital depreciation rate of sector i. We further assume that the capital depreciation rate is exogenous, and the total amount of new fixed capital formation is determined by the investment–savings balance relationship and the allocation mechanism of investment among sectors, which means that the capital growth rate of each sector and total capital growth rate are endogenous. We also assume that population changes, changes in labor supply, and technological progress are exogenous.

2.2. *Data calibration and scenario design*

The period studied in this chapter is from 2007 to 2020. We set 2007 as the base period, and drawing on the methods of Dixon Rimmer (2002),[2] treat the period from 2008 to 2012 as the period of historical simulation,

---

[2] Dixon & Rimmer (2002) put forward four simulation (analysis) functions of CGE, i.e., historical simulation, decomposing simulation, prediction simulation, and policy simulation.

and the period from 2013 to 2020 as the period of prediction and policy simulation. We establish a social accounting matrix (SAM) table based on the input–output tables of 42 sectors in 2007 released by the National Bureau of Statistics. The quantities of domestic and imported products domestically absorbed and utilized in the middle, and the carbon emission coefficients of various fossil energy products consumed by different sectors are calculated according to the method of Zhang (2010). This chapter distinguishes eight kinds of energy inputs, namely, the seven kinds of fossil energy of coal, crude oil, natural gas, petroleum processing products, coke, coal gas, thermal power generation and heating, and clean energy (hydropower, nuclear power, and wind power). We refer to the method of Sue Wing (2008) for the estimation of the input–output coefficients of the energy production sector.

According to the definition of substitution elasticity, we have preliminarily estimated the Armington substitution elasticity for domestic and imported products by using the comparable price (import) non-competitive input–output tables of 2007 and 2010, the mill price index of various products in the *China Statistical Yearbook* over the years, and the import price index of various products published in *China's External Trade Indices* compiled by the General Administration of Customs (see Table 13.1). The substitution elasticity between various factors and energy resources and the elasticity of capital conversion come from Zhang (2013).

Through historical simulation, we update the SAM matrix to 2012, and estimate the historical changes of various hardly observable variables (e.g., technological progress rate and consumption preference). The exogenous variables used are mainly observable macro- and industrial variables (e.g., population, total labor supply, GDP, consumption, investment, total output, value added, import and export, etc.). These variables are endogenous variables in the standard CGE model, but they are regarded as observable exogenous variables in historical simulation. We have determined the growth rates of various exogenous variables in the historical

Table 13.1 Armington substitution elasticity

Products	Agricultural products	Industrial products	Construction	Service
Elasticity	16.12	3.63	0.25	2.27

simulation period based on the relevant data in the *China Statistical Yearbook* 2013, *China's External Trade Indices* over the years, and the input–output tables of 2010.

We determine the baseline scenario of the system evolution of economy, energy, and environment from 2013 to 2020 through prediction simulation. In the prediction simulation, the actual GDP is still regarded as an exogenous variable, and its value is set with the expert investigation approach. In the meantime, the average efficiency of labor-capital-energy synthesis input is regarded as an endogenous variable. In addition, we assume that government subsidies to residents and enterprises vary proportionally with government revenues, while dividends of enterprises to residents vary proportionally with enterprise revenues, and various tax rates and resident savings rates remain at the base level. The values and sources of key exogenous variables in the baseline scenario are shown in Table 13.2.

In the policy simulation, we mainly examine the carbon emission intensity constraint, the mandatory greenhouse gas emission reduction policy. We thus treat the intensity of carbon emission as an exogenous variable, while carbon tax, total carbon emissions, and the total energy consumption are endogenous variables. China had announced that it would reduce carbon

Table 13.2 Values of major exogenous variables in the baseline scenario (%)

Variables	Annual average	Variables	Annual average
Actual GDP	7.6 (2013–2015); 7.0 (2016–2020); 6.0 (2021–2030);	International oil price[c]	1.1
Population[a]	0.5 (2013–2015); 0.3 (2016–2030);	International coal price[c]	3.7
Total labor supply[b]	0.14 (2013–2015); −0.53 (2016–2020); −0.68 (2021–2030);	International natural gas price[c]	2.0

Notes: [a]estimated on the basis of the data of *China Statistical Yearbook* and *World Energy Outlook* 2007: *China and Indian Insight* (the International Energy Agency); [b]estimated on the basis of the data of *China Statistical Yearbook* and the results of Qi (2010); [c]set according to the prediction released by EIA (2013).

emissions per unit of GDP in 2020 by 40%–45% in 2020, on the basis of 2005. China's 12th Five-Year Plan had also proposed that the intensity of carbon emissions in 2015 would be 17% lower than that in 2010. Based on this, we estimated for the intensity of carbon emissions to decrease by 3.7% annually in 2013–2015 and 3.1% annually in 2016–2020.

3. Macro-Impact of Carbon Intensity Constraint

Figure 13.1 shows the main macroeconomic indicators and the development trend of energy consumption and carbon emissions in 2007–2020 under the baseline scenario. With continuous economic growth, the consumption, investment, trade, energy consumption, and carbon emissions will also increase. In terms of the final demand, in the past few years, China's consumption (including resident consumption and government consumption) has exceeded investment and exports, and the gap between them is widening day by day. In the future, the gap between consumption and investment may remain at a relatively stable level, while the gap between

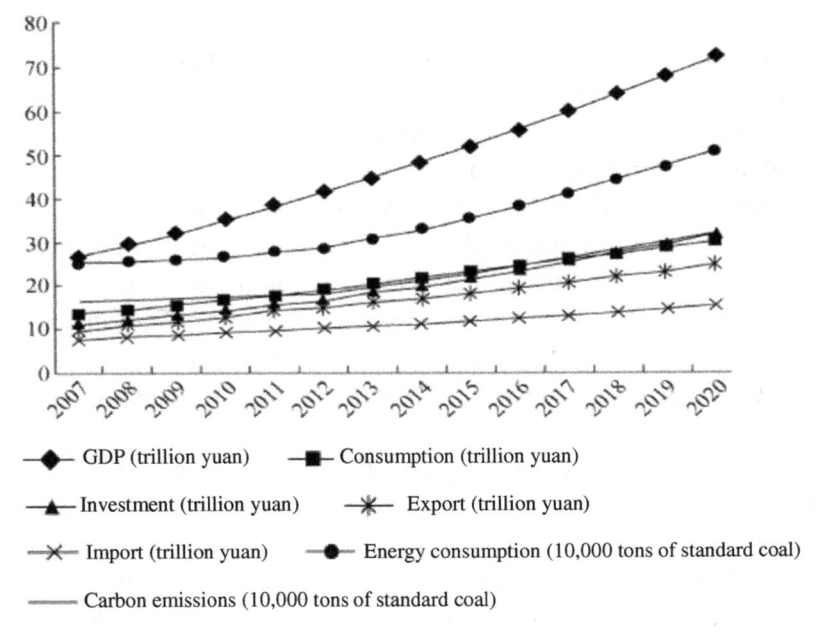

Fig. 13.1 Trends of major macro-variables under the baseline scenario

them and exports may be further widened. The above changes in the final demand structure are in line with the current series of macroeconomic control strategies (such as emphasizing the role of domestic demand, especially consumption, in promoting economy) and the international economic environment (it is difficult for developed countries to fully recover from the impact of the financial crisis, which in turn affects China's exports). In addition, under the baseline scenario, the proportion of non-fossil energy in primary energy consumption in China will slightly rise, reaching 9.8% and 10.4%, respectively, in 2015 and 2020.

Table 13.3 shows the macro-impact of carbon intensity constraints. Although the carbon intensity in the baseline scenario will gradually decrease, its annual decrease is obviously lower than that in the policy scenario. We can see that the carbon intensity constraint will slightly reduce China's total economy. This is because GDP can be simply regarded as a function of capital, labor, and carbon emissions. Given the capital and labor input, a larger decrease in carbon intensity will surely lead to a decrease in output (Zhang, 2013).

At the same time, consumption and investment will also fall due to the implementation of carbon intensity constraints. The decline in consumption is mainly due to the fact that as output falls, the wage will drop, thus affecting resident income. In comparison, the decrease in investment is significantly greater than the decrease in consumption. It is quite understandable in that the carbon emission intensity of investment products is significantly higher than that of consumer goods (Zhang, 2010). With the carbon intensity constraints implemented, the price increase of investment products will be even greater, and the impact on the demand for investment products may also be greater. We can see that the rate of investment return will also fall, partly because of the rise in the price of investment products, and partly because along with the decline of output, the rate of capital rent will decrease.

As the overall level of economic activities falls, the demand of China for imported products will also decrease. However, while China's domestic demand falls due to carbon intensity constraints, exports will increase slightly. This is not surprising, because although carbon intensity constraints lead to a decline in the export of carbon-intensive products, they may stimulate the export of labor-intensive and technology-intensive

Table 13.3   Macro-impact of carbon intensity constraints (in comparison with the baseline scenario, %)

Year	2013	2014	2015	2016	2017	2018	2019	2020	2013–2020
GDP	−0.0296	−0.0643	−0.1040	−0.1425	−0.1849	−0.2314	−0.2820	−0.3370	−0.1878
Consumption	−0.0186	−0.0376	−0.0570	−0.0737	−0.0906	−0.1079	−0.1255	−0.1448	−0.0872
Investment	−0.1346	−0.2767	−0.4251	−0.5587	−0.6972	−0.8403	−0.9884	−1.1433	−0.6917
Wage	−0.0994	−0.2030	−0.3100	−0.4056	−0.5037	−0.6042	−0.7072	−0.8121	−0.4806
Rate of capital rent	−0.1631	−0.3347	−0.5133	−0.6743	−0.8410	−1.0132	−1.1913	−1.3737	−0.7518
Ratio of investment return	−0.3215	−0.6623	−1.0195	−1.3427	−1.6789	−2.0276	−2.3898	−2.7657	−1.5260
Export	0.0232	0.0416	0.0548	0.0615	0.0638	0.0613	0.0540	0.0456	0.0516
Import	−0.0946	−0.1917	−0.2911	−0.3795	−0.4705	−0.5642	−0.6610	−0.7613	−0.4528
Terms of trade	−0.0045	−0.0076	−0.0093	−0.0093	−0.0083	−0.0060	−0.0026	0.0014	−0.0058
Energy consumption	−2.9075	−5.6962	−8.3622	−10.5629	−12.6791	−14.7093	−16.6594	−18.5320	−12.0861
Carbon emissions	−3.7191	−7.3194	−10.7916	−13.6902	−16.5030	−19.2266	−21.8683	−24.4302	−15.7750
Energy intensity	−2.8787	−5.6355	−8.2668	−10.4353	−12.5173	−14.5115	−16.4237	−18.2566	−11.1426

products and services. We can also see that the terms of trade of China will undergo little change, which means that carbon intensity constraints have little impact on the combined relative prices of China's exports and imports.

Under the carbon intensity constraints, the decline in energy consumption and carbon emissions in China will far exceed the decline in GDP. This is because, given the capital and labor input, the marginal output of carbon emissions conforms to the law of diminishing. When the carbon intensity constraints imposed force the carbon intensity to decrease even further, the decrease in carbon emissions will far exceed the decrease in GDP (Zhang, 2013). In the meantime, because the total carbon emissions mainly depend on energy consumption, they have a high degree of consistency in terms of change. Thus under the carbon intensity constraints, the decrease in energy consumption will also be much larger than the decrease in GDP, and the energy intensity will be significantly reduced. However, the decrease in energy consumption is lower than the decrease in carbon emissions. This is because under the carbon intensity constraints, China will make more use of clean energy, thus reducing carbon emissions faster than that of energy consumption.

It is worth noting that with the passage of time, the macro-impact of carbon intensity constraints shows a gradually increasing trend of change. For example, the impact of carbon intensity constraints on GDP increases eightfold from 2013 to 2020. This is because the continuous implementation of carbon intensity constraints will result in the annual GDP growth rate being a little lower than the growth rate under the baseline scenario; thus, the evolution trajectory of GDP under the policy scenario will increasingly deviate from that under the baseline scenario. In the same way, the difference between the values of other variables under the policy scenario and those under the baseline scenario will become bigger.

4. Impact of Carbon Intensity Constraints on Sectors

4.1. *Impact of carbon intensity constraints on output prices of different sectors*

Table 13.4 shows the average impact of carbon intensity constraints on the output prices of various sectors from 2013 to 2020. With the carbon intensity constraints implemented, the domestic sale price of coal mining and

Table 13.4 Changes in sectoral output price under carbon intensity constraints (in comparison with the baseline scenario) and contribution of energy conservation and carbon reduction (%)

Sectors	Comprehensive output price	Domestic sale price	Export price	Contribution of energy conservation	Contribution of carbon reduction
Agriculture, forestry, animal husbandry, and fishery	−0.0569	−0.0572	−0.0180	1.3159	3.1083
Coal mining and dressing	1.8777	1.8957	0.3474	3.7504	3.0819
Oil mining	−0.0054	−0.0058	0.0295	0.4270	0.2556
Natural gas mining	0.1255	0.1265	0.0454	0.1446	0.1075
Non−energy mineral mining and dressing	0.0230	0.0228	0.0326	0.1006	0.2263
Food production and tobacco processing	−0.0574	−0.0591	−0.0189	0.4893	0.5951
Textile, clothing, shoes, hats, leather, down, and their products	−0.0428	−0.0477	−0.0328	0.3711	0.2668
Wood processing and furniture manufacturing	−0.0360	−0.0402	−0.0201	0.0152	0.0380
Papermaking, printing and cultural, educational, and sporting goods manufacturing	−0.0203	−0.0233	−0.0027	0.6014	0.4232
Petroleum processing and nuclear fuel processing	0.2737	0.2757	0.0417	0.4897	0.3855
Coking	1.6156	1.6971	0.2483	0.4507	0.9483
Chemical industry	0.0277	0.0283	0.0229	1.1033	1.6729
Non−metal mineral products	0.1076	0.1101	0.0603	2.3721	2.3831
Metal smelting, rolling, and processing	0.1288	0.1323	0.0729	1.9081	9.6816
Metal products	0.0478	0.0501	0.0379	0.0383	0.0424
Manufacturing of general and special equipment	0.0116	0.0093	0.0256	0.1900	0.2120
Manufacturing of transportation equipment	−0.0113	−0.0140	0.0115	0.2653	0.2164
Manufacturing of electrical appliances, machines, and equipment	0.0175	0.0168	0.0197	0.0462	0.0331

(*Continued*)

Table 13.4   (*Continued*)

Sectors	Comprehensive output price	Domestic sale price	Export price	Contribution of energy conservation	Contribution of carbon reduction
Manufacturing of communication equipment, computers, and other electronic equipment	−0.0265	−0.0300	−0.0223	0.1166	0.0366
Manufacturing of instruments, meters, and machines for culture and office articles	−0.0250	−0.0351	−0.0174	0.0009	0.0031
Artware, scrap products and materials, and manufacturing of other products	−0.0651	−0.0752	−0.0150	0.0250	0.0298
Clean energy production and supply	−0.1179	−0.1179	−0.0860	−0.0055	0.0000
Thermal power generation, heating, and supply	0.6557	0.6561	0.3074	81.4917	73.9512
Fuel gas production and supply	0.4580	0.4580	0.0000	0.0713	0.0480
Water production and supply	0.0475	0.0475	0.0000	0.0025	0.0082
Construction	0.0186	0.0186	0.0252	0.2081	0.2658
Transportation and warehousing	−0.0055	−0.0089	0.0134	2.2695	1.1132
Posts	−0.0498	−0.0523	−0.0118	0.0256	0.0083
Information transference, computer service, and software	−0.0991	−0.1033	−0.0326	0.0028	0.0034
Wholesale and retail trade	−0.0929	−0.1070	−0.0360	0.1290	0.2809
Accommodation and catering	−0.0625	−0.0652	−0.0165	0.3579	0.2863
Finance	−0.1170	−0.1176	−0.0336	0.0082	0.0105
Real estate	−0.1395	−0.1395	0.0000	0.0097	0.0097
Rental and commercial services	−0.0513	−0.0590	−0.0351	0.3513	0.0310
Research, experiment, and development	−0.0523	−0.0529	−0.0097	0.0078	0.0029

Table 13.4 *(Continued)*

Sectors	Comprehensive output price	Domestic sale price	Export price	Contribution of energy conservation	Contribution of carbon reduction
Comprehensive technological services	−0.0777	−0.0777	0.0000	0.0278	0.0139
Water conservation, environment, and management of public facilities	−0.0570	−0.0570	0.0000	0.0529	0.0219
Resident services and other services	−0.0667	−0.0690	−0.0172	0.1872	0.0357
Education	−0.0563	−0.0564	−0.0181	0.0352	0.0324
Health, social security, and social welfare	−0.0301	−0.0301	−0.0062	0.1088	0.0321
Culture, sports and entertainment	−0.0730	−0.0789	−0.0223	0.0239	0.0131
Public management and social organizations	−0.0600	−0.0601	−0.0201	0.4123	0.0840

dressing and coking will have the sharpest increase. That of energy production sectors such as thermal power generation, heating and supply, gas production and supply, petroleum processing and nuclear fuel processing, and natural gas mining will also increase significantly. The prices of coal mining and dressing, coking, gas production and supply, and petroleum processing and nuclear fuel processing have increased, because the fossil energy provided by these four sectors is mainly used for end consumption and is the most important and direct source of carbon emissions. As discussed earlier, we assume that the government implements carbon intensity constraints mainly by imposing carbon tax, and thus the carbon intensity constraints will directly lead to an increase in the domestic sale prices of the above four sectors. The significant rise in domestic sale prices of thermal power generation, heating, and supply is because the sector consumes a large amount of fossil energy such as coal, oil, and natural gas and generates a large amount of carbon emissions to provide electricity and heat. It is the most typical carbon-intensive sector. The carbon intensity constraints are to indirectly push up the domestic sale price by increasing the input cost.

The domestic sale prices of other carbon-intensive sectors, such as non-metal mineral products, metal smelting, rolling, and processing, and metal products, have also increased, but not as significantly as the sectors mentioned earlier. Although oil mining belongs to the fossil energy supply sector, its domestic price has increased by a small margin. This is largely because the products provided by the industry are mainly used for intermediate inputs in petroleum processing and nuclear fuel processing instead of end consumption (combustion), and will not directly produce a large amount of carbon emissions, thus being relatively less affected by carbon intensity constraints.

While the domestic sale prices of the fossil energy supply sector and the carbon-intensive sector have increased, we can easily observe that of most labor-intensive sectors (such as agriculture, forestry, animal husbandry and fishery, textile, and most service sectors) and technology-intensive sectors (such as clean energy production and supply, and manufacturing of communication equipment, computers and other electronic equipment) have decreased. One possible reason is that carbon intensity constraints lead to a decline in the overall level of economic activities, which will reduce the demand for labor and capital. If we want to keep the demand for labor and capital unchanged, the only way is to reduce wage rate and capital rent rate. For labor-intensive sectors and technology-intensive sectors, labor and capital account for the major part of their element-energy input, while the share of energy input is relatively small. The impact of the decline in wage rate and capital rent rate on the input cost of these sectors is likely to exceed the impact brought about by the rise in energy prices. Naturally, the domestic sale prices of these sectors will also decline.

The export prices of the vast majority of sectors are in the same direction as the domestic sale prices, but the range of changes is significantly different. The difference between domestic sale prices and export prices of different sectors is mainly due to the difference in the price decision mechanism. The domestic sale prices of various sectors are mainly determined by their input costs. Export prices are influenced by input costs on the one hand, and by the supply of various sectors and the demand of the international market on the other hand. For example, the domestic sale prices of coal mining and dressing, petroleum processing and nuclear fuel processing, and the coking industry have increased significantly more than their export prices. This is because the carbon emissions from fossil energy exports occur abroad and are not directly affected by the country's carbon intensity; thus, the price increase is also relatively small. In addition, the domestic sale prices of oil mining, manufacturing of transportation equipment, and transportation and warehousing change in a different direction from their export prices. This is still caused by the difference in the price decision mechanism.

The comprehensive output price of each sector is the weighted average of its domestic sale price and export price. For the vast majority of sectors, since their output is mainly sold in China, their comprehensive output prices are very close to their domestic sale prices. For example, the comprehensive output prices of coal mining and dressing, fuel gas production and supply, petroleum processing and nuclear fuel processing, and coking are almost equal to their domestic sale prices. There are also some sectors (e.g., manufacturing of communication equipment, computers and other electronic equipment, and manufacturing of instruments, meters, and machines for culture and office articles) whose exports obviously exceed their domestic sales. Their comprehensive output prices are thus relatively close to their export prices.

4.2. Influence of carbon intensity constraints on output of different sectors

Table 13.5 shows the impact of carbon intensity constraints on domestic supply, total output, exports, imports, energy consumption, and carbon emissions in various sectors from 2013 to 2020. Due to the decline in the overall level of economic activities leading to a decline in domestic demand such as intermediate demand and consumption and investment, domestic supply in most sectors has declined to varying degrees. Among them, the largest decline occurs in coal mining and dressing, with coking and thermal power generation, heating, and supply ranking the second and the third, respectively. Other sectors with significant decline in domestic supply (over 1%) include the gas production and supply, natural gas mining, petroleum processing and nuclear fuel processing, and oil mining. As mentioned earlier, these sectors either directly provide fossil energy or

Table 13.5   Cumulative impact of carbon intensity constraints on industries (in comparison with the baseline scenario, 2013–2020, %)

Sectors	Domestic supply	Export	Total output	Import	Energy consumption	Carbon emissions
Agriculture, forestry, animal husbandry, and fishery	-0.1135	0.4313	-0.1080	-0.6833	-4.0455	-15.0058
Coal mining and dressing	-12.2241	-8.1230	-12.1657	-9.8034	-26.5246	-26.7796
Oil mining	-1.4078	-0.6842	-1.3987	-1.4749	-6.7462	-6.7543
Natural gas mining	-2.0124	-1.0586	-1.9989	-1.7197	-5.6986	-7.3496
Non-energy mineral mining and dressing	-0.9381	-0.8031	-0.9349	-0.6816	-2.0082	-7.1925
Food production and tobacco processing	-0.1118	0.4585	-0.0865	-0.6837	-5.8970	-9.9973
Textile, clothing, shoes, hats, leather, down, and their products	0.0917	0.7856	0.3247	0.0895	-4.8210	-5.2559
Wood processing and furniture manufacturing	-0.4710	0.4862	-0.2588	-0.5317	-0.9388	-3.5040
Papermaking, printing, and cultural, educational, and sporting goods manufacturing	-0.2221	0.0768	-0.1791	-0.4393	-9.1606	-8.6878
Petroleum processing and nuclear fuel processing	-1.6581	-0.9571	-1.6508	-1.2381	-1.9435	-2.7464
Coking	-6.7871	-5.7876	-6.7170	-3.3331	-7.8526	-26.2304
Chemical industry	-0.4582	-0.5364	-0.4667	-0.0531	-1.4840	-3.4427
Non-metal mineral products	-0.7313	-1.4169	-0.7650	0.2860	-3.9109	-5.3905
Metal smelting, rolling, and processing	-0.8999	-1.7269	-0.9492	0.3379	-1.2766	-7.9985
Metal products	-0.7331	-0.9032	-0.7655	-0.2499	-1.3912	-2.7804
Manufacturing of general and special equipment	-0.8526	-0.6043	-0.8171	-0.7512	-2.3752	-3.6524
Manufacturing of transportation equipment	-0.6468	-0.2683	-0.6064	-0.7689	-6.0983	-7.3809
Manufacturing of electrical appliances, machines, and equipment	-0.6126	-0.4510	-0.5711	-0.4490	-2.7077	-3.5082

Manufacturing of communication equipment, computers, and other electronic equipment	0.1886	0.5336	0.3498	−0.0985	−6.6808	−4.3860
Manufacturing of instruments, meters, and machines for culture and office articles	−0.4305	0.4212	0.0744	−0.7711	−0.3217	−2.3619
Artware, scrap products and materials, and manufacturing of other products	−0.4925	0.3869	−0.3456	−1.1929	−1.9151	−3.7950
Clean energy production and supply	1.6982	2.1786	1.6989	0.4478	1.5405	#
Thermal power generation, heating, and supply	−2.5088	−7.6665	−2.5161	4.0273	−24.8754	−26.4314
Fuel gas production and supply	−2.4484	#	−2.4484	#	−5.5104	−6.5524
Water production and supply	−0.6544	#	−0.6544	#	−0.7042	−8.0245
Construction	−0.7009	−0.5894	−0.7001	−0.7008	−1.3939	−2.8454
Transportation and warehousing	−0.6435	−0.2911	−0.5919	−0.6439	−2.9460	−2.2674
Posts	−0.2900	0.3055	−0.2506	−0.2932	−5.5408	−2.7243
Information transference, computer service, and software	−0.2403	0.8074	−0.1813	−0.2472	−0.5989	−2.4163
Wholesale and retail trade	−0.3094	0.8278	−0.0963	#	−2.3271	−8.1746
Accommodation and catering	−0.2978	0.4061	−0.2592	−0.3037	−6.8160	−9.0004
Finance	−0.4050	0.8321	−0.3965	−0.4229	−0.7279	−1.9710
Real estate	−0.0381	#	−0.0381	#	−0.9966	−1.7070
Rental and commercial services	−0.2960	0.8789	0.0694	−0.2961	−11.6685	−1.7056
Research, experiment, and development	−0.3787	0.2398	−0.3686	−0.3693	−4.4351	−3.1196
Comprehensive technological services	−0.6855	#	−0.6855	#	−3.3001	−2.7037

(Continued)

Table 13.5 (Continued)

Sectors	Domestic supply	Export	Total output	Import	Energy consumption	Carbon emissions
Water conservation, environment, and management of public facilities	−0.2479	#	−0.2479	#	−6.5915	−4.6094
Resident services and other services	−0.3312	0.4302	−0.2989	−0.3435	−10.0499	−3.1197
Education	−0.1162	0.4311	−0.1153	−0.1163	−1.1955	−2.1006
Health, social security, and social welfare	−0.1894	0.1525	−0.1881	−0.1863	−7.2014	−3.4838
Culture, sports, and entertainment	0.2741	0.5424	−0.1906	−0.2733	−5.5842	−5.7041
Public management and social organizations	−0.0919	0.4805	−0.0907	−0.0920	−7.7933	−2.7448
Average	−0.6993	0.0516	−0.6125	−0.4528	−11.4609	−15.1729

Note: #: non-trade products.

provide secondary energy through massive consumption of fossil energy. Under the carbon intensity constraints, their output price increases significantly, so their output has a significant decrease. The decline in domestic supply in the non-fossil energy sector is generally proportional to its carbon intensity: the higher the carbon intensity, the greater the decline. However, the domestic demand for clean energy production and supply has increased significantly. This is mainly because the carbon intensity constraints have led the production sector to make more use of clean energy instead of fossil energy. In addition, the domestic supply of textile, clothing, shoes, hats, leather, down, and their products; communication equipment; computers; and other electronic equipment has increased. Further analysis shows that the increase is mainly brought about by the intermediate demand of the two sectors for their own products.

The export quantity of each sector changes in a direction opposite to its export price, which is consistent with the basic assumption of the model. It is easy to see that the sectors where exports fall under the carbon intensity constraints are mainly fossil energy production sectors and carbon-intensive sectors. The largest decline in exports is still in coal mining and dressing, followed by thermal power generation, heating and supply, and coking ranks the third. Other sectors where exports fall significantly (more than 1%) include the metal smelting, rolling and processing, non-metal mineral products, and natural gas mining. Also, exports of most labor-intensive and technology-intensive sectors increase due to the implementation of carbon intensity constraints. The highest increase, more than 2%, is found in the export of clean energy production and supply. The smallest increase is in papermaking, printing, and cultural, educational, and sporting goods manufacturing. Furthermore, there is also a significant difference between the changes in the export of most sectors and the changes in their domestic supply, while the changes in the export of most labor-intensive sectors (including agriculture, forestry, animal husbandry, and fishery, most light industries and service) and some technology-intensive sectors (such as manufacturing of instruments, meters, and machines for culture and office articles) are in the opposite direction to the changes in their domestic supply.

As discussed earlier, the total output of each sector consists of its domestic supply and export, and the domestic supply of most sectors far exceeds its export, so the total output of most sectors is close to their domestic supply. For example, coal mining and dressing, with the largest decline in domestic supply and export, is also the sector with the largest decline in total output, while the change in its total output is almost equal to the change in its domestic supply. It is easy to see that the total output of most sectors has also decreased due to carbon intensity constraints. However, the domestic supply and export of clean energy production and supply; manufacturing of communication equipment, computers, and other electronic equipment; and textile, clothing, shoes, leather, down, and their products all increase, and thus their total outputs also increase. In addition, the export of manufacturing of instruments, meters, and machines for culture and office articles, and rental and commercial services is significantly more than its domestic supply, and the margin of export growth is larger than that of the decline of domestic supply, and thus its total output increases.

The impact of carbon intensity constraints on imported products of different sectors can be divided into two parts: income effect and substitution effect. The income effect is mainly because the carbon intensity constraints will affect the income of various domestic economic entities, which in turn will affect their demand for various synthesis products (domestic products and imported products). The substitution effect can be further divided into two parts: one is that the carbon intensity constraints change the relative price among synthesis products, leading to their mutual substitution; the other is that the carbon intensity constraints change the relative prices of domestic products and imported products, leading to their mutual substitution. We can see that the import changes in most sectors are the same as the changes in domestic supply, that is, the import of most sectors also decreases. This means that the impact of carbon intensity constraints on imports in most sectors mainly lies in income effect. However, the import of three carbon-intensive sectors, that is, thermal power generation, heating and supply, metal smelting, rolling, and processing, and non-metal mineral products, increases, which is different from the changing direction of their domestic supply. This means that the substitution effect of carbon intensity constraints on these sectors exceeds the income effect. The import of manufacturing of communication equipment, computers, and other electronic equipment also decreases slightly, in a direction opposite to that of domestic supply. In addition, the import of clean energy production and supply, and textile, clothing, shoes, hats, leather, down, and their products changes in the same direction as that of domestic supply, but it increases rather decreases.

4.3. *Impact of carbon intensity constraints on energy consumption and carbon emission of different sectors*

As discussed earlier, as producers, all sectors need to employ labor, invest capital, and consume fossil energy and clean energy to carry out production activities and yield output. The carbon intensity constraints will directly lead to an increase of fossil energy prices, and thus their impact on investment decisions of various sectors can also be divided into income effect and substitution effect. On the one hand, the increase in fossil energy prices will reduce the purchasing power of the producers' original input budgets, which in turn reduces their demand for various types of inputs. On the other hand, the increase in the price of fossil energy relative to labor, capital, and clean energy will make producers consider employing more labor, capital, and clean energy to replace fossil energy inputs. Both effects will reduce the demand of producers for fossil energy, and possibly increase their demand for clean energy. Changes in energy consumption in various sectors depend on changes in their demand for fossil energy and clean energy. The results of this chapter show that the energy consumption of all sectors except clean energy production and supply has decreased. In the meantime, in addition to clean energy production and supply (this chapter assumes that carbon emissions in this sector are negligible), carbon emissions in other sectors have also decreased.

Table 13.6 shows the contribution of various sectors to the national energy consumption and carbon emission reduction under the carbon intensity constraints. The sector of thermal power generation, heating and supply, as the most important fossil energy consuming sector, has the most significant decrease in its fossil energy consumption. This is followed by metal smelting, rolling, and processing, which is also a major consumer of fossil energy. The reduction in fossil energy consumption of the two sectors taken together accounts for about 74% of the total reduction in the entire production sector. In addition, coal mining and dressing, non-metal

Table 13.6 Sensitivity analysis of carbon intensity constraints (in comparison with the baseline scenario, %)

	Promoting clean energy	AEEI			Elasticity value	
		0.5% increase	1% increase	2% increase	25% decrease	25% increase
GDP	−0.1676	−0.1812	−0.1747	−0.1619	−0.1144	−0.2171
Consumption	−0.0794	−0.0840	−0.0810	−0.0751	−0.0720	−0.1035
Investment	−0.5795	−0.6720	−0.6527	−0.6141	−0.5708	−0.6965
Wage	−0.4097	−0.4685	−0.4562	−0.4316	−0.4974	−0.4134
Capital rent	−0.6411	−0.7316	−0.7113	−0.6708	−0.7242	−0.6707
Capital return	−1.3580	−1.4816	−1.4373	−1.3495	−1.3831	−1.3949
Export	0.0182	0.0510	0.0510	0.0507	0.1275	0.0193
Import	−0.3874	−0.4421	−0.4313	−0.4094	−0.3604	−0.4741
Terms of trade	−0.0005	−0.0060	−0.0062	−0.0065	−0.0302	0.0031
Energy consumption	−9.8130	−11.8051	−11.5226	−10.9532	−8.8734	−13.7376
Carbon emissions	−13.5216	−15.4199	−15.0623	−14.3403	−11.4572	−18.0390
Energy intensity	−9.0909	−10.8853	−10.6265	−10.1053	−8.1904	−12.6770

mineral products, and agriculture, forestry, animal husbandry, and fishery have also seen large reductions in fossil energy consumption, which together account for about 15% of the total reduction.

Since carbon emissions are mainly caused by fossil energy consumption, the sectors with the largest reduction in fossil energy consumption are also the sectors with the largest reduction in carbon emissions. The sector of thermal power generation, heating, and supply alone accounts for about 72% of the total carbon emission reduction in the entire production sector, the sector of metal smelting, rolling, and processing accounts for about 7%, and the sectors of coal mining and dressing, non-metal mineral products, and the agriculture, forestry, animal husbandry, and fishery industry account for about 10%. The remaining 37 sectors account for only about 10% of the total carbon emission reduction in the entire production sector.

4.4. *Discussion*

Many findings of this chapter are consistent with previous studies. Similar to Wang *et al.* (2009), Dai *et al.* (2011), Lu *et al.* (2013), Zhang *et al.* (2013), and Zhang (2013), the results of this chapter also show that carbon intensity constraints have little impact on the total economic volume. This chapter finds that carbon intensity constraints can significantly reduce carbon emissions. Similar results are also reached in Lu *et al.* (2013), Zhang *et al.* (2013), and Zhang (2013). Certainly, due to the differences in model structure and some basic assumptions, there are still obvious differences in numerical values between the results of this chapter and those of previous studies. Take the impact of carbon intensity constraints on GDP in 2020 as an example. The result here is –0.26%, a value greater than that of Wang *et al.* (2009) (–0.04%) and Zhang (2013) (–0.1%),[3] but significantly smaller than that of Lu *et al.* (2013) –3 to –2%.

In order to test the reliability of the simulation results in this chapter, we conduct three more groups of sensitivity analysis. The results are shown in Table 13.6. In the first group of sensitivity analysis, we assume that China will achieve the established clean energy development target while achieving the established targets of carbon intensity constraints. According to the *12th Five-Year Plan for the Development of Renewable Energy* issued by the National Energy Administration in 2012, the proportion of non-fossil energy in primary energy consumption in China in 2015 and 2020 will reach 11.4% and 15%, respectively, significantly higher than the proportion under the baseline scenario. This means that China needs to accelerate the development of clean energy, which will help reduce the negative impact of carbon intensity constraints on China's economy. However, with the increase of the proportion of non-fossil energy, the reduction in energy consumption needed for achieving the established targets of carbon intensity constraints will decrease, because energy structure optimization will contribute more to carbon intensity

---

[3] The present chapter is different from Zhang (2013) in that a dynamic model is adopted here, while the latter conducts a static comparative analysis. Besides, there is also a difference in the division of sectors.

reduction. In the meantime, with the decrease of the total economic volume slowed down and that of the carbon intensity remaining constant, the decrease in the total carbon emissions will also be slowed down.

In the second group of sensitivity analysis, we assume that the autonomous energy efficiency improvement (AEEI) is 0.5%–2.0% higher than that of the original simulation. Comparing Table 13.6 with Table 13.3, we can easily see that the value of energy efficiency has little impact on the simulation results, that is, the impact of carbon intensity constraints is not sensitive to energy efficiency. However, with the continuous improvement of energy efficiency, the impact of carbon intensity constraints on China's macro-economy, energy consumption, and carbon emissions also shows a declining trend, which is in line with the intuition, for with the improvement of energy efficiency, the carbon intensity will drop more sharply under the baseline scenario. This means that the difference in carbon intensity between the baseline scenario and the policy scenario will be reduced, and the difference in other variables will also be reduced accordingly.

In the third group of sensitivity analysis, we have expanded the range of values for various elasticity coefficients, including the transformation elasticity of domestic supply and export, the substitution elasticity of factors and energy inputs, the elasticity of export prices, Armington elasticity, and consumer preferences. When we reduce the values of these elastic coefficients to 75% of the original values, the impact of carbon intensity constraints significantly decreases. When the values of all elastic coefficients increase to 125% of the original values, the impact of carbon intensity constraints is significantly enhanced. This group of analysis shows that the impact of carbon intensity constraints is more sensitive to the values of various elastic coefficients. Therefore, in understanding the impact of carbon intensity constraints, we must pay attention to the uncertainties caused by the changes in the values of various elastic coefficients.

5. Conclusion and Policy Recommendations

This chapter analyzes the impact of carbon intensity constraints on China based on a dynamic CGE model. Different from previous studies, the present study discusses in detail the impact of carbon intensity constraints on economy, energy, and environment at the industry level, and analyzes it in combination with the macro-impacts of carbon intensity constraints. The results show that under the carbon intensity constraints, the total economic volume of China and the output of most sectors, especially carbon-intensive sectors, will decline. In the meantime, fossil energy inputs and carbon emissions will be greatly reduced, with most of them contributed by thermal power generation, heating, and supply. Based on the above conclusions, we put forward the following policy recommendations:

(1) Sufficient attention should be paid to the negative economic impact of carbon intensity constraints, despite the simulation results which show that the short-term impact is not obvious. On the one hand, it should be noted that due to the limitations of the calculation method itself, it is difficult to fully consider the costs incurred in the process of structural adjustment, and the actual negative impact will be greater than the simulation results. Special attention should be paid to the fact that when the carbon intensity constraint continues to be implemented, their influence will become stronger. On the other hand, we should consider the fact that China is facing the pressure of economic downturn.

In this case, in order to reduce the negative impact of carbon intensity constraints on economic development, it is necessary to introduce some strategic or revolutionary measures. At present, China's main efforts to optimize the energy structure are to "suppress coal use" and accelerate the development of new energy sources. But we should keep a sober mind as there can hardly be any major technological breakthroughs in a short period of time and that the policies to subsidize renewable energy do not prove very successful. The realization of China's target of carbon intensity constraints should take the national conditions into consideration. It has been fully demonstrated by practice that the dominant position of coal in the energy structure will not change for a long time. Thus, China's energy strategy needs to be adjusted appropriately. It should shift from the current excessive focus on new energy to paying more attention to changes in coal mining and usage patterns instead of simply "suppressing coal use". China should vigorously develop clean coal technology and promote the industrialization of underground coal gasification so as to embark on the road of "green coal" as soon as possible. This is not only beneficial to the realization of the carbon intensity constraint targets but can also effectively relieve the pressure of economic downturn brought by the carbon intensity constraints.

(2) In order to ensure that the targets of carbon intensity constraints can be achieved, China may consider imposing carbon tax, accelerating the improvement and expansion of carbon emission trading market, and subsidizing the carbon emission reduction of units and individuals. On the one hand, carbon tax can be tried out in pilot regions and then implemented nationwide. The tax can be collected at a low rate in the beginning, and then gradually increased. In order to make tax collection less difficult, carbon tax can be levied in the purchase of fossil energy. On the other hand, China should sum up the experiences and lessons learned from the trials of carbon emission trading in seven provinces and municipalities of Beijing, Shanghai, Tianjin, Chongqing, Hubei, Guangdong, and Shenzhen, and establish a national carbon emission trading market as soon as possible. In the meantime, the government's income from carbon tax and carbon emission trading should be applied to subsidize the research and development of energy-conserving and carbon-reducing technologies, equipment updating, and other carbon reduction behaviors.

(3) In view of the decisive role of thermal power generation, heating, and supply in the reduction of fossil energy consumption and carbon emissions in China, measures such as management (e.g., shutting down small units and further raising the entry threshold of the industry), technological upgrading, and equipment updating (e.g., increasing the proportion of cogeneration units, and safely and effectively promoting the construction of power grids to realize cross-regional power regulation) should be adopted to improve the energy efficiency of the industry.

(4) In international trade, we should continue to restrict the export of high energy-consuming, high environment-polluting and resource-intensive products, support the export of high-tech products and service, and encourage the import of carbon-intensive products.

It should be pointed out that there are still some shortcomings in this chapter that need to be overcome in further research. First, the impact of carbon intensity constraints is sensitive to the values of various elasticity coefficients. We can collect a large amount of data, then use appropriate methods to estimate these elasticity coefficients, and predict their future trends more accurately. This is conducive to improving the accuracy of the simulation results. Second, we can make technological progress endogenous, which can simulate the positive incentive effects of carbon intensity constraints on technological progress of various sectors. Finally, this chapter only depicts endogenous carbon tax, which, in fact, is a policy mechanism to reduce carbon intensity. We may also consider other mechanisms such as subsidies and carbon emission trading, and compare their effects.

References

Armington, P., *A Theory of Demand for Products Distinguished by Place of Production*. IMF Staff Papers, 1969, 16 (1).

Dai, H., Masui, T., Matsuoka, Y. & Fujimori, S., "Assessment of China's Climate Commitment and Non-fossil Energy Plan Towards 2020 Using Hybrid AIM/CGE Model". *Energy Policy*, Vol. 39, No. 5 (2011), pp. 2875–2887.

Dervis, K., De Melo, J. & Robinson, S., *General Equilibrium Models for Development Policy*. 1982. Cambridge University Press, Cambridge, UK.

Dixon, P. B., & Rimmer, M. T., *Dynamic General Equilibrium Modelling for Forecasting and Policy: A Practical Guide and Documentation of MONASH*. 2002. North-Holland Publishing Company, Amsterdam.

EIA, 2013, Annual Energy Outlook 2013. http://www.eia.gov/forecasts/aeo/.

Jung, H. S., & Thorbecke, E., "The Impact of Public Education Expenditure on Human Capital, Growth and Poverty in Tanzania and Zambia: A General Equilibrium Approach". *Journal of Policy Modeling*, Vol. 25, No. 8 (2003), pp. 701–725.

Lu, Y., Stegman, A. & Cai, Y., "Emissions Intensity Targeting: From China's 12th Five-Year Plan to Its Copenhagen Commitment." *Energy Policy*, Vol. 61 (2013), pp. 1164–1171.

Qi, M., "China's Labor Supply and Demand Forecast 2010–2050". *Population Research*, No. 9 (2010).

Qiu, J., "China's Climate Target: Is it achievable?" *Nature*, Vol. 462, No. 3 (2009).

Stern, D. I., & Jotzo, F., How Ambitious are China and India's Emissions Intensity Targets? *Energy Policy*, Vol. 38, No. 11 (2010).

Sue Wing, I., "The Synthesis of Bottom-up and Top-down Approaches to Climate Policy Modeling: Electric Power Technology Detail in a Social Accounting Framework". *Energy Economics*, Vol. 38, No. 2 (2008), pp. 547–573.

Wang, K., Wang, C. & Chen, J., "Analysis of the Economic Impact of Different Chinese Climate Policy Options Based on a CGE Model Incorporating Endogenous Technological Change". *Energy Policy*, Vol. 37, No. 8 (2009), pp. 2930–2940.

Zhang, D., Rausch, S., Karplus, V. J. & Zhang, X., "Quantifying Regional Economic Impacts of CO_2 Intensity Targets in China. *Energy Economics*, Vol. 40 (2013).

Zhang Y., "A Comparison of Performance between Carbon Intensity and Total Restraint: An Analysis Based on CGE Model". *The Journal of World Economy*, No. 7 (2013), pp. 138–160.

Zhang Y., "The Impact of Changes in Economic Development Patterns on the Intensity of China's Carbon Emissions". *Economic Research Journal*, No. 4 (2010), pp. 120–133.

Zheng Y., Fan, M., *et al.*, *China CGE Model and Policy Analysis* 1998. Social Sciences Academic Press, Beijing, China.

Chapter 14

Potential Impact of Carbon Tariffs and Their Collection Standards on China's Economy and Carbon Emissions[1]

Youguo Zhang, Shilin Zheng, Li'an Zhou and Guang Shi

Institute of Quantitative & Technical Economics,
Chinese Academy of Social Sciences

1. Introduction

In recent years, with climate change becoming a hot issue, more discussions have been made on carbon tariffs. Carbon tariffs, also known as "carbon border adjustment tax",[2] are a kind of policy measures designed by policymakers and scholars in some developed countries to avoid or reduce the so-called carbon leakage that may occur in international trade and to protect the competitiveness of their own products. Although no country or region has formally implemented carbon tariffs so far, they have in fact been put on the agenda of many developed countries and even implemented in disguised forms. For example, Directive No. 101 of 2008, approved by the EU in November 2008 and formally implemented in January 2012, attempts to incorporate international aviation into its emission trading system (EUETS), which amounts to imposing carbon tariffs on flights entering the EU.[3] In April 2009, the EU approved

---

[1] A brief version of the present chapter has been published in *The Journal of World Economy*, No. 2, 2015.

[2] Dong (2010) summarizes other versions of explanation for carbon tariffs.

[3] For more details, see http://ec.europa.eu/clima/policies/ets/documentation_en.htm.

Directive No. 29 of 2009, which further incorporates importers within the EU into the EUETS, requiring these importers to purchase carbon emission targets for their imported products, in effect imposing carbon tariffs on imported products. For another example, in June 2009, the US House of Representatives passed the *American Clean Energy and Security Act*, deciding to impose carbon tariffs on imports from some countries[4] starting from 2020. These documents issued by the US and the EU have aroused widespread concern and questioning all over the world.

At present, the researches on carbon tariffs mainly focus on two types of problems: one concerns the legal rationality of carbon tariffs. Some scholars believe that carbon tariffs do not go against WTO regulations, and put forward suggestions to make carbon tariffs conform to WTO regulations (De Cendra, 2006; Ismer & Neuhoff, 2007). Some other scholars argue that carbon tariffs are not in line with WTO principles (Shen, 2010), and that even if carbon tariffs can bypass WTO regulations, it is very difficult to manage and implement them (Medina & Lazo, 2011). The second is about the impact of carbon tariffs, including their impact on carbon leakage, and on the competitiveness, economic development, and carbon emissions of relevant countries. Many recent studies are focused on this problem, coming to different conclusions. Some studies find that carbon tariffs have no or little impact on carbon leakage, competitiveness, and welfare (Peterson & Schleich, 2007; McKibbin & Wilcoxen, 2009; Dong & Whalley, 2012), while some other studies reach the conclusion that the impact of carbon tariffs cannot be ignored (Mattoo, Subramanian, van der Mensbrugghe & He 2009; Hübler, 2012; Shen & Li, 2010; Lin & Li, 2012).

In terms of research methods, computable general equilibrium (CGE) is the main tool to analyze the impact of carbon tariffs. Many researches have used the CGE model to simulate the impact of carbon tariffs at the global or international level (Peterson & Schleich, 2007; McKibbin & Wilcoxen, 2009; Burniaux *et al.*, 2013), many of which involve discussions on China (Mattoo, 2009; Dong & Whalley, 2012; Lin & Li, 2010, 2012). Other studies focus on or specifically discuss the impact of carbon tariffs on China based on the multinational CGE model. Huang & Li

---

[4] Countries which do not set a limit on total carbon emissions, including China.

(2010) and Luan & Yang (2014) apply the Global Trade Analysis Project (GTAP) to simulate the impact of carbon tariffs imposed by the US on China's energy and export-intensive products on the macro- and sectoral economies and carbon emissions of China. Lin & Li (2011), Li & Zhang (2012) and Li, Zhang, Cai & Peng (2013) and others simulate the impact of carbon tariffs imposed by OECD countries on the overall and different regional economies (with economic characteristics) and carbon emissions of China. Hübler (2012) simulates the impact of carbon tariffs imposed by developed countries and all the trading partners of China on the economy, carbon emissions, and terms of trade of China.

There are also many studies that assess the impact of carbon tariffs on China based on the single-country CGE model. Research by Shen & Li (2010) shows that if all trading partners collect carbon tariffs, China's industrial exports will drop significantly. The simulation results of Li & Zhang (2012) show that when all trading partners levy carbon tariffs, their impact on China's carbon emissions is greater than on the total economy and exports. Yuan (2013) also simulates the impact of carbon tariffs imposed by all trading partners on China's economy, finding that carbon tariff will reduce China's total economy regardless of the rates, but the reduction will be small. Bao *et al.* (2013) focus their analysis on the impact of carbon tariffs imposed by the US and the EU in 2020 on China's sectoral carbon emissions, and discuss the sensitivity of the impact of carbon tariffs to technological progress. In addition, some studies based on partial equilibrium models also find that carbon tariffs will have a negative impact on China's economy and carbon emissions (Qu & Wu, 2011; Pan, 2012).

The multi-country CGE model can be regarded as the "parallel connection" of multiple single-country models (Zhang, 2009). The advantage of the model lies in its ability to simultaneously depict the impact of trade policies on multiple countries (or regions), while its disadvantage lies in the relatively lagging data and the inconsistency in sector division standards and trade data between different countries. Although the single-country CGE model cannot simulate the impact of a trade policy on multiple countries (or regions) at the same time, it can more fully depict the responses of various sectors within a country to a trade policy, and there is no problem of difference in sector division standards or inconsistent trade data. In the research on international trade, the multi-country CGE model mainly focuses on those multilateral trade policies that play a role in an economic zone (e.g., the EU) and is mainly used to analyze the resource allocation and welfare effects of trade policies, while the single-country CGE model focuses on the detailed characterization of domestic economic structure and is mainly used to analyze the sectoral effects of various trade policies (de Melo & Robinson, 1989; Bergman, 2005; Roland-Holst & van der Mensbrugghe, 2009). Thus, the choice of a research model, multi-country or single-country CGE, depends on the purpose and scope of the study (Wobst, 2001). If a research focuses on the impact of a certain trade policy on several countries or some international issues (such as carbon leakage), it is obvious that the multi-country CGE model should be adopted. If researchers only focus on the impact of a unilateral trade policy (e.g., carbon tariffs) on a particular country, especially at its sectoral level, then the single-country CGE model is undoubtedly an appropriate tool, which is more conducive to improving the availability and reliability of data.

It is necessary to point out that no collection standards of carbon tariffs at present have been agreed upon by policymakers nor scholars. The so-called collection standards in this chapter mainly refer to the carbon coefficient related to trade products. On the one hand, there is still much controversy over whether carbon tariffs should be calculated on the basis of the embodied carbon (emission) coefficient of trade products, the direct carbon (emission) coefficient, the carbon coefficient of importing countries, or the carbon coefficient of exporting countries. On the other hand, there is no uniform method and standard for calculating these carbon coefficients. As far as the authors know, most studies choose a certain collection standard to simulate the impact of carbon tariffs, which is somewhat arbitrary. Most of them take the direct carbon coefficient of the exporting country as the standard, while few choose the embodied carbon coefficient of the exporting country. It seems that only Mattoo *et al.* (2009) involve multiple collection standards. They simulate the impact of carbon tariffs based on the embodied carbon coefficient of importing and exporting countries, respectively, but do not consider the direct carbon coefficient of trade commodities. Thus, the current discussion on the impact of carbon tariffs under different collection standards on a country's economy is not sufficient.

The main contribution this chapter attempts to make is to compare the impacts of carbon tariffs under different collection standards. In the meantime, this chapter also attempts to analyze the impact of carbon tariffs on trade between China and different regions, an issue which is seldom discussed in the existing literature. Specifically, this chapter will distinguish the impacts of carbon tariffs on exports between China and the US, the EU and other regions. With the focus being the potential impact of carbon tariffs on China's macro, and sectoral economies and carbon emissions, this chapter adopts the single-country CGE model.

2. Diversity and Uncertainty of the Collection Standards of Carbon Tariffs

Carbon tariffs not only face the problem of inadequate legal basis, and even being "illegal", but also the problem of whether they can be implemented or operated. One of the key issues to be solved in implementing carbon tariffs is about setting their collection standards. The collection standards of carbon tariffs have not received clear specification or definition from either academic documents or policy documents (such as the *American Clean Energy and Security Act*). Judging from the relevant literature (as mentioned in the Introduction), there are many possibilities for such standards (see Table 14.1). On the one hand, carbon tariff-collecting countries can choose either the direct carbon coefficient or the embodied carbon coefficient of imported products as the collection standard. The embodied carbon coefficient of a product refers to the sum of the direct and indirect carbon emissions per unit of the product. On the other hand, countries can collect carbon tariffs on imported products with reference to the direct or embodied carbon coefficients of similar products of their own. In addition, carbon tariff-collecting countries can also take the difference between the direct or embodied carbon coefficients of imported products and similar domestic products as the collection standard.

When taking the direct carbon coefficient of imported products as the collection standard, we need to know the amount of various types of fossil energy consumed in the production process of imported products, and then estimate their direct carbon coefficients. However, manufacturers of imported products usually do not voluntarily disclose their energy

Table 14.1   Possible collection standards of carbon tariffs

Type	Standards	Methods for estimation
Embodied carbon coefficient	Embodied carbon coefficient of imported products; embodied carbon coefficient of domestic products; difference between the embodied carbon coefficients of imported products and domestic products	Base on the direct carbon coefficient of products, there are such methods as input–output tables, ISO/TC207/SC7, GHG Protocol, and PAS 2050.
Direct carbon coefficient	Direct carbon coefficient of imported products; direct carbon coefficient of domestic products; difference of direct carbon coefficients between imported products and domestic products	Currently, the accouting framework of IPCC (2006) is the most authoritative.

consumption information. Even if such information is required by importing countries, its reliability cannot be guaranteed. Although many countries (e.g., China) publish energy consumption data at the industry level, the industrial sectors are not finely divided. Moreover, different enterprises of the same industry may have great differences in their technological level and the quality of the energy consumed. Therefore, based on such information, the direct carbon coefficient of each type of import can only be estimated very roughly. Besides, energy statistics in many countries, especially in developing countries, are not complete, and sometimes even fail to provide energy consumption data at the industry level.

If the embodied carbon coefficient of imported products is chosen as the collection standard, it is not only necessary to know the direct energy consumption in the production process of each type of imported products but also the energy consumption indirectly caused, that is, the energy consumption in all upstream production activities necessary for imported products. In the meantime, we also need to understand the detailed technological relevance between each type of imported product and their upstream products. At present, many countries have input–output tables, which reflect the technological relevance among their industries. It is a common practice for scholars to calculate the embodied carbon coefficients of various products on the basis of the input–output tables. However, the level of detail in the input–output table will have a significant impact on the estimated value of the embodied carbon coefficient. Moreover, for many countries, input–output tables are not prepared every year. For example, China prepares an input–output table (basic table) every five years based on survey data, and another extension table during the period.

Furthermore, in addition to the input–output method, there are many other methods for calculating embodied carbon, such as the standards formulated by the Greenhouse Gas Management Standardization Branch of the Environmental Management Technological Committee (ISO/TC207/SC7), the Greenhouse Gas Agreement: Accounting and Reporting Guidelines jointly developed by the World Resources Institute (WRI) and the World Business Council for Sustainable Development (WBCSD), and the evaluation standard for greenhouse gas emissions in the life cycle of goods and services (PAS 2050) developed by the British Standards Association. The results obtained by different methods will also be different.

In order to deal with the difficulty in obtaining information, carbon tariff-collecting countries may consider taking the direct or embodied carbon coefficient of domestic products as the collection standard. Although there are many uncertainties in estimating the carbon coefficient of domestic products, it is much easier to obtain relevant information. In particular, carbon tariff-collecting countries are mainly developed countries, whose statistical systems are fairly complete, making it easy to obtain relevant data. For example, the US publishes its current-year input–output table every year. However, the classification of products or the division of industry sectors of carbon tariff-collecting countries is usually different from that of importing countries. They have to adopt appropriate methods to reasonably match the types of imported products with their domestic products. Furthermore, if they take the difference between the carbon coefficients of imported products and similar products of their own countries as the collection standard, then they have to possess information about all kinds of energy consumption of their domestic products and imported products. They also need to classify imported products according to their own standards.

As for the same product, the embodied carbon coefficient, which takes into account both the direct and the indirect carbon emission, is much greater than the direct carbon coefficient. When carbon tariff-collecting countries choose the embodied carbon coefficient, instead of the direct carbon coefficient, of imported products as the collection standard, the impact of carbon tariffs on the economy and carbon emissions of the producing countries will be much greater. Even in countries where carbon tariffs are collected, the embodied carbon coefficient of domestic products is usually significantly higher than the direct carbon coefficient of similar imported products. Thus, when the former is taken as the collection standard, the impact of carbon tariffs on the producing countries of imported products will be significantly greater.

When the embodied (direct) carbon coefficient of the carbon tariff-collecting country, instead of that of the imported products, is taken as the collection standard, the impact of carbon tariffs on the producing country is usually significantly lower, because the producing country is usually a developing country, while the carbon tariff-collecting country is usually a developed country (such as the US and the EU). The latter enjoys a higher level of technology, and the carbon coefficient of its products is much lower.

Taking the difference between the carbon coefficients of imported products and similar domestic products as the collection standard is obviously in line with the original intention of carbon tariffs, that is, as a guarantee of fair competition and a way to reduce carbon leakage. When this standard is adopted instead of the carbon coefficient of imported products, the impact of carbon tariffs on producing countries will usually be lower, but not necessarily so in comparison with the carbon coefficient of similar domestic products of the tariff-collecting country as the standard.

In short, the collection standards and calculation methods of carbon tariffs are diverse, but the relevant data are not sufficient, which makes the choice of collection standard full of uncertainties. Due to the diversity and uncertainty of collection standard, the impact of carbon tariffs on the economy and carbon emissions of the taxed countries is also uncertain. We will conduct a quantitative analysis of this issue based on the policy model.

3. Model, Data and Scenario Design

3.1. *CGE model*

The CGE model adopted in this chapter draws on the modeling ideas of Dervis *et al.* (1982) and Zheng *et al.* (1998). On the one hand, energy synthesis products formed by various fuels combine with capital to form capital-energy synthesis products, which combine with labor to form element-energy synthesis inputs. These inputs then combine with other various intermediate inputs, thus enabling enterprises to produce products demanded by the market. On the other hand, enterprises determine the proportion of domestic sales and exports of products according to the international and domestic prices of the products, and those products for domestic sales together with similar imported products meet various final domestic demands (including resident consumption, government consumption, investment and inventory, etc.) and intermediate input demands. Some of the key behavior equations of the model are given in the following.

3.1.1. *Production behavior*

The production behavior of this model can be expressed as follows:

$$X_i = \min(A_{z_{ji}} Z_{ji}, A_{Q_i} Q_i) \tag{14.1}$$

$$Q_i = \left[\alpha_{L_i} \left(A_{L_i} L_i \right)^{\frac{\sigma_{Q_i}-1}{\sigma_{Q_i}}} + \left(1 - \alpha_{L_i}\right) \left(A_{N_i} N_i \right)^{\frac{\sigma_{Q_i}-1}{\sigma_{Q_i}}} \right]^{\sigma_{Q_i}/(\sigma_{Q_i}-1)} \tag{14.2}$$

$$N_i = \left[\alpha_{K_i} \left(A_{K_i} K_i \right)^{\frac{\sigma_{N_i}-1}{\sigma_{N_i}}} + \left(1 - \alpha_{K_i}\right) \left(A_{F_i} F_i \right)^{\frac{\sigma_{N_i}-1}{\sigma_{N_i}}} \right]^{\sigma_{N_i}/(\sigma_{N_i}-1)} \tag{14.3}$$

$$F_i = \left\{ \sum_j \left[\alpha_{Z_{bki}} \left(A_{Z_{bki}} Z_{bki} \right)^{\frac{\sigma_{F_i}-1}{\sigma_{F_i}}} \right] \right\}^{\sigma_{F_i}/(\sigma_{F_i}-1)} \tag{14.4}$$

wherein, Z_{ji} represents the category j intermediate synthesis input (including fossil energy used as raw materials), Q_i represents the labor-capital-energy synthesis input, Z_{bki} represents the category k fossil energy used for power generation, heating, and terminal consumption of various sectors, N_i represents the capital-energy synthesis input, and L_i, K_i, and F_i, respectively, stand for labor input, capital input, and energy synthesis product.

A indicates the efficiency of various inputs, and its changes reflect technological progresses; α and σ, respectively represent the share coefficient and the elasticity of substitution. Expressions (14.1) and (14.4) mean that the total output is not only a multi-layer nested CES function of labor, capital, and fossil energy synthesis products but also a Leontief production function of intermediate inputs (including various non-fossil energy products and services, and fossil energy used to produce secondary fossil energy products).

It is easy to know that the intermediate input demand of each sector is in direct proportion to its total output. Moreover, we assume that the producers, i.e., each production sector, want to obtain the established total output at the minimum cost. By solving the first-order conditions of this optimization problem, we can obtain the optimal labor, capital, and energy requirements of each sector, and then obtain the carbon emissions of each sector and the total carbon emissions of the production sector. In the meantime, we assume that each sector supplies a product or service, and determines its domestic supply and export volume based on their domestic sale price and export price so as to maximize their income. In this way, the relationship between the total supply of the products and services and their domestic supply and export can be characterized by using a fixed elasticity coefficient of transformation (CET) function.

3.1.2. *Resident consumption*

Suppose that residents pursue utility maximization under certain expenditure budget constraints, and the utility is a Klein–Rubin function of various synthesis products or services

$$\max \prod_i \left(Z_{H_i} - z_{H_{subi}} \Psi \right)^{\beta_{luxi}} \tag{14.5}$$

$$\text{s.t.} \, P_{Z_{H_i}} Z_{H_i} \leq (1-s)\left[(1-t_H)(wL^s + U_{HP}) + U_{HG} + U_{HF}\right] = W_H \tag{14.6}$$

In the expressions, z_{H_i} represents the total consumption of synthesis product i, $z_{H_{subi}}$ represents the basic demand per capita for synthesis product i, ψ represents the total population, $P_{Z_{H_i}}$ represents the price of synthesis goods consumed by residents, β_{luxi} represents the share coefficient of various goods in total luxury consumption, L^s represents the total supply of labor, w represents the wage rate, U_{HP} represents the property income of residents from enterprises, U_{HG} represents the government transfer payment, U_{HF} represents the net overseas remittance, s represents the savings rate, t_H represents the income tax rate, and W_H represents the total expenditure of residents.

3.1.3. *Investment behavior*

We assume that each sector obtains investment according to their respective capital stock and the rate of static expected relative return. Drawing on the method of Jung & Thorbecke (2003) and making appropriate simplifications, we establish the following equation for the investment of a sector:

$$Z_{V_i} = \alpha_{V_i} \left(R_i / \Omega \right)^{\delta_i} K_i \qquad (14.7)$$

wherein, K_i, Z_{V_i}, and R_i, respectively, represent the capital stock, the investment, and the net capital return of sector i; Ω represents the interest rate, Ri/Ω represents the static expected relative return rate of sector i, and α_{V_i} and δ_i, respectively, represent the coefficient of investment scale and the coefficient of investment elasticity. It should be noted that we assume that the investment elasticity coefficient of the public investment sector is 0, that is, their investment is proportional to their capital stock ($Z_{V_i} = \alpha_{V_i} K_i$). Like most studies, we further assume that the share of each sector's demand for various investment products $Z_{V_{ji}}$ is fixed in its total investment demand. At the same time, we assume that each sector's inventory is in proportion to its total output.

3.1.4. *Government behavior*

The government obtains income through income tax, consumption tax, investment tax, customs duty, environmental tax, and other channels, and spends through subsidies to enterprises and residents and purchases of various products. We assume that the government may levy a carbon tax on fossil energy to reduce the intensity of carbon emissions. Then the price of fossil energy with carbon tax can be expressed as follows:

$$P_{F_i} = P_{FO_i} + \xi_i T_c \qquad (14.8)$$

In the expression, P_{F_i} represents the price of fossil energy with carbon tax, $P_{Z_{FO_i}}$ represents the price of fossil energy without carbon tax, ξ_i is the carbon emission coefficient of various fossil energy sources (carbon emissions per unit of fossil energy consumption), and T_c represents the specific carbon duty.

3.1.5. *International trade*

We assume that there is a substitution elasticity relationship of Armington (Armington, 1969) between domestic products and imported products, that is, the total domestic demand for a certain product is the CES function of the corresponding domestic products and imported products. After determining the demand of producers, residents, investors, governments, and other various entities for various types of synthesis products, the demand function of category i imported products can be obtained from the first-order condition of cost minimization as:

$$M_i = \left(1 - \alpha_{D_i}\right)^{\sigma_i} \left(P_{Z_i} / P_{M_i}\right)^{\sigma_i} Z_i \qquad (14.9)$$

wherein, M_i represents the domestic demand for category i imported products, Z_i represents the total demand of a country for category i synthesis products. P_{Z_i} and P_{M_i} indicate the prices of Z_i and M_i, respectively; α_{D_i} represents the share coefficient, and σ_i $(\sigma_i > 0)$ represents the substitution elasticity of domestic products for imported products. The import price P_{M_i} is determined by the international market, i.e., exogenously given.

We partially relax the assumption on small open economies, i.e., the assumption that the price of domestic export products is determined by the supply of domestic export and the demand of the international market. As mentioned above, we assume that each sector makes decisions as to the distribution of their products based on their domestic sale price and export price. Then export supply of a sector can be expressed as follows:

$$E_{S_i} = \left(1 - \alpha_{S_i}\right)^{\sigma_{s_i}} \left(P_{E_i} / P_{X_i}\right)^{\sigma_{s_i}} X_i \qquad (14.10)$$

wherein, E_{S_i} represents the export supply of product i, P_{E_i} represents the export price without carbon tax, P_{X_i} represents the comprehensive output price, and α_{S_i} represents the share coefficient, and σ_i ($\sigma_i > 0$) represents the transformation elasticity coefficient.

The demand of region r for domestic product i can represent the decreasing function of export price and carbon tax of the region.

$$E_{D_i}^r = \beta_i^r P'_{E_i}^{r-\theta_i} \qquad (14.11)$$

In this expression, $E_{D_i}^r$ represents the demand of region r for domestic product i, β_i^r represents the scale coefficient, $P'_{E_i}^{r-\theta_i}$ represents the sale price of products in region r with carbon tax collected, and θ_i ($0 < \theta_i < \infty$) represents export price elasticity. P''_{E_i} can be expressed as follows:

$$P''_{E_i} = P_{E_i} + \eta_i \tau_{E_i}^r \qquad (14.12)$$

wherein, η_i represents the carbon coefficient of product i, i.e., the collection standard of carbon tax. As discussed above, there are many choices for the collection standard, such as the direct carbon coefficient ξ_i of domestic product i, the embodied carbon coefficient c_i of domestic product i, and the embodied carbon coefficient c_i^r of product i of the carbon tariff-collecting country. $\tau_{E_i}^r$ represents the carbon tax rate of region r. Under the equilibrium state, we have

$$E_{S_i} = \sum_r E_{D_i}^r \qquad (14.13)$$

3.1.6. *Equilibrium conditions*

We assume that the market is in a state of equilibrium, which means that all kinds of economic entities will optimize their objective function (e.g., utility maximization) under their respective constraints (e.g., the constraint of resident budget) and the market will be clear. The specific equilibrium conditions include the following: producers obtain zero net profit; the demand and the supply for all products and elements are equal; income and expenditure are in balance for residents and the government, that is, their expenditures are equal to their respective disposable incomes minus their corresponding savings; international payments are in balance, that is, the total imports at international prices are equal to the sum of the total exports at border prices, net foreign transfers, and net foreign capital inflows; investment and savings are in balance, i.e., the total investment equals the sum of domestic savings and foreign capital inflows.

3.1.7. *Macro-closure*

We assume that government consumption and resident consumption change in the same proportion, and that government transfer payments (subsidies) and various tax rates are exogenous, which means that government savings and deficits are endogenous. We assume that the rate of household savings is fixed and the exchange rate is chosen as the baseline price, while the net inflow of foreign capital is endogenous. Thus, the adjustment of the net inflow of foreign capital can ensure the balance between investment and savings.

3.1.8. *Dynamic model*

The model can be made dynamic through the accumulation of production factors and technological progress, and by adopting a recursive form. We assume that the total capital supply at the end of the period is equal to the depreciation of the total capital supply at the beginning of the period plus the total amount of fixed capital formation added in the current period.

$$K_i^* = K_i \left(1 - d_i\right) + Z_{V_i} \tag{14.14}$$

In the expression, K_i^*, K_i, Z_{V_i}, and d_i, respectively, represent the final capital stock, initial capital stock, new investment, and capital depreciation rate of sector i. We further assume that the capital depreciation rate is exogenous, and the total amount of new fixed capital formation is

determined by the investment–savings balance relationship and the allocation mechanism of investment among sectors, which means that the capital growth rate of each sector and total capital growth rate are endogenous.
We also assume that population changes, changes in labor supply, and
technological progress are exogenous.

3.2. Data and scenario design

The period for which policy simulation is to be carried out in this chapter is 2007–2030, of which the year of 2007 serves as the baseline, with
years from 2008 to 2012 as the historical simulation period, and years
from 2013 to 2030 as the prediction and policy simulation period. We
establish an SAM table based on the input–output tables of 42 sectors in
2007 released by the National Bureau of Statistics.[5] The quantities of
domestic and imported products domestically absorbed and utilized in
the middle, the carbon coefficients of various fossil energy products, and
the embodied carbon coefficients of various sectors are calculated based
on Zhang's (2010a, 2010b) method and the input–output table of 2007.
Specifically, embodied carbon coefficient is estimated with the following equation:

$$c = \Gamma^T L \tag{14.15}$$

wherein, c represents an embodied carbon coefficient vector and its element is c_i; Γ represents the direct carbon coefficient vector of a sector, and
its element is ζ_i; L represents the Leontief inverse matrix, and its element
is l_{ij}. The superscript T indicates the transposition of a vector or matrix. It
is thus easy to get the following expression:

$$c_i = \sum_i \zeta_i l_{ij} \geq \zeta_i \tag{14.16}$$

---

[5] The input–output table of 2007 is compiled by the National Bureau of Statistics based on
a large number of basic surveys. Although the National Bureau of Statistics has released
the input–output table of 2010, the table is only an extended version based on that of 2007,
and its reliability is lower. Thus, we adopt the input–output table of 2007 as the data basis
for our research.

Figure 14.1 shows the estimated direct and embodied carbon coefficients for each sector. It can be seen that the thermal power generation, heating and supply, gas production and supply, metal smelting, rolling, and processing, non-metal mineral products, transportation and warehousing, posts, coal mining and dressing, petroleum processing, coking and nuclear fuel processing, chemical industry, and oil and natural gas mining enjoy higher direct carbon coefficient and embodied carbon coefficient, and they can thus be regarded as carbon-intensive sectors. The two carbon coefficients of labor-intensive sectors (such as agriculture, forestry, animal husbandry, and fishery), technology-intensive sectors (such as manufacturing of communication equipment, computers, and other electronic equipment) and most service industries are very low, and can thus be regarded as clean sectors.

Table 14.2 shows the estimated trade elasticity coefficient. The Armington substitution elasticity for domestic and imported products is estimated based on the definition of elasticity of substitution. The data used include the comparable (import) non-competitive input–output tables of 2007 and 2010 compiled by the authors, the mill price index of various products in the *China Statistical Yearbook* over the years, and the import price index of various products published in *China's External Trade Indices* compiled by the General Administration of Customs. We also estimate the elasticity coefficient of export prices for various sectors on the basis the four-digit industry code of the Chinese Customs. In order to unify the data caliber, we adjust the classification of other data according to the division of 42 sectors in the input–output table of 2007. Other important elasticity coefficients, such as the substitution elasticity between various factors and energy sources and the elasticity of capital conversion, come from some recently published studies (Zhang, 2013; Bao *et al.*, 2013)

Through historical simulation,[6] we update the SAM matrix to 2012 and estimate the historical changes of various hardly observable variables

---

[6] Dixon & Rimmer (2002) put forward four simulation (ananlysis) functions of CGE, i.e., historical simulation, decomposing simulation, prediction simulation, and policy simulation. When using CGE model to conduct policy simulation, it is usually assumed that various hardly observable variables (e.g., technological progress and consumption preferences)

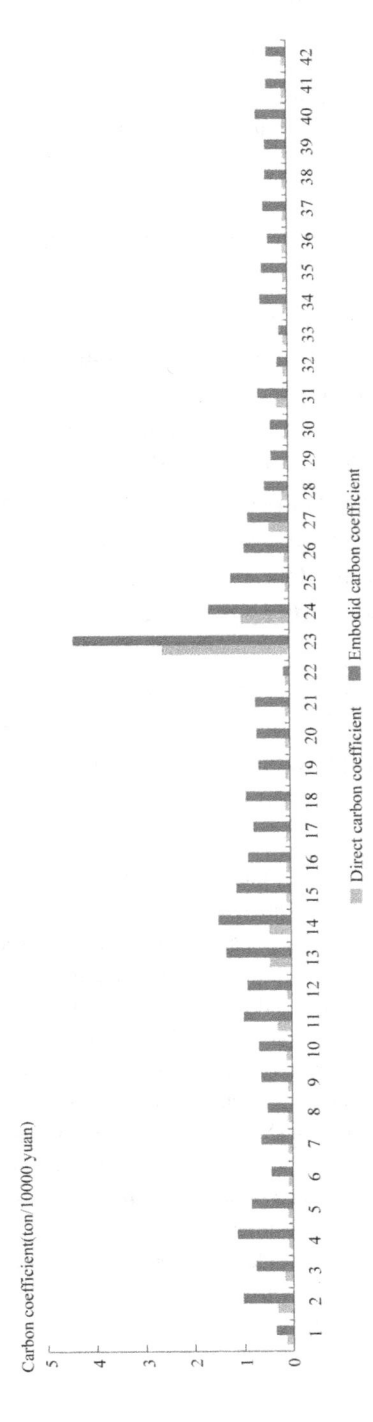

Fig. 14.1   Sectoral carbon coefficient (2007)

Notes: 1. Agriculture, forestry, animal husbandry, and fishery; 2. Coal mining and dressing; 3. Oil and natural gas mining; 4. Metal mineral mining and dressing; 5. Non-metal mineral mining and dressing; 6. Food production and tobacco processing; 7. Textile, clothing, shoes, hats, leather, down, and their products; 9. Wood processing and furniture manufacturing; 10. Papermaking, printing, and cultural, educational, and sporting goods manufacturing; 11. Petroleum processing, coking, and nuclear fuel processing; 12. Chemical industry; 13. Non-metal mineral products; 14. Metal smelting, rolling, and processing; 15. Metal products; 16. Manufacturing of general and special equipment; 17. Manufacturing of transportation equipment; 18. Manufacturing of electrical appliances, machines, and equipment; 19. Manufacturing of communication equipment, computers, and other electronic equipment; 20. Manufacturing of instruments, meters, and machines for culture and office articles; 21. Artware and manufacturing of other products; 22. Scrap products and materials; 23. Thermal power generation, heating, and supply; 24. Fuel gas production and supply; 25. Water production and supply; 26. Construction; 27. Transportation and warehousing; 28. Posts; 29. Information transference, computer service, and software; 30. Wholesale and retail trade; 31. Accommodation and catering; 32. Finance; 33. Real estate; 34. Rental and commercial services; 35. Research, experiment, and development; 36. Comprehensive technological services; 37. Water conservation, environment, and management of public facilities; 38. Resident services and other services; 39. Education; 40. Health, social security, and social welfare; 41. Culture, sports, and entertainment; 42. Public management and social organizations.

Table 14.2   Trade elasticity coefficient

	Agricultural products	Industrial products	Construction	Services
Armington substitution elasticity	16.12	3.63	0.25	2.27
Export price elasticity	−0.12	−1.12	−1.52	−1.52

(e.g., technological progress rate and consumption preference). The exogenous variables adopted are mainly observable macro- and industrial variables (e.g., population, total labor supply, GDP, consumption, investment, total output, value added, import and export, etc.). These variables are endogenous variables in the standard CGE model, but they are regarded as observable exogenous variables in historical simulation. We have determined the growth rates of various exogenous variables in the historical simulation period based on the relevant data in the *China Statistical Yearbook* 2013, *China's External Trade Indices* over the years, and the input–output tables of 2010.

We determine the baseline scenario of the system evolution of economy, energy, and environment from 2013 to 2020 through prediction simulation. In the prediction simulation, the actual GDP is still regarded as an exogenous variable, and its value is set with the expert

are exogenous variables, while macro-indicators such as GDP, consumption, investment, and total trade, and easily observable variables such as input, output, and price at the sectoral level are endogenous variables. The so-called historical simulation refers to updating the SAM matrix of the baseline period to the latest year (e.g., 2012) by using the facts that have occurred in the past few years (e.g., 2008–2012) and the data generated thereof. In historical simulation, we usually treat the above endogenous variables as exogenous variables, and their values can be obtained through various statistical yearbooks and other published statistical data. The values of these variables each year constitute the SAM matrix for the corresponding year. The purpose of the historical simulation is to make the best use of the information known in the real world so that the values of those significant variables (such as the above mentioned macro- and sectoral variables) are consistent with the facts that have occurred as much as possible, thus improving the reliability of the policy simulation. In the meantime, by substituting the values of these variables into the model, we can solve those variables that are not easy to observe.

Table 14.3   Values of major exogenous variables in the baseline scenario

Variables	Annual average (%)
Actual GDP	7.6 (2013–2015); 7.0 (2016–2020); 6.0 (2021–2030)
Population[a]	0.5 (2013–2015); 0.3 (2016–2030)
Total labor supply[b]	0.14 (2013–2015); –0.53 (2016–2020); –0.68 (2021–2030)
International oil price[c]	1.1
International coal price[c]	3.7
International natural gas price[c]	2.0
International prices of other products[d]	2.0

Notes: [a]estimated on the basis of the data of *China Statistical Yearbook* and *World Energy Outlook 2007: China and Indian Insight* (the International Energy Agency); [b]estimated on the basis of the data of *China Statistical Yearbook* and the results of Qi (2010); [c]set according to the prediction released by EIA (2013); [d]with a reference to Zhang (2013).

investigation approach.[7] The average efficiency of labor-capital-energy synthesis input is regarded as an endogenous variable. In addition, we assume that government subsidies to residents and enterprises vary proportionally with government revenues, while dividends of enterprises to residents vary proportionally with enterprise revenues, and various tax rates and resident savings rates remain at the base level. The values and sources of key exogenous variables in the baseline scenario are shown in Table 14.3.

In view of the diversity of the collection standards of carbon tariffs, we set up seven carbon tariff scenarios, which belong to two major categories, in the policy simulation (see Table 14.4) to compare the impacts of carbon tariffs on China under different collection standards. Reference is also made to previous studies (Mattoo *et al.*, 2009; Lin & Li, 2012; Yuan, 2013; Bao *et al.*, 2013). We assume four grades of tax rates, that is, 20 US dollars per ton of carbon equivalent (TC), 30 US dollars per ton of carbon

---

[7] We have adopted the results of the research group of analysis and prediction of economic situation and policy, Chinese Academy of Social Sciences.

Table 14.4   Collection standards of carbon tariffs

Category	Carbon tariff-collecting region r	Collection standard η_t	Export price after tax
Embodied carbon coefficient	US and EU	Embodied carbon coefficient of the exports of China	$P''_{E_i} = P_{E_i} + c_i \tau^r_{E_i}$
		Embodied carbon coefficient of the exports of China, decreasing annually	$P''_{E_i} = P_{E_i} + \tilde{a}_{it} c_i \tau^r_{E_i}$
		Embodied carbon coefficient of the exports of the US and the EU	$P''_{E_i} = P_{E_i} + c^r_i \tau^r_E$
		Difference between embodied carbon coefficient of the US and the EU and that of China	$P''_{E_i} = P_{E_i} + \left(c_i - c^r_i\right)\tau^r_{E_i}$
	All trading partners	Embodied carbon coefficient of the exports of China	$P''_{E_i} = P_{E_i} + c_i \tau^r_{E_i}$
Direct carbon coefficient	US and EU	Direct carbon coefficient of the exports of China	$P''_{E_i} = P_{E_i} + \varsigma_i \tau^r_{E_i}$
	All trading partners	Direct carbon coefficient of the exports of China	$P''_{E_i} = P_{E_i} + \varsigma c_i \tau^r_{E_i}$

Note: $\tilde{a}_{it}$ represents the annual adjustment coefficient of embodied carbon coefficient.

equivalent (TC), 50 US dollars per ton of carbon equivalent (TC), and 80 US dollars per ton of carbon equivalent (TC), and assume that China's exports will be subject to carbon tax starting from 2020.

The first category of scenarios assumes that the collection of carbon tariffs is based on the embodied carbon coefficient of exports. Specifically, we set up the following five scenarios:

(1) We assume that the US and the EU collect taxes based on the embodied carbon coefficient of China's exports.

(2) Considering that carbon tariffs may induce Chinese enterprises to promote technological progress in order to reduce carbon emissions, we assume that when the US and the EU start to collect carbon tariffs

on the exports of China, they will reduce the embodied carbon coefficient of Chinese exports year by year according to the annual technological progress. Upon our calculations, from 2007 to 2010, the embodied carbon per unit of export will decrease by 4% annually, and the rate may decrease further. Based on this fact, we assume three grades, 1%, 2%, and 4%, of average annual decrease rate of embodied carbon in exports.

(3) Suppose that the US and the EU collect taxes on China's exports based on their own production technologies, that is, their own embodied carbon coefficients of exports. According to the carbon emissions for various countries released by the Carbon Dioxide Information Analysis Center (CDIAC), the US Department of Energy, and the total economic volume for various countries released by the International Monetary Fund (IMF) database, the carbon emission intensities of the US and the EU, respectively, account for about 44% and 16% of China. We assume the same ratio of the embodied carbon coefficient of the US and the EU exports to the embodied carbon coefficient of Chinese exports.

(4) We assume that the US and the EU collect carbon tariffs based on the difference between their embodied carbon coefficient and that of China.

(5) We assume that all trading partners collect carbon tariffs on the exports of China according to the embodied carbon coefficient of Chinese exports.

The second category of scenarios assumes that the collection standard of carbon tariffs is the direct carbon coefficient of the exports of China. We specifically set up two scenarios: (1) the US and the EU collect carbon tariffs according to the direct carbon coefficient of Chinese exports; (2) all trading partners collect carbon tariffs according to the direct carbon coefficient of Chinese exports.

In addition, we have also set up two carbon tax scenarios related to carbon tariffs. In the first scenario, we assume that China will levy a carbon tax to achieve the reduction of carbon emissions when the US and the EU collect carbon tariffs based on the embodied carbon coefficient of Chinese exports, while no such tariffs are actually imposed on Chinese exports. The scenario may be called "carbon tax scenario one". In the second scenario, we assume that China will levy a carbon tax to make its carbon coefficient on par with that of the US in 2020, so that the exports of China will not be subject to carbon tariffs. The second scenario may be called "carbon tax scenario two". In order to make things simple, we further assume that when the carbon emission intensity of China is equal to that of the US, their carbon coefficients are the same. Then, carbon tax scenario two will mean that the carbon emission intensity of China needs to decrease at an average annual rate of 8.6% from 2013 to 2020.

4. Results

4.1. *Macro-impact of carbon tariffs imposed by the US and the EU based on the embodied carbon coefficient of the exports of China*

Table 14.5 shows the impact of carbon tariffs imposed by the US and the EU on the macroeconomy of China. Carbon tariffs will directly increase the price of Chinese products (the price including carbon tariffs) exported to the US and the EU markets, resulting in a sharp drop in China's exports to these two regions. At the same time, we have noticed that China's terms of trade have deteriorated. Since the import price is exogenous, the deterioration of the terms of trade means that the basic price of China's exports (the price excluding carbon tariffs) will fall due to the influence of carbon tariffs. As a result, the demand for China's exports in other regions that do not impose carbon tariffs will rise. It follows that a part of China's products, which may otherwise be exported to the US and the EU, will be diverted to other regions, and China's exports to these regions will increase considerably. However, due to the fact that China's exports to the first two regions have fallen too much, its total exports will still fall under the impact of carbon tariffs.

Since the Reform and Opening Up, and especially since 2001, China's economic growth has been characterized by a relatively obvious "export-oriented" feature, and exports will remain an important engine for China's economic growth for a period in the future. The negative impact of carbon tariffs on exports will thus inevitably affect all aspects of China's economy. A decline in exports will first directly lead to a decline in total

Table 14.5 Impact of carbon tariffs imposed by the US and the EU on the macroeconomy of China (in comparison with the baseline scenario) (%)

	Cumulative impact of different rates of carbon tariffs (2020–2030)				Impact of different years based on the rate of 50 US dollars/standard ton		
	20$/standard ton	30$/standard ton	50$/standard ton	80$/standard ton	2020	2025	2030
GDP	−0.141	−0.195	−0.279	−0.367	−0.059	−0.268	−0.415
Consumption	−0.487	−0.685	−1.006	−1.363	−0.171	−0.963	−1.618
Investment	−0.644	−0.913	−1.349	−1.839	−0.218	−1.262	−2.129
Export	−0.482	−0.673	−0.978	−1.299	−0.215	−0.957	−1.411
Export to the US and the EU	−17.747	−25.100	−36.974	−50.004	−6.859	−36.074	−56.893
Export to other regions	7.597	10.759	15.868	21.494	2.986	15.542	23.916
Import	−2.348	−3.311	−4.874	−6.621	−0.882	−4.726	−7.706
Terms of trade	−1.558	−2.194	−3.221	−4.365	−0.623	−3.398	−5.602
Energy consumption	−0.680	−0.939	−1.328	−1.723	−0.245	−1.282	−2.037
Carbon emissions	−0.670	−0.925	−1.309	−1.701	−0.244	−1.268	−2.006
Energy intensity	−0.490	−0.680	−0.967	−1.263	−0.186	−1.017	−1.629
Carbon emission intensity	−0.481	−0.667	−0.950	−1.244	−0.185	−1.002	−1.597

economic volume, and then affect resident income and curb consumption, and in the meantime reduce the demand of various domestic economic entities for investment and imported goods. Compared with exports, the decline in imports will be greater, which means that carbon tariffs will not have a substantial impact on China's trade surplus. Due to the decline in total economic volume, the energy consumption and total carbon emissions will drop accordingly.

With the increase of the rate of carbon tariffs, their negative impact on China's macroeconomy will become more serious. Yet their marginal impact will turn less: if the rate is doubled, its impact will be less than doubled. This is in line with the basic assumptions of neoclassical economics on which the CGE model here is based.[8] At the same time, in the simulation based on the dynamic CGE model, the results of the previous period provide the basis for the simulation of the subsequent period, that is, the impact of the previous period will be deferred to the subsequent period, and thus the impact of carbon tariffs will accumulate. As a result, with the passage of time, the impact of carbon tariffs increases, making the value of each variable in the policy scenario increasingly deviate from that in the baseline scenario. For example, the impact of carbon tariffs with the standard of 50 US dollars per standard ton in 2030 on GDP is equivalent to seven times its impact on GDP in 2020. In general, carbon tariffs do have "energy-conserving and carbon-reducing" effects on China, but they will also have obvious negative impacts on China's economic development.

4.2. *Macro-impact of carbon tariffs based on other collection standards*

Table 14.6 shows the cumulative macro-impact of carbon tariffs under other collection standards from 2020 to 2030. If during the process of

---

[8]Zhang (2013) noted similar findings when analyzing the total amount of carbon emissions and carbon intensity reduction, that is, the marginal cost of carbon emission reduction increases with the increase in carbon emission reduction. In other words, with the increase of carbon tax (equal to the marginal cost of carbon emission reduction in a state of equilibrium), the marginal effects of carbon emission reduction decrease.

Table 14.6 Cumulative impact of carbon tariffs with the standard of 50 US dollars/ton under other scenarios (2020–2030, in comparison with the baseline scenario) (%)

	Embodied carbon coefficient						Direct carbon coefficient			
	Carbon tariffs by the US and the EU						Carbon tax scenarios			
	Coefficient of China decreases annually			Coefficient of the US and the EU	Difference between embodied carbon coefficient of the US and the EU and that of China	Carbon tariffs by all trading partners	The US and the EU	All trading partners	Carbon tax scenario one	Carbon tax scenario two
	−1%	−2%	−4%							
GDP	−0.271	−0.265	−0.257	−0.112	−0.219	−1.122	−0.034	−0.187	−0.005	−1.484
Consumption	−0.983	−0.960	−0.916	−0.379	−0.772	−4.163	−0.108	−0.456	−0.008	−1.013
Investment	−1.318	−1.285	−1.221	−0.500	−1.029	−5.057	−0.097	−0.308	−0.068	−4.929
Export	−0.947	−0.926	−0.894	−0.383	−0.761	−3.499	−0.040	−0.265	0.017	−0.538
Export to the US and Europe	−36.021	−35.092	−33.312	−13.805	−28.316	−5.965	−3.100	0.559	0.010	−1.042
Export to other regions	15.467	15.064	14.277	5.898	12.135	−2.345	1.392	−0.651	0.020	−0.303
Import	−4.756	−4.642	−4.426	−1.831	−3.734	−16.260	−0.320	−1.158	−0.049	−3.367
Terms of trade	−3.151	−3.082	−2.948	−1.215	−2.471	−11.925	−0.297	−1.161	−0.002	0.233
Energy consumption	−1.304	−1.279	−1.226	−0.535	−1.046	−5.467	−0.163	−0.608	−1.274	−49.695
Carbon emissions	−1.286	−1.261	−1.209	−0.527	−1.031	−5.296	−0.160	−0.599	−1.309	−52.144
Energy intensity	−0.953	−0.935	−0.896	−0.383	−0.757	−3.976	−0.116	−0.385	−1.169	−48.879
Carbon emission intensity	−0.936	−0.919	−0.880	−0.376	−0.744	−3.822	−0.115	−0.378	−1.202	−51.374

imposing carbon tariffs the US and the EU take into consideration the changes in the embodied carbon coefficient of China's exports, and suppose that the embodied carbon coefficient of China's exports decreases year by year with technological progress and optimization of energy structure, the negative impact of carbon tariffs on China's macroeconomy will decrease. It is easy to understand, under the above premises, that the faster the rate of decline of the embodied carbon coefficient of China's exports, the more it can suppress the negative impact of carbon tariffs.

If the US and the EU collect carbon tariffs on China's exports according to the embodied carbon coefficient of their own exports, the impact of carbon tariffs on China's economy, energy consumption, and carbon emissions will decrease significantly because the embodied carbon coefficients of their export is far lower than that of China. If the two regions collect carbon tariffs according to the difference between their embodied carbon coefficients and that of China, the impact of carbon tariffs will rise significantly compared with the previous scenario, but will still be significantly lower than the scenario where carbon tariffs are collected according to the embodied carbon coefficients of China's exports.

Compared with the situation where only the US and the EU impose carbon tariffs, carbon tariffs imposed by all trading partners according to the embodied carbon coefficient of China's exports will have a worse impact: an impact on China's macro-indicators about four times that of the former. It is not difficult to understand that although the US and the EU are the two most important trading partners of China, China's exports to them account for only about one-third of the total exports after all. Thus, carbon tariffs imposed only by the US and the EU have much less impact than by all trading partners. Although the decline in China's exports to the US and the EU will slow down when all trading partners impose carbon tariffs, exports to other regions will change from a significant rise to a significant decline, and eventually lead to a considerable decline in total exports.

Since the direct carbon coefficient of the exports of China is far lower than the embodied carbon coefficient, carbon tariffs collected by the US and the EU according to the direct carbon coefficient of China's exports have much lesser impact than according to the embodied carbon coefficient of China's exports, and even less than that according to the embodied carbon coefficient of the exports of the US and the EU. Even if carbon tariffs are collected by all trading partners according to the direct carbon coefficient of Chinese exports, their impact is still significantly less than carbon tariffs collected by the US and the EU alone according to the embodied carbon coefficient of Chinese exports. It can be speculated that if the US and the EU collect carbon tariffs on Chinese exports according to the direct carbon coefficient of their own exports, China will be less affected.

If China imposes a carbon tax so that it has the same impact on China's carbon emissions as that of the carbon tariffs imposed by the US and the EU, the rate of carbon tax needed is relatively low. We might as well call it low carbon tax. The impact of low carbon tax on the GDP, consumption, investment, import, and other macroeconomic indicators of China will be significantly less than the impact of carbon tariffs imposed by the US and the EU. Low carbon tax may even promote China's exports, because under low carbon tax, China's carbon-intensive exports will decline, but labor-intensive and technology-intensive exports will rise.[9] However, the impact of low carbon tax and that of carbon tariffs on China's total energy consumption are basically the same. Since the negative impact of low carbon tax on GDP is much less than that of carbon tariffs, and both have the same impact on energy consumption and carbon emissions, low carbon tax will bring about a greater decrease in energy intensity and carbon emission intensity.

There are roughly two reasons for the difference between the impacts of low carbon tax and carbon tariffs. On the one hand, the tax income generated by low carbon tax will be counted into GDP as a part of government income, while that generated by carbon tariffs is the income of foreign governments instead of the Chinese government. This is equivalent to transferring a part of welfare of the producing country to the importing country. On the other hand, the two exert impacts in different ways. The object of low carbon tax is all fossil energy used as fuels, which directly affects production behavior and then indirectly affects demand. The object

---

[9] Owing to the limited space, the results for the sectoral impact of "equivalent carbon tax" are not presented here. Interested readers may consult the authors for relevant information.

of carbon tariffs is the direct or embodied carbon coefficient of export products, which directly affects demand behavior and then indirectly affects production behavior.

If China imposes a carbon tax to reduce the intensity of its own carbon emissions to the level of the US in 2020 so that it will not be subject to carbon tariffs, then the level of carbon tax that needs to be set is relatively high. We might as well call it high carbon tax. The impact of high carbon tax on China's macroeconomy, especially on energy consumption and carbon emissions, will be significantly greater than that of all trading partners imposing carbon tariffs, and far greater than that of the US and the EU imposing carbon tariffs. Under the impact of high carbon tax, the carbon emission intensity of China will fall far beyond the established target, 40–45% lower than that of 2005 in 2020. Therefore, the high carbon tax is a relatively radical low-carbon development scenario for China. It can be predicted that China's economy will be hit even harder, if its carbon emission intensity is reduced to the lower level of the EU by imposing a carbon tax.

4.3. *Sectoral impact of carbon tariffs imposed by the US and the EU*

Table 14.7 shows the impact of carbon tariffs with the standard of 50 US dollars per standard ton, which is based on the embodied carbon coefficient of China's exports, on various sectors of China from 2020 to 2030 (in comparison with the baseline scenario). It is easy to see that exports of tradable sectors to the US and the EU have all decreased significantly, and the decrease is basically consistent with the carbon intensity of various sectors, that is, the higher the carbon intensity, the greater the decrease. Out of all sectors, 11 carbon-intensive sectors such as chemical industry, metal smelting, rolling, and processing, and metal products see their exports to the US and the EU drop by more than 50%. Also, exports of tradable sectors to other regions have increased, but the increase is much less than the decrease to the US and the EU.

The changes in the total exports of tradable sectors are determined by the changes in their exports to the above two regions, with the former being the weighted average of the latter two. In the 16 sectors with lower total export volume, there are not only high carbon-intensity sectors

Table 14.7 Cumulative sectoral impact of carbon tariffs with the standard of 50 US dollars/ton imposed by the US and the EU (%)

Sectors	Total output	Domestic supply	Export Total	Export US and EU	Export Other regions	Import	Carbon emissions
Agriculture, forestry, animal husbandry, and fishery	0.654	0.617	6.632	−16.221	14.863	−9.200	−0.676
Coal mining and dressing	−1.078	−1.079	−0.494	−47.184	18.172	−8.162	−2.298
Petroleum and natural gas mining	0.786	0.767	3.853	−52.214	12.927	−7.391	−0.805
Metal mineral mining	1.561	1.713	−4.277	−66.880	23.849	−5.729	0.354
Non-metal mineral mining and dressing	−0.372	−0.281	−4.702	−44.179	26.103	−7.834	−1.557
Food production and tobacco processing	0.249	0.115	4.837	−20.682	14.639	−8.604	−0.961
Textile	0.520	0.121	1.739	−30.120	18.654	0.116	−0.697
Textile, clothing, shoes, hats, leather, down, and their products	−0.373	−0.353	−0.424	−20.341	19.581	−0.348	−1.739
Wood processing and furniture manufacturing	−1.703	−0.994	−5.905	−28.298	28.164	−8.193	−2.935
Papermaking, printing, and cultural, educational, and sporting goods manufacturing	0.261	0.349	−0.575	−37.232	16.565	−6.063	−0.927
Petroleum processing, coking, and nuclear fuel processing	−1.468	−1.491	1.010	−53.448	9.824	−10.418	−2.055

(*Continued*)

Table 14.7   (*Continued*)

Sectors	Total output	Domestic supply	Export			Import	Carbon emissions
			Total	US and EU	Other regions		
Chemical industry	0.311	0.697	−2.686	−55.206	19.822	−8.986	−0.422
Non-metal mineral products	−1.154	−0.934	−5.847	−64.911	22.734	−7.883	−2.035
Metal smelting, rolling, and processing	−1.233	−1.123	−5.033	−69.773	16.146	−6.754	−2.303
Metal products	−2.062	−0.960	−8.994	−52.207	26.880	−6.585	−3.465
Manufacturing of general and special equipment	−1.491	−0.448	−7.810	−43.306	25.431	−5.872	−2.968
Manufacturing of transportation equipment	−0.820	−0.444	−3.380	−38.613	18.564	−6.296	−2.251
Manufacturing of electrical appliances, machines, and equipment	−2.779	−0.631	−9.321	−50.130	15.405	−5.860	−4.195
Manufacturing of communication equipment, computers, and other electronic equipment	0.440	1.309	−1.329	−20.967	10.570	−2.701	−0.758
Manufacturing of instruments, meters, and machines for culture and office articles	1.648	2.619	0.630	−25.986	11.693	−2.231	0.395
Artware and manufacturing of other products	0.133	−0.563	2.683	−24.602	17.997	−8.150	−1.168
Scrap products and materials	−0.980	−1.021	−0.516	−30.845	16.507	−1.021	−2.746

Table 14.7   (*Continued*)

Sectors	Total output	Domestic supply	Export Total	Export US and EU	Export Other regions	Import	Carbon emissions
Thermal power generation, heating, and supply	−0.488	−0.488	−0.834	−93.088	7.571	−7.868	−0.817
Fuel gas production and supply	−1.584	−1.584	#	#	#	#	−1.374
Water production and supply	−0.442	−0.442	#	#	#	#	−1.884
Construction	−1.149	−1.189	3.058	−53.962	8.253	−1.189	−2.781
Transportation and warehousing	−0.087	−0.548	4.355	−51.261	9.422	−0.547	−1.079
Posts	−0.262	−0.589	5.249	−47.909	10.092	−0.567	−2.120
Information transference, computer service, and software	−0.974	−1.412	4.873	−26.331	7.716	−1.390	−2.374
Wholesale and retail trade	2.070	−0.601	12.405	−20.504	15.403	#	0.082
Accommodation and catering	−0.297	−0.466	7.055	−25.500	10.021	−0.455	−1.934
Finance	−0.177	−0.234	8.347	−14.355	10.415	−0.226	−2.291
Real estate	−0.347	−0.347	#	#	#	#	−2.236
Rental and commercial services	2.420	−0.167	9.469	−29.277	12.999	−0.165	0.506
Research, experiment, and development	−0.459	−0.596	5.185	−33.098	8.673	−0.610	−2.148
Comprehensive technological services	−0.586	−0.586	#	#	#	#	−2.344
Water conservation, environment, and management of public facilities	−0.615	−0.615	#	#	#	#	−2.370

(*Continued*)

Table 14.7 (*Continued*)

Sectors	Total output	Domestic supply	Export			Import	Carbon emissions
			Total	US and EU	Other regions		
Resident services and other services	−0.619	−0.725	5.871	−25.558	8.735	−0.701	−2.462
Education	−0.829	−0.838	6.643	−25.967	9.614	−0.838	−2.460
Health, social security, and social welfare	−0.929	−0.940	5.026	−36.704	8.828	−0.940	−2.363
Culture, sports, and entertainment	−0.055	−0.616	6.442	−26.301	9.425	−0.618	−1.801
Public management and social organizations	−0.985	−0.998	6.930	−22.224	9.586	−0.998	−2.733
Average	−0.428	−0.388	−0.978	−36.974	15.868	−4.874	−1.329

Note: # represents non-tradable goods or services.

(e.g., power, heat production and supply, metal products and non-metal mineral products, etc.), but also those with low carbon intensity (e.g., manufacturing of communication equipment, computers, and other electronic equipment).[10] Because the export of electrical appliances, machines, and equipment, metal products, and non-metal mineral products to the US and the EU has greatly dropped, and the export of these sectors to the above regions has a larger proportion in their total export, their total export volume has dropped most significantly. For the same reason, in the remaining 21 tradable sectors whose total export volume has increased, most of them enjoy relatively low carbon intensity (e.g., agriculture, forestry, animal husbandry, and fishery, and most service sectors), while a few of them enjoy relatively high carbon intensity (such as petroleum and

---

[10]The export of communication equipment, computers, and other electronic equipment to other regions is 1.65 times that to the US and the EU, while the decline of these exports to the US and the EU is 1.79 times that of their growth to other regions. Thus, the total export volume has decreased.

natural gas mining). Generally speaking, the sectors that see a decline in exports are carbon-intensive sectors, while those that experience a rise are mainly relatively clean labor-intensive and technology-intensive sectors.

Since carbon tariffs reduce the overall level of economic activity in China and suppress domestic demand, domestic supply of most sectors also declines. A few sectors see their domestic supply increased, including service sectors (e.g., finance) and technology-intensive sectors (e.g., manufacturing of communication equipment, computers, and other electronic equipment), which are relatively clean, as well as carbon-intensive sectors (e.g., metal smelting, rolling, and processing). Changes in the total output of various sectors are weighted averages of the changes in their exports and domestic supply. The domestic supply of most sectors far exceeds their exports, which means that their total output changes mainly include domestic supply changes. For this reason, the total output of most sectors also shows a decline. Similarly, due to the decline in domestic demand, China's demand for almost all imported products also decreases, with only a slight increase in textile imports. Further analysis shows that textile imports (about 52%) are mainly utilized as intermediate inputs in the production of textile industry itself; thus, the quantity of change is greatly influenced by the output of the textile industry. As the output increases, the textile imports also slightly increase.

The change of carbon emissions of different sectors mainly depends on the change of their output, so the relative decrease of carbon emissions of different sectors is basically the same as the relative decrease of their total output. However, other factors also contribute to the change, such as the substitution of production factors for fossil energy inputs and changes in the energy structure. If in the production process of a sector, production factors substitute fossil energy to a large degree, or if the energy structure is optimized to a greater extent, then the decrease in carbon emissions will obviously exceed the decrease in total output. Due to the above-mentioned possibilities, we can see that most sectors, especially some service sectors (e.g., culture, sports, and entertainment) have a larger decline in carbon emissions than their total output. Some sectors (e.g., agriculture, forestry, animal husbandry and fishery, textile, and chemical industry) even see their carbon emissions slightly reduced while their total output increased. Of course, there are also some sectors, such as the metal mining and dressing, manufacturing of instruments, meters, and machines for culture and office articles, the wholesale and retail trade, and rental and commercial services, experiencing an increase in carbon emissions, because their total output greatly increases.

It should be noted that the sectoral impacts of carbon tariffs imposed by the US and the EU under other standards and tax rates are similar to the results shown in Table 14.7, but to different degrees. Furthermore, when all trading partners impose carbon tariffs, total exports, domestic supply, total output, imports, and carbon emissions of most sectors change in the same direction as when the US and the EU alone impose carbon tariffs. However, when all trading partners impose carbon tariffs, China's exports will not show obvious regional difference, that is, exports to the US and the EU will not decline while exports to other regions rise.

4.4. *Comparison with previous studies and sensitivity test*

Table 14.8 summarizes the researches on the impact of carbon tariffs on China based on CGE model. In terms of the impact of carbon tariffs on GDP, in the scenario where some or all developed countries impose carbon tariffs according to the embodied carbon coefficient of Chinese exports, the results of this chapter are obviously lower than Mattoo *et al.* (2009) and Luan & Yang (2014). In the scenario where all trading partners impose carbon tariffs according to the embodied carbon coefficient of Chinese exports, the results here are lower than Hübler (2012). In the scenario where some or all developed countries impose carbon tariffs according to the direct carbon coefficient of China, the results here are close to Yuan (2013), but significantly lower than Lin & Li (2011), Li *et al.* (2013), Huang & Li (2010), and Lin & Li (2012). In the scenario where all trading partners impose carbon tariffs according to the direct carbon coefficient of China, the results here, if converted to the same tax rate, are significantly lower than Li & Zhang (2012).

In terms of the impact of carbon tariffs on total exports, in the scenario where some or all developed countries impose carbon tariffs according to the embodied carbon coefficient of Chinese exports, the results here are also significantly lower than Mattoo *et al.* (2009), but significantly higher than Luan & Yang (2014). In the scenario where all trading partners

Table 14.8 A summary of the researches on the impact of carbon tariffs on China based on CGE model

| Research | Method | Research period | Specification of carbon tariffs | | | Impact of carbon tariffs in the report period (%) | | |
			Tax regions	Standard	Tax rate	GDP	Export	Carbon emissions
Mattoo *et al.* (2009)	M	2004–2020	IC	Cid	66	−3.7	−15.8	−1.7
Lin & Li (2011)	M	2007	OECD	Cd	10–40	−6.72 – −1.72		−9.57 – −2.45
Dong & Whalley (2012)	M	2006	EU+US	Cd	6.8–54.5	0.004–0.033		0.101–0.816
Hübler (2012)[a]	M	2004–2030	ALL	Cid	17.7–28.3	−21.7 – −16.8		−5.0 – −4.2
Li & Zhang (2012)	M	2007	OECD	Cd	2.7			−0.77
Li *et al.* (2013)	M	2007	OECD	Cd	13.6	−2.62		−2.76
Huang & Li (2010)	M	2001	US	Cd	30–60	−3.62 – −1.84		
Lin & Li (2010)	M	2007	OECD	Cd	10–50			−1.545 – −0.319
Lin & Li (2012)	M	2007	OECD	Cd	50	−2.62		−2.76
Luan & Yang (2014)	M	2007–2020	US	Cid	30–60	−1.30 – −0.69	−0.24 – −0.13	−0.24 – −0.13
Bao *et al.* (2013)	M	2007–2030	EU+US	Cd	20–80			−0.04 – −0.01
Shen & Li (2010)[b]	S	2002	ALL	Cid	30–60		−6.95 – −3.53	
Li & Zhang (2012)	S	2007–2012	ALL	Cd	7.2	−0.12	−0.08	−0.45
Yuan (2013)	S	2011	ALL	Cid	10–100	−0.23 – −0.04		
The present chapter	S	2007–2030	EU+US	Cid	20–80	−0.53 – −0.24	−1.30 – −0.76	−2.00 – −0.96

(Continued)

Table 14.8   (*Continued*)

Research	Method	Research period	Specification of carbon tariffs			Impact of carbon tariffs in the report period (%)		
			Tax regions	Standard	Tax rate	GDP	Export	Carbon emissions
The present chapter	S	2007–2030	ALL	Cid	20–80	−1.54 – −0.52	−4.93 – −1.58	−8.56– −2.13
The present chapter	S	2007–2030	EU+US	Cd	50	−0.03	−0.04	−1.27
The present chapter	S	2007–2030	ALL	Cd	50	−0.19	−0.27	−2.01

Notes: (1) "M" refers to the multi-country CGE model, and "S" refers to the single-country (China) CGE model. (2) "Tax regions" refer to the regions where carbon tariffs are imposed on imported goods. "EU" refers to the European Union, "US" refers to the United States, "OECD" refers to OECD countries, "IC" refers to developed countries, and "ALL" refers to all trading partners of China. (3) "Cd" means the direct carbon coefficient of China's exports; "Cid" indicates the embodied carbon coefficient of China's exports. (4) The unit for tax rate is unified as "USD/tc". (5) [a]calculated based on the results of the origi- nal study; [b]the exports studied in this document are limited to industrial products. (6) This chapter only summarizes part of the results of previous researches. For example, Mattoo *et al.* (2009) and the carbon tariffs in this chapter include both the collection method based on the carbon of Chinese exports and that based on the carbon of domestic products of importing countries. For another example, Dong & Whalley (2012) set up various scenarios such as carbon tariffs imposed by the US, carbon tariffs imposed by the EU, and carbon tariffs imposed by both the US and the EU. The present chapter only takes the results of the scenario where the US and the EU impose carbon tariffs at the same time.

impose carbon tariffs according to the embodied carbon coefficient of Chinese exports, the conclusions of this chapter are significantly lower than Shen & Li (2010). In the scenario where all trading partners impose carbon tariffs according to the direct carbon coefficient of Chinese exports, the conclusions here, if converted to the same tax rate, will also be significantly lower than Li & Zhang (2012).

In terms of the impact of carbon tariffs on total carbon emissions, in the scenario where some or all developed countries impose carbon tariffs according to the embodied carbon coefficient of Chinese exports, the conclusions here are close to Mattoo *et al.* (2009), but significantly higher than Luan & Yang (2014). In the scenario where all trading partners impose carbon tariffs according to the embodied carbon coefficient of Chinese exports, the conclusions here are still significantly lower than Hübler (2012). In the scenario where some or all developed countries impose carbon tariffs according to the direct carbon coefficient of Chinese exports, the conclusions here are in a similar direction to Lin & Li (2011), Li *et al.* (2013) and Lin & Li (2012), with small differences. In the scenario where all trading partners impose carbon tariffs according to the direct carbon coefficient of Chinese exports, the results here, if converted to the same tax rate, may still be lower than Li & Zhang (2012).

In general, all studies except Dong & Whalley (2012) find that carbon tariffs have negative impacts on China's GDP, exports, and carbon emissions, but the results of different studies are quite different due to differences in methods, research periods, and specification of carbon tariffs.

Furthermore, we also conduct a sensitivity test of the research results in the scenario where the US and the EU collect carbon tariffs with the standard of 50 US dollars/ton according to the embodied carbon coefficient of Chinese exports. Specifically, we first reduce all elasticity values (including the transformation elasticity of domestic consumption and export, the substitution elasticity of production factors and energy inputs, export price elasticity, Armington elasticity, and consumer preference) by 10% to simulate the impact of carbon tax, and then increase all elasticity values by 10% and simulate the impact of carbon tax again. Figure 14.2 shows the ratio of the impacts of carbon tariffs under the value changes to the impacts under the original values. It is easy to find that with the exception of import, the impact of carbon tariffs on all macroeconomic

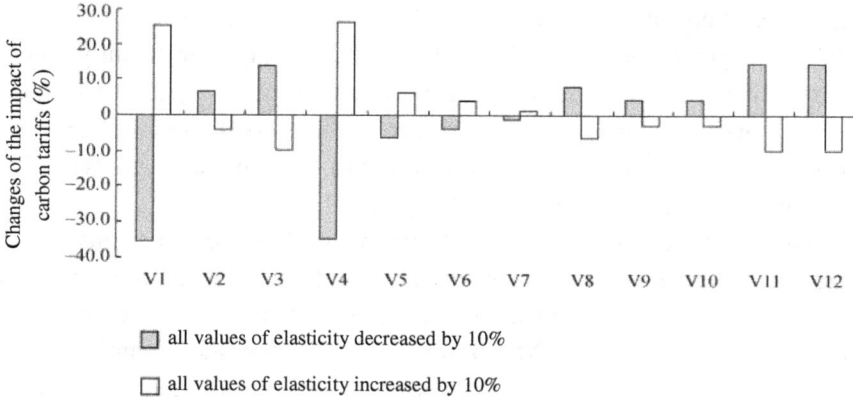

□ all values of elasticity decreased by 10%

□ all values of elasticity increased by 10%

Fig. 14.2   Sensitivity test of the impact of carbon tariffs imposed by the US and the EU with standard of 50 US dollars/ton, which is according to the embodied carbon coefficient of Chinese exports

Notes: V1. GDP; V2. consumption; V3. investment; V4. exports; V5. exports to the US and the EU; V6. exports to other regions; V7. imports; V8. terms of trade; V9. energy consumption; V10. carbon emissions; V11. energy intensity; V12. carbon emission intensity.

variables, especially GDP and export, is sensitive to the value of elasticity coefficient. Therefore, when evaluating the impact of carbon tariffs, we must make clear the uncertainty brought about by the value of elasticity coefficient.

5. Conclusion and Policy Discussion

Based on the dynamic CGE model, this chapter simulates the impact of carbon tariffs under different collection standards on China's economy and carbon emissions from 2020 to 2030. Regardless of which collection standard is adopted, carbon tariffs will lead to a decline in China's total economic volume, consumption, investment, trade volume, energy consumption, and carbon emissions. However, different collection standards lead to different degrees of impact. When carbon tariffs are imposed by the US or the EU, the embodied carbon coefficient of China as the collection standard gives rises to the greatest impact, followed in order by the difference between the embodied carbon coefficient of the US and the EU and that of China, and then the embodied carbon coefficient of the US and the EU, and the least impact is caused by taking the direct carbon coefficient of China as the collection standard. When other trading partners follow the example of the US or the EU in imposing carbon tariffs, the impact of carbon tariffs on China will increase dramatically.

When achieving the same amount of carbon emission reduction, the impact of carbon tax on China's economy is far less than that of carbon tariffs imposed by the US and the EU. Thus, carbon tariffs are not a cost-effective or reasonable way to slow down "carbon leakage". If China reduces the carbon coefficient of its own products to the level of the US in 2020 in order to avoid carbon tariffs, the economic losses thus caused for China will be far greater than those caused by carbon tariffs. Therefore, in the face of carbon tariffs, China should not reduce the intensity of carbon emissions too quickly, but should gradually improve the efficiency of carbon emissions according to the established targets.

Since carbon tariffs are an unreasonable trade barrier and have a great impact on China's economy, China should resolutely resist carbon tariffs of the US and the EU through various legal channels. China should also actively take measures to deal with possible unilateral carbon tariffs imposed by the US and the EU. First, China should vigorously facilitate the innovation-driven development strategy to realize the transformation of economic development, especially to promote the research, development, and support of energy-conserving and environmental protection technologies and products, which is conducive to quickly ending the reduction of the embodied carbon coefficient of China's exports, thus easing the impact of carbon tariffs. Second, China can consider introducing a carbon tax policy in due course to promote the development of low-carbon life, but the carbon tax rate should be set at a low level to avoid stepping into a radical low-carbon development process. Imposing carbon tax will not only help China save energy, reduce carbon, and improve China's adaptability to carbon tariffs, but also provide political bargaining chips for China to resist carbon tariffs. Finally, China should actively optimize its trade structure. If clean products account for a large share of exports, this will greatly reduce the impact of carbon tariffs. In addition, the implementation of the carbon emission trading system will also help China to improve carbon emission efficiency to cope with the impact of carbon tariffs. At present, China has already started the pilot work of carbon emission trading in seven regions, on the basis of which a national carbon emission trading system should be established as soon as possible.

References

Armington, P., "A Theory of Demand for Products Distinguished by Place of Production". *IMF Staff Papers*, 1969, 16, pp. 159–178.

Bao, Q., Tang L., Zhang Z. & Wang S., "Impacts of border carbon adjustments on China's sectoral emissions: Simulations with a dynamic computable general equilibrium model". *China Economic Review*, Vol. 24, No. 1 (2013), pp.77–94.

Bergman, L., "CGE Modeling of Environmental Policy and Resource Management". In K. G., Mler, J. C., Vincent, (eds.), *Handbook of Environmental Economics*, Vol. 3. 2005. Elsevier, The Netherlands.

Burniaux, J., Chateau, J. & Duval, R., "Is There A Case for Carbon-based Border Tax Adjustment? An Applied General Equilibrium Analysis". *Applied Economics* (2013), pp. 2231–2240.

De Cendra, J., "Can Emissions Trading Schemes Be Coupled with Border Tax Adjustments? An Analysis Vis-à-vis WTO Law". *Review of European Community and International Environmental Law*, Vol. 15, No. 2 (2006), pp. 131–145.

de Melo, J., & Robinson, S., "Product Differentiation and Foreign Trade in CGE Models of Small Economies". *Journal of International Economics*, Vol. 27 (1989), pp. 47–67.

Dervis, K., De Melo, J. & Robinson, S., *General Equilibrium Models for Development Policy*.1982. Cambridge University Press, Cambridge, UK.

Dixon, P. B., & Rimmer, M. T., *Dynamic General Equilibrium Modelling for Forecasting and Policy: A Practical Guide and Documentation of MONASH*. 2002. North-Holland Publishing Company, Amsterdam.

Dong, Y., & Whalley, J., "How Large Are the Impacts of Carbon Motivated Border Tax Adjustments". *Climate Change Economics*, Vol. 3, No. 1 (2012).

Dong, Y., "A Research on Measures for Carbon Border Adjustment in the Game of Global Climate Change". *World Economics and Politics*, No. 7 (2010), pp. 5–82.

EIA, *Annual Energy Outlook* 2013. http://www.eia.gov/forecasts/aeo/.

Huang, L., & Li, X., "The impact of Carbon Tariffs to Be Imposed by the United States on China's Economy: An Empirical Analysis Based on GTAP Model". *Journal of International Trade*, No. 11 (2010), pp. 93–98.

Hübler, M., "Carbon Tariffs on Chinese Exports: Emissions Reduction, Threat, or Farce?". *Energy Policy*, Vol. 50 (2012), pp. 315–327.

IPCC, *2006 IPCC Guidelines for National Greenhouse Gas Inventories*. Prepared by the National Greenhouse Gas Inventories Programme, Eggleston, H. S., Buendia, L., Miwa, K., Ngara, T., & Tanabe, K. (eds.). IGES, Japan, 2006.

Ismer, R., & Neuhoff, K., "Border Tax Adjustment: A Feasible Way to Support Stringent Emission Trading". *European Journal of Law and Economics*, Vol. 24, No. 2(2007), pp. 137–164.

Jung, H. S., & Thorbecke, E., "The Impact of Public Education Expenditure on Human Capital, Growth and Poverty in Tanzania and Zambia: A General Equilibrium Approach". *Journal of Policy Modeling*, Vol. 25 (2003), pp. 701–725.

Li, A., & Zhang, A., "Will Carbon Motivated Border Tax Adjustments Function As A Threat?". *Energy Policy*, Vol. 63 (2012), pp. 81–90.

Li, A., Zhang, A., Cai, H., Li, X. & Peng, S., "How Large Are the Impacts of Carbon-motivated Border Tax Adjustments on China and How to Mitigate Them". *Energy Policy*, Vol. 63 (2013), pp. 927–934.

Li, J., & Zhang, Y., "A Quantitative Analysis of the Impact of Green Barriers to International Trade on China's Economy Based on CGE Model: A Case Study of Carbon Tariffs Imposed by Developed Countries on China's Exports". *Journal of International Trade*, No. 5 (2012), pp. 105–118.

Lin, B. Q., & Li, A. J., "Impacts of Carbon Motivated Border Tax Adjustments on Competitiveness across Regions in China". *Energy*, Vol. 36 (2011), pp. 5111–5118.

Lin, B., & Li, A., "The Impact of Carbon Tariffs on Developing Countries". *Journal of Financial Research*, No. 12 (2010), pp. 1–15.

Lin, B., & Li, A., "Where does the Rationality of Carbon Tariffs Lie in?". *Economic Research Journal*, No. 11 (2012), pp. 118–127.

Luan, H., & Yang, J., "The Impact of Carbon Tariffs Imposed by the United States on China's Carbon Emission Reduction and Economy". *China Population, Resources and Environment*, No.1 (2014), pp. 70–77.

Mattoo, A., Subramanian, A., van der Mensbrugghe, D. & He, J., "Reconciling Climate Change and Trade Policy". Peterson Institute for International Economic Policy Working Paper 09-15, 2009.

McKibbin, W., & Wilcoxen, P., "The Economic and Environmental Effects of Border Tax Adjustments for Climate Policy". *Brookings Trade Forum*, 2008/2009, pp. 1–23.

Medina, V. D., & Lazo, R. P., "A Legal View on Border Tax Adjustments and Climate Change: A Latin American Perspective". *Sustainable Development Law & Policy*, Vol. 11, No. 3 (2011), pp. 29–34, 43–45.

Pan, H., "The Impact of Carbon Tariffs on China's Export Trade and Countermeasures". *China Population, Resources and Environment*, No.2 (2012), pp. 41–46.

Peterson, E. B., & Schleich, J., "Economic and Environmental Effects of Border Tax Adjustments". Working Paper Sustainability and Innovation No. S 1/2007, 2007.

Qi, M., "China's Labor Supply and Demand Forecast 2010–2050". *Population Research*, No. 9 (2010), pp. 76–87.

Qu, R., & Wu, J., "On the Welfare Effect of Carbon Tariffs". *China Population, Resources and Environment*, No. 4 (2011), pp. 37–42.

Roland-Holst, D., & van der Mensbrugghe, D., *General Equilibrium Technique for Policy Modeling*, translated by Li Shantong, Duan Zhigang and Hu Feng. 2009. Tsinghua University Press, Beijing, China.

Shen, K., & Li, G., "The Impact of Carbon Tariffs on China's Industrial Exports: An Assessment Based on Computable General Equilibrium Model". *Finance & Trade Economics*, No. 1 (2010), pp. 75–82.

Shen, K., "Carbon Tariff Dispute and Its Impact on China's Manufacturing Industry". *China Industrial Economics*, No.1 (2010), pp. 65–74.

Wobst, P., *Structural Adjustment and Intersectoral Shifts in Tanzania: A Computable General Equilibrium Model*. International Food Policy Research Institute (IFPRI), Research Report 117, 2001.

Yuan, Y., "A Quantitative Analysis of the Impact of Carbon Tariffs on China's Economy Based on CGE Model". *Journal of International Trade*, No. 2 (2013), pp. 92–99.

Zhang, X., *The General Equilibrium Theory and Practical Model*. 2009. Renmin University Press, Beijing, China.

Zhang, Y., "A Comparison of Performance between Carbon Intensity and Total Restraint: An Analysis Based on CGE Model". *The Journal of World Economy*, No. 7 (2013), pp. 138–160.

Zhang, Y., "Carbon in China's Trade and Its Influencing Factors: An Analysis Based on (Import) Non-Competitive Input–Output Tables". *China Economic Quarterly*, No. 4 (2010b).

Zhang, Y., "The Impact of Changes in Economic Development Patterns on the Intensity of China's Carbon Emissions". *Economic Research Journal*, No. 4 (2010a).

Zheng, Y., Fan, M. *et al.*, *China CGE Model and Policy Analysis*. 1998. Social Sciences Academic Press, Beijing, China.

Index

CPSIA information can be obtained
at www.ICGtesting.com
Printed in the USA
BVHW090244260220
573339BV00007B/15

9 789811 202902